Rebel Without a Clue

Magical Thinking, a Motorcycle Journey, and The Great Teenage Diaspora

Jonathan Robertson

Aided and abetted by
Tom Duncan

Rebel Without a Clue
Magical Thinking, a Motorcycle Journey,
and The Great Teenage Diaspora

Copyright © 2024 Jonathan Robertson

ISBN 978-1-61170-317-7

Memoir • Sociology

All rights reserved. No part of this publication may be reproduced, stored in a retrieval system or transmitted in any form or by any means, electronic, mechanical, photocopies, recording or otherwise, without the prior written consent of the publisher, except in the case of brief quotations embodied in critical reviews.

Published by:

www.RobertsonPublishing.com

Printed on acid-free paper.

For Tom
Lifelong friend
who helped me help him
bring both of us back alive,
keeping up the flow of wit
and dry observation throughout.

For Alicia
You transcribed our journals,
listened patiently over coffee,
and provided the occasional eye roll
to keep me grounded:
a voice of reason and encouragement
from start to finish.

ACKNOWLEDGMENTS

A number of quite generous people helped me with editing, advice, and fact-checking, including Nicolette Lategan, Lauren Lewis, Cathee van Rossem-St.Clair, Jim Asher, Laura Howard, Jessica Rohan, and Glen Robertson.

To write this book, I relied upon our journals, my own writings, consulted with my riding partner, researched facts and place names, and called upon my own memory. I changed a few names to retain privacy.

I didn't include footnotes or a bibliography, but information was gleaned from a number of sources, including the Dept. of Veterans Affairs, The Heritage Foundation, Kaiser Permanente, Pew Research, the Office of Financial Management, the Centers for Disease Control and Prevention, Gallup Analytics, The Week Junior Magazine, YouGov.com, Brookings Institution, WalletHub, the Dept. of the Treasury, Snopes, FiveThirtyEight, NPR, PolitiFact, Skeptical Science, Association of Statisticians of American Religious Bodies, The Atlantic, the ACLU, USAToday, The Guardian, The American Conservative, ReaganLibrary, Robert Reich, and the letters and diaries of Edith C. Robertson. Additional sources are noted in the text. Thanks to Kevin Stroud for his permission to quote from The History of English podcast.

I am aware that the United States of America is a collection of states which happen to be in America, and are not "America" any more than Peru, Canada, the United States of Mexico, Costa Rica, or any of the other countries on these two continents. I used the common nickname since it's less cumbersome and carries the weight of my intent, despite the entitled undertone. We live in America, but so do the people of Ecuador.

The cover photo is from a different trip, with different bikes. Same attitude however. *Photo by Betty Carpenter.* The photo on the back cover of me with Molly was taken by my wife, Alicia. The one with the Trihawk was taken by Mary Courtney. Illustrations of myself and the ProColor Magic Bunny were by Barb Kyger.

Rebel_Clue@icloud.com • RebelClue.blogspot.com

CONTENTS

Preface

PART I ~*Struggle for Identity & Reason*

Kid *vs.* World 1
My Life of Crime 15
How to Make a Quilt 29
The Spring Steel Kid 39
Words & Music 45
The Two Bards 57
Thoughts on Paper 71
Fuse, Meet Match 87
The Ugly Truth 111
Ducks & Dinosaurs 129
Ode to Yellow Line 159

PART II ~ *Breakout & Experience*

Kickstart 179
The Wet Shoe Journals ~ 9,847 Miles by Motorcycle 193
Map & Legend 348
Fifty Years Later 351

PART III ~ *Synthesis*

The Great Teenage Diaspora 407
Common Sense 423
    Thoughts on Thinking 433
    Rich Man, Poor Man 441
Final Thoughts 451

RebelClue.blogspot.com

PREFACE

This portmanteau of history, narrative, and observation is inextricably linked to how I learned to recognize injustice and wend my way past arbitrary rules. It is the tale of a motorcycle trip and what I learned from it—a homemade education in ethics and socioeconomics.

This is also a story of two road maps. The first is for those who suspect their life might hold unusual patterns or be trailing down dotted lines that fade into abject nothingness. The second map is provided by *The Great American Dream Machine*, which traces out the grey and blue history of our national unease and the primary reasons for it.

I have written all my life, usually for other people. That was my job. But *Rebel Without a Clue* is for all the van Goghs who end up in business instead of pouring out their soul onto a thousand frames of canvas, the Homeric rebels who question authority and fight for fairness despite the odds, and the quiet ones who would rather ride out in search of life with not much more than a toothbrush and a nervous grin.

About the Journals

Tom and I each kept a journal on the trip, notes we jotted down at the end of each day. Sentence fragments, really. I had a compact hardbound ledger; Tom's was a small binder. Many years later, my wife Alicia typed both journals into her iMac as a gift, with the idea I might someday write about our experiences. This book is the result.

When I finally started to write about the trip, it took a while to figure out that the journals in and of themselves didn't really tell the full story. I kept adding brief comments and asides until it became obvious I needed to rewrite everything as a unified piece. So I combined the journals to make it more readable, made myself the primary voice for simplicity, and added enough backstory to explain my situation in the context of the trip and the times I lived in. I then wrote an afterword to explain what I'd learned *from* the trip—as a series of individual monographs—which I eventually made separate, and reformatted into a sequel, *The Great American Dream Machine*.

That said, you might not have bargained for forthright commentary. You saw an old photo of a couple of guys on motorcycles and thought it would be interesting to find out how we managed to maunder our way from California to New York and back by way of Albuquerque without slamming into something or running out of money. Well, I hear you. I even sympathize, which is why I shoved my more spirited insights online. But don't fret; the volume you're holding now is complete unto itself. The gleanings from the aftermath just make it that more interesting.

"Better than pirates!"
– *T. Sawyer*

"Tis not so deep nor so wide as a church door, but 'twil serve, 'twil do."
– *Wm. S.*

"Hardly any typos."
– *Gene Faucher*

Kid *vs.* World

When I was a kid, I didn't talk right away. For years. No daddy, no mommy — nothing. I was this happy, animated, mute child. You might be thinking, *poor kid,* right? Like maybe there was something wrong with my larynx or maybe even my *brain,* and I had to have this huge operation with some hotshot doctor they called in from New York (and my parents were poor, so my father had to sell his antique pocket watch that was handed down from his grandfather, who was a famous railroad guy from way back, just to pay for the operation). No, nothing like that. I was mute because I was too *happy.*

See, I was surrounded by all these older kids, and I was the only child in the family. The boarders were the same age as my brother and sister — teenagers. I was evidently a very winning child, so they gave me constant attention. It was piggyback rides whenever my little arms went up, and *Jonny, do you want this? Jonny, do you want that?* and I didn't *have* to speak. Well, until I did. Because one fine day, I wanted Edith (my mother) to open the back door so I could go outside. (I didn't have the skill necessary to turn the doorknob.)

"Edith, would you please open the door?" I was a polite kid; that's how I was raised. And totally unspoiled, even in my youth — *amazing.*

Okay, well yes, there is a point to all this other than how obnoxious I was as a kid. The point is, I didn't "spake as a child," which is what scripture tells us we're all supposed to do until we grow up and put away childish things. I never had to do any of that stuff because I was already grown up by the age of two. And *totally* unspoiled; remember that.

So, during the first three years of my life, I was the only child, surrounded by up to ten teenagers at any given time, with no baby talk. (It was against our religion.) Being a toddler in this milieu gave my developing intellect a lot to consider. I was in the catbird seat watching all these young adults interact, both with each other and with my parents, and my parents with each other. There was no television in our house at that time, so my attention was (however unwittingly) focused on some very complex systems at work.

That kind of childhood has far-reaching consequences. In any dynamic system, early changes can create wildly divergent outcomes. The sooner you turn the rudder, the less effort you have to make.

I was born in 1950, when the U.S. economy was shifting into overdrive. My older siblings, Glen and Sheri, were born eleven and twelve years earlier, when there were empty fields behind our house, clear up into the Los Gatos foothills.

Our family took in other children as boarders (similar to foster children today), and we raised goats (for the milk) in the backyard. Sheri, Glen, and I were taught to call our parents by their given names, Edith and Ray, even as children. This was for the sake of all the other kids living with us. Our parents felt that anything else would have been elitist and wrong. That was the way of it, and I thought nothing of it at the time, but to this day I think of them that way, as Edith and Ray Robertson, individuals who happened to be my parents.

By the time I hit the second grade, the boarders had gone back to live with their parents and Glen and Sheri were off to college. So all of a sudden there I was, home alone, with parents.

I was just a kid, and nobody thought much about what I did with my time. So, I took things apart and made my own inventions. I built forts in trees and attics and hunted for pollywogs in the creek. I made a few small bombs like most other kids. All perfectly normal.

Every spring, Santa Clara Valley was white with the blossoms of fruit trees. My brother Glen had picked prunes to earn spending money. Sheri had cut cots, and so did I. (To "cut cots" is to pit apricots with a short paring knife and place the fruit face-up on a wooden drying tray while making every effort to avoid stabbing either yourself or the kid standing next to you.) Lots of kids cut cots during the summer, and the money was pretty good for the ones who didn't get too much blood on the fruit.

The rules at table were the same for all of us. We had to take at least one bite of everything on our plate before we could leave the table (so we wouldn't end up as picky eaters later in life). When we left, we could only leave with both hands full—holding dishes or cutlery to take back to the kitchen. A common enough reminder getting up from our dining room table was that dry admonition from Edith, "Two hands full."

Our family didn't go out to eat very often, and at the end of one meal in a restaurant, I picked up my plate and glass and was off my chair looking for the kitchen before anyone spotted what I was doing. In our family, some concepts never changed. But even though the work ethic and the two hands full rule were the same for my older siblings, other issues became decidedly different.

Skeptics Inc.

I was taught to identify corporate trickery from a young age. It was a never-ending education. Edith poked fun at television commercials with the same vigilance and determination as she did everything else. In our home on Englewood Avenue, the television was turned on for just a few programs: the evening news, *Walt Disney's Wonderful World of Color*, and *Bonanza*. (Plus, I got to watch a few other shows on my own that weren't considered completely dreadful.) So, the television wasn't on all that often. There were two sixty-second ads at the top and bottom of each hour, and Edith had an acerbic comment for many of them—and for some of the more infantile dialogue in the programs, as well. Nobody got away scot-free. The word, "Hollywood," delivered in a dry undertone of derision, was common enough.

Would we all grow up to be handsome and beautiful and have a joyful golden retriever (it was always a golden retriever) to run and play with on the beach if "dad" (who always wore a cardigan sweater) smoked a certain brand of cigarette? Or perhaps we should aspire to ride the range as Marlboro Men and pause our horses on a ridge, backlit by the setting sun as the music swelled and we puffed on a cigarette. Because that was the implication. Forget about cancer, play with the puppy! Free horses and sunsets in every pack!

Would we all become witty and smile wonderful smiles if we ate a certain brand of cereal or drove a specific car? Our family was perfectly aware of the connection between cigarettes and cancer, the necessity for seatbelts, and the dangers of too much sugar by the early 1950s. Most people were.

Edith called it brainwashing, and she wasn't wrong.

Her one-woman tirade against stupidity and manipulation was indefatigable, allowed for few exceptions, and I'm absolutely certain that my early education into the mendacity of anonymous people gave me the kickstart I needed to draw my own conclusions.

I don't think that Edith planned it, but her little boy was never going to grow up to become a True Believer. So when I started questioning my parents' religion, she didn't contradict me. She wanted me to question everything, just as she did.

Edith's science experiment

I was able to take thirteen vitamin tablets in one swallow by the time I was thirteen years old. I know this only because the numbers matched, and I thought I'd accomplished something at the time. At breakfast I got three powders: Tiger's Milk, brewer's yeast, and Carnation Instant Milk. Edith stirred these into a half-full glass of water, then augmented this concoction with 1% skim milk of uncertain vintage.

Uncertain, because Edith didn't drink milk or use it in her coffee, and sometimes it got a little long in the tooth. Or a lot. Which taught Edith's little boy how to engage his gag reflex from an early age since the powders didn't always mix that well, and I had to face these slimy clumps from time to time. All by myself. Along with bad milk.

This witch's brew was all for my personal benefit. It was fried liver for breakfast, or sometimes a scrambled egg. I could have one bowl of cereal (covered with Kretschmer wheat germ) on Saturday mornings as a treat. Without sugar. This went on for years.

I think Edith bought bread by the pound, even though Ray (my father) had been a baker. She liked her bread to have a good solid heft to it, and the longer it lasted, the better. Dense and hard was her motto, probably from growing up as a child of the Oklahoma Dust Bowl. Good tasting food wasn't against Edith's religion per se; it just wasn't high on her list. It wasn't against mine, but I was too young to vote.

But breakfast did have a downside — cleverly disguised. Edith allowed me to eat my orange juice frozen, straight from the cardboard tube. It took less time because she didn't have to mix it or pour it or anything. I found out over the ensuing years that the ascorbic acid in my Donald Duck orange juice concentrate was even more powerful than the orange juice, and it neatly removed all traces of enamel from my teeth. Teeth that were supposed to last a lifetime.

And of course, we exercised each morning before we left for school. Jumping jacks, knee bends, sit-ups, push-ups, and I had a chinning bar in my bedroom doorway — all to the tune of *Chicken Fat*, a catchy song composed by the same guy who wrote *The Music Man*. Edith's kid was going to know he'd been through a full-blown childhood, no matter what.

Instead of candy, I got chunks of carob from the health food store, which was very good — like chocolate. Maybe a couple of times a year. Or she would buy me a piece of sugarcane to chew. Or a pomegranate to pick apart. Sometimes a chunk of honeycomb in a four-inch wooden frame. Childhood was interesting, but dental visits were a nightmare.

Reading Lesson

Until I got past the second grade, I didn't have much reason to exist beyond watching *The Adventures of Rocky and Bullwinkle*. I ate and I slept. I went to school and learned some stuff, but I wasn't a very good student. I didn't know anything or think about much beyond my next bowl of Cheerios. I was just an eight-year-old kid getting by on his good looks until that summer, when my mother announced her next little project.

Edith called me into the house, sat me down, fixed me with one of her looks, and laid down the law.

"I will not have a *non-reader* in this family," she said firmly. "Understand? You are going to learn how to *read*."

Okay, she was my mother. What's the big deal? Fourth-grade teacher who used a whistle and stopwatch for almost everything, Edith Coffin Robertson brooked no disrespect or dissenting opinion whatsoever. It was her way or a lengthy discussion guaranteed to go her way in the end. I was toast no matter what. Nobody messed with Mrs. Robertson—not her fourth-grade students, not their parents, and certainly not me, sitting there kicking my heels on our living room couch.

Now, I already *did* know how to read; I just wasn't very good at it, and it wasn't something I could fake. What Edith wanted was *fluency*. She wanted me to love reading as she loved it, as our entire family loved it. She wanted her kid to know the joy of being transported to another time and place, and she wanted me to gain all the knowledge and second-hand experience that reading could provide. She wasn't kidding around. I had no real choice here. When you were good, she was strict, but when you were bad, she was the Spanish Inquisition. Edith was focused, verbal, and relentless.

Anywho, that afternoon, on that couch, with the sunlight streaming through our dining-room windows and dust motes doing their Brownian motion thing in the still air of summer, I was hit with a rude reality. Our family had standards, I was somehow in violation of them, and I was expected to live up to them. Not just expected—I had no other option. I *would* live up to them. I was crying there on the couch because my insignificant smudge of a life just got *ruined* and I didn't know why. *No summer vacation?* I still remember the tears running down my face while I sat there trying to wipe them with my sleeve, listening to Edith go on and on about what my life was about to become and wondering why I had to die so young.

"You will read aloud to me for an hour each day," she was saying. "You will follow me wherever I go and read loudly enough for me to hear you *at all times*. If I'm running the vacuum cleaner, you will *read louder*. If I go outdoors, you are to stay with me and *keep reading*. Shout if you have to. It will not be my job to hear you; it will be your job to make sure you get heard. At all times. Do you understand? Nod your head that you understand. Good. We start tomorrow." And then she handed me a book. A nice thick casebound book.

Edith was no dummy. The book she put into my hands was *Lad, A Dog,* by Albert Payson Terhune, and it had a picture of a collie on the front. A perfect book for a little boy to start with.

Years later, Edith told me that after three or four days of this, well, one day she couldn't hear me. My voice had just sort of petered out.

"I was going to come yell at you, and I came looking. I found you on the couch, engrossed in the story, silently moving your lips. You hadn't noticed me, so I tiptoed back out of the room. It was in that moment that I knew I'd won." And she had. From that point on, I was hooked on books.

Adventure stories, science fiction, and novels. Big books, little books, and mysteries. I was suddenly exploring abandoned houses with hidden doors and staircases that climbed into darkness and old men who rarely spoke but knew a lot and lighthouses and coves that might have hidden treasure.

Danny Dunn and the Homework Machine. Pippi Longstocking. The Hardy Boys. The first ones were like candy bars, and then I got into more adult fare, such as *Æsop's Fables,* Agatha Christie, and books on chess. I went right through the *Horatio Hornblower* series. Edith had handed me the keys to her kingdom. And now it was mine. The result was terrifying and wonderful.

The little speech that changed everything

I was trundling along like any kid my age, when something odd happened. I was at home with my mother. It was during the day, probably on the weekend, probably summertime when, as a schoolteacher, Edith would have been home. Let's say it was around noonish. I know we were in the living room because I remember how the light streamed in from the windows facing the driveway, framed by those hideous yellow curtains we had. Yet again, the dust motes danced in the sunlight as I stood on our pea green carpet, lost in the magic haze of childhood, forever poised in those few minutes that changed my life.

Edith turned to look at me, and then she paused. It was a little odd, and I wouldn't have noticed, except she caught and held my attention. My mother did not pause very often; if a thing wanted doing, she did it. On this day, however, she was weighing something, rolling it over in her mind. She kept looking at me, her lips a tight line of thought.

I remember feeling curious about her staring at me because it was as if she were sizing me up for a new pair of jeans or a haircut. And then she spoke.

"Do what is *right*, no matter what."

She just flat out said it, with a hard edge on the word right. It was out of the blue. I stood there, transfixed and wondering.

"I'm not telling you to break the law, but if the law is wrong, there are times you have to break it — when it's the right thing to do. Remember that," she added.

End of conversation, or pronouncement, or whatever the hell it was. I had no idea what was going on in her life, nor what law she was getting ready to break, but I heard what she said and it made perfect sense.

Edith's brief message did more to change my life than anything I can think of. Not that I always *did* the right thing, but that lesson became a solid buttress against my back when nudge became push became shove with the Selective Service, the FBI, and an amoral Uncle Sam.

Edith had told me to pursue "the right thing" in its truest form: the truth I already knew. I was to question any authority. The draft, the church, and even — *gulp* — whether to participate in school if I wasn't being taught something worthwhile. I'd heard the message before, but never with such dire commitment or drama. Edith had decanted a simple, yet strict moral code into my somewhat random soul, and it was her spine I used when my own was too young to take the weight.

My mother had me tested

When I was in the third grade, my brother Glen switched his major from theology, after graduating from Moody Bible

Institute, to psychology at Wheaton College (also in Chicago). He then entered the Psychology Master's Degree program at San José State College. One of his classes required him to administer twenty intelligence quotient tests. The vacation trailer in our backyard had a kitchen table, which is where he gave me the Stanford-Binet I.Q. test. I was homework.

I remember the stopwatch he used and the one joke I made when he asked me the name of the type of tree which is *not* evergreen. The answer was supposed to be *deciduous*, but I just couldn't think of it. And the stopwatch was ticking, and I was running out of time, and he was my big brother, just sitting there trying not to look at me, trying to keep his face professionally neutral. *Ticka, ticka, ticka, ticka.* When the pressure became insurmountable, I blurted out the only thing I could come up with.

"Autumn prone."

Which made perfect sense to me. My trying-very-hard-to-be-serious brother was absolutely still for a moment, holding it in, but then the dam burst, and the moment fell apart into laughter and giggles, and we couldn't continue until the following day.

"You know it was supposed to be deciduous, right?"

"Yeah, but I couldn't think of it."

Between my mother being a teacher who wanted to know how I was doing, regular district testing, and my big brother's homework, by the time I was in the seventh grade, I had probably taken four or five such tests of one kind or another.

I had gotten pretty good at it. Quite the little test-taker, I could tell in the little drawings of "things that are alike" that the television set and the clothes iron were both unplugged, which meant they were both powered by electricity but without power at the moment, which made them (arguably) *more* alike than the other items. I could do so without really thinking about it—which gave me more time for all the other stuff, the more difficult stuff. The remaining answers got easier as well, because I'd seen these kinds of tests so many times that at a certain point, *any* performance test put in front of me was just another bicycle I hadn't ridden yet.

Not only were all the tests rather alike, but many of the answers were subjective. I didn't agree with the criteria, but it was pretty easy to see how I was expected to respond. The TV set was unplugged, just like the iron, but in that same group was a drawing of a closed book. Was the unplugged TV more like the closed book because they were both informational conduits not providing information? The unplugged clothes iron wasn't providing information either, but it never would (other than "hot" or "room temperature") because it was just an iron—which now made *it* the odd guy out.

And that wasn't the only instance. The psychologists who designed tests such as the Wechsler and Stanford-Binet hadn't thought things through, and their slip was showing. Cultural bias and home environment were key issues. A large part of my youth seemed to be spent in a dance involving the book, the clothes iron, and the TV set, and my ability to recognize the differences between them.

The tests of that era had been designed with assumptions that attempted to force "correct" answers that were only correct if you used the test maker's world view—a kind of amorphous circular reasoning. That's what these tests often tried to do. I think the test designers assumed that the sheer quantity of questions would average out anomalous issues to make a workable score, but their cultural bias could never be averaged out because it existed throughout the test.

I was perhaps reading more into them than expected, but that's what happens when you give test after test to a bright kid who's bored and getting a little annoyed by all the shortsighted assumptions. He starts coming up with different and better answers. It was almost a challenge.

Why shouldn't the answer have been "autumn prone?" Deciduous was the correct and proper answer sitting upright in its little chair with folded hands and feet flat on the floor, but "autumn prone" was e.e. cummings coming right at you with a grin. If you want forest management, you get deciduous and lumberjacks, but if you want to paint the forest in its most vibrant and true colors, *autumn prone* was the way to do it. My brother knew that instinctively, which is why he couldn't stop laughing. My answer broke the test because the test couldn't account for it, either specifically or generally.

It was just like being in church, where you were expected to accept one right answer when there may have been many possible explanations — or none. *But forget about searching for the truth; that's too confusing. Let's help you by narrowing your choices to one. There you go. Doesn't that feel better now?*

I started trusting books more than adults, but I didn't trust all the books either. I did have faith that if I read *enough* books, my overall understanding and knowledge would go up.

This ignorance was similar to the false assumptions that underpinned the tests I was given, skewing everything. The I.Q. tests and performance evaluations weren't measuring what their designers thought they were measuring. They were measuring my ability to *take tests*. I was starting to wise up.

Another test?

When I entered the seventh grade at Fisher Middle School, there was a school-wide test. Another *test*. They didn't say what it was for, just that we all had to take it. And I was in no mood. I don't know if I didn't have my Cheerios that day or what, but I was fed up — I wasn't having it.

I marked the test as wrong as I could on the ones I knew automatically, and marked everything else with a repeating pattern, like **A, B, D, C**, over and over down every page, then turned it in when the others did. Just my little way of saying "thank you" to the world.

It felt scary as I did it, like the bottom had fallen out. I felt a kind of sick horror even as I marked the forms. But no matter which mule it is, if you prod it and push it enough times, at some point it's going to kick. Well, that was my first real kick. The first kick that landed, anyway.

I got yanked into the school office so fast... The school guidance counselor (all the kids called him adder-adder because he was so annoying) said I'd tested so *low* that he knew there was something wrong. So, he spent twenty minutes trying to figure out what I was up to after having the school nurse determine that I wasn't, in fact, sick or dying. When the nurse said I was fine, he assumed I was just being a brat and tried to shame me about how I was letting down America and *what had I been thinking?* He had me take another test right there in his office.

I didn't have the emotional moxie to thumb my nose at him. I just kept my head down and nodded when I was supposed to nod and got out of there as fast as I could after retaking the test. I wasn't particularly afraid of adder-adder, but Edith was at the other end of this situation, and she was the real force I would have to reckon with—like that shark in *Jaws* you know is coming because of the music...

~ Da ***dum*** ~

That would be my mother: *Jaws* in a sensible blouse and skirt. When Edith heard about my little experiment in civil disobedience, she marched down to the school, pulled rank, and got hold of the results. She told me later I had tested at eighty-five the first time and oh, a lot higher the second time. If I could hold my own for twenty-three moves against Koltanowski in San Francisco when I was in the fourth grade, Edith knew there was no way on this green Earth I tested that low. She was furious, but also puzzled. *What had I been thinking?*

The whole situation irritated me, and I felt very much alone. It seemed I'd let down the entire known universe, including the alternative ones we only speculate about. I was tired of taking tests and knew I was going nowhere. My life was stupid and pointless. Looking back on it, the level I tested at normally should have been lower. Not because I knew the answers (I didn't actually—all the tests were a little different), but because I knew what the right answers *looked like*. I was scoring high because I knew how to score high. I had a good feel for what the answers ought to be, and I knew how to pace myself throughout each test to save time and go back over the more troublesome questions. I've used that skill throughout my life.

Expectations were high, but I wasn't as smart as everyone seemed to think I was, and in my heart, I kind of knew it. That was the fear that haunted me. That I would never be as smart, as educated, or as talented as I *should* be.

Our whole family was bright and capable. My mother was a teacher, Ray owned a retail business downtown, and my older brother and sister had both gone off to college. Glen was studying *Aramaic,* for crying out loud. I was surrounded by success. But somehow I didn't get with the program. I was frustrated beyond belief. My frustration had grown over time, and I didn't know how to overcome it. That test was my breaking point. The adults could say whatever they wanted, but I didn't care for the conversation.

I didn't know it at the time, but I was in survival mode. That test was another case of me getting my feet wet with unheralded truth, and my start to taking matters into my own hands. The actions I would soon employ to wrest my education out of the control of others were at least partly seeded by all these damn tests. One after the other, they were designed to assure everyone that I was on the right path — the common path to success — and that the groove I was in would soon be deep enough to keep me in it. But I was sick of the groove, and I wanted out.

My brother mentioned something years later, that intelligence is not just the ability to do math problems or word puzzles, but also the ability to get along with others and function well in society — to succeed in life. I kinda sorta knew that, and at least part of my frustration stemmed from being so late in maturing. Plus, none of the tests were measuring for that. But nobody said anything, and I knew I was falling behind.

I was smart enough to rebuild an automobile and I could run track well enough to set a middle-school record, but my social skills were mostly internal admonitions to keep my head down and my mouth shut. I was questioning way too many accepted norms like religion, school, and the pressure to succeed, and I was dwelling overlong on the obvious conflicts.

Despite these limitations, there were a few things I had some control over: reading, music, and late-night television. I was like a vacuum cleaner with a special attachment for books and records, and that worked for me because I could learn about stuff outside of family, church, and school.

Besides hanging out at my brother's house, another source of information was Johnny Carson, who took over *The Tonight Show* in 1962. I have no idea how I found out about him, but he was on from 11:30 to 1:00 am, and I was determined to watch. Somehow I got hold of a 15 inch TV set and installed it in my closet at eye level, across from my bed. When the door to my room opened, damage control was automatic: the cord was pulled out of the wall socket by a thin rope (causing an immediate cessation of sound), the closet door swung shut (hiding the evidence), and I appeared to be fast asleep (of course). It worked a charm from middle school until my parents didn't care anymore. Carson taught me a lot about self-deprecation, grace under pressure, and what everyone in the real world was doing and thinking—valuable stuff.

There was another issue. My mind kept wondering about other people and what they were thinking. What their issues were. Did other people concern themselves with how they fit in the world as much as I did? It was hard to describe.

I was alone in this, perhaps afraid to even mention it. And perhaps everyone was like this; I had no idea, but they didn't seem to be concerned. I was somewhat aware of the boy-girl relationship mystery: "Does she like me, does she not?" but this was more than that. When I thought about it, my perspective rotated, and I could pretend to be the other person. I finally decided I just had a knack for putting myself in other people's shoes. It was probably a good thing, but it made me more observant than was probably good for me, and my mind never let up.

During this time, I started high school. Which I hated, but slogged through until my sophomore year, which is when I got two kinds of sick. Which wasn't fun. But all of these issues overlapped like a "this is your life" Venn diagram. And right in the middle of that overlap was a perfect idea, rolling its eyes at me and daring me to test the limb I was about to venture out on. It required a simple ruse, but I had some skills. And I had Edith's moral code burning a hole in my back pocket.

My Life of Crime

Several things happened during my sophomore year of high school to allow me to become the hero of my own life. First, I had to have my appendix removed—no biggie, right? But just after that *(drum roll, please)*, I got pertussis, otherwise known as whooping cough. The path I followed from that point forward was narrow and led in risky directions, but I took it anyway. I was too sick, too tired, and I just didn't care about the rules anymore. I allude to the sinister affair involving a small metal die, about a million books, and my personal moral compass.

There was no vaccine or cure for whooping cough at that time; you just had to suffer through it. If you were reasonably healthy and not too young or too old, you lived. But if you'd just had your appendix removed, you could tear out your stitches and maybe bleed to death before they could get you to a hospital, which the doctor said with measured tones, would not be good.

Sometimes the coughing was non-stop and a little violent, what with the repeated *whoops* as I tried to get more air into my lungs and the spasming of my diaphragm up and down and up and down until the contents of my stomach started coming into my throat and... well, until it finally stopped.

And I was always left exhausted. Then the next bout would hit me, which was unpredictable, but guaranteed to put me through the wringer all over again. And then again. And this would go on for quite a while. One fit led to the next. It was *not* fun, plus I was clutching at my right side to hold the stitches together, like a cowboy in a bad western who just got shot.

This resulted in a very stern medical letter "To whom it may concern..." that brooked no questions and allowed me to walk out of any class at any time so I wouldn't start coughing uncontrollably, throw up my breakfast, rip my stitches, and bleed out in the middle of World History.

Over time, I was able to suppress the gag reflex and eventually the cough itself, but it took a lot of practice (of course, I *got* a lot of practice). There was a kind of meditation I went into while I "lived with" that deadly tickle in my throat. Strange skill to learn, but I could never transfer it over to my *talk* reflex, which would have made it far more useful later in life.

I was taken out of school for several weeks when I first got sick. I was reading up a storm, and (important point) realized I didn't *want* to go back to school and trudge from classroom to classroom, sitting in each like a lump for fifty minutes. I wasn't up to it; my chest hurt and I was tired all the time with what my body was going through. What I really wanted to do was *read*. Turns out there was a solution, but it was going to take a devious kid to figure it out. I was my own perfect tool.

My mother was a schoolteacher, but the family business was my father's bailiwick: Los Gatos Office Equipment and Supply on North Santa Cruz Avenue, which is where I worked most days after school. Along with everything else, we sold custom rubber stamps—two to three every day. Actually, we had them made for us by Mercury Rubber Stamp in Santa Clara. Pretty straightforward. When we got the rubber stamps back by mail, it was my job to check them for accuracy, price them out, and call each client.

Occasionally, someone would want something unique, such as a stamp of a signature or a logo—in which case we had to send out for a metal die to be made, which was used instead of movable type to make the stamp. This cost more, and we always put the die in the same bag with the stamp. The customer had paid for it after all, and it could always be used to make a new stamp if something happened to the original.

Being the observant kid that I was, I knew the die itself was far more accurate than the rubber stamp, but you had to be careful to ink it and imprint the paper perfectly by coming straight down and square to get a usable impression. How did I know this? Well, it looked logical, and after a few simple experiments, I convinced myself it was true: it worked.

I had the bright idea to have a rubber stamp made of my mother's signature, just to get that die. It became quite handy when our doctor's letter finally lost its mojo. Instead of going to school like everyone else, I elected to forge medical excuses on an as-needed basis so I could skip most of my classes and read six to ten hours a day before going on to college. From that point on, I was either at the park or our local library, reading. I had opted out.

The tension in my soul was almost overwhelming when I began this little adventure. I knew exactly what I was doing, and I had a good idea where it might lead. I had an idea of what my parents and the entire known universe would have thought of my brilliant little strategy (had anyone found out), but I did it anyway. It was my ticket to the future.

In my defense, I had been taught to make my own decisions. Indeed, it was part of our family culture to do so. I had Edith's emphatic little speech about doing the right thing lodged in my subconscious, along with the example of my father's independent business spirit. All of which caused me to pause, evaluate the facts as I saw them, and take a stand. Right or not, wise or not, I picked a weedy, overgrown fork in the road and started jogging. And then I picked up the pace.

Back in high school, nobody even noticed I was missing. I was one of many, and not of particular importance in the grand scheme of things. I had attended enough classes by the spring of 1968 to graduate, although I'd missed so much that my grade point average was just scraping by. Like a ghost, I had flitted in and out of Los Gatos High. My body had been there on occasion to take a critical test or two (and to show my face), but my mind had never been—not after I made that great leap out of the frying pan. In the end, I refused the diploma. The school hadn't educated me, *I* had. *Gulp.*

So, I created my own education from scratch. Kind of like deciding the standard white bread from the grocery store just wasn't good enough and I should instead try combining flour, water, yeast, a little salt, and my own special starter to bake a sourdough so full of flavor and texture it could aspire to greatness. I didn't go through the normal teenage coming-of-age program because I took charge of the official agenda—school, football games, the big dance—and scribbled all over it.

My high school experience (what there was of it) had been lecture-driven, which didn't work for me at all. I wasn't learning much, and it seemed like nothing more than an elaborate babysitting program. At that point in my life, I wanted the stories that explained the facts. Giving me a bunch of unrelated information wasn't helping. Where was the real history, the actual science, the literature of life I'd been promised? *Great Expectations* and Chemistry 101 — that's all ya got? I was appalled.

One-way ticket to Palookaville

I'd been brought up as a voracious reader in a family of voracious readers who believed reading books every day for one's entire existence was not only normal but expected, and that anything less was a disservice to our family, the country, and our own brains. And maybe our local librarian. Anyone who didn't appreciate books as a natural conduit of entertainment and education didn't know what they were missing and had probably been raised by wolves. So there was that.

When I started reading down at Oak Meadow Park, I knew it was a one-way ticket and I had no idea whether there was anything for me at the end. It was a massive gamble. I was staking my entire future on my own ability with no end in sight at a very early stage in life's journey. Everything I'd been taught, all the common wisdom shouted, *You fool — do not go down this road!* But the stars were aligned, and the opportunity was right there in front of me, daring me to pick it up and put it to good use. I had the die of my mother's signature; I knew how to use it without leaving smudges; school was utter nonsense, and I had something better to do.

I justified my actions by reading the good stuff, the works of accomplished writers who (presumably) had something to say, something important for me to read. We didn't have a set of the Great Books at home like some families, but it wasn't that hard to find the classics at our local library, and although I found lists of such books, many of the authors' names were common knowledge anyway.

Names such as Henry James, Virginia Woolf, and Charles Darwin. This wasn't some gigantic mystery. I didn't know who

Christopher Marlowe was (yet), but I'd heard Shakespeare's name bandied about so much I couldn't remember when I *hadn't* known who he was. And there were many others on the list, including physicists, philosophers, and archeologists.

I took a passing glance at sociology with Abraham Maslow's hierarchy of needs and B. F. Skinner's *Walden Two*. I also knew something of the anthropologist Margaret Mead and what she found regarding cultural issues in New Guinea and coming of age in Samoa. This foundation was sketchy at best, but it made me wonder about behavioral issues, social forces, and motivations later on when I returned from the motorcycle trip.

I got books from the library and a few from bookstores with the money I made at my father's store, and I borrowed a few from my brother's collection (most of which I returned). I lugged all these books around in a cardboard box I kept with the spare tire and a few tools under the back cowl of my car.

There was blue sky above me each day at the park and I could hear the birds in the trees. In my mind I was in one of Richard Feynman's famous lectures, struggling to understand the two-slit experiment of quantum mechanics or watching in my mind's eye when he loosed a bowling ball on a long wire to swing down the center aisle of a lecture hall to impress his audience with the laws of physics. (He didn't die on the return swing.) Right brain teaching. Smart guy.

I may have been sipping a Coke and eating a PB&J sandwich under an oak tree in Bachman Park, but I was also sifting dirt with Louis and Mary Leakey in Olduvai Gorge in Tanzania when they made discoveries that would transform our understanding of human ancestors.

A few years later, I would be hiking with Donald Johanson and Tom Gray through the dust and rocks of the Rift Valley in Ethiopia when they discovered the bones of Lucy, a tiny lady three feet tall who (by the look of her hip, knee, and ankle joints) had managed to walk fully upright some 3.5 million years ago. Her head was the size of a softball, and everyone on this planet traces their DNA back to someone just like her.

Langston Hughes, Thomas Wolfe, Rollo May, John Updike, Carl Rogers, and Sylvia Plath; Saul Bellow, Rachel Carson and

Ayn Rand; Cervantes, Sabatini, and R.D. Laing. For me, these authors constituted an unbroken chain of heroic mentors who knew each other in some nebulous metaverse of wisdom and sagacious writing.

I devoured their ideas, their characters, and their way of looking at the world—a more sophisticated view than mine. All while sitting under a tree at the park, all during the hours that would have been (to my mind) misspent in school. I read *Look Homeward, Angel* so many times I had to tape the book back together.

Part of it was a slog, I'll admit. Writers can't create the great stuff all the time; it comes in short bursts and passages that occur between the rolling swells of prose and poetry. Not every paragraph can be a full-rigged ship plunging through the spray of our lives, but when those ships are sighted, our lives change a bit—as did mine. They mark our existence with a truth we recognize, even if we ourselves have never been on that ocean, down that road, or in that courtroom.

For if a writer can get me to clamber up the ratlines and over the tumblehome to somehow get myself on board and see the ocean through *his* vision? That is gold. That is the dream, to be so engrossed in an alternative universe that for a time we become someone who doesn't have a paper due the next day, or a mean coworker, or a thoughtless spouse.

I became Horatio Hornblower on a ship of the line, chasing down a shrewd French captain rounding the peninsula just off the harbor at Brest. I was Frodo Baggins picking his way through the Dead Marshes with Sam at this side, on his journey to Mordor to throw the One Ring into oblivion. Whatever the story, gifted writers brought me in, made me see, provided the texture, glamor, anxiety, and taste of something I could not otherwise have experienced. It was my second existence, my education, and my freedom.

I had educated myself by reading an incredible variety of books, one right after the other, but there were two very large subjects still out there staring straight at me: Shakespeare and the Bible. I wasn't sure how I would tackle Shakespeare, but I had long familiarity with the Bible.

The urgent imperative

The only question in my mind was how much time I would have to accomplish this endless task of self-education. That was a big factor in this little equation of mine. Would I run out of road before I could achieve anything useful? I didn't want to be stopped in the middle (wherever and whenever that might be), but I knew the long arm of authority could reach out at any moment to snatch me off that park bench, admonish me severely, then plop me right back into high school with gyves upon my wrists and ankles.

Someone would recognize me at the park or library and wonder what I was doing, or see through my ruse in some other way. Somebody in the high school office would get suspicious of identical signatures. (If I'd been smart about this little crime spree from the beginning, I would have made two or three dies from different samples of both my mother and father's signatures and intermixed them.) So, there was that disaster lurking in the background. I had all the time in the world, but I was forever on the cusp of losing my entire universe, which drove me to read many books I would have passed on. I had to read them now because I might never again have the chance, and I assumed I needed the kind of depth I would get from such literature.

Vocabulary lesson

I had acquired a decent enough vocabulary even at an early age because of the family I was born into—*deciduous, right?*—but that put even more pressure on me to develop my own depth of knowledge. Given the authors I was reading, I kept running into words I'd never encountered.

At some point, I got a four-foot-tall reading stand and a massive casebound dictionary, then put the latter atop the former. This setup allowed me to keep a decent dictionary open day and night. I made a little vow to myself to look up words I didn't know, and used that reference even after search engines such as Google replaced it. I felt guilty if I skipped over a word I didn't know or just assumed its meaning by context. A book without a dictionary is like pants without a belt, and sloppy attire didn't work in our family. I would often read beyond the original words and halfway down the page out of curiosity and momentum, a habit that eventually sparked my interest in words, word origins, and the interrelatedness of languages.

Bertrand Russell

One thing I did get out of high school was a very critical, very particular assignment. I was to study something from recent world events and write a report. I chose the Cuban Missile Crisis, which had occurred a few years before. That report was like that grain of dust every raindrop and snowflake must have to precipitate from a cloud.

In the autumn of 1962 (when I was in the seventh grade), the world came close to nuclear war when the United States and the USSR turned a dispute over the Soviet installation of missiles in Cuba into a dangerous game of chicken. Everyone on Earth faced unthinkable horror for thirteen days.

Two years after that event, I wrote my paper, and in that process, discovered a couple of things that would enable my efforts to educate myself. I learned the mechanics of discovery and research at our public library. That was important, but I also found that in addition to Kennedy and Khrushchev, there had been a crucial *third* party involved in the negotiations: Bertrand Russell, a British private citizen, who had tried desperately to defuse the situation by sending telegram after telegram to the parties involved, plus others who might have been able to help.

I read the telegrams he sent to the UN Secretary-General U. Thant, and British Prime Minister Harold Macmillan, and the telegrams he sent back and forth to Kennedy and Khrushchev. But that wasn't the main lesson.

I'd never heard of Bertrand Russell, and discovering him was revelatory. He was a person of wide-ranging knowledge, a philosopher, logician, mathematician, historian, social critic, and political activist. Russell wrote essays, which were published by magazines and gathered into books. He won the Nobel Prize for Literature in 1950 "in recognition of his varied and significant writings in which he champions humanitarian ideals and freedom of thought."

I'd heard of the Nobel Prize and knew of its origin story, of Alfred Nobel inventing dynamite and then having second thoughts about the whole idea, and I knew of the Pulitzer Prize for journalism. But I'd never heard of anyone who simply wrote essays to express his thoughts, then got them published. That was new and different. I was quite naïve; I just hadn't thought it through. Did I have any thoughts I wanted to express? No—not yet. But later, yes, and Bertrand Russell became my archetype.

The anti-jump muscles relaxed

With my insatiable curiosity and desire to create, I realized I was on some kind of mission in life, and that the common road everyone else seemed to be traveling wasn't going to get me anywhere. I don't know why I felt that way, but I did, and it was a little scary. Actually, it was a lot scary, but I did it anyway. It was that kick in the pants I got from Edith in our living room that gave me the gumption I needed. And I would get no recognition for any of this because no one could know about it. My redemption had to come from the clarity of my actions, how much I retained, and the life I created from it. I was desperate to learn as much as I could for as long as I could. Although I couldn't yet see my future, I wanted it to contain some version of myself who wasn't puzzled at every turn.

It was a strange time. I was attempting to walk a dangerous path; I felt as though one wrong step and my life could blow up. But I was also the only one in charge. My parents cared about me, but they could never have understood my reasoning or motivation. I had no allies I could talk to about it. I was pretty darn sure no one would have approved or kept quiet once I'd told them what I was up to. So I was on my own, a naïve kid exploring a jumbled landscape with dire consequences if I so much as stumbled.

Or... Edith might have been on to me all along. It would have been right up her alley. She had no truck with outside authority and asserted her own brand of practical wisdom as a matter of course. Edith could have pulled rank with a librarian to see what I'd been reading, figured out what I was up to, and then secretly relished the thought of having such a Promethean in the family.

She told me years later that she had never had a problem with hiding her agenda from Ray. Whenever she did something he didn't agree with they fought for a bit, and then she usually acquiesced for the sake of familial harmony. After a stage wait, she went right back to doing whatever it was she had been doing, figuring her husband would reassess the situation and decide it wasn't worth the bother. And, if that wasn't going to work, her policy had been to drop it, knowing she had other irons in the fire and that it was more important to fight the battles she could win. So, she might have been secretly cheering me on—who knows?

I was attempting to be my own educator, my own teacher. But I was also my own taskmaster. To put it more accurately, the authors of the books I was reading were my teachers, and I was the one setting the curriculum. And hey, what did I know? I was in the midst of inventing a completely made-up, secret education. I knew what I was doing had explosive consequences attached. And a diploma no one would ever see. But it was also very important.

I trudged through book after book, many of them deathly dull. Virginia Woolf wrote sentences longer than my arm, like many writers of her era. Sometimes the prose was beautiful and mellifluous, but at other times it was just boiled cabbage, day after day. I wondered why some of these authors were supposed to be so great. Many of the books seemed somewhat pointless, but I read them anyway. I was a foot soldier in my own private army of one, trudging through the halls of literature, science, and history. I was looking for any scrap of humor, interesting emotion, or storyline that would spark my imagination. Thank goodness I was a fast reader.

Why did I put myself through it? I aspired, perhaps not to greatness, but to understanding. I wanted to *know* stuff, and even though I wasn't sure what that stuff was, I was pretty darn sure I could find it in books if I only read enough of them. I was like a quilter who buys fabric because it sparks something inside where imagination lives. The quilter doesn't know yet how they are going to use it, or indeed if it will ever be used. but they buy it anyway. I also wanted to be a more complete human being. I discovered the word *mensch,* and knew I didn't (as yet) measure up, but it got me to reading books on psychology and philosophy.

I had been taught that nothing is free in this existence, that I'd have to work hard to achieve anything. If reading Henry James, Flann O'Brien, Thomas Mann, and Flannery O'Connor right along with Arthur C. Clarke and C. S. Forester was the price I had to pay, so be it. Not completely painful of course, (these are very skilled writers with significant ideas), but I was not at a level, either in life experience or intellect, where I could properly appreciate what I was reading other than the fun of it all. I was force-feeding myself stuff I didn't understand. Brilliant, eh? *Oh well,* I thought, *perhaps some of this will sink in.*

If I'd known what I was looking for, I might have had a better handle on it. I mean, I recognized the names; the authors were mostly familiar to me and I discovered their peers as I went along, but I didn't know what *made* their writing great. It was a mystery that wouldn't get solved until several years later, when I managed to introduce Bill Shakespeare to Bob Dylan in a cloud of wonder and sudden comprehension.

All I had at the beginning was a sense of story and a ton of motivation because reading in the park was far better than sitting in some classroom that smelled of teenagers and listening to some uninspired teacher who didn't have a clue how to motivate anyone. I had to justify what I was doing and the only way I could do that was by reading the good stuff. Which I did. Plus a bunch of other stuff that was often a lot more interesting.

Working the puzzle

My reading regimen certainly followed our family culture, but by skipping so much high school—like a flat stone flung across a quiet pond, creating small ripples from time to time—I was clearly living outside the law. At least I was honest about it; I ate all my vegetables. I had been taught there was a consequence for any behavior, good or bad, and I was (perhaps unconsciously) weighing that against my own personal truth.

Not that I could have told you what that personal truth actually *was*; I was silent on that point, even with myself.

I was angry with my assumption of my parents' relentless expectations, by the hypocrisy of our church, and by the government's relentless enthusiasm for their war over in Vietnam.

I was also frustrated by my ignorance and lack of ability. Why I thought I should have known more than I did or been able to learn at a quicker rate, I have no idea, but that's the way it was. Perhaps it was the reading. I was going through some very accomplished authors, people who had done wonders with their lives and with the written word. And who was I? A shallow teenager with a shallow teenager's worried brow, attempting to pound his way through strange books with subject matter he often got the gist of, but never seemed to master. I was a fool on a foolish mission, but there had to be some benefit, even if I didn't get the full benefit right away.

Of course, for there to be any real benefit, I'd have to *retain* what I'd read, and more importantly, *understand* it. And even more important than that, be able to synthesize new concepts using my own intellect and apply those ideas to life in a meaningful way. Right.

Between work, home, and the various parks of Los Gatos, I lived in the society of adults. I sold business machines to local business owners, listened to an interesting variety of folk and protest music, and read a somewhat whimsically curated list that constituted my own version of the Great Books. So, I may have known a ton about spinning tops, the history of the Soviet gulags, Thomas Young and his two-slit experiment, and what had made James Joyce tick so loudly, but my quiet search for meaning continued unabated.

Some of these books I most decidedly did not understand, but I plowed through them anyway, figuring my unformed intellect might be able to assemble the pieces into something that made sense later, like a ship in a bottle erected by a judicious pull on a bit of thread.

I felt that general reading would generate a much needed level of complexity and depth to my pint-sized soul, and books on science would sharpen my mind like a knife on a whetstone.

When my brain began to overheat, I switched to other subjects and writers, none of whom were being taught in the high school where I was supposed to be sitting with a dutiful but vacant smile on my face for six hours a day.

I became Jude the Obscure, attempting to puzzle out my existence. I went from one book to another like a magpie, often engaged with several subjects at any given time. I wasn't skilled at anything in particular, but I was extraordinarily curious. And in my little corner of the world, that worked.

I read Frank Herbert's *Dune* and *Seven Pillars of Wisdom*, by T. E. Laurence — both of which gave some insight into the culture and long-held tension we saw boiling up in the Middle East in 1967, during the Arab-Israeli Six-Day War. Seeing Seven Pillars as the epic movie *Laurence of Arabia* by David Lean gave me even more perspective on that area of the world. It dovetailed with *The Source*, by James Michener, which chronicled Israel all the way back to pre-history.

I read any number of books on physics, paleontology, and books that explored the history of science and the scientific method while explaining Darwin's Theory of Evolution and natural history. I even read something on sea snails. It was quite interesting, but more importantly, explained natural selection far better than anything else I'd read, including Darwin.

Some were obscure, like the one about spinning tops. I was interested in why gyroscopes and bicycles didn't just fall over, given, you know, gravity. The quantum mechanics concept of non-locality also puzzled me, implying something too weird to believe. That what happened to an electron miles away or even on the other side of the galaxy could immediately influence an electron at a local level seemed bizarre. What Einstein called "spooky action at a distance." It defied all our current notions of natural law. It made me read even more.

The idea of continuous engagement of all matter came to me as a possible solution — as if everything were, in a transcendental way, rubbing shoulders with everything else.

But I didn't call it that and never wrote it up as a paper. I wasn't pursuing physics as a career, so it was just a nice idea, like many other nice ideas I had at the time. But I remembered it, and when I finally did read that Erwin Schrödinger had proposed quantum entanglement as a solution (long before I was even born), I felt a bit of validation. I didn't have the math to work the problem, but I did have the right sort of imagination. And for my purposes, that was enough.

So, while erstwhile classmates grappled with acne and algebra, I was devouring galaxies with interstellar architects and discussing unproved theories with philosophers and paleontologists. So much fun. It made me an oddity, a creature concocted of curiosity and quiet rebellion. I wore the same jeans as everyone else, but my mind danced to a different dimension.

Pyramid power

The social structure in high school has at times been compared to a pyramid. Popular kids on top, regulars in the middle, and a thin layer of nerds along the bottom. But graduation isn't the final scene. After high school, the smart ones often rise to the top of society, while the kids who peaked early find themselves at the bottom, working the hardest. The regulars rarely change. By sidestepping most of high school, I bypassed the pyramid. I leapfrogged my way directly into college, with afternoons and Saturdays in my father's business to pay for books (and much-needed accouterments for my 1960 Bugeye Sprite).

On the bell curve of life, I put myself far over to one side. I had no idea which end that was, but I was well aware of the indefensible nature of my position, which I suspected was only going to get worse. I just hoped my singular path would lead to something decent and that I wouldn't end up in a sanitarium at some point, weaving baskets and muttering to myself, getting occasional visits from sad, but sympathetic relatives. Or out on the street, refusing to be rescued.

I was able to fool most of the people most of the time, which worked for me. I related best with people who liked to speculate on subjects beyond the everyday, but I didn't meet many until I started talking to college professors who, for the most part, treated me as a peer. That's when I discovered that I'd been on the right track from the very beginning.

How to Make a Quilt

Edith's television set was on a high shelf at the front of her fourth grade classroom, where I found myself perched one fine day — twiddling knobs and wiggling wires — trying to get Channel 9, our local PBS station. (I was her Mr. Fix It whenever the school custodian wasn't handy.) Suddenly, her California Gold Rush program came in sharp and clear. I was a genius. Quicker than I'd planned actually. So for about ten more minutes, I just sat up there in my three-piece business suit like a natty gargoyle, looking down on her classroom. Which turned out to be a bit of a mystery.

There was a spelling test going on. One of the students — a girl — was standing at the front of the class, facing the students. Obviously a spelling test, because the girl would say a word, the kids would write something, and then she'd say another word, and again the kids would write, and so on until the end.

I was rather startled when she suddenly yelled *"FRONT!"* and whipped her arm in a big circle. Every kid scrambled out of their seat, bumped and jumbled their way to the middle aisle, and somehow made themselves into a single file of boys and girls — from the front of the class to the back.

When everyone was still, the kid at the back of the line handed his paper to the kid in front of him. And that kid took it, added his own paper to the top, and handed both on to the next kid. This continued like a human conveyor belt until the kid at the front of the line handed the entire stack to the girl who'd given the test. The line of kids was quiet while all this was going on.

Once she had the stack of papers, the girl yelled "GO!" and the kids scrambled and bumped and jostled their way back to their desks as if their lives depended on it. There wasn't any talking; this all happened with only the sound of feet moving, chairs squeaking, and paper rustling.

When everyone was back at their desks, the girl in front said "DONE!" (not quite as loudly this time), and whipped her arm in a circle again. She wrote something with a bit of chalk on the blackboard, then took the papers over to Edith's desk and set them down. Edith never looked up.

The girl went back to her desk. Edith stood while reading her book and never skipped a beat. She walked to the front (still reading) and started to teach as if nothing had happened. "Turn to page 128, second paragraph from the top."

After a bit, I came down the ladder and went over to the door. I finally got Edith's attention and she followed me outside. We walked toward the parking lot, and I had to ask, "Okay, so... what was all *that?*"

"You mean the spelling test?" she said.

"No. I could see it was a spelling test. I mean all the rest of it—the kids in the line and the arm waving and so on." I looked at my mother. She did look like my mother. Same eyes, same hair and all that, but this was her domain, and it was as if I was no longer her son with all that baggage—but just a guy who happened to be her son, seeing her with different eyes.

"Oh *that*," she said. I swear she smirked. "You mean all the other stuff that went on?" She was being *cute*, for crying out loud. I'd never seen her like this. Here was a woman who —back during the boarder years—had nailed clothing to the floor that one of us had left without thinking. No one did that again. This was the force of nature who had dumped an entire pitcher of water on one of our heads because we'd gone back to sleep after the alarm had sounded. Nobody did that again either. And she was *smirking?*

"Yes, Edith. All the other stuff." We were next to the car. She looked at me and paused for a second.

"Well, I'm a highly paid public servant, right?"

I nodded as if this meant something.

"And the school district doesn't pay me to give spelling tests," she said. "That would be a waste of taxpayer money. Plus, I've got better things to do. So I always have the kid who got the most right answers on last week's test give it the next time. It's a reward. That way I can be doing something useful, like prepping for the next lesson. Kids this age are very reward-driven, so I give rewards for everything I can think of.

I was nodding right along. It was all very logical.

"The district doesn't pay me to sort papers, either," she added. "And almost all teachers put the kids in alphabetical order because it's easier to learn their names that way. And I teach the fourth grade."

"So?"

"So, by the time they get to me they've had three years of sitting in the middle of the same four classmates because their teachers were too lazy to put them where it would do them the most good. And they've gotten to know each other and formed little cliques, and they're entirely too comfortable, and they tend to whisper, and it makes for a difficult classroom.

A car drove through the parking lot and I followed it with my eyes, then came back to my mother.

"The real problem is that the ones who need my attention are sometimes in the back and the ones who are used to being called on all the time are usually somewhere in the middle — so I mix it up a bit." She looked at me and then continued.

"I put the slow ones right up front where I can see if they're getting it, and the bright ones I put in the back where they can work on other projects if they need to, like setting up the film projector. I have a film strip and a TV program almost every day."

While she had been talking, I had been absorbing it all, standing there in the school parking lot with the sun shining down on the two of us. I was curious and fascinated as well. This was my mother, explaining her teaching methods to me as if I was a colleague. It was a little odd.

I was being non-committal; she could see it in my face.

"Yes, well. You see, I have this theory," she continued. "My theory is that with fourth graders, their brains are connected to their *heinies*. And if they sit for longer than twenty minutes, they go brain dead." She smiled.

It all made perfect sense, her brain|heinie theory, I mean. I just kept my face straight.

"And so I use every excuse I can think of to get them *out* of their seats on a regular basis—at least every twenty minutes or so. All of them; not just the bright ones. And every student has at least one special responsibility they need to get done sometime during the school week.

"So, kids just get up and move around while you're teaching?" This was new to me.

"Yes. It seems odd, doesn't it? It may get a little chaotic at times, but the kids are happy because they don't feel nailed to their chairs, and they're learning, which is the main thing. And I like to use contests because it makes it more fun."

"Contests?" I asked.

"Sure," she said. "The girl who was giving the test waved her arm because she had a stopwatch in that hand; she was clicking it. She was just being dramatic. Kids that age like to be dramatic, especially when everybody's looking.

"When all the kids got into that line and passed their papers forward, they were standing in alphabetical order. So, when the papers got to my desk they were already alphabetized and I don't have to waste my time getting them in order."

"What did the girl write on the blackboard?"

"Their score. They get points out of it." Edith had that tight smile of a little girl who'd gotten away with something. I was grinning too. For most of my life I'd never seen my mother in a playful mood. It was certainly novel. Heck, she might have been grinning that time she nailed all the clothing to the floor, but nobody was around to see it.

Edith liked innovation, and she wasn't afraid to try new techniques. She'd read some of B.F. Skinner's work on behavior modification (an idea that might have sparked from a conversation with my brother), and loved the very idea of it—that it might be possible to control behavior via mechanical means. At one point Edith was carrying around little pieces of candy to hand out to students. She was rewarding basic behavior, such as class participation and hand raising, trying to even the playing field between the haves and have-nots through positive reinforcement.

She tried all kinds of things with her students; having them march to music on the playground while chanting their times tables, and rewarding students by letting them play chess during recess if they got enough place names right on a blank outline of California. Some could name over two hundred cities, mountains, and rivers from memory by the end of the year.

Edith was singularly unmusical, but her sister Dorothea, also a teacher, had a beautiful singing voice. So she asked her sister to sing to her trusty Wollensak reel-to-reel tape recorder. Two generations of fourth graders sang their folk songs in harmony with my Aunt Dorothea's voice and got their art appreciation by proxy. Edith had a million ideas.

She taught typing for about four years by putting a working typewriter on every desk (Ray sold typewriters, and these were older trade-ins he had no other use for, and again I was Mr. Fix It, since I attended the same school where she taught during that time). Every single paper had to be typed, using the touch system. She didn't allow hunt-and-peck. She had Ray order one of those window-shade key charts and mounted it over the blackboard. It came with a long pointer with a rubber tip so she could indicate various keys on the chart while the kids learned to type.

She told me years later that the school board would send observers to sit in on her class. They wanted to find out if any of her methods could be used to improve teaching throughout the district, since her class had—by a wide margin—the highest number of double-promoted students each following year. Edith tried to raise every student at least two grade levels.

We learn by example from many sources, but intrinsically from our parents, and this was the woman who had drawn the short straw when it came to dealing with me, the third kid from the sun. She was a law unto herself. Difficult, demanding, and she set a high bar, but she taught me well.

Edith's better half

My father had tried many careers and business ventures before he found one that really clicked, and there were stories of how he'd resorted to unusual methods to succeed. A few years after World War II, he bought the Polly Prim Bakery in downtown Los Gatos, when sugar was at a premium. It was too expensive for sweet rolls and donuts, so all the bakeries were substituting honey. But honey didn't taste the same, it grew to be cloying, and people got tired of it.

In his previous job, Ray had worked as an accountant for the Eatmore Ice Cream plant, right across the street, and he knew they used sweetened condensed milk to make ice cream. Boiling it down to refine his own sugar from fifty-gallon barrels of the stuff was an experiment that paid off. My father was running his delivery truck into other cities twice a week to other bakers who didn't know his secret and were mystified by the low cost and great taste of his glazed donuts, raisin snails, and other baked goods. How the dairy industry got the sugar to make sweetened condensed milk at that time didn't worry him. He was a practical man who knew how to take risks.

I got that story, like many others, as the background of my life. I future years, I too would try unusual solutions. All learned early on, and with no thought in mind to the consequences.

How to make a life

To overcome doubt, we must somehow overcome our own instinct for survival. Something everyone learns firsthand on a motorcycle. That stretch is the essence of creativity. It is the root of the root, the core of who we are when we take that risk and reach into the future. I read something once which I'll repeat here as best I can.

> **You want to be a quilter, so you make a quilt.**
> **It isn't a good quilt, but you made a quilt.**

When we create something, that something comes from inside. It is ourself we put out into the world. It is both separate from us and connected at the moment we create it.

It is the making of our first quilt that's the most difficult for any of us, and it is critical. It takes us from wishing to do something all the way to achieving it. Without that first quilt, we haven't done anything. Not really. It's a binary issue: we either made a quilt or we didn't, and *trying* doesn't count for anything except insofar as it describes the beginning of the process.

When Tom Duncan and I started out on our motorcycles that day in 1970, we were giddy with daring. It was a leap of faith, a gamble on our own abilities, and everything was new. We kinda sorta knew what we wanted to do, and we kinda sorta knew where it would take us, but we were writing our future on a clean slate. In those hours and days, we were doing something out of the ordinary; it was the stuff of dreams.

Both of us were out in mid-air, daring gravity to take us down. And that's the beauty of it. It's also the scary part. When we risk like that we become purified *in defiance of our doubts*. We are reaching beyond the edge, and in that stretch, we become our quintessential selves.

The courage to create

I believe our *ah ha!* moments come when one side of our brain shares information with the other and we put something together we never realized before — because our conscious side had only half of what was needed to form our final, inspired, triumphant idea. And that's why it happens so unexpectedly and feels so magical. It's like the punchline of a perfect joke; we are surprised by the unexpected, and our epiphany comes out as laughter.

When I wrote the prose poem *"Angel of Deliverance,"* those feelings were part of the process. I was firing on all cylinders, clipping the apex of every thought, braking just right into every verse, and accelerating out with brio and enthusiasm as if I'd been born to write that piece in just that way.

This isn't to say I didn't write and rewrite draft after draft as I created it, but those rewrites were joyous. I was filled with a fantastic belief in myself, and that feeling of doing something "right and true for its own sake" was quite real. I understood why the Greeks put such value in their muses.

And there was another emotion: self-conscious irritation for such presumption on my part. But I countered that thought with a question: *Who else to write it?*

Creative thinking and great writing don't have to have a gilt title or heavy binding, they can also be found in advertising, podcasts, or comic strips like *Calvin & Hobbes*. The heavy binding and gilt title just mean that somebody *else* has sanctified it as great, and in some cases they're wrong. If the writing isn't accessible to a wide enough audience, I think it's flawed in the same way that an intelligence test measuring a person's ability to handle numbers is flawed if it doesn't also measure our ability to laugh with others and at ourselves.

Our emotion, life, and creative power are our own, and we need no one else's judgment to know whether or not what we've created in that moment is "right and true for its own sake." For without the courage to create, to overcome our doubts, to overcome the voice in our head admonishing us that we don't have enough experience or training or native skill or whatever it is we think we lack, it *cannot* be done.

> "If you think you can do a thing or think you can't do a thing, you're right." — Henry Ford

It takes no courage whatsoever to watch television, read a book, or do a job for which we've had specific training, and it doesn't take courage to obey the rules and toe the line. But it does take moxie to attempt an untried approach to teaching or sign a five year lease on a commercial building knowing you have nothing but your wits to make it work, because we are often battling doubt, fear of failure, and the history of our own life reminding us that we've never done such a thing before and could quite easily fail at it.

In my early and middle years, I was trying to understand the *process* rather than the result. What was going on within that allowed me to create those moments and hours of creative harmony, and could I duplicate it? I really wanted to repeat that feeling of mastery and congruency with the task at hand, but it was difficult to pin down. The difficulty I had with my triple life of being in business *and* wanting to create (primarily via writing and painting), *and* being present for my personal life with family formed one of the main struggles of my life.

I tried to overcome it, but the voice in my head grew louder when I wasn't doing my "real" job properly, and getting around that nagging voice proved nearly impossible. The examples I'd been given by my father, mother, sister, and brother were too strong, too much a part of our history, and too respected.

There are times in our lives when we take measured risks: when we start a business, propose marriage, try out for a new job, or start a risky journey of self-discovery on a motorcycle. We don't usually think of our actions as art, but they carry many of the same attributes. What I didn't realize was simple: I had been creating all along, just as my parents had. I just didn't see it as such.

The virtue of discontent

Two templates for how to create a meaningful life were on full display from my parents: Ray with all his business efforts, and Edith with her teaching innovations. They gave me unique models to follow. As resident witness to two quietly competent adults busy carving out their lives with passion, I was inspired to view my own life as an experiment-in-progress and an opportunity to make it my own. Given how much they expected from themselves and the efforts they made, it's no wonder I whistled a similar melody.

Edith and Ray weren't content to hold down a job. They were serial entrepreneurs in the real world, and I watched their works in progress. I saw the struggle, I heard the discussions, I saw the tight belts and the problems. But I also saw what they were doing and how well they did it. To start a new business, to invent a teaching technique that had never been tried, to keep at it when things were clicking and abandon them when they weren't and go on to something else — those were attributes I aspired to, and they were attributes that I took on for myself. I didn't become my parents, but I did learn from them. I think they both knew that, in the end.

My parents shared their life experience as living examples. Parts of it were told to me as stories, but I got most of it just by being in the right place at the right time. And I chose the right family to be born into, obviously.

When I was a child and came up with an excuse about my homework or something else I was perfectly capable of doing, Edith had a standard answer, always stated deadpan, "Well, stand on a chair." This was always tossed at me in a beanbag sort of way as if anyone with a bit of sense knew this tiny bit of folk wisdom. It was her way of telling me I was being silly and she wasn't going for it; I needed to stop complaining and grow up a bit.

She was also telling me that if whatever I was doing wasn't working, I needed to try something completely different, perhaps even extraordinary.

When I had that metal die made and plotted to overcome the powers that be by crafting my own education, that was my first quilt. I was following her advice and the examples set by both my parents. I certainly wasn't operating in a vacuum. I don't know if this is how other supervillains began their careers, but it was mine.

The Spring Steel Kid

Twang!

That would have been me, circa 1964. Or actually, the sound I created by plucking the center typebar of an Olympia SM9 to demonstrate how it sounded (when vibrating), compared to every other typewriter on the market. And I was pretty good at it. I was a half-pint salesman who seemed to know entirely too much about high-quality business machines.

My father sold the Polly Prim Bakery and purchased Los Gatos Sewing Machines in 1957. He expanded into business machines, office supplies, and office furniture to survive. By the time I was ready to do my bit, Ray had moved the firm into the downtown area, and the staff had grown from two to six.

Edith and Ray shared the keys to their office supply company when I reached the wizened age of twenty, the only real admonition being to not run it into the ground. I was told that if I didn't screw up, I'd gain an ownership position someday. I hired a variety of people over the years, we had lots of anxiety and fun, and cash flow was horrible. But we did survive, one way or another.

I had first started working in my father's office supply store on a regular basis, after school and on Saturdays, in 1962. I was twelve. The Beatles had just released their first song, Johnny Carson had recently started hosting the Tonight Show, and I could be found most afternoons straightening merchandise for fifty cents an hour. I was the kid who made all the Scotch tape straight. I corrected all the incorrect typewriter ribbons in their tiny little boxes. I aligned the desk organizers, paper clips, and cartons of paper. I was the son of the boss, but not particularly important. It was entry-level work that any idiot could do, and my father had found the ideal person for the job.

Up to this point, my work ethic had been based primarily on getting by; I had no larger goal in life. My father (and boss) sometimes found me reading in the far aisle along the right wall where he kept a residual inventory of religious books from his Christian bookstore in San Diego—an early attempt at retail.

It was in that section, sitting on one of those rolling kick-step stools where I first discovered that reading—no matter what about or who the author was—was better than almost anything else. I read a lot of theology back then. I seemed to be the one guy on the planet attempting (in my own way) to make reading obscure texts into a recognized sport. I was just beginning my life of crime, and although I hadn't mastered the finer points, I was well-motivated. But I knew nothing of business machines, typebars, or spring steel.

One day in 1964, my father decided it was time I learned how to sell typewriters. He brought me up to the demonstration table in the front of the store and had me sit next to him. He then proceeded to teach me The Olympia SM9 Twelve Point Sales Demonstration. That's what he called it, anyway.

Ray started with the ribbon selector, then went around the typewriter counter-clockwise, describing every feature, some of them unique to his pride and joy. Which, to hear him tell the tale, was the finest piece of machinery devised by the hand of man. Term papers and novels practically wrote themselves if you were lucky enough to own one. He then had *me* do it. Again and again.

Sitting there, going through this with him, I realized something rather odd. *This was just like with Edith and the book.* I woke up to the idea that Edith and Ray were like two sides of the same coin, and they were on a joint mission to improve *me*.

"Remember the eraser table: demonstrate how it works. And the automatic paper gauge that tells the typist how far they are in typed lines and inches from running out of paper. Pull up one of the stainless spring steel typebars and pluck it so the customer can hear it buzz, then tell them why that's so important.

"Be careful not to pull it too far, or you'll go past the point of no return! The springiness of the steel in that typebar can only take so much before it deforms, and suddenly you've ruined a beautiful piece of machinery."

Each of those twelve features was supported by reason and logic. What does this do? Why is that important? In what way does it help the typist? He patiently guided me through his presentation over and over until I could do it with understanding. Not from rote, but from considered thought and appreciation. Features and benefits. He kept asking questions to see if I really understood. It took him two days.

Over the course of two afternoons, a boy in jeans and an older businessman in a suit sat side-by-side going through all the pros and cons of that classy little typewriter. I had no idea those sessions would be my introduction to high quality and a very specialized track into my own future.

This was all new to me and a bit strange. My father and I had always been a bit wary of each other. Ray, who I didn't know well at all, who I had never spent much time with, who had never paid much attention to me since I was two, was showing me (a) that he cared for something other than *The Kiplinger Letter*, and (b) he wanted me to care about it in the same way he did—just as my mother had with books during that whole "follow me around the house reading out loud or die" episode.

I was born in 1950; Ray was born in 1908. Which made him fifty-six years old to my fourteen that afternoon. To my eyes, he was the quintessential business man: stuffy, obscure, and perpetually worried. He had arthritis, thinning hair, and was growing older and more careworn. He was overweight, wore rimless spectacles with bevelled-corner trifocal lenses and gold wire temples.

He carried a three-inch ring of keys the size of his fist in each pocket in case he lost a set. In Edith's words, he had the obnoxious condition of *lockitis*. Which meant he went around locking and unlocking everything, and the lining of his pockets suffered for it. One year for Christmas she gave him a case of Master padlocks, all keyed the same: #2035. It was probably the most thoughtful gift he ever got. His life was dedicated to running the business (Los Gatos Office Equipment & Supply), and doing the books—the accounting—for his firm.

In two afternoons at the front of our store, I didn't just learn about a typewriter. I learned that my father cared about quality, that what he sold was quality, and that quality *mattered*. More importantly, he wanted it to matter to *me*. An American rite of passage, circa 1964.

And that's when I started selling business machines — at the age of fourteen. My customers were laughably older than I was, and I'm sure some of them wondered why this kid kept talking so much when they were there to buy an expensive piece of equipment, but after a while, they didn't wonder anymore. I was solving their problems. And as much as anything else, that was what catapulted me into adulthood, because I understood for the first time a major part of what it was to *be* my father, and it all made perfect sense.

When my father sold someone an Olympia SM9, he was offering the highest quality typewriter on the planet along with his very best intentions. It was an elegant device, extremely well-made, and presented to each client by an honorable man who cared about what he sold. And I did the same.

Stainless steel spring steel typebars didn't get out of alignment, even when crashed together by clumsy fingers. Part of my demonstration included pulling up a typebar and plucking it to make it vibrate. Honestly, you could hear it *sing*.

I would gain eye contact with my customer, who would invariably nod with experience — yes, they had jammed a few typebars in their time. Then I'd move a few machines over and pluck the typebar of an IBM or a Smith-Corona.

thud

It was a remarkable demonstration. There was no denying that sound, nor could anyone deny the logo on the front of the machine that made it. These were major brands, using pot metal for critical parts. Absolutely ridiculous. *What were they thinking?* I never had to explain it twice.

I hit the books down at our library. I found out a lot about typewriter development and the methods people had invented to put words on paper throughout the centuries. I did the same thing when business machines started going electronic, so I could speak with authority on their inner workings. It was all part of the story. I loved stories and I loved to tell them.

By the time I was through, every customer knew they'd been in a serious conversation with someone who wanted to know about *their* workload more than he wanted to sell them a machine. I sent people directly to other vendors on a regular basis, knowing that most of them would be back. I was no longer a high school kid with bad hair. I had become a problem solver.

And it was fun! I was helping people, and I knew my stuff upside down and backwards. I even went to work in our Service Department for a full year so I would have a working knowledge of common issues.

I had no advertising budget, so I displayed the hell out of them. When people walked into our store, I had a hundred Olympias, all in one massive display, their silver paper supports up like flags. More than anything, it was a show of confidence. People knew they were in the right store.

After the SM9 came the Report deLuxe electric, and I went head-to-head with IBM in our corner of the universe, garnering almost every sale. We ended up selling more Olympia typewriters than anybody in the United States at one point, and our family got a twenty-pound box of horrible chocolates with marzipan and weird jelly centers from Olympia Werke AG every Christmas to remind us.

Identity

Up to that point, my life had meaning only in the books I read and the music I listened to, which was really *other* people's meaning that I stepped into via the waking dream that art gives us. But working at my father's store during the 1960s stayed with me. I learned to ask questions and listen for the answer, since that was the process for solving problems. There was real satisfaction in that, and the customers loved it.

I gained a personal identity that somehow aligned with my father's, which meant that the family business was no longer the dead-end I'd always thought. I wasn't just working at a job. Heck, I was making the world a better place, one client at a time.

Neither my father nor I were ever in business to sell anything. Or at least, not just for that. We were in the business of teaching the concept of quality and precision to anybody who would listen, and offered products that met that criteria. We took the time to impart our knowledge because there was tremendous meaning for us in that. So in a way, we were a family of teachers as much as we were business owners.

Observation also became important to me in a larger sense. If I didn't understand something, how could I measure its worth? The point was well taken only because Ray had taught it to me with enough reasoning and detail that I was able to make sense of it and incorporate that knowledge into my view of the world.

Application

Because I worked at my father's company and ran it for many years and eventually transformed it into other corporations, and because I did almost all the hiring, the company culture was centered on helping people and solving their problems. That is what I created during that part of my life. It was true and right and clean and honest, and everybody liked us and it felt good to work there. It was *great*.

The quality thing is why I have a very old amplifier creating spectacular music through studio speakers from vinyl records. So, when I listen to Joan Baez singing the *Bachianas Brasileiras #5* aria in Portuguese, or Isaac Stern playing *Brahm's Concerto in D Major*, it's as if I'm right there.

It's not that I don't listen to music on our Amazon Echo when I'm busy in the kitchen. The Beach Boys will always sound like the Beach Boys, with that "CD" quality where all the high notes are strangled off into attenuated nothingness. But that isn't really listening to music, is it? That's just hearing it.

Really listening to music means experiencing it in such a way that it lifts our emotions beyond this mortal coil and elevates us to a better plain. It means listening with *intent*. Which was also how I wanted to drive my life. Spring steel bends, but it also bounces back.

Words & Music

My spin on life came from many sources, but my education in ethics started early, with a story about a dragon. A song, actually. You've probably heard it. It was my quiet introduction to the darkness at the edge of town.

I first heard *Puff the Magic Dragon* when I was about twelve years old, and it hit me pretty hard. *Puff* enthralled me and broke my heart, all in one car ride home with the radio going. It was the story of a dragon and the kid he had adventures with—Jackie Paper—who grew up and never came back to his lifelong friend. It was wonderful, and colorful, and incredibly sad.

The land where *Puff* lived was an album called *Moving*, by Peter Yarrow, Paul Stookey, and Mary Travers, and they were a very big deal, both to myself and the rest of the world for many years to come. They were a good-looking team of folk singers with a justified sense of social outrage and childlike whimsy delivered in two- and three-part harmony.

My first Peter, Paul & Mary record album was like that book, *Lad A Dog*, my mother had handed me back in the mists of my illiterate youth. It gave me new ways to understand the world and started me on a road I would travel the rest of my life.

I grew up reading any book that looked interesting, edifying, or entertaining until my eyes bugged out and my hair needed cutting, but it just wasn't enough. I had ears, didn't I? Music formed the other half of this wide-eyed experiment of mine. And it was the lyrics, not the music, that made me come alive and pound the table over new and important ideas. I didn't admire books for their typography any more than I admired music for its melody. The melody was just the carrier wave that got the songwriter's ideas to my ears. The lyrics were what I remembered and pondered over. It was the lyrics that made me question life and what I planned to do with my own.

Flash forward

Two years later and I finally got an inexpensive record player and started listening to modern folk music. Some of it was traditional folk and blues of the Pete Seeger | Woody Guthrie | Josh White variety, but most of the songs were written by singer-songwriters and small groups just out of college, like Peter, Paul & Mary. This new folk music was made popular by Joan Baez, Tim Hardin, Judy Collins, The Rooftop Singers, Gordon Lightfoot, Phil Ochs, The Brothers Four, and others.

It was important to me because it had meaning, or at least it *sounded* as if it had meaning. It certainly wasn't about moon rhyming with spoon and the merry old month of June. I was a callow youth with no wisdom of my own, but no one could listen to this kind of music without seriously thinking about the content. I was moving up in knowledge and understanding, and it was an amazing education. Wisdom borne out of experience would come later.

Folk music had an underlying theme running through many of the songs about standing up for a cause greater than yourself. It was about fighting for freedom, speaking up to the ones in charge, and breaking out of the morass of hypocrisy the world seemed to be trapped in. That's why it was called folk music in the first place; it was music "of the people," giving voice to the issues of the common man. It felt underground and subversive, as if I were part of a secret society, an ethical society of young people moving up through the ranks whether the establishment wanted to accept our ideas or not.

Listening to folk music of the 60s might not make sense nowadays unless you identified with the spirit in which it was written or had a solid sense of the motivation driving it. The songs might sound old-fashioned or irredeemably romantic. But that would be a cynic's viewpoint of songs like *Blowin' in the Wind* or *Where Have All the Flowers Gone?* The disparagers are way off base. Folk music told heart-felt truths and motivated people beyond all expectation. Gospel is the only other music that comes close. When people marched in their thousands from Selma to Montgomery, Alabama in 1965, they were singing *We Shall Overcome* by Pete Seeger, and they absolutely meant it.

An entire generation of young people was waking up. A tectonic shift away from complacency was in progress, and people were leading that shift through music, consciously using lyrics that invited a lot more consideration than anyone was used to. People didn't have to think of course, it was optional. But since they'd never had to think before, this was entirely different. And that changed everything.

There was a social awakening so basic and powerful that the force of it changed history, our culture, and politics. While everyone else in the Los Gatos school system seemed to be *Surfin' USA* and emoting to the Beatles, I was learning about Emmett Till, the Ku Klux Klan, Dr. Martin Luther King, and Medgar Evers. I heard of Carole Robertson and her friends—Addie Mae Collins, Cynthia Wesley, and Denise McNair—all blown apart by racists one Sunday in the 16th Street Baptist Church in Birmingham, Alabama. I think the haunting terror and sadness of that song—*Birmingham Sunday*—stayed with me through thick, thin, and everything else, because of Carol's last name. She was a Robertson and I was a Robertson. She and her young friends were just 14 years old. So was I.

I am of Clan Donnachaidh, of Scotland. Our clan's first recognized chief, Donnchaidh Reamhar (Stout Duncan), son of Andrew Atholl, was a minor land-owner and leader of a kin-group around Dunkeld, Highland Perthshire, and an enthusiastic and faithful supporter of Robert the Bruce (King Robert I) during the Wars of Scottish Independence. Duncan was succeeded by Robert, from whom Clan Robertson takes its name. All Robertsons and Duncans trace their lineage back to Stout Duncan, with tartan, coat of arms, badge, and motto: *Virtutis Gloria Merces*. Carole Robertson from Alabama obviously didn't.

I'd read how slaves brought over from Africa were given new names based on the plantation they worked or the name of their owner. What better way to demoralize someone than to take their personal identity and rip it to shreds? It occurred to me that one of my ancestors (or a cousin thereof) had at one time *owned* Carole Robertson's family. Which made me a slave owner by proxy via lineage. Which made me think a lot harder about who I was and what kind of life I wanted to lead.

I was learning that there were three main classes of powerless people: people of color, women, and the poor. They were suffering, didn't feel heard, and the people who cared didn't have the power to leverage anything. Later I would add other categories (and realize myself as part of one such class due to the draft), but this was enough to go on.

The stories of these people and others like them changed me. It redirected who I wanted to be, and it gave me an awareness I would not have had otherwise. No one knew any of this; I had no need to share it. I simply assumed it was something I needed to learn. But a lot of it was incredibly sad. Besides the love songs and stories of redemption, I was learning about the casual abuse of power and man's inhumanity to man.

These songs were like that quiet person who says little, but everyone listens carefully when they finally speak. They helped a lot of us bond until there was a feeling of camaraderie in our hearts and in the air. When Tom and I rode into Syracuse and walked into that student union at the university and heard Dylan playing, it felt like home.

The youth of our nation was dealing with a government that had its collective head stuck up its cold war with Russia, its open war upon Vietnam, and how to send a man into space. Congress was attempting to perpetuate its pet myth of American superiority and the moral high ground of Capitol Hill, but their hollowed out ethics had no hope against who we were or the music we embraced, for unbeknownst to all the lawmakers and generals and industrialists, their sons and daughters had seized their almighty high ground. And there was nothing they could do to stop us.

They had momentum, but we had ideas. They had empty promises dressed up in crisp uniforms, but we had poetry and guitars. They had money, but we were as cocksure as Peter Pan and twice as natural. People who are perpetuating a lie are often aware of it, deep down; to be found out is the fear that haunts them. We had no such fears. We lived in a Camelot built by the Kennedy brothers, and the certainty of our righteous indignation made us feel invincible. Our music was our saving grace, binding us together to heal the world we lived in.

Roots

It started as a creative amalgam: a medium dose of genuine English folk music passed down from the Middle Ages, some gospel from Black Baptist churches, and a few ancient ballads from the Blue Ridge Mountains where people from Scotland and Ireland had settled early on. All of this mooshed together to form modern folk music: the rhythm of our struggle, and the lyric of our lives.

At first we called it folk music, but that wasn't quite right, because although that may have been the major ingredient at first, that was just the foundation we built on. Then the term protest music was used to categorize it, but that didn't work either, because what we were creating had a mercurial quality; first it seemed one thing, then another. Mostly it was *our* music. Not the songs of our parents, and most decidedly not that of racist America, that nameless corpse plant that blossomed so easily in the South before putting forth its insidious tendrils and shoots throughout the land.

Anybody with a clear head and an eye for history would have been flummoxed. Folk music came at us out of left field, but it came for a reason; it was driven by our thirst for knowledge and our need for ethics. Segregation, voting rights, the war in Vietnam, and the belittlement of women were root causes. Common sense discovered it and creative energy propelled it forward.

America was facing enormous problems that the 50s had tried to gloss over with a thin coat of Corvette Stingrays and stock options, but we weren't buying that kind of pablum anymore. The hypocrisy went so deep that almost everyone not immersed in the ruling culture of the time could recognize it. We were damned if we'd be Mr. Jones just to please our parents and the jackboots of history. We wanted a new way of life for ourselves and everyone else going forward.

I started with Peter, Paul & Mary because of *Puff*. Then I found Judy Collins, with her dirty blonde hair and sad voice of reason. Leonard Cohen and Simon & Garfunkel added a pinch of literate poetry to the mix. I listened to Joni Mitchell with her two-sided clouds, Buffy Sainte-Marie and Gordon Lightfoot out of Canada with his twelve-string guitar and wilderness | railroad stories, and Leonard Cohen with his *Famous Blue Raincoat* and *Suzanne*. Willy Nelson and Dolly Parton shared their story songs of difficult love and growing up in hard times. And then there was Janis Joplin, standing there all by her lonesome, with that raspy laugh and fixin'-to-die voice of outrageous heartache.

Then I discovered St. Joan. With her acoustic guitar, long black hair, and clear, heartrending soprano, Joan Baez created a musical space unparalleled by anyone. I could hardly believe such a person existed. She was concerned about social justice in a way that brought it all back home and was as honest as the voice in your head that never stops telling you *wrong* from *right*. Baez became the conscience of young America — like JFK, his brother Bobby, and Dr. King. She was only 22 years old when she linked arms with Dr. King to lead 250,000 people in the March on Washington in 1963. Every time she went to prison for her beliefs, she was leading by example. How many people do that?

Across all of this, she liked to make fun of herself, laughing out loud at how serious she was, and doing vocal imitations, sometimes right in the middle of a song, which made her all the more real. It has always seemed to me that people who can laugh at themselves with dry wit and gusto understand life at a more fundamental level.

And then her voice would climb three octaves a cappella and transport us all into another universe where it seemed possible and even probable that justice would prevail and we would vanquish the forces of utter stupidity and evil and consign them to the rubble heap of history. She was an exemplar to the world — for anxious parents and uncertain teenagers alike.

I was able to set my own path because of people such as her. It was the right thing to do, and that formed the forward path, but St. Joan was right there in front, on television and in the news, showing me and everybody else what was possible. She was one of the ones who stood up to be counted, willing to take the heat for their humanity. They were the archetypes, the pathfinders. Then a few more stood up. And then a lot more, and suddenly it was a movement. And all that sarcasm, hypocrisy, and bloated patriotism became exposed for what it really was when we all sat down on the Group W bench, folded our arms, and refused to move.

I listened to a number of Vanguard's spoken word recordings as well. Dylan Thomas, T. S. Eliot, Allen Ginsberg, J. R. R. Tolkien, and others, reading their own short stories and poems. To hear these writers express their thoughts in their own voices was incredible. Dylan Thomas telling *A Child's Christmas in Wales* was magic. These recordings created a bridge in my mind that crossed over to Bertrand Russell's writings, and the thought came to me: *If they can do it, so can I.*

Out of that epiphany I started writing my monographs, which caused me to think my way through problems instead of dismissing them as too difficult. I was starting to feel my way through a forest of ideas, symbols, and logic, developing skills I would require to understand my own moral code. By writing my ideas out on paper, I was learning to express myself in logical fashion, in an accepted form.

I also wrote songs and composed the music by sounding out the notes on my guitar and marking blank sheet music. Recording equipment and a professional microphone allowed me to make cassette tapes. I eventually hired a recording studio and pressed a CD. I assembled this material into a binder, which I handed out; an early form of self-publishing.

Later on, I would listen to Country Joe and the Fish *(Fixin' to Die Rag)*, Linda Ronstadt, Led Zeppelin, Grace Slick of Jefferson Airplane, The (Rolling) Stones *(Painted Black)*, The Byrds *(Mr. Tambourine Man)*, Pink Floyd *(The Dark Side of the Moon* album*)*, and Jimi Hendrix *(All Along the Watchtower, The Star-Spangled Banner, Purple Haze)*. And there were many others, including the Moody Blues, Creedence, and the Supremes, who seduced everyone with the silken voice of Diana Ross. *Baby Love* was a constant reminder.

But I was also listening to more difficult songs. Buffy Sainte-Marie is an indigenous Canadian singer who taught me about the Trail of Tears with songs such as *My Country 'Tis Of Thy People You're Dying*, a lengthy narrative song that describes how the United States Army provided tens of thousands of Native Americans with unwashed blankets from hospitals treating patients infected with whooping cough, typhus, diphtheria, and cholera, then marched them at gunpoint over two thousand miles during the 1830s, expecting most of them to die along the way. Many of them did.

Historians estimate that over three thousand Cherokee died in their tracks on that journey. All because of the arrogance and greed of settlers who wanted their land. Or their oil. Or maybe they just wanted to get them out of sight: our *Might Makes Right* ideology of nation building made manifest by our actions.

Buffy Sainte-Marie's song came out in 1966 and was an indictment of American greed and racism, similar in tone to *The Lonesome Death of Hattie Carroll* by Bob Dylan. Both songs were in my mind as Tom and I rode across the Midwest. Much of what I was learning during those years spoke to the intolerance mankind has suffered under since history began, almost all of it due to ignorance, stupidity, fear, and greed.

Up to speed

I was learning the history of mankind, and found it rather lumpy: our road had always been full of rocks. But I was curious, and didn't gloss over the substance of the music by dismissing it into the background. I looked up the Trail of Tears to find out what really happened, and I read books on World War II, the Nazi Party, the horror of the concentration camps and the Holocaust. I read about Joseph Stalin, and of the Irish Rebellion, prompted by a Peter, Paul & Mary song, *The Rising of the Moon*. I read about the French Revolution, the Industrial Revolution, and our own early history as well: the Founding Fathers, their struggles, and how they rejoiced to have created a government without a monarchy or an established religion, both of which they equated with persecution.

I wasn't reading history books usually; that would have been horribly dull. I read historical novels, then used our World Book Encyclopedia to confirm what I'd read (as far as that was possible), and to see photos of what had taken place.

There was one over-arching theme that ran through everything I listened to and read: *social justice*. Between the books and the music, the idea of how we took care of each other (or didn't) was rising up to meet me head on. I could either ignore society's ills and pretend, like Gottfried Leibniz, that I lived in the best of all possible worlds, or I could ascribe to Voltaire's idea that mankind needed to spit on its hands, grab a shovel, and clear the road...

Those rocks are necessary, my dear fellow. Without them, it would be all smooth walking and we'd learn nothing at all!

It seemed to me that many people wanted to get rid of *Might Makes Right,* and change it out for something far more humane, but we kept struggling with it, despite our democratic and humanitarian ideals.

Overcoming brute instincts is difficult, ongoing work. It takes introspection and constructive thought that many people are just not willing to attempt. So they don't. They often explain the necessity for *injustice* with religion (sinners don't deserve justice), finance (we can't afford that much justice), the momentum of history (but we've never had that much justice), or the twisted logic of peer pressure (nobody else provides that much justice).

As my life progressed, I had many opportunities to take a stand, but none more visible or with such far-reaching consequences as my interaction with the Selective Service and, by proxy, the Vietnam War. Which was a pretty big rock in the road. I may not have wanted to become political, but it was thrust upon me by the times in which I lived.

From what I could tell, everyone starts out with what they think are good intentions. There is always some redeeming factor. Even the executives in the tobacco and oil companies who hid all that research on cancer and climate change and lied to

Congress repeatedly must have started out with good ideas; people aren't born evil, no matter what St. Augustine said.

But some people bought into their own nonsensicalness so thoroughly and dragged so many down with them that years passed before the public could install corrective measures. When such people have real power, especially if they are narcissistic or sociopathic (or both), humanity suffers, wars begin, and planets begin to tilt.

The Vietnam War probably started like that: people in power genuinely scared that the communists were going to swallow the Earth and them with it, and a small group got together over drinks at somebody's house. I could see it even then: a dark paneled room, red leather chairs, the dark amber courage tilting in their glasses. And the low rumble of conversation: three men, maybe four, all very respected, very credentialed, discussing how to deal with the wave of communism they thought was very much on the way.

Empathy 101

The Lonesome Death of Hattie Carroll told the story of a man who killed a barmaid with his cane because she didn't serve him fast enough at a social gathering in Baltimore. The refrain of the song admonishes those who would philosophize about such a death; that such a death might be regrettable, but nothing much to worry over. She was just a waitress who cleaned up the ashtrays on a "whole other level," and anyone taking such a thing to heart was being overly sensitive.

For myself, this was an answer to all those people who talk *over* tragedies with *blah, blah, blah* remarks that bury the importance of what's really going on. *"Well, of course that's true, Bob, but we have to remember that..."*

People like that don't *want* to face the truth, they don't want to deal with it, they just want it to go away. They belittle those who point out such issues and try to evoke change. Sarcasm, scorn, and misdirection are the common tools of closed and indifferent minds. "All Lives Matter" and "Blue Lives Matter" are perfect examples of such unthinking arrogance. For crying out loud, of course *all* lives matter, but that isn't the point, is it? It isn't *everyone* who's being singled out, stomped into the ground, and murdered by the police (and drunk rich guys). It's people of color. So saying "All Lives Matter" with unctuous piety is the same as saying, "Black lives *don't* matter." "Make America Great Again" is the same thing. It's racist because it states that America *was* great back before the larger population started empathizing with people who didn't have it so great. Which is why some people want to return to a time when they didn't have to think about police brutality or slum conditions or racism because no one was complaining loudly enough to be heard above the background noise of life. A time when they didn't have to think about anybody but themselves.

Such people with their elitist attitudes just make me tired. They need to grow up and try, for once in their lives, to show a little courage. It's simple. The ones who criticize despair are the cowards, and those who attempt to address the underlying issues are the heroes.

If I had known about my cousin Maria's efforts to register Black voters in the South, it would have given me heart. Only four years older than I was, she was moved to travel to Wilcox County, Alabama in 1965 to go door-to-door talking to strangers, despite being shot at, jailed, and vilified. She faced death at the age of nineteen and wrote a book about it later, now used as a textbook: This Bright Light of Ours: Stories from the Voting Rights Fight, Maria Gitin. *University of Alabama Press - 2014.*

Waist Deep in the Big Muddy (and the Big Fool Says to Push On) is a song from 1967 by Pete Seeger. It's about the idiocy of the Vietnam War, President Johnson's policy of escalation, and Nixon's desperate incursions into Cambodia. It was just one of many anti-war songs at that time, but it was quite clear about the politics involved. The American people were being lied to repeatedly, and Seeger's song hit hard, deep, and true.

Sometime the message is hidden in plain sight. *Bad Moon Rising* by Creedence warned of imminent danger. It wasn't clear what the danger was or where it came from, but it didn't take much effort to see that John Fogarty's "bad moon on the rise" *might* refer to a specific political danger. It was easy to substitute "right" for "rise" to evoke the meaning nearly everyone got from it. I say nearly, because John Fogerty himself didn't get it right away. The Creedence band members understood the song better than Fogerty did—they heard "right" *in addition to* "rise," and had to explain the more layered meaning to him, since he obviously wasn't getting it.

Poetry and music can move us in ways that prose cannot. I was influenced in my views on war and my moral obligation to oppose it by many of these songs. Prose gave me an intellectual understanding, but hearing similar concepts expressed in poetry and song was experiential, visceral, and fundamental. It was something I could *feel*, which made me think and react on a different level. I made my own decisions and figured out my own path forward, but I was certainly inspired by others.

Aside from figuring all this out, I had one more task ahead of me. Somehow, I had to synthesize all this into a single, cogent argument to make my case, both to the FBI, and the last step in this chain of improbable events, an unknown judge in some unnamed courtroom, somewhere in the future. Because if I could not articulate my thoughts *and* my passion, I wouldn't be able to communicate who I was relative to the war and my reasons for refusing. And if I couldn't properly defend my ethical position in my own words, I'd be lost.

But now I had my own, somewhat amalgamated, self-generated conscience, and it goaded me into action. I had taken my basic understand of right from wrong from my parents and that strict admonition from Edith directly, but the combination of reading all that history, plus listening to music by and for the people and synthesizing that into my own philosophy provided a new way to see the world. No more myths or sin or magical thinking, but good and bad behavior starting at the dawn of man and funneling its way down to me. Metaphysics and ethics, triggered by a story about a dragon who lived by the sea.

The Two Bards

While I was listening to music and after I'd read everything there was on the album covers, I glanced at the names of the songwriters and musicians, and one name cropped up again and again. It was 1965, and Bob Dylan was writing many of the important songs of that time.

It was like the entire world had gone nuts over this guy who sang and played his guitar and harmonica down in the Village in New York, and wrote incredible, compelling music, much of it almost un-unravelable, and written at a completely different level from anything that had come before.

I was at McCool's Music store in downtown Los Gatos one day and browsing the record bins, learning about music as I *flip, flip, flipped* through the various albums. I happened upon the Bob Dylan section, and I can remember the visceral shock when my eyes met his new album, *Bringing It All Back Home.* I kind of knew who Bob Dylan was at that point (I'd seen his name enough times on the record labels), and I'd heard *Blowin' in the Wind,* and *The Times They Are A-Changin',* and I knew he was sort of important, but I wasn't at all prepared for the bizarre montage of concepts and images I was facing in the front photo of that album. I remember thinking, *"This is like cigarettes or liquor. I'll have to get permission."*

I was young and, no matter how many books I'd read, terribly naïve. I also knew I had to listen to Dylan directly, from the source. With that outrageous cover, this was not just another album. Looking at the list of song titles on the back, it was one unblinking thing after another, staring right at me and daring me to listen: *Subterranean Homesick Blues, Love Minus Zero/No Limit, Outlaw Blues, Bob Dylan's 115th Dream, Mr. Tambourine Man, Gates of Eden, It's Alright Ma (I'm Only Bleeding),* and *It's All Over Now, Baby Blue.* Multiple publications still describe that one record as the greatest vocal album of all time across all genres. No wonder it looked dangerous; Bob Dylan was breaking *all* the rules.

I bought it the next day, and that was the day I started a second, far more meaningful journey into literature. I'd always been a reader (from three to five books a week), but I'd experienced nothing to prepare myself for what was going on inside that guy's head. It was a mental and cultural shock when I put the needle down and played that record that first time. It was right there in the sounds and ideas spun out by a sarcastic, whiney-sounding guy who had a hell of a lot to say, and almost all of it beyond my reach.

Dylan poked fun at consumerism, advertising, preachers, teachers, political parties, money, moralizing judges, and the President of the United States. But mostly he changed the conversation. This kind of music had never been created before — *not ever*. Folk music had protested against injustice, but it had never done this. Dylan wrote in color while everyone else was stuck in shades of gray. The songs were sarcastic, biting, snide, cogent, complex, street smart, *and made a hell of a lot of sense*. No wonder The Beatles were playing his music day and night. When you break all the rules, the people whose rules you're breaking take notice.

Dylan's more intricate songs really threw me for a loop, but as I grew older and became familiar with his references and symbolism, I finally caught on to the river flowing through them. Like learning to appreciate red wine or asparagus, I suppose. His songs were so entangled and so *layered* I was able to find new meaning, even after listening to them many times.

Dylan's poetry crashed over me like stained glass windows shattered in a church of my own devising, and in their ruin became a more accurate reflection of a world I hadn't understood before. He knew how to break and rebuild language such that I could see my own truth — like Plato's Forms — clearly, and for the first time. His work evolved to whatever new interpretations I could decipher as I gained perspective, like reading *Finnegans Wake*, or realizing with a start that the clock ticking away in the crocodile chasing Captain Hook had always been more than just a clock.

These songs stayed new and fresh to me as the years passed because they resonated with my life experiences just as they happened, as we experience with the paintings of Joan Miró and Vincent van Gogh. What I got from them when I was sixteen had little to do with my understanding at age twenty, and little to do with what I understood from them when I passed thirty-five or when I became fifty. Only a few other writers did that for me, and none of them held up to the same degree.

Shakespeare used natural imagery throughout many of his plays to buttress the central theme of his stories. The rose metaphor in Romeo and Juliet. The "unweeded garden that grows to seed; things rank and gross in nature," from Hamlet. He even speaks of the process directly in yet another play:

> "The poet's eye, in a fine frenzy rolling, doth glance from heaven to Earth, from Earth to heaven; and as imagination bodies forth the forms of things unknown, the poet's pen turns them to shape and gives to airy nothing a local habitation and a name; such tricks hath strong imagination."
>
> – *A Midsummer Night's Dream*

Shakespeare's imagery was similar to Dylan's, and they were both concerned with how things seemed versus how they really were. But I was getting both barrels from a very modern voice at an early age and, being written in song format by someone of Dylan's caliber, it was far more condensed and to the point. Dylan used everything under the sun, moon, and stars and threw in a kitchen sink or two if he thought it would help get his point across. He was an order of magnitude different from all other modern writers, but just as Shakespeare described him in *A Midsummer Night's Dream*.

Dylan didn't compromise with his poetry, and he refused to explain it. I purchased books to study up on him, thinking this was like anything else; you buy one or two good books on the subject and you learn it. But that didn't work. There were no shortcuts through Dylan's back pages. This was existential stuff, and Dylan spoke his truth to whoever was listening. Or not. It didn't seem to matter to him. It was *all* in the poetry. If I didn't take the time to think about what he said, he wasn't going to spell it out for me. Dylan winked at me, inviting a shared moment of irony in the chaos of life. I wasn't certain yet just what that wink was all about, but I was up for just about anything back then, and willing to give it a go.

The other bard

I felt it was necessary to understand Shakespeare's plays to consider myself educated, and I was intrigued by the Dylan | Shakespeare connection. There were far too many references to Shakespeare in Dylan's work to ignore.

I struck pay dirt with Professor Barrett. He taught using the Socratic method, and his course was Shakespeare 101. It was organic, refreshing, and fun. We all got involved. It was what education should be, but rarely is.

Our world exploded with ideas we hadn't known existed, and the class was so charged up we started holding impromptu meetings outside of class. "You bring the chips, I'll bring the drinks." We learned to recognize and understand symbolism, metaphor, simile, and the genius of Shakespeare's writing, primarily by deconstructing *Hamlet, Richard III,* and *Romeo and Juliet.*

Hamlet is Shakespeare at the peak of his powers. It is his most philosophical play; he asks the biggest questions about the nature of human beings and taps into universal experiences that span all of history.

Without knowing how I got there (and yet I'd done the work myself, with highlighters and my Big Book of Shakespeare), and as unexpected as it was fresh (as though 350 years had not gone by), I suddenly found myself in that candlelit room with the man himself as he wrote into long winter nights, burnishing the mirror between Hamlet and Ophelia so his audience could understand Hamlet better in the time it takes for the play to be performed.

That moment was like I'd cheated death itself *and* invented chocolate cake. Throughout the play, if Hamlet was up, Ophelia was down; if one was uncertain, the other just knew. She was a backwards doppelgänger: an inverted echo of Hamlet. With the evidence right there before me, I realized Ophelia was not more nor less than Hamlet turned inside-out and wearing a dress.

Barrett concurred. He confided that he'd never seen that analysis before in any of the literature, and that I had explained a conundrum that had bothered Shakespearian scholars from the beginning: the reason for Ophelia and her odd behavior. I didn't know whether Barrett's praise was accurate or not, but I took it as validation for the pattern of logic I was using in all of this. Not just with Shakespeare, but Dylan's writing, social issues, religion, and everything else. If, in figuring stuff out, I could come up with my own conclusions, that would be huge.

Shakespeare didn't expect his audience to parse out his metaphors and similes any more than a painter wants someone to focus on his brush strokes or the frame that holds his masterpiece. I suspected that Dylan didn't either, but his writing was (and is) incredibly dense, very connected, and so ripe with references that anyone not noticing is simply not listening.

On any given day, over half the population of Elizabethan London, rich and poor, educated or not, went to see a play. Shakespeare wanted his audience to understand Hamlet — his plays were not being read, they were being acted on a stage in rather flowery verse and prose — and most people would see his plays only once. So with Ophelia, he crafted an *anti*-Hamlet to show contrast. Like Hamlet, she has choices. But she doesn't understand what Hamlet understands. She doesn't act in the same way, and she dies because of her passivity and inability to discern the agendas of those around her.

It was a character study by contrast. It was action or lack of action and how things *seemed* that so concerned Hamlet in the first place. They both die in the end, but it was their approach to life that Shakespeare contrasted to flesh out his characters.

He used multiple references to nature throughout the play to bind these two characters together even tighter, even as he inverted their personalities to show his audience who they were. Shakespeare was hammering his Hamlet character home to the audience by revealing Hamlet as he might have been, reflected in the mirror of Ophelia.

Suddenly, I understood a large part of what Shakespeare had done with the language, all of which came down like a torrent when I reread writers I'd been attempting to understand. And I understood Bob Dylan far better, which was unheard of. Nobody understood Dylan. There was a connection between their writing I hadn't seen before, and it was like a bright light came upon me.

I got it. I tore it up. I was suddenly *in my element.* But could I take it further? Could I use this method to puzzle out shaded meanings other writers might have buried between the lines of their text? But more than anything else, I wanted to know if Dylan's verse was, like Elizabethan English, impenetrable at first glance, but perfectly understandable with a little thought and common sense.

Reckless abandon

At this point in time I had my own approach to life to flesh out, my own demons to face. I was twenty years old and could either stay in college to keep my comfortable little deferment, or I could put myself in harms way. The government made it easy: attend class and you're safe, do anything else and you become cannon fodder. Either way, we were all little soldiers marching to someone else's tune. I would be the odd man out.

There is a turn of mind that comes to anyone who believes in his ideals so strongly as to stand up for justice against the weight of government and society. It doesn't happen that large that often. Most of us only get a few tries in life to throw ourselves against the bulwarks.

Like Hamlet, I was out to catch the conscience of the king despite the slings and arrows, so I went back to work, and notified the FBI that I was no longer enrolled. Hamlet had his day and I would have mine; I had a government to stare down. But in the mean time, there were other mysteries and other songs.

All the world's a metaphor

Desolation Row is a song recorded on August 4, 1965, and released as the final track of Dylan's sixth studio album, *Highway 61 Revisited.* The song was a crazy, mixed-up conglomeration of images—and powerful beyond all imagination. It is arguably Dylan's most lyrically sophisticated song, impossible to completely understand, and yet we get it over the transom—our psyche comprehends what our consciousness cannot.

Dylan was at the height of his bottle rocket, parabolic powers as a writer and musician. In this eleven-minute marathon of a song, he references a motley parade of world-class characters, including Nero, Einstein, Cain and Abel, Ophelia, Romeo, Cinderella, T.S. Eliot and Ezra Pound, Bette Davis, Robin Hood, Noah, and a host of minor characters falling like accidental grace notes from a careless god's sleeve.

It is also Dylan's most misunderstood song, which makes sense, given its lack of a clear narrative and wild, surrealistic imagery. My initial bewilderment came from my own assumption about desolation row itself. The title (and repeated refrain) led me to think of a bad and unattractive neighborhood of row housing—a ghetto of sorts. It is anything but.

Dylan describes it as a place where all intellectually honest people live—everyone who rejects the standardized morality of conservatism and the shallow glitz of glamour and success. *Desolation Row* is home to the outsider, the intellectual outlaw, the artist. And to me the song is a requiem for a heavyweight—America itself—when our nation became like a family learning to disassociate themselves from one another after we had our guts punched out with the unconscionable murders of our three great modern exemplars: JFK, Dr. King, and Bobby Kennedy. Once I got this through my head, the rest fell into place.

I pried it open line by line, and all the connections were there. It took a lot more work because Dylan juxtaposed his references in such unusual ways, and I had to either know or look up their historical and social context, but my methodology worked in much the same way.

The people who live on *Desolation Row* know the score, or are at least engaged in finding out. Shakespeare's Ophelia only takes a peek, allowing herself a voyeuristic view of those living outside of society's (and her own) constraints. Shakespeare painted her as passive, as does Dylan. A passive life translates into death by drowning in both folios, which is perhaps why she has her eye on "Noah's great rainbow." She is wasting her time in this world hoping for a better life in the next.

Who was selling postcards of the hanging? What hanging? And what did it have to do with people painting their passports brown? (It had everything to do with it, and yes, it was a real hanging. And documents that have turned yellow or brown are old. But if they have been *painted* brown, someone is faking their age — and perhaps their authenticity.)

Why would Einstein be playing an electric violin? Did that connect him to Nero? (Of course it did. $E=mc^2$ is the writing on the wall for all of us, just as Nero fiddled while Rome burned.) Cinderella, whose true beauty was never understood or appreciated by conventional society, sweeps up all the broken bits while Bette Davis, the blind commissioner, the riot squad, and Einstein's jealous monk take part in a joyous symphony: everything connected, the center held, and although I didn't get all of it down to the last jot and tittle, I was filled with a rush of understanding of what was possible with language, history, and the magic of metaphor.

Desolation Row offers a chillingly accurate microcosm of society. Dylan delves deep into the chasm separating the affluent elite from the struggling masses, painting a stark portrait of a world divided by privilege and power. But the song's scope extends beyond mere class disparity. It is a poignant commentary on the human condition, exploring themes of empathy, control, and the pursuit of meaning.

By placing a magnifying glass on the lives of the marginalized, Dylan forces us to confront our own complicity in a system that often devalues the struggles of others. The song challenges us to question the nature of our connections, the depth of our compassion, and the kind of society we are collectively constructing. Ultimately, it is a call to action, urging us to step beyond mere spectatorship and become active participants in shaping a better, more equitable world.

I found other connections between Shakespeare and Dylan, most notably in *Love Minus Zero/No Limit,* and *Sonnet 130,* which was a kind of inverted love poem. It implied that Shakespeare's girlfriend might be exquisite indeed, but to paint her with colors too bright could never do her justice. It was far more important to view her as she truly was—just as Dylan did.

There were other parallels as well. Would my life be measured out like that blind commissioner's, one hand tied to the tightrope walker, the other fiddling away in my pants? Would the balance of my life be nothing more than a cheap and gaudy carnival, with me—always in the wrong place, always some echo of Mr. Jones—watching Cinderella in her glass dancing slippers, sweeping up after everyone had gone home?

Dylan employed all the colorful characters of *Desolation Row* as allegory for everything going wrong, asking us to think about our own place in society. The recurring question, "Which side are you on?" underscores the central theme: conformity *vs.* rebellion, mainstream *vs.* fringe.

What was it I saw nested in these disorderly words, these raucous verses—and was I the one looking out upon the destruction and the sorrow? Would I lose the name of action or embrace it? Spitting into the wind isn't all what it's cracked up to be, and I wasn't so naïve as to think I'd get away with it, but the choice was there in front of me, nevertheless. Do, die, or wither away as hollow men do.

The Paint in Spain

There are two paintings that made an impact on my life and education: *Guernica* by Pablo Picasso, and *Persistence of Memory* by Salvador Dalí. I got to view both paintings on the same day at the Museum of Modern Art in New York about a year after I came back from my motorcycle trip. I was surprisingly and profoundly moved, finding personal validation in both pieces. Seeing these paintings in person was revelatory.

Standing in the presence of Picasso's *Guernica* was to stand in the presence of greatness. It hit me like a weight. *Guernica* is a huge cubist work of art—painted all in gray—that depicts the stark terrors of war. It came from a depth of experience and understanding of the human condition I had never seen before.

I had referenced it in my letters to the draft board and the FBI. The painting is enormous: twenty-five feet wide by eleven feet tall. Seeing that huge painting up on the wall felt surreal.

It brought home the great truth I'd found within it and within myself, and I found validation at the moment I saw it. It also resonated with my walk through Dylan's music, with his fractured vision of a world that makes no sense until we realize the irony and truth of it all.

Persistence of Memory (the one with the melting clocks), I'd always found intriguing. Dalí teased me in a way similar to Dylan. *What was going on? Why are there ants on the watch? What is this horrible blob in the middle of the painting?* Perhaps just as important, but subliminal in its message, *why is this painting so darn famous?* Ironically, the painting is quite small for all its impact on the world: only thirteen inches wide by nine inches tall. To view it properly, one must bend from the waist and lean in; viewing from a distance gives no detail. It is another way of expressing what *Desolation Row* says with words.

It took me years to connect the dots between Dalí, Picasso, Shakespeare, and Dylan. The past is never just said and done: the memory persists.

Integration & synthesis

Songwriters bring it down-to-earth so we can look directly into the truth of who we are, how we got here, and what we might do about it. I was learning about man's inhumanity to man, and it made me *angry*. I felt deceived and cheated that I wasn't learning this from regular sources.

The education I got by listening to all of this music and studying the history behind the songs became a lodestone that tugged at my moral compass, swinging my attention to what I might stand for, what I believed, and what I would have to do when my number was drawn. It made me *think*.

And so there I was, all of fourteen, sixteen, eighteen years old, figuring this stuff out. The music was a catalyst, an educational conduit. Bob Dylan, Peter, Paul & Mary, Pete Seeger, Bertrand Russell, and Joan Baez were all about choice. They showed me how any one person could and should question established values whenever necessary. And if they could do it, I could do it. Choices I might never have gotten to on my own came to me out of paper and vinyl and my own subsequent constructs, and I created a working social conscience in the process. Listening to records and reading books was all passive, all just interesting and inspiring theory. Protesting the war by standing up to the draft board despite the consequences was how I used it. Such ideas became my map.

Over the years I listened to many groups and individual musicians to see if anyone else wrote with the same thundering, heart-wrenching genius. I even looked into the lyrics of Tupac Shakur, in deference to my daughter, who insisted on the value she found in his talking blues. Many had individual songs with dazzling lyrics, but none had such layers of literate meaning, metaphor, symbolism, and oblique suggestion to make me look at life in unexpected directions. Like Shakespeare, Dylan created in his own lane.

Like Dylan and Shakespeare, I pulled out all the stops I knew. I wielded my knowledge of history and man's inhumanity to man to shift the momentum of deadwood I found around me. It started with books and records and my mother's strict admonition to do the right thing, but the empathy and knowledge and anger generated by injustice stayed with me and had other uses I discovered later on, particularly in business when I was able to stand up for what was right and true over a span of many years, many people, and many companies.

Making it all pan out

I was heading toward serious difficulties in two ways. There was the Vietnam War on one hand, and our family's business on the other, with Yours Truly stuck right in the middle, still half-baked and attempting to understand William Shakespeare, T.S. Eliot, Arthur Rimbaud, and Pablo Picasso so I could get a better grip on Bob Dylan's caustic insights into the human condition. And I had to face the music whether I liked the tune being played or not.

I secretly wanted to grow into some combination of Thomas Wolfe, William Turner, and Henry Higgins (carrying on with Eliza Doolittle—as played by Audrey Hepburn of course), but I had serious doubts. I had written poetry and a few articles, but hadn't received much feedback, and I had a sneaking suspicion I wasn't nearly as smart or as talented as I aspired to be. My plan had a hole in it, and the hole was me.

To write or sell business machines, that was the question. Would I live my life out in my father's office supply business, or tear the heavens with prose and paint? My sense of self was high, but I didn't want to starve in the gutter, either. The alternative was another kind of half-life: to take my place as the dutiful son, but live out my life forever in search of lost opportunity and time, like a modern day flying Dutchman.

So, just in case—despite all logic and all odds—my plan to create myself as the masterpiece of my own existence might someday succeed, I kept reading the good stuff. Not as an exclusive diet. That would have been crazy. Just every once in a while, like a snack. And I kept writing, listening, and evaluating.

Big Bang

Amid all the reading and music and Shakespeare and Dylan; between the faces of lovely girls and stained glass constructs hollowed out within the halls I walked when I was still in-between who I was and who I wanted to be but couldn't; and during all the events and moral issues crashing down upon me, something happened. Something clicked. Something fell into place.

I had been writing for years. Self-absorbed poetry (the kind you know is bad even as you write it) plus my thought-pieces on logic, philosophy, and physics that I called monographs. The monographs worked, but my poetry was lousy. I was a shallow teenager with not much to say, and it showed.

Bad as my poetry was, I was learning from it. By writing my thoughts out in poetic form, I got into the rhythm and arc of each line, each thought and stanza. In this fashion I developed an internal ear for prose that read well and occasionally soared.

I kept plugging away, and from time to time I would happen upon a phrase, a line, a glimmer of words that worked. I tried building on those, writing and rewriting, attempting to break through to something finer. It was a long slog, but I kept at it. And then I wrote something that hit the page with everything I had.

It was a wet winter, and the rain kept coming down that year. I had set myself up out in our vacation trailer, where Glen had given me that I.Q. test years before. I had a typewriter, a box of paper, and that massive dictionary, and was spending hours every day, trying like hell to put one foot in front of the other. I pushed myself to focus, to create anything that wasn't pure dreck. Short stories, poetry, fragments of thought.

The process itself was what did it, either that or I simply lost my peach fuzz, because at some point the combination of tired fingers, drizzle of rain, and mind over emotion came together with everything I was as a person, and it clicked. I wrote one line and then another until whole paragraphs began pouring out of me, and suddenly the world made sense and I was in the middle of a prose poem that tore the curtain and hit me with furious passion as I fought it into crude form, screaming, reaching, crying out, and breathing new life into being.

And as I crafted this thing, this being into existence, I found myself supported by fine threads hung from stars by another version of myself so long ago that the reality of it had become irrelevant. For yes, I did confront the world in my righteousness and anger. Coherencies whirled up through the air, to be taken like lightning by the hands of the accuser, to whirl up and crash down, to thunder down crashing and be nailed to the page by the might and the glory and the tears and the hammering fury of this crazy dream man-child who sought only so much as to glimpse into the face of that which he had no name for.

As the rain came down outside that trailer, I knew I'd made an original. I was ecstatic and in awe—not of myself, but of what it felt like. I had created something altogether new, and it was better than good. It was great. I had branched out and become something more.

It was a birth, a resurrection, a benediction, an absolution. It was something I had no other way to express that came to me then and stayed with me as a child sits with a parent through the necessary night, and gleamed softly all the while as brightly shone the pages I'd crafted and hammered and bled into for days without sleep, then stumbled into the light in search of food. And when it was done, I just knew.

I knew what the creative frenzy felt like. I knew then what it was to work all night and burn bright with the fever of organic purity when everything snicks into place and the stars align. It gave me a taste for what Shakespeare, Picasso, Joyce, and Dylan—what everyone who came before had known.

It also made me curious as to what had really happened, and I made efforts to find that out over the coming years. What was this process called creativity, and what could I do to make it happen again and again and yet again? That was something I wanted very much indeed, and yet hard work alone didn't seem to be the answer. There was something else at stake. Something more fundamental, perhaps.

Fork split personality

My deep dive into books, music, and writing paid off, and I became charged with intent. But more than that, I took on the meaning and substance of what I'd learned and started to resemble the person I wanted to be, forming a conscience and focus during those thoughtful hours, an ethos that matched that fundamental lesson I got years before from Edith. I took a stand in the wilderness and cleared the brush. I chopped down a few stunted, gnarly trees and planted new ones. I was a pioneer on property I owned because I had done the work. I'd made the effort and found inspiration, new muscles, and new abilities—developing all those nooks and crannies I wanted along the way. Not that I had any idea that this was going on while it happened—as usual, I was clueless. But my intent and effort seemed to be paying off.

All of this culminated in what I was able to do later when push came to shove with the Selective Service and star-spangled thinking run amok. I was able to stand alone with my toes to the line and state my case knowing I would be sentenced to five years in federal prison. I was scared to death, but adamant because I knew my own mind. Plus, I now had a pretty good idea I would not be forced by the fact of my own existence to lead a life without purpose.

Thoughts on Paper

Questions large and small filled my brain. Human behavior, religion, science, finance—all were open topics. For those with no convenient answer, I attempted to decipher with logic and sheer determination. I contemplated, deliberated, and pondered. I made suppositions, stumbled into conclusions, then questioned all of it again, endlessly spinning out my mind in a fantasyland of curiosity. My questions were as ponderous as Kilimanjaro, my conclusions as deep as I could make them. I was the kid who decided to climb them, claim them, and make them his own.

Writing a short piece on creativity got me started, and I began to jot down my own thought experiments—my monographs—attempting to answer the imponderables that came to me from time to time.

Like the idea that language itself might preclude the concept of death, which became my seminal piece, established my concept of independent thinking, and inspired me to continue. My thesis on this one was simple:

- Our instinct for self-preservation causes us to fear what we don't understand,
- We cannot know what we haven't experienced, and
- We have never experienced death, therefore...
- We fear death.

One obvious consequence to this was mankind inventing religion as an anodyne for our collective fear of death and then getting stuck with the check.

That was just one of my papers, and I mailed it, and others like it to friends and a few family members from time to time. My idea of peer review, I suppose.

I wrote a number of these thought pieces on various subjects over the years, from philosophy to physics—whatever was puzzling me that I couldn't find in the books I was reading. None of these were rigorous papers with footnotes and references, mind you. I was simply trying to work through a number of ideas and concepts because I knew it could be done. If we have all the information, we can figure stuff out by writing and thinking about it until the concept at hand becomes clear.

I've heard it said that ninety percent of life is just showing up. Well, the moment I finished that first piece was the moment when I showed up in my own life. I have no idea what prompted it other than curiosity and a sort of devil-may-care, *Well – what the heck, let's try this and see what happens.* But I did make a beginning, and I saw my inner thoughts on paper for the first time. But I also knew it wasn't enough just to begin. It's the *follow-through* that creates a pattern of repeatable behavior.

In the movie *Serendipity*, written by Marc Klein, the main character's sidekick makes a comment that rings true. He says, "You know, the Greeks didn't write obituaries. They only asked one question after a man died: 'Did he have passion?'"

Years after I first heard it in the movie, I took the time to look it up. It sounded just a little too neat, a little too much, and I was right. The Greeks had nothing to do with it. These were the words of the screenwriter speaking through a character, expressing perhaps what he (the screenwriter) felt, but misattributing it to the Greeks to provide the gravitas needed to make it stick in the minds of his audience.

Nevertheless, it is a powerful concept, isn't it? Forget money, power, social stature, and all that jazz, just live your life with *passion*. That's the ticket! To a certain extent that is exactly what I was trying to do. I discovered my life in bits and pieces by experimenting with different ideas. It was like trying on different clothes to see what fits, what feels right to the man inside. The writing helped clarify and sort my ideas, and get myself in the habit of exercising critical judgment with my guard up against the slough of confirmation bias my brother had warned against.

Few people knew anything about this part of my life, and those who did were those I trusted. I don't mean I grayed it down, because my inner life did manifest itself in my behavior and appearance. I had way too much going on inside. Thus, the three-piece suit with watch chain, spectacles for glasses, a full beard, and lines through my 7s and Zs (once I knew the purpose for it). And I refused to wear logos.

Wearing someone else's insignia was just obsequious nonsense: free ads for whatever company or band was in vogue, and it would have been advertising *me* as nothing more than another empty-headed sycophant.

I ran track, so I started wearing my black, crepe-soled track shoes as regular footwear. They weren't that comfortable, but they were different, and I continued with them until I noticed other kids doing the same. Something like that had happened once before. Happy Gilbert, one of our borders, had remarked that he wasn't all that popular. My mother dared him to wear non-matching socks for two months just to see what might happen. It became a local fad. Edith mentioned it after it happened to me.

That type of footwear later evolved into what would later be called "trainers," and today they're ubiquitous—Nike, Reebok, Adidas—almost everyone wears some version. Wearing those shoes was similar to my habit of carrying schoolbooks straight down from a tight grip instead of tucked under the arm as everyone else did. I wanted to be different to the point of pain.

I stopped swearing. I had heard it was an indicator for a lack of intellectual rigor and didn't want to live my life looking like a fool. All the choices I made and all the things I did fed a voracious appetite that drove and pounded me down the tracks of my life. I wanted to be Onion Boy, with all the best layers.

All these attributes came from decisions I made, but they were like the color of my eyes or the wave in my hair (back when I had a wave in my hair). They were all just part of the fabric, texture, and pattern I was attempting to weave for myself *out* of myself. And yes, I did it on purpose; I did almost everything on purpose. But I really didn't know where that purpose was taking me. It seemed to me that of all the people on the planet, it was only the artists and philosophers who were doing something similar. I was wrong in that, but you can see how limited my worldview was up to that point.

In his *Equilibrium of Planes,* Archimedes could have been talking about me. I don't know if the books were the fulcrum and my thirst for information was the lever or the other way around, but it certainly worked. I have read great (and not so great) works throughout my life, but I often didn't recognize the level at which I was reading; I just took it all in. There I was, diamonds and rust right in front of me, blithely skipping through as if it were all the same, all grist for my mill, just a few more interesting rocks in a world filled with interesting rocks. But every rock got counted, and a structure began to form.

It was Tolkien who caused me to reconsider the sound of words and language. He used *cellar door* as an example of a phrase that sounded beautiful to him, aside from its literal meaning. He described it as having a rich sonority and a sequence of vowels and consonants pleasing to the ear. This made me think about phrases and paragraphs I'd run across (separate from poetry and song) that drew me in with rich, mellifluous notes and cadence. Which, in turn, caused me to notice such text in regular reading, making me hit the brakes, go back, and reread. In some cases, like with *LOTR* and *Portrait of the Artist as a Young Man,* that involved an entire book. I realized that some authors were attempting something beyond basic communication. And that I should pay attention.

I'm not saying that if we were to eat our language, *cellar door* would be the mushroom gravy of phrases or the Sees Candy of sounds... But the reader's ear is involved, even when reading quietly in the corner, and the sound of our thoughts can create a swell of emotion that carries the words on the page. That lesson changed how I wrote first paragraphs in particular, last paragraphs, and important writings. It made me craft the language to suit my meaning instead of simply typing out whatever I wanted to say. I was not always successful, but it helps to have a plan.

Thomas Wolfe held Blue Ridge emeralds up to the light with rolling paragraphs charged with a symphony of life and the struggle of living in *Look Homeward, Angel.* I would later read *The Prince of Tides* by Pat Conroy, who made me gasp at the beauty of words and the span of great narrative. Less poetic perhaps, but Bill Watterson spurred me to think around corners with his grand opus—and to look up the original philosopher namesakes for *Calvin & Hobbes* to see if I should read them. In *The Once and Future King*, by T. H. White, King Arthur was depicted as a political innovator, attempting to temper traditional force and strength with justice. White was a philosopher who cleverly disguised himself as a novelist, just as Tolkien had.

My homemade process, once started, never stopped.

It took practice and repetition, but I only solved my dilemma through *active thinking*. I had come to that point in my life, a kind of mental and emotional state, where I began to wonder why a certain phrase or passage was so loaded with meaning.

I'd created a way of being in the world to keep me from just stumbling through it. All that reading and speculation and writing and abject failure were distilling me into the person I wanted to become. Except not as good looking.

Thoughts about thinking

As I started to question authority and generate my own ideas, I also started to wonder about these ideas and how they came to me. Why was I questioning authority? Why did I care what a writer wrote or why they wrote it? Why did I care what was going on in my own mind?

I started rummaging around and became curious about belief systems, emotions, and the interactions between myself and others. This "thinking about thinking" was a large part of my self-awareness. And that scared me a little at one point. What was I doing? Could I get lost in the labyrinth of my own thoughts? Was there a madness inside this odd box of parts that I called me? Was there some critical mass I might inadvertently reach, upon which there would be a small pop and a puff of smoke—and my family would be struck by flying debris that looked suspiciously like parts of Jonathan?

Glen was a psychologist, and I thought about asking him if a person could drive himself mad just by thinking about thinking about thinking, but decided not. He'd probably be very polite, appraise me over his glasses for a second or two, then ask me quietly if I thought I was a danger to myself or others. I'd just embarrass myself. So I decided to stop worrying about it.

It's not like I was sitting there with a pad and pencil making notes, but I was trying to figure it all out. The world of people (including girl-type people), books, art, science, history, and music was right there, waiting for me to understand all of it.

First Ellipsis...

After a few years of writing, I duplicated everything into a common binding. A kind of homemade book of everything I'd been working on—several hundred pages of adolescent gunk. I had learned just enough guitar to accompany myself, bought some blank lined sheet music, and started learning how to time music. I learned how to write the various notes, and where to place them on a five-line staff. I had some popular music books for guitar and figured out which chords made the sounds I wanted. It was tedious, but not all that difficult.

When technology changed to compact disk, I upgraded the recordings to CD, which I repackaged as *First Ellipsis...* I only found out later that one of my poetry | music collections had been duplicated en masse and shared by women rangers throughout the U.S. Department of Forestry.

First Ellipsis... came to me as a prequel, since the literary magazine I started in 1988 was named ***Ellipsis...***, so named due to my idea of helping under-published writers get their work into print. The three dots of an ellipsis signify the omission of text. The three dots of *my* ellipsis signified the omission of under-published, and therefore unknown writers. I did not include my own writings since I didn't want *Ellipsis...* to carry the stigma of a vanity press; the only place I appeared was on the editorial pages in the back. It took close to six months, but when the first edition came out, I found myself standing with no apologies right next to the publishers and editors of *The New Yorker, The Paris Review,* and *Granta*.

About the monographs

I wrote about a dozen articles during these years, all single subject pieces. I kept coming back to them, adding or subtracting ideas as my thinking matured and new information became available. Topics included anything that puzzled me enough to work the problem. In some cases, like my lengthy piece on politics and monetary policy, the information was out there, in the wild so to speak, but scattered in so many articles and books that making sense of it was difficult. I put pieces together and wrote them out logically so I could understand the subject matter, often creating informal thought experiments on the fly.

In general, my topics were subject only to gathering the correct information and applying logic. If A equals B and B equals C, doesn't A equal C? If not, why not? What if A is green and spins to the left? Writing in this particular way forced me to sharpen my ideas and made me feel that I was in charge of something — my own mind, I suppose. *I think, therefore I figure stuff out* was the dictum I followed, and it worked well enough.

Written mostly during the late sixties and early seventies, my early writings were sent off just as I typed them, like messages in bottles floating through the postal service to anyone who might respond to such esoteric pontifications. I wanted comments and criticism but rarely got more than "Interesting idea, Jon. Now, explain why you're doing this. Are you taking some kind of class or something?" Among a number of subjects, I wrote about:

- How we communicate our thoughts
- Why language is intrinsic to our fear of death
- Whether the gravity of a mass is focused as a locus of points along a spherical plane (or shell) within that mass, or at its center, given that gravity's effect diminishes over distance.
- How to determine if a statement is true, false, or wishful thinking.

An enquiring mind

If we can function in society just fine without changing our thinking, we tend to rely on momentum to get us where we want to go. For myself, that wasn't working. I wasn't a cute little kid any longer, but an unsettled teenager with questions.

The issue probably came up because of religion (which began to lose its bright patina when I was quite young), and I began casting about for answers to basic questions.

The physicist Richard Feynman was once interviewed by Yorkshire Television, and he used the ritual of brushing teeth as an example of established thought.

> "What ceremonies do we believe in? Every morning we all brush our teeth. What is the evidence that brushing our teeth does any good against cavities? And you start wondering. Are we all imagining that, as the Earth turns and the orbit has an edge between light and dark, that along that edge all the people are doing the same ritual—*brush, brush, brush*—for no good reason? Have you tried to picture this perpetual line of toothbrushes going around the Earth?
>
> "Now it may well be that brushing the teeth is a very good thing because it gets rid of cavities, but you can try to find out whether it does or doesn't. You ask your dentist. He says, "Of course." And you say, "What about evidence?" I have not found the evidence from dentists, because they just learned it in school. I am not even trying to argue if it is good or bad to brush teeth. What I am trying to argue for is to think about it. Think about it from a new point of view."

That's all I'd been trying to do with this part of my life, think about things we take for granted, but from a different point of view. Just because we've always done something a particular way doesn't mean we have to continue down that road. And just because we've always believed something is true doesn't make it so.

And Bob's your uncle

In 1974, astronomer Brandon Carter pointed out that if our universe weren't hospitable to life, then we wouldn't be here to wonder about it. This idea came to be known as the *anthropic principle*. Similar to René Descartes's first principle, "I think, therefore I am," but with a bit more topspin.

I took it a bit further. If our universe did not have beings capable of wonder such as ourselves, then there would be no one available to invent a deity capable of creating it. I had suspected from an early age that the gods were created by man in his own image primarily to explain the meaning of life and the wonders of the universe. That one phrase, "And God created man in His own image..." (Genesis 1:27) was just too pat, too much of a coincidence to not be questioned, toyed with, and then reversed by my wandering mind.

The capper to all that was axiomatic: "And man said, 'Let there be God.'" *KABOOM!* And although that didn't actually explain the Big Bang, it certainly parsed out the how and why of biblical creation. We found ourselves in a hostile world and invented something to balance the universe as best we could. It all made a ton of sense. The god of Abraham was way too much like a vain, embittered old man for it to be coincidence.

It also occurred to me that if we created God in our own image, then we probably endowed him with our own attributes as well—including our sense of right and wrong. (We also exaggerated him into a comic book version of a man: more powerful, more angry, and more perfect in every way.) In fact, it is not a belief in gods and demons that defines our moral values, but just the opposite. Christians (as with people of other religions) once burned witches at the stake, enslaved people, tortured people on the rack, and stoned adulterers to death, thinking that was what God wanted. But we don't do that anymore. Did God change, or did we? As Shakespeare put it, "The fault lies not in our stars, but in ourselves."

So, what if... our invention of one or more deities was really nothing more than the fact that we were capable of inventing them? Believing in something for the sake of believing in it is circular and makes no sense. There are only two ways of knowing something: logical reasoning and experience (which includes observation). Believing and feeling are not the same as *knowing*. If the only task is to drive a nail, everything begins to look like a hammer, even that big rock over there.

Extending that idea, one could imagine that for there to be a deity there would have to be a life form to conjure it into being. People do not require a deity, but a deity most certainly requires people. After all, Chinese food is just food in China. If deities didn't have lesser beings to create, bless, and dominate, why would they be deities? They might exist and have powers we don't have as human beings, but in a world where everyone is superwoman, who cares? So to my mind, the idea that we were really just projecting our *own* image into the clouds like a bat signal lighting up the midnight sky as a call for help made a lot more sense.

I didn't know about the anthropic principle or what "projection" might have meant to a psychologist, nor do I think I could have expressed either idea to anyone, including myself, but the thoughts were there, hovering over my head like thought balloons of possibility.

Synthesis

Carter was a bright guy, but I was a happily worried kid. I thought about it and thought about it until I *finally* got to an age where thinking led somewhere and I could come to at least a few more conclusions of my own.

I put two and two together and got—*death*. I wondered about death. All kids do; we just never talk about it because nobody likes weird kids. But we all secretly think about it. And one of the things I wondered about was this: Everything that has ever been alive has experienced dying, but nothing has ever experienced death, since the complete death experience (including the "being dead" part) requires a mind to record it, and a functioning mind requires life. It seemed logical. I mean, the idea does have internal consistency and everything. But I didn't stop there. I kept pulling at it. And I came up with the following:

> Since we cannot understand what we have never experienced, and death is a one-way ticket, there is no mechanism to know it. It's all just speculation. As human animals, we have evolved to fear what we do not understand in order to survive, and have invented elaborate life-after-death scenarios to ameliorate our fears and mitigate the finality of it. For many people the end of our life can only

be explained with magic (we aren't really dead, we just look that way), and we have after-life destinations such as Valhalla and Heaven to solve that problem.

Good stuff. But I wasn't done, because I felt it necessary to explain it in such a way that it would make sense to an impartial observer (not just me). Remember, this is just me talking to me at this point; I was only just starting to write things down.

The entire process was new. The discovery of *new* knowledge all on my own, without having read about it in a book somewhere. By writing this paper and following each thread to my own conclusion, I had resolved a huge mystery.

And perhaps just as important, I had followed Bertrand Russell into the realm of philosophy in a real way. I was no longer just reading this stuff, I was *writing* it. I was making up new ideas from scratch. And that was amazing to me. Instead of the passivity of learning, I was doing something more. I was assembling words on the page and solving problems in the moment I conjured them onto the page.

Of course, my thesis on language and death wasn't complete. The fear of death haunts us like nothing else, and to a great extent it is driven by our own self-esteem and fear of decrepitude and pain. We spend half our time denying the inevitable and the other half attempting to overcome it through vitamin supplements, exercise, diets, and religion in our collective and individual search for meaning.

And there is instinct of course, which we share with all the other animals. I strongly suspect the gazelle fears the cheetah when it's running flat out to avoid being taken down. But most of us are removed from dealing directly with cheetahs, and I wasn't speculating about the pain and suffering sort of fear anyway. I was talking about a simple end to life.

In the spirit of Darwin, it is a species' lot to avoid extinction. We humans are just the only animals who agonize over our own existence and the meaning of life. The problem comes with language, contemplation, and self-awareness. All the other animals just live in the moment. Except perhaps dolphins, orcas, and whales. And maybe an octopus or two.

People fear death for reasons that transcend their ability to conceptualize it in a satisfying way. But this monograph of mine was a new *way* of looking at the issue, at least for me. And it created a path for me to walk with other ideas.

That other path included the rather liberating thought that whatever moral compass I did have, it could be my own, and that I didn't have to clone someone else's to have one.

Man's Fear of Death

Reprinted from *First Ellipsis... 1967*

What happens at death is the great unknowable thing. It is an intrinsic part of our lives, yet not part of our experience. And if we can't experience something, it just isn't there — it isn't part of us, and we can only understand it from a distance on some intellectual plain. Death is like infinity; we use imperfect models (such as a möbius strip or a wedding band), to describe what we can only imagine. And some things are beyond even that, even by analogy.

Nobody gets out alive, and we all figure that out as soon as we get to a certain age. Truth is, we all want to live forever. We know it, the neighbors know it, and the local minister absolutely knows it. For many of us, the shadow of death creates an urge to leave a legacy, some mark on the wall of life that says we were here, damn it, and you can't take that away. Without our common fear of death, we might never have invented religion.

But there are other clues into all of this. English and — as far as I have been able to find out — every other Indo-European language, doesn't have a way to describe death without using words that involve or imply life.

The sentence, "Sara Jenkins is dead." uses the verb "is" to describe Sara's relationship to death, and the word "is" happens to be a verb, and all verbs describe an action of some sort taken by the subject of the sentence. And since the subject of the sentence is a person, and she does something, that indicates life.

A basic sentence is constructed: subject | verb | object. In the sentence "Sara Jenkins is dead," the word "is" is a form of the verb *to be*, and "being" is something that we *do*.

The English connecting word "is" (and related forms) is a verb, and so is "die | died." Various criteria allow one to argue that "be" and "die" are verbs, also that "dead" is an adjective. A very basic test for the verb status of "be" is subject-verb agreement: the connecting word must agree with the subject. English sentences can't describe anything without using a verb — this is a basic structural issue. Some languages have sentences without any verbs, however, the verbs are *understood by context* — it's implied. Mankind's existence is founded on this idea of doing something, and if nothing happens, it's as if we don't exist.

How to be dead

"Being" is an activity just as much as talking, eating, running, and thinking. But we aren't "being" anything when we are in that state called death — we have become *inanimate*. Our language doesn't have words to describe existing in a state of death, so we use what words we do have, even if they aren't accurate. In fact, the word "existing" implies life as well, so we can't even create an oblique description of the situation.

In that, our language imposes an assumption upon all of us that "being dead" doesn't involve death so much as it does some weird alternate form of life in which we can't move. Like going to sleep and never waking up — the Sleeping Beauty syndrome, where we wait for Prince Charming and True Love's Kiss to pull us back into wakeful existence. (The part of Prince Charming to be played by whatever "god" happens to be in vogue at that time).

And I think this is where all the fear comes in. The fault lies in our inexperience with and subsequent ignorance of something outside our existence and understanding. No wonder we are afraid of it; we can't even describe it without euphemisms and a lot of mumbo-jumbo. "Mommy's just asleep, dear." or "Mommy is with God and the angels." Part of this is out of respect for who mommy was and that we didn't want her to die in the first place, but still...

The horror

So when we imagine ourselves after our own death, we default to thoughts of some sort of macabre stasis where we are perfectly aware of everything, but unable to move—*for all eternity.* Not a good place to be. Or we think we're in a cloud-like place with harps and wings, grateful to our parents for twisting our little ears and forcing us to go to church when we wanted to work on our model airplane. Or, *shuddering thought,* what if we'd miscalculated—missed the boat (via arrogance, most likely)—and wind up in that *other* place our parents had warned us about, filled with the acrid smell of brimstone?

All of which gives rise to the notion that when we die we don't *really* die, but have a kind of life-after-death that continues on forever, and all because we cannot *language* it properly.

Of course, you may have spotted the hole in my thesis, and are quietly (or loudly) laughing to yourself over what an idiot I was at whatever age I was when I wrote this piece.

To put not too fine a point on it, everybody dies. And if we die early, we don't get to pass on our genes. No kids, no grandkids, no nothing, forever and ever. Which means all the little goodies (and weird bad stuff) our own particular DNA managed to pick up over the millions of years since time began for the naked ape are lost forever. Gone. Pfffft. Kaput. Siblings would pass most of it on, but not us personally.

It's almost like genes have a mind of their own. Like that old joke about the chicken being the egg's way of producing another egg. Darwin's survival of the fittest, plus the anthropic principle combine to create our fear of death because without it, we wouldn't be here. But we are here. Thus, it is so. You're still laughing. Okay, so I didn't have it all together back then, but... like an expensive medicine about to go off patent, I *can* repurpose it as a wonderful example of incomplete logic!

Think about it. All those conspiracy theories swirling and bumping through conservative society without any solid footing. They make sense in an odd way to the ones who repeat them, but they lack evidence, ignore the obvious explanation, and are generally preposterous. As everyone knows who isn't hunkered down in a fever-swamp basement with all the other conspiracy nut jobs. Because people (including me) don't always think things through logically. *Ta da!*

A few years ago I revisited my idea on an open forum of scholars I belong to. I asked if anyone knew of a language construct of death that does *not* imply life. This resulted in a rather interesting discussion over several years as I visited the thread from time to time. I got a fair number of suggestions, but only a few (in my own mind) came close to answering the intent of my original question. But there were gems among the dross.

One writer noted that the Bantu language Matuumbi does not always require verbs to express meaning. He wrote that one can convey the present state "The person (muundú) is dead" either using a verb — muundú a-wíile, or using an adjective without any verb — muundú η-waá. The adjective η-waá agrees with the noun muundú, and the prefix for agreement η- is used only on nouns and adjectives, but not on verbs. It may be just as common for languages that do not require a verb to require a connecting word. He also noted that tenses don't line up perfectly across languages, but "good enough" might be possible.

But for my thesis, I don't think "good enough" is actually good enough. While Matuumbi may not language the Bantu people into the existential corner I describe, it remains an obscure language spoken only south of the Rufiji River in Tanzania, and I have no idea if the Bantu fear death the same way everyone else does or not. They probably do fear cheetahs, however.

Oh well. It was a long shot to find a language construct of death that doesn't somehow imply life. Man's fear of death is at least partly driven by the limitations of how we can express such concepts, rather than by something intrinsically scary about death itself.

During my reading, I discovered that Parmenides, a Greek philosopher who lived around 500 BCE, argued that "nothing cannot exist," since "To speak of a thing, one has to speak of a thing that exists. Nothing cannot exist because nothing isn't real." Which sounded similar to what I was saying.

I also remembered being taught that the number "zero" had only been made real by historical edict—that mathematicians use it despite it's dubious reality simply because it works. They use imaginary numbers in the same way. (Zero is considered to be both sort of real and imaginary.)

There is not a single observable entity that has no properties. By definition, if it did, it would be unobservable. The closest things to "zero" we get is empty space, but quantum indeterminacy prohibits completely zero energy in space. All of this is oblique to my main thesis here, but fits within the greater idea that we often don't know what we don't know—but if we think about it long enough and hard enough and ask enough questions, we can often figure it out.

Provenance

All of this thinking and writing led me down my own road, deriving at least some of my own conclusions. I now stood for something that I myself had created. I was now *me*, a person unto himself. A necessary step. Not only for life in general, but for what I was about to do.

Part of that was my own memory, which helped me puzzle through. I have always been able to remember (almost verbatim) when the subject matter was important enough. I can remember prior to being able to speak or talk, for instance, because things happened at that time to impress me. And I remember a lot of what I've read over the years. When putting the pieces together, that ability to recollect came to my aid. It wasn't perfect, and I didn't always know where an idea came from, but it worked well enough to facilitate what I had to do.

Fuse, Meet Match

The Vietnam War seemed to be driven by an existential fear that communists would soon take over the world (whereupon everything would soon be painted gray and there would be no more Sunday School or peanut butter sandwiches), plus the widespread assumption that our nation was a paragon of ingenuity and virtue, particularly entitled to tell other people how to live their lives. The whole thing was sketchy.

Why was our pastor telling us in his Sunday sermons that it was our duty to God and country to travel halfway around the world to kill a bunch of subsistence farmers working ten hours a day in rice paddies? Half the Bible told us to slay the Amalekites (and by extension, anybody else that didn't believe in God), but the other half said to turn the other cheek, reforge all our swords into farm implements, and invite the neighbors over for dinner. From my frame of reference, it was spectacularly bipolar, but nobody was owning up to it. I was growing up in Bizarro World with everyone pretending it was all quite normal.

Throughout my young life, religious teachings had been a tangled mystery. Too many things just didn't add up, and no one I knew was willing to acknowledge any of it—with the exception of my older brother.

Glen had gone to Moody Bible Institute, and my sister Sheri had gone to Westmont. In our family, you could graduate from home and get on with your life if you went to a religious college. At least, that's what it looked like from my perspective.

Glen had studied biblical texts in the original Greek and Aramaic (an ability to translate at least some of the original text was part of the curriculum). He told me stories of his college days, especially after I came to live with him and his wife Suzy, as a teenager. College hijinks mostly, but he also went into some of the biblical issues he'd come up against.

While translating, comparing, and contrasting ancient texts back and forth between different versions in Greek, Aramaic, and Elizabethan English, Glen had stumbled upon passages of original scripture that had been mistranslated (or reinterpreted) by whatever forgotten scholar had done the work. Sometimes it was just one word. And it made a difference.

These botched translations—some quite fundamental to western theology—had changed the meaning of a number of critical passages, and in result had scattered small caches of misinformation throughout the scriptures. People think a particular translation stands on its own, but they rarely do. They are put together from other translations. The King James Bible wasn't a new translation at all. It was cobbled together from other English translations. That is how these incorrect translations kept multiplying. *They were reusing bad code.* Calling it the "Word of God" kept it from being questioned.

Translations can get tricky when words and phrases go from one language to another, especially when there are competing dialects. A phrase meaning *seventy-two raisins* can end up as *seventy-two virgins* faster than you can say "Deluded terrorists reading from Arabic interpretations of the Qur'an instead of Aramaic or Syriac thinks they will be rewarded with virgins in paradise."

Take any system that has no governor, push it gently at the beginning, and you wind up with something very different at the end. The wobble at the start overwhelms the result if there is no way to correct for error along the way. It made me think of a kid learning to ride a bike. Without the automatic self-corrective skill that comes from repetition and muscle memory, controlling any bicycle is difficult and rudimentary. The kid usually ends up in the ditch. Like Jerome of Stridon.

It's the Early Middle Ages. You're a scholar named Jerome of Stridon who has just been hired by Pope Damasus to translate scripture from Greek and Aramaic into street Latin (Latin Vulgate) so everybody can understand it. You run across a word you're not sure of. It might mean one thing or it might mean something different. You wonder what to do. You scratch your head. Maybe you take a break and have lunch. But finally you make a decision and keep going. And of course, the rest of what you translate might get shifted just a little by that one word. This happens many, many times because you don't have a Greek to Latin or Aramaic to Latin dictionary. Nobody does. You're going by your own memory and the memory of those who taught you. Plus your own opinion, of course. Your own idea of what the Bible *should* say. And you were never perfect.

You hand in your work, get paid, and find another patron. Bibles are copied by hand and beautifully illustrated. A thousand years later, a guy named Gutenberg invents moveable type. New translations are made, but your work (which is older) is used in the new stuff too. In fact, now long dead, you are being cited as an authority on critical passages. Presses crank, and your little interpretation of history ends up all over the world in Bibles now declared to be the Word of God.

My brother had questioned one of his professors about passages he knew were mistranslations. He was told, "Look, you're a biblical scholar, educated in the text. The general public isn't, and if we started explaining every single thing, there will be all sorts of questions. The Bible would be thrown into a sea of ambiguity. It would be a mess!"

Dangerous information upsets the balance of power; don't release it into the wild or we'll all reap the whirlwind. Pay no attention to that man behind the curtain! My takeaway was the same as my brother's—when in doubt, doubt.

The inconsistencies weren't little, and my brother knew it. So, obviously, did his professors. Glen quit that university and enrolled elsewhere. He changed his major from divinity to psychology and pursued a completely different career.

Ten years later, he and I are sitting in his livingroom in Willow Glen discussing the stuff and nonsense of life, including any *ologies* interesting enough to merit consideration, and this comes up like a row of ancient coins.

Glen imparted to my untutored ears such tales and mysteries that made my eyes, like glowing orbs, distend in wonder and my mind to swirl in rude awakening and enthusiastic curiosity. I asked question after question, and in that livingroom we traveled from the Earth to the stars and back again, touching on everything that mattered.

His explanations made a lot more sense than the religious cant I'd been spoon-fed by Sunday School, church, Vacation Bible School, and family. His answers matched my questions in any number of places, but his scripture knowledge was fascinating. Apparently, I'd been grossly mislead. I'd always suspected as much and simple logic had led me to believe so, but the evidence Glen imparted was specific and overwhelming.

My brother's intellectual tenacity impressed the hell out of me. I didn't have his intuitive ability, but I could read. I had a decent enough brain, and I figured that might be sufficient. I wanted to swing for the fences just as he had.

It looked to me like some of these botched translations had created a codependency between the established church and the military, going clear back to the crusades. The church had legitimized war and, perhaps even worse, made it sound noble.

The way I figured it, we language our understanding of existence from our collective and individual experience, then create the deities we must have to make that reality work and to assuage our fears. Organized religion uses fear because fear drives religion. Fear of death, fear the crops will fail, fear we won't win the big football game: the list is endless.

Read to live, live to read

I was raised on this stuff, so it felt like part of my DNA, but it also felt foreign. The Bible is like a shopping cart of ancient beliefs; I understood a little of it, but felt that I should know a great deal more. For good or for ill, the language and morality of the Bible is interwoven throughout Western literature like never-ending threads of cultural identity. Dismissing such an enormous influence on mankind out of hand without at least reading its primary text would have been stupid or lazy or both.

I was already familiar with the Bible, having had various passages and themes preached at me over the years, and I'd read many key verses in church as well, so I wasn't a blank slate. But I didn't have a complete front-to-back understanding of it, which is what I felt I needed if I were to comprehend it as a whole.

Reading the Bible as a study project would be a huge, mind-numbing chore and I certainly didn't relish the idea, but with the hubris of youth, I made it one of my tasks, along with the yet nebulous goal to get a grip on Shakespeare. Elizabethan English in large doses isn't fun, but I felt it was necessary if I were ever to consider myself truly educated. Putting religion into perspective might be near to impossible, but I was young and relatively pure, so I saw no reason not to try.

Any connection between my understanding of Christianity and my issue with the draft board and the Vietnam War wasn't immediately obvious, but both dealt with ethics and behavior, and I had a notion that they were deeply interrelated.

I took a deep breath and did it. This all happened during my self-education years when I was supposed to be in high school. It took me two tries, front to back. The first time was just a run through, because I knew I'd been secretly skimming from time to time. Cheating, basically. It was an arduous task and I wasn't getting anywhere, but I had the goal of finishing, so I did. And surprise, surprise, I learned virtually nothing.

So I refocused my mind and read it again. But the second time I got smarter about it; I had a *strategy*. There are problems with reading the King James version (which is the version I chose because that's the one our family used): it's big, it's repetitious, and it was written in an archaic form of English from earlier translations written by many different people, from one language to another several times at different periods in history. There was a concordance, but that wasn't a lot of help.

So, I found two reference books at the library. One each for the New and Old Testaments. I took pages of notes as I went, filling my notebook going back and forth between the Bible and my reference materials. I also got a map of the holy land from my father's store, with all the old place names.

In addition, I consulted the collected works of Josephus — a massive tome, which I referenced down at the library. Frankly, I had never heard of Flavius Josephus (37-100 CE) before, but my historical guides mentioned him so many times that I felt driven to find out who he was and what he'd written. So I looked him up; he was surprisingly readable.

And there was one more guy: St. Augustine. I only knew about him peripherally, from listening to Bob Dylan. *I Dreamed I Saw St. Augustine* was the song, and it raised questions. All these things seemed to connect with one another, like some English maze garden I found myself winding through. I could touch the hedge on either side, I could see the path in front and behind me, but I had only a rude idea where it was going.

One day I'm browsing this used bookstore I liked in Willow Glen off Lincoln Avenue. Thousands of books, all stacked higgledy-piggledy in general sections on a labyrinth of raw wooden shelves, with that wonderful musty odor you only get in libraries and old English sports cars. And somewhere between the Andre Norton paperbacks and a moth-eaten set of Punch in multiple volumes, I ran across *The Confessions*—by, you guessed it, Augustine of Hippo, the African theologian and philosopher with ties to Rome. A doorstop in a red cover. So I bought it.

Bottom line? A sixteen-year-old boy and his father go to a public bath house together and Augustine (still a boy), got an erection or was showing some hair growth, which his father noticed. His father was positively giddy about it when they got home, told his wife, and embarrassed Kid Augustine no end. When he grew up, that embarrassment, along with the story of the bathhouse, went right into his Confessions, which I read when I read the Bible the second time.

See, he wasn't considered "of age" yet, so puberty was there *prior* to his ability to tell right from wrong, which meant (using a little reverse engineering), that it had to have been there *from birth* since there was no other event prior to coming of age that he could point to. We all grow up, right? Well, Augustine took that simple fact and somehow managed to convolute it to a whole nother level.

Twenty-seven years later, Augustine publishes his memoir in the form of one long letter to God, including a lot of considered opinion, plus the bath house incident.

That experience became the basis for his invention of original sin, which isn't really in the Bible itself. It's an *interpretation* of the Bible, and the Catholic Church made him a saint for coming up with it. Talk about revelatory. My brother had some stories about the stuff he found out, but now I had my own. Some kid gets embarrassed in public, and now we've got original sin? Wow. I felt like Vasco da Gama, gazing out at the Pacific. It's true I wasn't reading any of this in Greek or Aramaic — or Hebrew, for that matter, but I found plenty to keep me occupied. I had found my element.

My theory with all this back and forth was pretty basic. If I got different perspectives from a variety of source material and wrote my thoughts into a notebook, I would have a fair-to-middling chance of getting some of it to stick, plus I'd be less likely to glaze over somewhere in the middle of the begats.

And maybe, just maybe I'd be able to figure out the politics going on that was about to send me into harm's way via bootcamp and eventually the Vietnam War — there was a connection in there somewhere.

I remembered my mother teaching her fourth graders, and how big she was on context. It wasn't just about what happened, but why it happened and what lead up to it. I was asking the "Five Ws" — *who, what, where, when,* and *why* — as such questions were often called. A reporter's catechism for making sure nothing important got missed.

Reading the Bible for the second time (at a much slower pace), I started running into stuff I hadn't noticed the first go around — or in church or Sunday School, for that matter. And some of it was awful. Shockingly bad, in fact.

At first, I dismissed it because I knew the Bible described a culture and time different from my own. And I knew something of cruelty from what I'd read about the Nazi death camps in World War II. But it stood out completely at odds from what I'd been taught (God is good, God loves you, God's got your back, etc.), and I could no longer ignore it.

So I made some notes, and in a few cases tried to find some explanation other than the straight reading of the text, either in books I already had, or in Charles Spurgeon, an old time Bible-thumper, who could explain anything, given enough ink and paper. My father had a whole shelf full of Spurgeon's sermons.

"Slaves, submit yourselves to your masters with all respect, not only to the good and gentle, but also to the cruel."
— *1 Peter 2:18*

"If two men are fighting and the wife of one of them comes to rescue her husband from his assailant, and she reaches out and seizes him by his private parts, you shall cut off her hand. Show her no pity." — *Deuteronomy 25:11-12*

"No one who has been emasculated by crushing or cutting may enter the assembly of the Lord." — *Deuteronomy 23:1*

"The men of her town shall stone her to death [*for adultery*]."
— *Deuteronomy 22:20-21*

"Anyone who curses their father or mother shall be put to death." — *Leviticus 20:9*

"The people of Samaria must bear their guilt, because they have rebelled against their God. They will fall by the sword; their little ones will be dashed to the ground, their pregnant women ripped open." — *Hosea 13:16*

The problem was, these verses (and many other like them), didn't jive with what I'd been taught. The whole idea of God telling people to rip open pregnant women wasn't right in *any* time or culture, and I knew that much even at the ripe age of sixteen.

And the kicker? The kicker was that Jehovah himself was supposed to be all powerful and omniscient, in all places and times at once, and yet he couldn't edit his own book.

Gimme that old time religion

From an early age, I had been suspicious of the concept of hell. I remember asking my parents about it because it didn't make sense that a person (or even a child!) would be thrown into a fire to burn forever just because they weren't willing to bow down to a mediæval god. It seemed like a good place to start. What I gleaned from our local library only added to the bits and pieces I'd learned from my brother. Took some work, but it was all there. I just had to put the pieces together.

Hell (or hades) is an embellished translation from a Greek word that doesn't really mean what we think it means: ἅδης. It originally meant death or grave, but in various languages has been translated as trash heap, the place they put the bodies, or the city dump—called a *midden* by archeologists.

Ancient people didn't have bulldozers to bury their trash; it just built up over time. And the garbage dumps outside all large cities became breeding grounds for vermin, wild animals, and disease. They weren't that far from where people lived either, and transportation was by donkey or you walked.

So, back when the Bible was being written garbage dumps were a health problem just waiting to explode with bubonic plague, cholera, typhoid, and other nasty surprises. And even though they didn't have modern medicine, common sense told people to get rid of the garbage. Jews in Roman times were obsessed with purity, as shown by the number of *mikvehs* (ritual baths), and the use of stone vessels, assumed to be unaffected by impurity. In Jerusalem, everyone took their garbage out beyond the city boundary (because it was impure, and God didn't like that).

What did they do to keep the garbage from festering with disease? They set it on fire. The fire never went out; it kept smoldering unless there was a good rain. After which, the good citizens of Jerusalem scurried right out and set it on fire again.

Jerusalem lies on a plateau between two deep gorges. The people carted their garbage through the Harsith (Valley) Gate to the Valley of Hinnom, referred to as Gehenna, which was a dumping ground for the city. Residents called it the "valley of the sewer," or "hell." According to Josephus, there were about 50,000 people living in Jerusalem at that time, with a life expectancy of 35. So, lots of bodies. Almost all were taken care of formally, with a burial, but not everyone was so lucky.

So, the gorge at the edge of the city where everyone dumped their garbage was always on fire, and was known at that time as hell. And the kicker? The kicker was... that was the place where they threw the bodies of dead people when their families didn't have enough money to pay for a proper gravesite or if they'd done something really bad. Thieves and murderers ended up there. One of the worst things was to be left unburied when you died, so it was a kind of last punishment. Really, bad. Hence, the word hell was used to describe a place of final punishment because it was a really bad place of fire and death.

They carted or dragged the bodies out the Harsith Gate and threw them right onto the fire. That was the big deal with Jesus getting to borrow the rich man's tomb, because the carpenter from Nazareth would have been *cast onto hell* along with the two thieves who were also crucified that day — you know, because he was a poor guy and guilty of a whole list of crimes, including witchcraft and infuriating the priesthood with his itinerant preaching. Treason was the final verdict, but all were bad enough for him to go unburied. His disciples had to steal his body.

In the Old Testament, two words are used for hell: sheol, which means the grave or a pit; and Gehenna, which is the Valley of Hinnom, a garbage dump outside Jerusalem. What you don't find is a place of fire-and-brimstone, eternal torture and suffering, ruled over by the Devil — what we call hell.

The New Testament has three words for hell: Gehenna, sheol, and Hades and Tartarus, which are two words meaning the Greek underworld. The imagery of a fiery hell is used in many places, but in each case it refers to the Greek myth (not sheol), and is not intended to be understood literally.

Judea was conquered and ruled by Greeks from 332 BCE, and Greek education continued under the Romans. 350 years later, Jewish scholars were given a formal Greek education. This applied even to religious leaders such as Pharisees: for instance, we know Paul of Tarsus had a formal Greek education because of the proper Greek he used in his letters.

Greek ideas had seeped into Jewish thought throughout the New Testament. For example, First Corinthians 13:12: *"For now we see only a reflection as in a mirror; then we shall see face to face"* is a good description of Plato's allegory of the cave, which Paul would certainly have been taught.

The Greek underworld is another example. The Phlegethon River is the river of blazing fire associated with punishment. However, I doubt any educated Jew of the first century would have believed that the Greek Hades was real. They would have held tightly to the Old Testament ideas of sheol. Some of the common people might have believed it, in the same way as some Christians today believe we will be punished if our evil deeds outweigh our good. Both ideas: weighing-scales and fire-and-brimstone, may be useful for teaching but not mainstream doctrine or literal depictions.

In the King James Bible, the Old Testament term sheol is translated as "Hell" 31 times, and it is translated as "the grave" 31 times. Sheol is also translated as "the pit" three times. Modern translations render sheol as "the grave, "the pit," or "death."

In modern times, popular concepts about hell come from literal interpretation of scriptural allegory, as described above, or pagan ideas. For instance, the word *hell* comes from Old Norse Hel, Loki's daughter, who rules over the damned in Niflheim. Ideas about Niflheim have influenced our modern ideas about hell and images that were popular during the Reformation. Two classic instances are Dante's *Divine Comedy,* and Michelangelo's painting, *The Last Judgment.*

How much mythology has been built on that tower of linguistic Babel? Which scribe first made an ancient city dump equivalent to a lake of fire and eternal torment to put the heebie-jeebies into ignorant folk who just wanted to keep their heads above water, pay their taxes, and go to church the way their parents had? The Bible is riddled with this stuff.

The entire book of Revelations is one man's cryptic history of events that took place during his lifetime and how he felt about it. It had nothing to do with future events. The original audience would have easily recognized most of his flamboyant symbols and understood them within the context of their own era, much as Shakespeare's audience understood his references during their era. Prior to modern times, people were far more familiar with allegory and symbolic imagery.

John of Patmos was something of a crank, and he wrote his singular masterpiece — *Revelation* — as political allegory to reflect his own anger at the tumultuous state of the still-nascent Jesus movement in the late first century. Jerusalem had fallen, its main temple lay in ruins, and despite multiple promises to return within everyone's lifetime, Jesus had broken that promise—apparently abandoning his followers, including the writer. And John of Patmos was decidedly unhappy about it.

The priests at Nicaea who compiled the Bible were dubious about including it, but did so despite misgivings, seemingly because it was so colorful and provided a boffo ending to their big book. It was like the fireworks at the end of an evening at Disneyland: spectacular and inspiring. Empty calories perhaps, but still rather delicious to the Bible thumpers, who have been screaming its dire warnings at their wide-eyed parishioners ever since.

The purpose of the Christian religion seemed to be twofold: control behavior with the concepts of sin and punishment, but also promise a way out—an easy fix for all the problems of the present. Life was a bit of a slog for the common man back when this stuff was being creatively endowed.

I discovered that the idea of being saved for an afterlife in heaven or being sent to a hades ruled by a satanic figure came directly from Greek culture: Homer's *Odyssey* contains a good example—written about seven hundred years before the New Testament. As with almost everything else, the Greeks invented it first. Their original concept is still current in Mexican culture—exemplified by the Day of the Dead—in which the continued existence of the dearly departed is dependant upon their constant remembrance by the living. There's even a Disney movie about it, entitled *Coco*.

I became a familiar face at our library during this time—and to the librarians, who probably wondered what the heck I was doing out of school. By the time I'd finished the Bible a second time, I was ready to move on. I had planned to tackle the Qur'an, and I started the Torah, but quit after about twenty pages. My brain was turning south on me. I needed a break, and I was starting to feel concerned about spending so much time on a single subject. I had a lot more yet to plow through, including Shakespeare, somehow, all of it leading to the person I had to become in order to make my life work.

But all of my biblical studies were to help tremendously when I had to make that huge moral commitment about the war, which was based to a great degree on the same tenets that underlay religion. Not that I knew that then, of course; there was far more for me to learn before I could piece that quilt. At the beginning, I was just a curious kid barnstorming his own education the best way he knew how.

The One Ring

Right after the Bible, I started J.R.R. Tolkien's *The Lord of the Rings*, another tome focused on ethics. This was the second time I had re-started a book immediately after turning over the last page of the last chapter. I couldn't believe what I'd discovered. Tolkien revealed a moral clarity I hadn't experienced before except in conversations with my brother. I'm not talking about Good *vs*. Evil; that was the obvious theme, the storybook theme. Tolkien was far more subtle than that.

Frodo's quest was to *destroy* a treasure that had already been found (the Ruling Ring). In every other book of this nature, going back to *Treasure Island* by Robert Lewis Stevenson, finding the treasure and carrying it back to fame and an easy life was the implied goal. Tolkien made the treasure the root of all evil. He flipped the narrative.

He also wrote his ending with Frodo as a partial failure. Frodo succumbs to the Ring's temptation, and Sméagol | Gollum is the one who saves the quest through his own avarice at the last minute. So the main character gives in to the dark side, and Gollum saves the day. Frodo did not come home to a hero's welcome. He ends up a broken Hobbit, with far more pain than joy. Still a hero, but greatly diminished.

The Hobbits had seen the horror, cruelty, and the crushing despair of a war that ravaged Middle Earth and changed their world forever. They returned to find a war criminal, Saruman, had taken over the Shire and destroyed much of it. At the end of the adventure, there is a feeling of melancholy.

I have read comments by readers who loved LOTR but hated the long protracted ending, feeling that Tolkien should have cut it short with a heroic homecoming. They didn't get it, they didn't understand what he was saying. Tolkien had seen war first-hand as a second lieutenant, and he knew the horror of it. His battalion occupied front-line trenches at Beaumont-Hamel, Serre and the Leipzig Salient during World War I. It was an experience that changed him and galvanized him into creating books unlike anything the world had ever seen. Just as important, he came home from war, and he knew what happened after.

This ambiguity was a joy for me to discover in a world that seemed to crave heroes or villains with a chasm bereft of merit or logic in between — despite the reality of our lives. Tolkien's world wrestled with serious doubts, and his protagonists often did the wrong thing. They weren't always brave, and they didn't always win. His villains lost, but they didn't always perish, and sometimes they came back, more threatening than ever.

I myself would soon be embroiled in the test of a lifetime against the greatest power on the planet. Was I right? Was I wrong? Tolkien postulated that there was room for both and that it was possible to be okay with that. Such a refreshing change from so many other writers, who seemed to feel that stark contrast was necessary if their readers were to understand the truth they were attempting to convey.

All of which made *Lord of the Rings* one of the best-selling novels of all time, primarily because it's messy and dark and ambiguous and very much true to life. Tolkien was a contemplative man who poured himself into his books, creating paths through dark and tangled forests so others could follow.

I read that book over and over during the following years. Why? For the same reason everyone else did: it delineates some of the biggest lies we tell ourselves and reveals the truth we rarely like to face. Tolkien was right: the ends do not justify the means, life isn't perfect, things don't always work out for the best, heroes often fail, and absolutes are often short-sighted. I took these wisdoms and incorporated them as best I could into this new version of myself I was busy building. Aside from the documentary novel *Babi Yar* and Viktor Frankl's book, *Man's Search for Meaning,* Tolkien's classic did more to shape my attitude toward war and redemption than any other.

Interestingly enough, LOTR is the only book I've read that has its own score. I started reading it at the park, but later at home, often listening to music. I soon settled on a very specific album, which seemed to fit the tone of the book: *Wes Montgomery, Return Engagement*. Cool and plunky, Wes Montgomery's electric guitar was backed by a full orchestra, pianissimo.

I got tired of getting up to change the record all the time, so I took the turntable apart and rigged it to continuously replay without intervention. (Lord of the Rings takes a while to read.) Over the years my brain evidently associated that music so closely with the book that I always heard *Bumpin' on Sunset* when I read the part about Frodo and Samwise traversing the Dead Marshes. And whenever I play that album—I might be listening to *Tequila, Naptown Blues*, or *Con Alma*—I am right there with them at Sammath Naur, the Cracks of Doom. (My own little Pavlovian association.)

How to fight a bully

In 1965, there was an incident that acted on me like the click of an ignition key. Something started up inside me that I hadn't known existed or even could exist. And it shocked the hell out of me. I was in my freshman year of high school.

I'd always been leery of physical confrontation. No big deal; almost everybody is. I'd seen other kids struggle with it over the years, and dreaded coming up short if I had to box my way out of some situation. I was a reader, not a fighter. I even convinced Edith to let me take Kempo karate lessons, which gave me a much better sense of my body's position, movement, and limitations, but not much else. A bookworm with a yellow belt is, after all, still a bookworm.

There had been a high school assembly, and everyone was streaming out of the gym, walking back to class. The boy and girl in front of me appeared to be having a heated discussion. She said something; he said something; things got loud; she said something final, and he knocked her purse out of her hands. Fairly dripping with high principles, I picked up the girl's purse and handed it to her. No big deal. But the guy turned, and suddenly I was the enemy, meddling in his personal business. No wonder I pissed him off. He was my height but heavier and stronger, and had the look of a junkyard dog who liked to lift weights. Honestly, I was toast.

I couldn't believe I was doing this, but when he made some sneering remark, I spoke right back, pointing out that I was just handing the girl her purse. I didn't know either of them; I was just being a nice guy. I knew it and he knew it and I knew he knew it. But my speaking up wasn't what he wanted to hear just then, so he said something far more derogatory.

There is always some point when you realize the ice is iffy under your feet. You're at the far end of the pond, snow and ice all around, and suddenly the ice doesn't feel right. And then, for no reason, you take another step. That is what I did. I took it one more step.

I said something right back, and the ice broke. He slugged me in the jaw, hard. My glasses took a graceful journey of their own, arcing and sparkling into the sky. I stood there, stunned. This had gotten very serious, very fast. It was too serious for what it was, which made it funny, so I went beyond the edge of reason and *laughed*.

Now, anybody with a bit of sense knows you don't do that. You don't laugh at a bully in a schoolyard, and certainly not when he's just slugged you. I don't know if there was something off in my thinking or perhaps it was just the Cheerios talking. I was supposed to be in fight-or-flight mode and my brain told me to laugh. *Great decision, brain. You're gonna get us killed; you know that, right?*

It was lead, follow, or get out of the way, and I decided to punt. My Cheerios-addled brain told me to point my finger at him. And then laugh. Again. It was like I didn't know me anymore.

His only solution was to use his fists, and I sort of expected that. Thudding body blows staggered me back, but didn't hurt. I may have looked like an easy target, but my stomach muscles were incredibly strong from doing sit-ups nonstop when I had trouble sleeping; one more of my little projects.

I just stood there (a bit sideways—I was no fool, plus, you know, I had had all that karate training). And that's when I reached for the stars.

"How does it feel to be a bully?" I asked him. I shoved harder. "Are you nuts?" I was *Rikki-Tikki-Tavi,* clearing cobras from the garden.

Kids had started to gather around and I started to mock him. Hell, I was on a roll. I shouted to the other students, my arms up in the air, waving them in, yelling, "Fight! Fight!" The situation was bizarre, yet intriguing.

"I thought you wanted to fight! What's *wrong* with you? You're *chicken,* aren't you!" It was the ultimate triple-dog dare.

"Are we going to meet down by the bike racks? Are you going to beat me up? Come on, mister tough guy, hit me again. Is that all ya got?"

He hit me twice—right in the jaw. *Bam. Bam.*

I just stood there, dazed. I shook my head. He was standing there, like a boxer, watching me. He was waiting for me to do something. Hit him back? Run away? He was at an impasse. I looked right back at him. He was in the process of discovery. The fight was over.

I'm not sure where I got my attitude and reckless disposition, but I was fed up with people telling me what to do and I wasn't going to take it anymore—especially from some punk kid my own age, no matter how much weight he could lift. I wasn't going down and I wasn't going away. Quiet guys carry seeds of insurrection within them that can unexpectedly blossom if they're pushed too far too fast, and I suddenly discovered that I was one of those guys. I became my own hero that day.

The surrounding group had grown to thirty or forty students, with more gathering as they paused on their way back to class—a huge audience. It was surreal. The students around us probably thought it rather novel also, and an interesting finish to another boring assembly.

I'd never thought about the loneliness of bullies before, thinking of them only as one dimensional kids who enjoyed pushing other people around. But that need for attention and control had to come from somewhere. An absent parent perhaps, or some horrible experience. Or maybe it was just neglect coupled with opportunity. But this time was different because I saw the confusion in his eyes when I just stood there looking at him. His world had gone haywire. I looked around at the other kids, and during that brief glance, he slipped out of the group. I spotted him after a second or so, halfway across the basketball courts and moving quickly.

I looked at the girl. She was still standing there, but she wasn't Natalie Wood and I wasn't James Dean, so that wasn't going anywhere. The kids were still there, I was still there, but he wasn't. And I had *laughed* at him. It was amazing. My jaw hurt like hell and I ended up with swollen salivary glands for a week, but I was elated. I had won a fist fight. And I hadn't lifted a finger!

I had never stood up to anyone before. Not in that way. In retrospect, I got a visceral lesson on the *firmness in truth* protests of Dr. King and Mohandas Gandhi that I would learn about later in life. So I had stood my ground against a bully, found I wasn't the coward I'd always suspected myself to be, and got a solid lesson in human relations, all in one go.

I had always assumed a person had to act tough to have courage. Watch enough television and movies and that's what you get: brave guys acting tough. Well, maybe having a purpose was just as good, or perhaps even better. Which meant—*ding! ding! ding!*—I was on the right track. I was on my way to becoming a *mensch*, and this had been the hard evidence (rubbing my jaw) I'd been looking for.

I had seen individuals stand up to power. Not personally, but there were plenty of movies and books with that narrative. But movie stars and characters in books aren't so much brave as acting a part. To paraphrase Jessica Rabbit, *they're just written that way*.

I learned *what* I would fight for and how I would do it. Not at first, but it eventually came to me. I wasn't much for pushing my own agenda, but when I thought someone else was being bullied—like that girl with her purse—that made a huge difference.

This was a harbinger of decisions I would make and actions I would take over the years to come, when courage supplanted my sense of self and I spoke up for someone who had no voice. I was able to argue a case in Superior Court when circumstance placed me in a position to tip the balance and made a difference. Whatever personal insecurities I had fell away as I focused entirely on getting the point across to make sure a little girl didn't get steamrolled by the system.

The clue for me was when I forgot about myself. When I *became* the force people had to reckon with, beyond whatever embarrassment I might be feeling, and speaking out in reckless disregard for what others might think of me — that was the core of it. Fight-or-flight was the response written in all the psychology textbooks, but I had discovered another avenue. Stand firm and speak up; nobody's going to do it for you.

My own kind of music

Questions started to form; like airplanes circling overhead, waiting to land. I became interested in ideas that weren't in the books I was reading — or at least I couldn't find them. Some were philosophical in nature, and to a certain extent, I assumed I just hadn't read enough books yet. I figured that as long as I continued to read, I would eventually run into authors who wrote about such ideas. I was only partly wrong. Either I was really good at looking in all the wrong places, or I would have to come up with some of this stuff on my own.

Books I hadn't read and knowledge I didn't have looked like an endless row of cereal bowls, some with frosted flakes (history, murder mysteries, science fiction, and adventure), and many like bran flakes (nearly everything else). Some were akin to Grape Nuts (like chomping on granite — the Bible, Charles Spurgeon), and still others were more like Raisin Bran (T.S. Eliot, James Joyce, Bob Dylan, Djuna Barnes) — I knew it was good for me and the initial taste was often difficult to take, but there was a world of wonder if I could understand it. I read with quiet determination, knowing I had little with which to correlate all this new information. My lack of experience wasn't helping.

When I got to college, I was dumbfounded by an arbitrary limitation on the number of units I could take. I understood their reasoning, but thought it nonsensical to apply that to me personally. *What were they thinking?* I wanted to sign up for double the number of classes, then quickly drop those taught by droning, uninspired professors with little to offer.

I went to the administration office and explained my predicament; I wasn't interested in the units or in graduating, I just wanted an education, and I didn't have years to waste on dull classes or instructors who were there just for a paycheck. They thought that a little horrifying, but suggested an alternative.

I ended up working within their framework by signing up for as many classes as I could, then sitting in on the rest and adding the ones I wanted after convincing each professor how excited I was to be there. Sheer flattery, but it worked. Many of the rules in life are there simply to create order out of chaos, and I understood that, but I also had a knack for circumvention when I had a clear goal in mind. I took the greats, dropped the dullards, and sprinted for a finish line I could only imagine.

Wildcard

They accepted me at a university in England. There was a special exchange program, and my high school advisor must have wanted to get me as far away from her as possible. They also accepted me at our local West Valley College, because they took anybody who could fog a mirror and attendance was dirt cheap. I opted for cheap. And no, I didn't take any SAT tests. I'd taken way too many tests in my life. So I went to West Valley. Plus, it was just down the road in Saratoga. I had to take remedial English (ha!), a requirement for anyone who didn't have a high school diploma.

The English teacher I got must have wondered about my level of education and familiarity with English, because about two weeks into the semester, she asked me to stay after class. She came over after the other students had left and sat down at the next desk.

"What are you doing in my class?" she asked. "No, let me rephrase that. What the *hell* are you doing in my class?"

The entire story soon tumbled out. I had her spellbound, explaining the whole appendicitis | whooping cough | reading to get my own education at the park | refusing my diploma story. That was the first time anyone had heard what I'd done. At the end, she laughed and told me she was going to give me a passing grade (it was a pass | fail class) so I could get on with my life. She then put out her hand for me to shake, said her name was Sharon, and asked me for a *date*. That set me back.

Beyond any other consideration, I decided to attend West Valley because I knew I had to remain close to the family business. I needed to learn my father's accounting system and how he ran the store, plus my parents could never have afforded a school like Cambridge. They'd already put my siblings through college, and I honestly didn't see myself as college material. At least, not to spend serious money on. Years later I learned that my brother Glen had been accepted at Stanford — similar situation, with a comparable solution.

My best learning up to that point had always taken place on a park bench under an oak tree, in my self-directed classroom of one. No one mentioned that universities had teachers far more capable than what I'd experienced in grade school, or that their teaching methods might be different. Sheer ignorance. I didn't know what I didn't know.

So, I just ignored the "We are pleased to announce..." letter when it came. Tore it to pieces in frustration. Didn't tell a soul. But I probably got lucky in one regard: I would likely have gotten distracted by some bright young thing with a mellifluous English accent who had a thing for bad poets and ended up a completely different person. I like who I became, so anthropic principle strikes again.

But change was coming. My studies, writing, music, and the moxie I conjured up to skip school gave me something to think about beyond mere existence, and I wanted more — plus whatever might turn me into a real boy. It may well be that, by defying school authorities at an early age and the government a few years later at the Oakland Induction Center, I generated the gumption I wouldn't have had otherwise, flexing moral muscles of which I'd been unaware until I used them. Enough to carve out a life.

The knowledge I'd gained from all my reading, coupled with the moral outrage I gained from folk music and protest songs was building. I had just the right mixture of righteous indignation plus the untempered courage of youth to fulminate an ungovernable force. But reason kicked in, I brought my temperature down to simmer, and kept plugging away.

Getting there

Why did all this matter? By creating my own education and rejecting the dictates and standards of society and by subjecting the magical thinking of religion to critical thinking, I set the stage for the decisions I would need to make later and created the tone for my life. I may have been a rebel without a clue, but I was acclimating myself to tough choices. Instead of just reading, I was starting to *write*. I had turned the corner on the courage to create. Suddenly my passion had direction and magnitude. From that point on, I knew I would be a little different. But it was a comfortable difference, something I could live with, despite the drawbacks.

Each of us is the sum of all the people we've known, all the thoughts and dreams we've had, all the cuts and bruises along the way—all the love we gave or didn't. It is all these moments that become our history and the texture of who we are. A nudge here or there along the way and we follow a different path, become a different person. With music and books, I was attempting to elbow my way into the person I wanted to become. I had committed the perfect crime with that metal die, and in the process, saved myself from a life of misery and desperation. When it came time to graduate, I turned it down; Los Gatos High hadn't earned the right to say they had educated me. Because they hadn't. I had.

I was pretty determined, although it also brought up a series of unvoiced questions. Why couldn't I have gotten a decent education from the school everyone else went to? Why couldn't I have been like all the other kids in their caps and gowns and move my tassel from one side to the other? Why did I feel it necessary to force a conversation (on a very reluctant and rather bewildered school secretary) demanding that I not receive a diploma? What drove me to go through the quiet and lonely melodrama of mavericking my way into adulthood as I did? I was gambling my future on what... myself? That was a risky little game.

My distrust of school and religion was woven into my distrust of government, plus the fact that my own parents couldn't see through the transparent foolishness of believing in some mythic sky daddy who would provide angel wings and harps so they could sing praises to him while they walked streets of gold in the sweet bye and bye. So I didn't have much of a choice here. I knew too much. Like that kid who called out the king for wearing no clothes, I was doomed to create my own salvation, whatever that might be.

But there was something else going on as well. By refusing my diploma, I was making a statement to myself that my absence from school and the efforts I'd made toward my own education had been intentional. It hadn't started out that way. In the beginning, I was just a very sick kid who wanted to self-medicate by preoccupying himself with a world outside his own little corner of hell. Over time, my actions turned into resolve, and by refusing my diploma, I was in fact doing a sort of reverse graduation; an affirmation that by creating my own education, I had invented a perfectly valid (albeit unconventional) way to run my life, and that I should be proud of the heritage I'd made for myself. The stand I took to refuse my diploma *was* my diploma.

>That Robertson... chock full of insight.
>
>*Yeah, but he doesn't say enough to let anyone know.*
>
>Handsome as a Greek god on a fair day. With a breeze.
>
>*Yeah, but a complete schmuck the next. Listen, he bites his fingernails down to the quick. Is he completely stable?*
>
>Maybe not, but in a couple of years he might traverse the North American Continent and meet all kinds of people

and become a compete human being with empathy and his own spark of divine fire and stuff.

Yeah, but he'll probably keep falling over.

Yeah, but he'll probably learn from it.

You sure about that?

Yeahbuts were the bane and blessing of my entire existence. Without them clinging to me all over like sticky notes, I would surely have clicked with the cuter half of the population at an earlier age. Of course, the "not clicking" part was why I aged so gracefully, garnered such wisdom, and gained so much traction later on when it really mattered. And the falling down part just improved the flavor. So, mixed bag, but I hated those yeahbuts.

The Ugly Truth

Many years went by before I understood the full effect the Vietnam War had on our family. I was living with my parents when the war began to weigh upon my life, and with my brother's family in Willow Glen when I had to deal with the moral issues it presented. I was subject to the draft, and aware of the war from about 1964 onward, just after President Kennedy was assassinated. The government had instituted a lottery — *this one goes to war, this one gets to stay home* — and I had draft number 83 by the beginning of 1970.

Years later, my sister made an interesting comment regarding the fundamental differences which had arisen between my two older siblings and me.

"I try to remember you had a different upbringing," Sheri said. "But for the life of me, I just can't remember when you were dropped on your head."

At first, I thought, *No, I didn't; we had the same parents, and we grew up in the same house. And I wasn't dropped on my head.* Then I realized that, yes — Sheri got it right. I *did* have a different upbringing — at a very critical juncture in my life. My coming of age during the peak of the Vietnam War brought difficult decisions for my parents and me but left my much older siblings unruffled.

Like most of us, I was influenced by my parents and siblings via the osmosis of family interactions; comments made and actions taken add up over time. Edith was a chicken farmer's daughter who, with her family, had picked cotton for food and gas money to escape the dust bowl of Oklahoma and knew hardship firsthand. Ray had helped to support his parents and sister in New Mexico from a very early age, then made it to California on his own. Their life stories were different, but the melody driving them was the same.

I'd heard all the stories, knew all the lessons. Neither of my parents were tolerant of laziness — they hadn't the time or inclination. Sleeping-in had to be justified by the exhaustion of hard work. There was stuff to get done. Reading was dinner, television was dessert, and nobody survived for long on cake and ice cream.

My parents provided me by word and gesture with an entire laundry list of simple imperatives by which to live my life. Tell the truth; keep your word; don't steal; don't cheat; don't be wasteful or greedy; work hard; if you don't have something nice to say, don't say anything at all; always be kind to animals (and intolerant of those who are not); be polite to your elders; empathize with those who haven't had your advantages; and in a final, cheerful little Hail Mary kind of edict, do everything you're supposed to do and don't do anything you're not.

I was also taught that we didn't make fun of other people. Even people acting stupidly or people who had silly ideas; we just worked around them. It was the stupid and ignorant, the inadequate and bullies who made fun of others. Good-hearted people would never act that way; it wasn't right.

It was the way they were, and all that fitted snuggly into what my parents thought was a solid conservative mind-frame. But what didn't fit was their upset when people were treated poorly, couldn't get a decent education for their kids, or went hungry. That they couldn't square with anything. My father donated to the church, but also to the San José Rescue Mission, and although it was a Christian organization, it took care of anyone and everyone who walked in. It was my father's favorite charity, but I was also told that the people they treated were deserving of sympathy. Many had lost jobs and family. Some had lost their self-respect in the process.

Edith said very little about politics — she just kept to her fourth-grade classroom. Ray read *U.S. News and World Report, Time Magazine,* and *The Kiplinger Letter* in his recliner almost every night but made few comments. He was busy trying to survive as a local business owner in a small town with no guarantees of anything other than bills that had to be paid and a family that had to be fed.

But there was a ton of information conveyed in other ways, like the way they expressed themselves about people being treated poorly, or kids who came to school hungry. Edith saw it directly in her classroom. She got tight-lipped at times, and I was well aware of how she felt—about that and other things that went bump in the night but weren't spoken of directly.

I grew up in a smallish town in California to parents who believed they were concurrently conservative and Republican. Unbeknownst to them, this was an assumed identity. They may have voted the straight Republican ticket, but their actions and attitudes were decidedly liberal in a social sense. My father in particular seems to have conflated monetary concerns with social values, as if the two were joined at the hip, never to be considered different issues. In retrospect, that explains a lot about who I am and why I didn't have huge arguments with him; we were batting for the same team and didn't know it.

Direct observation

Some people identified with traditional conservatism but didn't act like it. My parents were great examples. Edith mentioned the fight she'd had with the town over two of her young boarders—Carol and Lettie—who happened to be Chinese, and not allowed to live in our house unless they were domestic servants. (She won the fight.) Edith also told me about the anti-Japanese rallies down on Pageant Way behind the Boy Scout cabin, and how our mayor had led the chanting. She'd been confronted with it one day going down to the library.

Ray told me of being witness to a lynching in St. James Park in San Jose, and of how he'd pressed himself as small as he could into a doorway while the mob took ignorance and anger into their own hands. He told me how terrified he'd been. I got it; I saw the darkness was everywhere, like termites eating away at the foundation of our lives.

The Vietnam War caused all of us to ponder our moral code. For some, it was simple; do what you're told and don't question authority, for we are Americans and Americans always do the right thing because we're American. This was the old "My country, right or wrong; my mother, drunk or sober." philosophy of life. It required no personal responsibility, little thought, and no anguish. Like living in a perfect snow globe.

It was a cookie-cutter morality that worked for people who desperately needed their lives to match that of their neighbors, and not unlike religion, the idea of questioning any part of it was inconceivable. Unthinking people embraced it, loved it, reveled in it, and wrapped themselves in Old Glory with it. Sent their children off to die with it.

The military was great at promoting this "morality of convenience," because uniformity was paramount. Old soldiers never die, they just wear baseball caps with their proud service emblems and get more crusty. Slam the screen door and walk back into the house. Shades of gray don't live here anymore. Perhaps they never did.

For others, it was just easier to go with the flow and ignore their own, internal questions. *It's the law; I have no choice, and besides, everyone else is going along with it, there must be morality in numbers, and who am I to question The United States of America?*

The Vietnam War was driven by the same wishful thinking and patriarchal mindset as religion. Both dealt with morality, behavior, severe curtailment of personal freedom, and adherence to established dogma. Both assumed that men should be in charge. Both assumed that killing people was a good solution to political problems. They were deeply interrelated. So, I wrote about it on several occasions, which clarified my thinking, and provided a lever with which I would later defy the world. Or perhaps just my part of it.

Right before our eyes

The Vietnam War was instigated by the one-sided arrogance of star-spangled privilege. It was not a humanitarian effort—not even close. It started with Napoléon Bonaparte initiating French colonial rule for commercial exploitation in 1887, was run by the United States as a political experiment in nation-building via napalm, bombs, and bullets, and ended with a blood-drenched whimper in 1975, our government lifting people off an embassy roof with helicopters to get them out of a place they should never have been in the first place. I'm not sure that Gen X, Y, or Z (and later, Alpha or Beta) would get this because it may not have been covered in school all that well, but the world had watched in fascinated horror as it imploded on national television.

Vietnam was a rich man's war fought by a poor man's army. It was a war of domination that used the poor, the ignorant, and the powerless as disposable nails and the Selective Service as a human nail gun. It was fairly obvious the supporters of the war didn't care about the Vietnamese or the soldiers any more than they cared about a box of nails they might use to build a deck in their backyard. They cared about being in control and being right. Empathy, or a lack thereof, had a lot to do with it.

Everyone could see a stark contrast between the plutocrats in Congress and the boys fresh off the farm or inner-city ghetto — hired to do their political wet-work at the rate of $78 a month and the option of an honor guard playing taps over their pine box, with a triangle of star-spangled cloth handed to a middle-aged mother or young wife in the end. All enforced by mandatory servitude. Yeah, I know; everyone gets in on the GI Bill, but who needs that when your legs are blown off and you're trying to exist with a colostomy bag and nightmares that won't stop? The reality of it didn't match the promise of righteous glory, and valor ideation had nothing to do with the experience.

There's this funny thing about empathy; it's a survival trait. Marriages fail and nations collapse for the lack of it. Heck, almost every country song in the past fifty years describes what happens when you don't have enough empathy for your nearest and dearest: a lot of slammed doors until there's nothing left but your truck, your dog, and a lot of heartache. Well, nations have relationships too. With their people, with other countries, and with morality.

Social conservatives said they cared so much about America, yet, based on what I saw of their behavior, they cared nothing about actual Americans except their voting behavior and their ability to pack a gun. People died in the gutter (or jungle) in the name of freedom without any hope of achieving it. Being free to die wasn't freedom, it was delusional thinking as far as I was concerned.

Not all conservatives were like that, but it made me wonder if the ones who weren't might not be a little confused about their identity. Maybe they weren't "conservative" in the social sense, but only thought they were because no one was taking the time to make the distinction. Maybe they cared about the national debt, which seemed reasonable and prudent, but were lumped in with all the other conservatives via casual thinking.

I suspected that religion was a large part of the equation. After all, there was no particular reason why being frugal in money matters should align with regressive social issues or the imperative to lord such doctrines over everyone else, but that was pretty much what their religion embraced—at least, the way they practiced it.

Some people grow more inward, crusty, and calcified as they get older, as if the frailty of their bones becomes a reflection of their inability to understand the world. For them, change is something to be fought at any cost—or denied, since ignorance seems to be a true handmaiden to bliss. To reevaluate their own belief system is a mountain they don't want to climb.

If you weren't for them you were against them, no holds barred and devil take the hindmost. In the meantime, shove these religious tracts into all the cars in the parking lot; they're obviously sinners or they'd be at church right now.

All of this threaded through the warp and weave of life, and I in my innocence thought it only described life outside the bucolic town I grew up in. How could it happen right here in River City? I realized over time that some of what I was seeing made very little sense. I knew a lot of people thought the war was terrible but necessary. They seemed to think that politics and religion could be forced onto other people by going to war and bombing the hell out of them, despite the horrors that would ensue. We're seeing that happen in Ukraine and Israel with the Gaza strip. Like the German people, who were indoctrinated into believing the ends justified the means.

But I had read up on Hitler and Stalin, and the picture I got was beyond horrible. I had read about the concentration camps and Babi Yar (which is located in Ukraine), and I had read what came out of the Nuremberg Trials. I realized that many Americans had good intentions but no rational control over their own fear, and that their fear took them far beyond sight of land, just as it had with Germany. At which point their devotion to peer approval (or the need to be right) took over and kept them there beyond all reason, transmuting their frustration into anger, hatred, and even outright malice.

Americans became willing to sacrifice their own children to the horror and slaughter of war so they could feel better about having stopped someone else's politics on the other side of the planet. I think it interesting that socialism is vilified by small-town traditionalists because they've been brainwashed into believing it's an existential threat to capitalism (it's not), that somehow capitalism is the last bastion of Christianity (it's not), and that without Christianity everywhere all the time, America will be canceled (it won't).

Some people feel oppressed by the freedom of others. The idea that one's neighbors might not believe in their god, or any god is anathema to them. They seem to think it's their fundamental right to have everyone conform to one standard — their standard. Men marry women; women are always virgins on their wedding day; rape isn't all that bad and women need to stop making such a fuss about it; black and brown people should keep to their place at the bottom of the ladder. And everybody goes to church on Sunday. It's *Onward, Christian Soldiers* all the way down, just like with the turtles.

Sometimes people think they're been driven to violence as if it's being done *to* them, and the actions they take are really not their fault. A "blame the victim" or "blame the system" mentality that uses a passive-aggressive denial of responsibility to white-wash the sins they know full well they're committing. And some of these are bright, educated people. And in the process of defending a religion that preaches "love thy neighbor," they've turned themselves into gun-toting terrorists who live on the poisonous manna of victimhood. Pure idiotic madness.

The True Believer

I was picking through my brother's office | library just off the dining room as I often did when the conversation had waned and I was looking for something different and interesting to read. Glen started glancing around with me, then picked out a book. He handed me *The True Believer,* by Eric Hoffer.

"It's a must-read," he said.

I put in on my little stack. I found out later that President Eisenhower had referred to *The True Believer* in a nationally televised address in the 1950s (which might have triggered my brother to read it). Eisenhower evidently kept several copies with him at all times and was in the habit of handing it out to people he met over the years.

Hoffer showed in great detail how fanatics think and the dynamics of a mass movement. He didn't pull his punches, and I loved it. His social concepts became my Rosetta Stone for unraveling the mysteriously polarized behavior I was witness to during the Vietnam War and beyond, with people following leaders without question for ideologies that transcended all morality and common sense.

The nation was being lied to, repeatedly, by politicians of both parties, and a lot of people were following along without questioning any of it. All the books have been written and everyone agrees on that now. Once the *Pentagon Papers* came out in 1971 — about 7,000 pages of documentation — they showed how four successive presidents had essentially lied about our involvement in Vietnam: Democrats and Republicans alike, but especially Johnson and Nixon.

Lyndon Johnson had so much remorse over his stewardship of the Vietnam War that he refused to run for a second term, despite having an outstanding social record. Johnson's "Great Society" included the *Voting Rights Act* of 1965; the *Elementary and Secondary Education Act*, providing federal aid for public schools; launched *Head Start* for the early education of low-income children; the Social Security amendments that created *Medicare*; increased welfare payments and rent subsidies; the *Water Quality Act* of 1965; and the *National Endowment for the Arts* and the *National Endowment for the Humanities*. In one session, Congress passed 84 laws. Forty million Americans were poor in 1960. By 1969, that had dropped to twenty-four million.

Conservatives hated him for it. They had fought for fifty years to end business regulation and social services and the taxes they required. Johnson blew that all up.

Johnson had been led around in a complete circle by the American ideology of benevolent power, and finally realized how he'd been bamboozled during his final days in office. By the time the war was over and the final tally taken, over a million Vietnamese had died. In addition to that was our own carnage. There are 57,939 American names inscribed on the Vietnam War Memorial.

And we all know about Nixon, the man whose heart was two sizes too small. He followed right after LBJ. Richard Nixon was the thin edge of the wood chipper for all the nonsense to follow. He would notoriously begin statements full of lies and self-excuses with the phrase, "Let me make one thing perfectly clear." His inferiority complex, bullying, and outright lies set the stage. And then it all began to fall apart.

I remember the look on my father's face when all this came to light a couple of years after I got back. Ray was befuddled. He felt betrayed. Perhaps not as much as he would have been if I hadn't been a conscientious objector, because the experience of being my father through those years had changed his thinking. But still, Nixon was a guy he had voted for and supported. It was hard for my father to watch the corruption unfold on national television. All the underhanded skullduggery of Nixon and his cronies was just heartburn he didn't need.

Tax the poor!

And then it happened again with President Reagan, and my father really liked Reagan. We were in the middle of buying and remodeling our downtown building when "Reaganomics" and his "trickle-down" experiment were pushed to slash taxes for the rich, on the theory that businesses large and small would thrive and get us out of an ongoing recession. Massive failure.

People wealthy enough to have benefited from Reagan's tax breaks put most of that money directly into real estate, municipal bonds, and the stock market—sequestering that capital for decades. No trickle-down from the vested interests, and very little benefit at the bottom of the pyramid. All for the ones who just wanted everything on the planet to accrue to them.

Reagan's tax cuts pushed inflation up like a rocket, and forced the Federal Reserve to move interest rates to over 20 percent, which provoked a severe double-dip recession, the worst since World War II. Our business almost foundered because our building remodel required us to borrow at rates well into loan shark territory, soaking up our cash like a sponge.

Ronald Reagan was one of the most popular presidents in modern history. As a former Hollywood actor, he had an uncommon degree of charm. He joked. He told stories. He laughed at himself, and the press corps ate it up.

I think my father liked him because he had been a cowboy actor, and Ray really liked the idea of the Old West. *Bonanza* was his favorite television program. There was a pattern in place, I watched it unfold, and it was fundamental to my moral position on the war. Nixon created an attitude and Reagan pushed it forward. It was all of a piece, and still is.

Wealthy conservatives absolutely adored Reagan. He said Social Security was a form of welfare. And he hated welfare. Hey, let's forget about grandma. That's okay, because people needed to be taught self-sufficiency. Poor people are no better than layabouts who should be put to work. Because grinding poverty is nothing more than being lazy, right? People who work hard can be rich, or even president!

Ronald Reagan's slogan about welfare queens riding around in Cadillacs (on your tax dollars!) classified all poor people as grifters. That simple phrase vaulted him all the way to president, so he repeated it as often as he could. He forged his political career by radicalizing and poisoning the very idea of social reform. It didn't much matter if people lived out their lives in poverty or died of drugs and disease or got shot; they were bad and wrong and belonged in jail or a grave. *They weren't like us anyway.* Your kid was never going to meet a welfare queen in a classroom at Harvard or Stanford. So, no accountability, and the cattle kept moving along, motivated by simple stereotypes.

Reagan and other conservatives became masters of dehumanizing people and treating them like children with slogans to make them seem dirty and incapable. Take away freedom economically. Make it difficult or impossible for certain people to vote so they remain powerless. Belittle them with sneers and call them names. Racism and our collective distaste for the poor empowered conservative politics like jet fuel. Recordings were released years later of a conversation between Nixon and Reagan. Sickeningly racist paranoia, with jokes all around.

The extremes America suffered from Nixon and Reagan would hit even harder in 2016, when conservatives would swallow the ghost of Goebbels along with their own political tail, and devour the body of their philosophy in defense of racism and hatred, becoming as circular and pointless as an ouroboros.

The power of one

Was I aware of any of this back then? Of course not. I wasn't even listening to politics except as it applied to the Vietnam War, the draft, and me. Oh, I knew Nixon was a jerk, but you didn't have to be working at NASA to figure that one out. It kind of crept up on me like a fog coming in (as it probably did for most Americans), but I had educated myself to the connections between seemingly unrelated people and events, and at a certain point I realized there was something rather odd about my position and circumstance.

I was powerless to stop the machinery of government and yet I was its most powerful foe. Not as an individual, of course. As an individual, I was nothing more than a speck, a statistic. But as a member of a large and growing group of similarly motivated young men and women, I represented a significant force. Something unions and guilds had discovered back in the Middle Ages.

To make any significant change in society, someone has to move in a different, and often difficult direction. I may have been following the example of others—Joan Baez in particular—but in my little world of one, I felt very much alone. I didn't know anyone personally who had stood up to the government like this, and it was scary as hell. Five years in prison? My parents' economic survival put in jeopardy because of my willful disobedience? I was falling through the ice into a swift current, and the issue right in my face shouted at me that I and I alone had stomped on the ice long enough and hard enough to make it crack, shatter, and collapse. I knew full well I was going to disappear into the surging waters below.

Plus, there was a solid possibility I'd be taking my parents down with me. Well, maybe — I couldn't predict the future, but I knew it was important for me to step into the business. The only ones available were my sister Sheri, her husband Miles, or myself, and I was the logical knight on the family chessboard. I was my father's transition into retirement if he would ever get one. It was going to get really bad, really fast at some point, and there could be no backing away, no do-over.

To get a handle on all of it, I made notes and started writing about whatever I couldn't figure out — adding to my monographs, as I called them. I eventually edited some of those writings down into a single thesis, which I presented to the Selective Service and the FBI.

It took time for me to understand that the seeds had been watered by Nixon and his ilk during the years when guys my age had to deal with their subversive behavior directly, most of it decked out in military garb with snappy salutes, firm handshakes, and manly tears for the dead and wounded. Just like the Marlboro commercials of my youth, boys were sent off to war with a grin and a wave, like cowboys riding off into a carcinogenic sunset. Business as usual, and the body count just kept climbing.

There was untoward behavior on both sides of the political aisle of course, just as there always had been. The problem wasn't Democrats or Republicans; the problem had to do with arrogance and a lack of empathy, which manifested itself in politics just as it did in every other facet of life.

It was tough to figure this stuff out, given the inside-out nature of fanaticism rigged out as patriotism, and I only got it by dribs and drabs. I was young and not terribly sophisticated, and there were no easy sides unless you picked one and stuck with it—often for reasons that had more to due with your parents than with your own considered viewpoints. Some of it became clear when I finally understood that the soldiers fighting the war were not the ones running it; they were the victims of it. When I finally understood that fundamental truth, everything made more sense and things started falling into place.

The ugly truth came home from the war in flag-draped coffins unloaded at military airports. Nightly footage of those caskets lingered long after Walter Cronkite had ended his broadcast of the CBS Evening News with his signature close, "And that's the way it is." Everyone in America knew he was giving us the unvarnished truth at that point, including my parents.

Cronkite actually went to Vietnam, put on a helmet, got himself embedded in an infantry division, and reported from the front lines. Actions unheard of for a news anchor at that time. He was the Conscience of America, and I still think of him as a hero. The military-industrial complex and the politicians had fooled him the same as everybody else, but he changed his thinking when he saw with his own eyes the evidence on the ground. When he reported what was really going on with his avuncular realism, including the incursions into Cambodia, America woke up. So it really did seem as though the grown-ups had bitten off more than they could chew, and the rest of us didn't want to swallow.

The problem wasn't Democrats *vs.* Republicans. Both parties disagreed on policy and the size of government, but at that time they were still together on helping the country. As I was starting to understand it, the conservatives and religious leaders wanted everything to stay mostly as it had been (in living memory) and championed the *Might Makes Right* version of geopolitics. Their lack of compassion allowed them to insulate themselves by spending everything on armaments and police and forget about all the threats that common folk face every day. The concepts of live and let live, the Golden Rule, social justice, police restraint, and negotiation between nations were for the foolish and faint-hearted.

They're not like us

Communists don't believe in God, so let's bomb the hell out of them. Let's sacrifice the youth of our nation – or at least those who can't get out of it by being in college or who can't afford a good enough lawyer to argue the bone-spur angle. It was Darwin's Theory of Natural Selection in real-time, driven by religious fervor and using the poor and uneducated as cannon fodder. If you were smart and well-connected, you got to stay home, you didn't die, and your line wasn't extinguished. Everybody else was fair game. A conservative's game. I watched it happen, as did my parents. It made my father very uncomfortable to be on that side of the ledger.

Over time, I came to realize that the one common attribute binding these true believers together and defining them as a relatively homogeneous group wasn't about lack of education, fear of change, religion, their absolute horror of ambiguity, or even social issues particularly. It was lack of empathy. It was a defining characteristic as true as it was during the Middle Ages and even before that.

Empathy is mostly a learned trait, taught by example. If your parents didn't exhibit at least some altruistic behavior, you weren't likely to learn it on your own. So conservatives begat conservatives with exclusionary social inbreeding, which (along with a general lack of education), is at least partly why they were so defensively tribal about their belief system, so prone to self-destructive behavior, and so insistent on limiting their world-view. It became self-perpetuating, like wealth or grinding poverty.

It's also a defense mechanism. If you don't have empathy, you aren't sensitive to and don't have to deal with the pain of others or the somewhat messy and complicated circumstances of life outside your own social sphere. That makes life a lot easier, particularly if you are in pain yourself. But it also means you don't have the tools needed to understand that your own suffering is somewhat universal and that although their circumstances may be different, others are in just as much pain. All of which makes it far easier to belittle the human condition and the real issues that others have to deal with. It also makes it a lot easier to send kids off to war knowing full well that a lot of them are going to get blown to flinders.

Edith and Ray understood that. So did my two older siblings. My sister started out educating kids as a schoolteacher, like Edith, and Glen went into a kind of social work, running a non-profit agency that housed and cared for the mentally ill. These were not jobs suited to people without empathy or a lack of education. That was the texture I was born into. A kind of village wisdom scaled down to family size. There was a hierarchy, and I was clearly last in line (they used to call me the Caboose). But I was also the last one available to take over the family business. That was on me, and it added to the weight.

Frag the vets!

What bothers me to this day is the massive gap between the lip service conservative gave to veterans and the actual help they offered. No matter what your politics might be, these soldiers fought for their country, many paid the ultimate price, and almost all of them came back gravely wounded in body *and* spirit. These soldiers were not fearless, yet they did it anyway. Being scared to death and going forward anyway is the very definition of valor. What bugs me (almost as much) is the blind belief on the part of veterans that the perversely unsupportive conservative behavior is excused by their patriotic flag waving. It's completely upside down, and most of them don't get it.

The horrors of war are literally that; our vets hadn't been playing some video game. But from time to time I would read that conservative politicians were fighting to cut the budget of the Department of Veterans Affairs (the VA), and it made no sense. And these aren't isolated incidents by a few misguided members of Congress.

In recent years they been pushing hard to privatize the entire agency so they could detach it from public funding and replace it with a simple health insurance policy. But that would shutter VA hospitals all over rural America, causing a massive drop in the number of veterans getting any health care whatsoever. The average age of veterans at death is 67, almost a decade younger than the national average of 76.4 years old. That isn't from battleground deaths, but from lack of post-service care. They need *more* care, not less.

Closing down the VA is like putting your wounded children on an ice floe and giving it a good shove.

And there was another aspect that perhaps only the veterans and the VA doctors know much about. The VA really knows how to help victims of war because they've been doing it a long time. They have the experience and resources. They've dealt with all the known issues brought on by Agent Orange, they've installed thousands of prosthetics, and they know about drug addiction, weight management, military sexual abuse, shell-shock | PTSD, depression, and all the other psychological issues veterans come home with. And now we have new illnesses caused by burn pits as well.

The VA doctors know about marital problems, what questions to ask, and how to refer their patients for the kind of help that works. Regular doctors do not; they don't even ask the right questions, feeling that such issues are outside their purview. There isn't an internship program in the world that prepares a regular doctor for what veterans have gone through, except war itself. And conservatives want to get rid of the only agency we have that has the depth of knowledge and day-to-day experience to treat any of this. *Take two Tylenol and make another appointment if it gets worse.*

And now we have ex-soldiers on television begging for medical attention, with fuzzy, logo-imprinted throw-blankets for anyone who sends in a few bucks. The private non-profits who support these men attempt to take care of their issues, but they cannot replace the VA. They vary in scope, don't have all the services required, and don't have the depth of knowledge and experience the VA does. These organizations think of themselves as conservative, but in every conceivable way, they are functioning as bulwarks against the *lack* of support from conservative politicians: one hundred and eighty degrees of irony.

I didn't see the imbalance then, but it goes all the way back to the war. Veterans mustered out carrying a personal legacy of heavy damage, only to find they'd been forgotten by the very people who'd convinced them to go fight in the first place. Worse than forgotten, they were vilified. And powerless.

Conservative politicians would authorize the Blue Angels to fly over football games to pump up feel-good patriotism, yet frag their own troops by turning a decidedly blinkered eye to all the vets coming home as if their wounds were in poor taste. It didn't happen after World War I or II, or even the Korean War, but from Vietnam on it's been a huge issue.

A high percentage of recruits go into the military with a conservative mindset, which is logical, considering that the military is all about solving problems through physical threat and capability. But they aren't so conservative when they muster out — studies show that the percentage drops after they've had a real world education. This is not to say that the military isn't necessary — sometimes a significant show of brute force is required when dealing with tyrants.

But the raw youth who go in are not the same after being transformed into veterans — particularly if they've been in direct combat positions. After seeing violent death, they become far more liberal. This showed up dramatically during the Vietnam War. A high percentage of returning vets opposed the war, and America was suddenly confronted with a fair number of ex-Army, acid-head street-poet visionaries and self-appointed social reformer consciousness-raisers, all demonstrating in their faded green fatigues with military badges and patches and making fired-up speeches about why the war was so very wrong in so many ways.

But as much as the government tried to hide the damage, there were no happy warriors coming home from Vietnam. Even the ones who hadn't been in combat were in awful shape from what they'd seen and what they knew. It was right in front of us on television almost every night.

I had friends and people I worked with who'd fought in Vietnam. They told me what they'd been ordered to do. Haunted eyes turned inward with the grim pain of remembrance. It was a nightmare.

Twenty-five percent of the boys sent into battle came home with PTSD, and over 300-thousand suffered the effects of Agent Orange, including their children and their children's children. Cancer, sterility, premature dementia: there are about fifty diseases and nearly twenty birth defects caused by Agent Orange, which contains 2,3,7,8-tetrachlorodibenzodioxin. *Unbelievably* toxic. It was disclosed in court documents that the U.S. Army knew full well what was in Agent Orange and used it anyway. They used it as if they were spraying for mosquitoes.

It was all of a piece. The lack of empathy, the patriotism without depth or post-service follow through, the eagerness to go to war for political reasons and capitalism run amuck to make money off of death and destruction with what amounted to blank-check fulfillment contracts. Although I didn't put all these pieces together until later in life (partly by talking to the friends who came back alive, and partly by filling other kinds of military contracts myself), it all added up to the same thing.

I was completely against the war, but ended up totally *for* the veterans — victims one and all — most of whom seemed to have no idea how or to what extent they'd been torpedoed by the very people who promised to have their back.

We watch the Blue Angels fly over the big football game and listen to a military band with ribbons and uniforms and medals for bravery, and it's all very patriotic, even romantic. But those who have seen combat know better. An insidious nightmare of death that never ends, that colors your existence, that follows you home.

Ducks & Dinosaurs

In the religion I'd been taught (our family was Baptist, therefore common as dirt in our part of the world) there was an omnipresent Greek chorus of three ghosts in a mysterious place called Heaven that existed somewhere high up over the clouds. And we were supposed to wish super extra hard for what we wanted by folding our hands together, closing our eyes, and using telepathy to contact the Main Ghost. Or, if you were a Catholic, the Second Ghost's teenage mother. It was all very mediæval and smacked of magic on a grand scale. And every bit of this fed directly into my decision regarding the draft, compliance to authority, and the Vietnam War.

My parents seemed to accept the precepts of their religion without hesitation, which to my mind was just plain crazy. I could trust my parents to be true to who they were — they were at least consistent in their own belief system — but the rest of it I had to figure out on my own. I mean, if they believed in Santa Claus (and I had a whole ton of logic to support the idea that there never had been a Santa Claus), how could I trust their judgment on other matters? Did their impaired judgment extend to business matters? Health and wellness issues? Social concerns? I had no idea.

When I was little, our family's church looked huge. It had oak beams supporting the roof, like the ribs of an upside-down ship we all huddled under. The pews were also oak, and upholstered in dark red fabric. I gazed up at those vast beams while the sermons droned on, running my fingernails absently in the texture of the cushions. There was a huge cross on the wall at the front of the church, symbolic of Christ's pain and suffering.

The building itself held no real mysteries because I had explored it over a series of mildly felonious Saturday afternoons, messing about with Jay, our pastor's kid. We'd climbed our way in and out of the baptistry tank above the choir loft, sampled communion grape juice from the church stores, and looked for treasure (in the form of overlooked change) in the offering bags we discovered one day. And whenever we heard a door open, we scrambled away, our hearts pounding like steam engines.

Sitting next to Edith and Ray for that hour every Sunday was part of the bargain of who we were, but also rather boring. We usually sat toward the back on the right side so Ray could ease himself out to count the offering and make the bank deposit; volunteer work for an accountant.

I stood when I was supposed to stand and sat when I was supposed to sit. And we sang *How Great Thou Art* and *Rock of Ages* from the hymnal, then went home to read *Time Magazine* (my father), Agatha Christie (my mother), or listen to folk music and read C.S. Forester (me). Between Sunday School, regular church, Bible classes, and prayer meetings, I had a pretty good handle on most of it. I knew my Assyrians from my Pharisees, King David from Herod, and I had a fairly good idea what had happened to Saul on his famous road trip to Damascus. There wasn't much you could surprise me with.

My mind was prone to wander. Our pastor was a good man who meant well, but his sermons were like a complex suspension bridge with strands of logic that lead everywhere and nowhere. One had to accept the entire concept as presented, since it was all held together by the spiderweb of faith that didn't make any sense when I thought about it.

I was told that God had always existed. Forever, and for no apparent reason. And then, after existing an infinite amount of time (which sounded more boring than watching reruns of golf), he decided to spit on his hands and create things so he could have a life populated by something more interesting than a bunch of one-note angels and a big empty room. He evidently needed to be adored, and the angels weren't enough.

So anyway, he touched off the Big Bang. (I knew about the Big Bang.) And then he did absolutely nothing for 14 billion years to allow atoms to form, gasses to coalesce, stars to ignite and grow old, go nova, scatter themselves into space and pull together (over and over) to form galaxies with stars, some of which ended up with a scattering of leftover material. Which clumped together into planets and formed solar systems.

And one of these planets happened to be Earth, just one of about 40 billion planets where its companion star was just hot enough (but not too hot), and the gravity was just strong enough (but not too strong), and there was enough free water on the surface so that life could evolve. *Bingo*.

So after dinosaurs and a whole bunch of other stuff came and went, mankind arrived on the scene. God thought humans were fascinating, and meddled wildly in our affairs for about 1,500 years by giving one tribal society a bunch of rules like "Thou Shalt Not Kill," then directed them to kill and enslave their enemies anyway. Rather bipolar, and very exciting.

But evidently, this wasn't enough. So he came down to Earth cleverly disguised as a carpenter to preach for three years before dying a super-painful death meant to atone for the flaws inherent in all human beings (which he created, via the Big Bang). Then Carpenter God goes to Hell for three days. But he bounces back and floats up to Heaven, where he stays with two other versions of himself and cuts off all communication for the next 2,000 years, leaving us with nothing but questions and a cobbled-together collection of metaphorical and contradictory instructions for eternal bliss. Which may or may not work, because the only way to find out if any of it is true or not is to die. Kind of a scaled-up Schrödinger Box the size of the universe.

Questions kept popping up and interfering with my indoctrination. I had been taught that God knows our every thought and action. So why do we need to pray? If he already knew everything, did he just want us to beg? All that Supreme Leader stuff bothered me, particularly after seeing films from World War II, with those huge columns of goose-stepping men, their arms upraised in the Sieg Heil salute to their Führer. To my mind it seemed one and the same. Were the angels doing that, up there in heaven? Because I was being told I had to do it. And if I didn't, I'd be thrown into an active volcano when I died — which could be tomorrow! Who knew?

A loving and merciful god grants a special prize to everyone who "worships" him—*God had to be a man, right?*—with proper and dutiful adoration. Not only do the lucky acolytes avoid going into the Volcano of Doom, but they get to sing their adoration along with the angels forever. A sort of stage musical with wings and streets paved with gold. We were supposed to adore him because he had saved us. But he had only saved us so we could adore him. *Huh?*

Bonus round: Go directly into the volcano! Do not pass Go; do not collect $200. *Hot! Hot! Hot! Hot! Hot!* This same merciful and loving tyrant consigns everyone to eternal torment for the cardinal mistake of using their own intellect to question all these unsupported ideas presented as facts. *Sorry, kid; you were a tad short in the sincerity department. In you go!*

Wow. I had to wonder about that. This God guy sounded like the most narcissistic, self-righteous grad student of all time, using a science-gone-haywire experiment (with us humans as lab rats) to get his doctorate in sociology or psychology. That seemed to be the primary reason for God's existence. What kind of creature needs constant adoration? Narcissistic men, obviously.

The idea that a benevolent god would create the entire universe as backdrop and populate the third rock from a mediocre star just to test our loyalty, and do it with the foreknowledge most of us would end up in a lake of fire for all eternity in some kind of bizarre game of cosmic chicken was beyond ridiculous. That everyone around me—including my parents and older siblings—could consider this stuff profound just seemed silly.

If we were given free thought and a brain capable of using it, why all the retribution? Why all the indoctrination? Telling everyone it's "my way or the highway" with a stern look and a wagging forefinger doesn't result in freethinking. It results in fear and adherence to dogma. I was not only raised to think for myself but also to accept whatever *natural* consequences there might be for my actions.

And why wasn't there a "Mrs. God," exactly? Oh, right. *Mary.* So, for all of eternity up to when little Mary became sexually mature, God made man in his own image but didn't get horny? I was horny all the time. Which made me wonder what kind of *thing* God actually was. Some kind of weird alien being with no hormones and nothing between his legs. Except for that one time, with a teenager named Mary, who turned out to be someone else's wife. *Cute.*

It was quite a puzzle, because to me the story didn't add up. I was taught that God was all powerful, existed everywhere all at once (and for all of time, which was infinite), and was morally perfect. But, if God was all powerful, then he must have had the power to eliminate Evil—or maybe not have created it in the first place. *Had there been a mistake in there somewhere?* And, if God was morally perfect, then he would have wanted to get rid of Evil. But if the anti-Good force of Evil still existed, then either God didn't have the power to eliminate it, or didn't really want to for some reason. But that would make him complicit. Codependent maybe?

Or… (I had a busy little mind) Good and Evil *had* existed for all time, just like God. Which, by their very existence, made them equal to God. Which meant—*ta da*—that God was not really all powerful. Maybe God needed Good and Evil to create contrast? "Hey, I'm with Goodness and Mercy. Worship me!"

But sometimes really bad things happen for no discernible reason. Therefore, God didn't exist. Either that, or he wasn't even up to kindergarten level in the morality department. And saying he was allowing Evil to exist just to teach us some kind of cosmic lesson or calling it all a big mystery was just a cheap dodge to avoid the issue altogether as far as I was concerned. People are smart, and even little kids know when things don't add up. I found out years later that Thomas Jefferson didn't believe it either, and for the same reasons.

If there is a reason for everything, then God must have a cause. If there can be anything without a cause, it may just as well be the universe as God, so there can't be any validity in that argument. It's similar to the Hindu view, that the world rests upon an elephant and the elephant rests upon a turtle. And when they ask, "How about the turtle?" they say, "It's turtles on top of turtles, all the way down."

There is no reason to suppose our universe had a beginning at all other than we know it's expanding, and at one point must have started with everything very close together. But the Big Bang might have been nothing more than a Big *Bounce*. What if the universe stopped expanding at some point in the distant past, collapsed, and exploded again? Maybe it's always done that. The idea that things must have a beginning is really due to the poverty of our imagination.

And then there was the Ten Commandments and all the schadenfreude that came along for that ride of a lifetime; lots of *that* to go around. "Look at her! Going to hell for sure; just look at how she's carrying on!"

The bridge built by our religion didn't touch ground anywhere as far as I could tell. It just seemed to float upon a never-never cloud of "belief in believing," like an elaborate bridge to nowhere. A lot of talk, but not much logic.

I'd been warned about the Pentecostals, who "spoke in tongues" when they got really excited, and handled venomous snakes like timber rattlers and copperheads during their church services (to prove the power and fidelity of their faith). My parents said darkly that such people took their religion *too far*. So what distance was too far? Was it just the snakes, or were there other signposts?

Perhaps it was just a matter of geography; the Pentecostals were mostly located in the Deep South. I figured that they'd been taught from a young age to have these beliefs and had just grown up that way, but it bothered me that they didn't question any of it. By that time I already knew about the different inquisitions during medieval times and how torture had been sanctioned by the Catholic Church. Now *that* seemed very much too far.

Edith was fond of how she handled Jehovah's Witnesses when they came to the door. She would smile sweetly and tell them, "We don't believe in the cults." And then she would firmly but gently shut the door. So she knew one sect from another but didn't seem to discern problematic issues within her own faith. Or maybe she did. Perhaps both my parents did, but were afraid to say anything for fear they would break the spell. Again, I had no idea, but I had my suspicions.

I also wondered about the obvious benefits. Was religion similar to a meditative state—like Zen perhaps? Both brought joy to people and seemed to give them purpose, but was that just a coincidence, or was religion actually a manifestation of that way of being? Were truly religious people (in the good way, not the horrible, destructive way) simply practicing Zen under the guise of something that carried a ton of ritualistic and magical baggage?

Power symbols

I noticed that religion was big on symbolism and ritual, as if these things are a valid substitute for substance. Holy water, chasubles with orphreys, menorahs, Bibles, the Holy Grail, an empty tomb with a giant boulder for a door. High angels, fallen angels, personal angels, archangels—they're all there. And let's not forget Satan (a fallen angel), dressed in his signature flame-red outfit, complete with pitchfork and barbed tail. The ultimate bad guy. Shadrach, Meshach, and Abednego, streets paved in gold, David and Goliath, manna from heaven, and Jacob's Ladder, all accompanied by stylized fish bumper stickers, the Easter Bunny, and every crucifix known to man.

Then there were the rituals: Confirmation, the Eucharist, ordination, marriage, reconciliation, Holy Communion, getting saved, Baptism, the missionary position, the list just goes on and on. And then there are all the holy holidays: Easter, Christmas, Ash Wednesday, Lent, Ramadan, Palm Sunday, Passover, Good Friday, Dia de los Muertos, Yom Kippur.

People love it. It's like they're addicted to the symbols and the rituals and the holidays. Or maybe it's just the sheer spectacle of it all. And the military is the same way. Badges and honors and uniforms and precision drilling. Purple Hearts, rank and file, rear admirals, lieutenants, battleships, stars and bars and chevrons, lots of guns, codes of honor, tanks, and everyone salutes everyone all the time everywhere.

Ritual is important because we want our lives to make sense and have meaning, and ritual seems to provide that. But not really. Ritual is the dressing without the salad. When ritual is all there is, that's bad. It's the empty calories our parents warned us against.

As I sat in church, there seemed to be the need for a lot of convincing. Our minister kept harping on certain subjects as if the congregation wasn't fully invested. Within a certain latitude, ministers could interpret ancient texts any way they wanted and make it sound significant, particularly if they ignored the context of the Biblical epoch when most of it took place—a period which was to a great extent driven by fear, superstition, and random death.

Sitting there every Sunday with nothing better to do, I began taking it apart, gossamer strand by gossamer strand. This is when I dove headlong into the Bible as a study project.

I learned early on that, in the vocabulary of the Robertson family, atheist rhymed with anarchist (or antichrist). But I strongly suspected that I wasn't the only one with serious doubts. It was "The Emperor's New Clothes" codified by a very old book full of flowery language and mediæval logic that people believed for no other reason than they believed. I had been taught by the same parents I sat next to each Sunday to put no truck in such nonsense, yet here it was, in full bloom, like a corpse flower in the garden of life.

Most people have no idea how many 'messiahs' this weary world has endured, but it's a lot. I've counted sixty-seven that have popped up throughout history. Some quite local and self-serving, others had significant followings. Most were obvious kooks, but many were quite sincere. A few of them are alive today and preaching their own particular brand of gospel to a choir of True Believers, willing to overturn everything in their single-minded zeal.

The mystery deepens

There were a few other cracks in the dam as well, like the whole thing about Catholics. Because the way I was taught, Catholics worshiped Mary instead of Jesus, and that was just horribly wrong. Not that Catholics were bad people, understand. They just got it very wrong early on and had persisted in their "Mary, Mother of God" thing down through the ages without looking at the evidence right there in front of their own eyes in the Bible (for crying out loud), which was the 𝕷𝖎𝖛𝖎𝖓𝖌 𝖂𝖔𝖗𝖉 𝖔𝖋 𝕲𝖔𝖉 already, and stated in *plain English* that Jesus was the Real Deal and Mary just happened to be his teenage mom. Along for the ride, so to speak. And what about Purgatory???

So if the Catholics were wrong in major suppositions like that, who else was wrong, and how wrong were they? Well, the Pentecostals with their rattlesnakes were nothing to write home about. As were the Jews because they still didn't believe that Jesus was the True Messiah, even after all these years. Heck, they didn't even put up Christmas trees. So they were nuts. And then of course you could go farther out on a limb with the other religions because they were all going to hell in a handbasket along with the non-believers because they were all just as wrong. So being a Baptist (evangelical) meant you got to go to heaven, but only if you "took the Lord as your personal savior and renounced all sin," plus you had to get bent over backward by the minister and hold your breath under water in front of everybody for a full Mississippi to make everything official. But then you got ice cream that night, so there was that.

Not unlike the ancient Egyptians, my father was concerned that even though he would be made whole during the Rapture (when everybody who's been saved, living and dead, goes to heaven), he would still be stuck in an old man's body, and if it deteriorated over time, he wouldn't look so good in heaven.

According to him, nobody actually went to heaven until the Endtime, and we all went together, including everyone who had ever died: Abraham, Isaac, Mary the mother of Jesus — all those guys. (That's one of the reasons the Baptists think the Catholics had it all wrong, by the way, Mary was still in the dirt somewhere, so how could anyone pray to her?)

All those movies where they speak of the dearly departed looking down from heaven? *Wrong.* They aren't looking down. They aren't looking anywhere. According to the Bible, they're all still stuck in the mud right here on Earth. Probably ground up by a glopita-glopita machine and incorporated into the cement of some high-rise apartment complex somewhere. There is one famous exception: one of the two thieves on Golgotha got a golden ticket when he was told, "Truly I tell you, today you will be with me in Paradise." So he got to go up with Jesus when he died, but nobody else ever has, including any of the twelve Apostles or your great aunt Helen.

What's all the fuss about?

Another thing that bothered me was *motivation*. Why in the world would anyone—or any god—want to be worshipped in the first place? It made no sense. I certainly wouldn't want that, and the people who do are narcissistic nut jobs with an inferiority complex the size and shape of Texas. What's the motivation? They had to be compensating for something.

Which meant to me that the Lord God Almighty was afraid nobody liked him and he'd never get a date to the big dance. Like a teenager with self-esteem issues. That's what it usually means. I was taught that respect has to be earned—that you couldn't just *command* it. But that's exactly what they put in the Big Book of Commandments. No choice. No options. Not even a little bit. *Bow down, puny humans!* God Almighty wasn't very mighty if he had to do all that just to get a little respect. The whole setup was in very poor taste.

Another issue was the whole creation myth at the back end of time, coupled with this huge 180° turn in religion. For umpty-ump years since creation, everything is going along just fine. There's the one hiccup when Moses comes down from Mt. Sinai with the Ten Commandments to find everyone having way too much fun, but then that gets fixed until about Zero BCE when this teenage girl named Mary gets knocked up by an incubus called the Holy Ghost and has a baby.

Mary's kid grows up, learns a trade, then starts to preach and gets some government people really super mad at him. They kill him, but then he wakes up and just floats away. What happened there? God's grand experiment wasn't going well, so he had to put in a change order? Why this method? Why this moment in time?

And of course, Jesus stated over and over that he'd be back within the lifetimes of those who knew him. But he didn't. Anyone who reads these repeated passages with a clear eye, unconcerned with the theological dictum that the Bible must be rescued from error no matter how contorted the reinterpretation, can easily see them for what they actually say and recognize the obvious: Jesus was no better than anybody else. He wasn't a god.

The Bible thumpers have been trying to explain this ad infinitum by parsing every possible interpretation to refute the reality check we've all been witness to. Like when President Clinton tried to redefine the word "is" so he could weasel out of admitting he had sex with Monika Lewinski, it states the obvious. Jesus never came back because he *couldn't*. And he couldn't because he was no different than the 67 other wannabe deities we've had to deal with over the past 2,000-odd years.

God seemed to be conducting a massive sociological experiment—winnowing the True Believers from the Infidels like rats in a maze. But then he went and changed the rules because he suddenly has this son who cares about *all* the people, even the Amalekites. The Jews weren't the Chosen People anymore, the True Believers who went into the river to get themselves dipped were. *Quite the flip.* So now instead of offering up blood sacrifices as the Jews did before *The Great 180*, we're to believe in Jesus because *ta da,* he's the second ghost! The ancient slayer of Amalekites, versus the peace-loving hippy from Nazareth. With obviously different agendas.

> "Now go and smite the Amalekites, and utterly destroy all that they have, and spare them not; but slay both man and woman, infant and suckling, ox and sheep, camel and ass." — *Samuel-1 15:3*

> "But thou shalt utterly destroy them; namely, the Hittites, and the Amorites, the Canaanites, and the Perizzites, the Hivites, and the Jebusites." — *Deuteronomy 20*

Genocide. All just crazy thinking that had nothing to do with what we ate that morning or whether the grass needed mowing. It also meant that I had to do my own reasoning. My parents (and older people in general) were just nuts in this one particular way which skewed how they looked at the world and each other. It was like they had all painted themselves blue for some reason, or were stomping around on peg legs which everybody pretended to ignore.

The problem with this particular fantasy is that it is a worldwide self-delusion and old as dirt. It was invented by mankind in prehistory and has come down through the ages, indexed and cross-indexed, and embellished by generations of True Believers, all fervent in their proselytizing that their particular god was the One True God (complete with capital letters and a long grey beard to denote wisdom) and that anyone believing anything else was dumb as a brick and destined to swim in the molten rock of an active volcano forever.

Common sense that we might be the same as any other plant or animal was completely rejected. Oh, no! We live on in perpetuity, either in heaven or hell, and common sense was for idiots. This massive self-deception has been invented and reinvented and sliced and diced into so many different religions and sects the mind boggles. 4,300 at last count. About 10,000 if we include the ones without a working website.

Denial in a teacup

"You really liked the exhibits?"

"Oh, the exhibits were great. Just like the museums up in the gold country. Everything in great detail," said my father.

I was talking with him in the living room in front of the couch and the big mirror. Ray had been reminiscing again.

"But these fossils... The animals... They never existed?"

"No; the Earth hadn't been created yet."

"Do you see any sabre-tooth tigers?"

"It saw its bones. And artist drawings."

I had no idea where this conversation was going, but since I rarely discussed anything with my father other than my not wanting to close the books at the end of the month, I kept it going. I was curious.

"It was fascinating," said Ray. "All those skeletons turned to rock. Animals got stuck in the tar and couldn't get out."

"Like sabre-tooth tigers?"

"And mammoths, and other animals."

"They've found older fossils too," I said. "Out in Utah. Dinosaurs." He looked preoccupied.

"How about Tyrannosaurus Rex?" I said. "And stegosaurs. Some taller than our house." And then I went for broke.

"But they couldn't have existed," I said. "Right? The Earth isn't that old. According to the Bible."

Ray gave me a look. He wasn't stupid, just stuck. He went back to his *Time Magazine,* temporarily disgruntled.

I had taken the conversation as far as I dared. I felt kind of bad that I'd done this, but Ray had started it. Somehow he'd gotten to talking about the La Brea Tar Pits he'd seen as a young man: the nature exhibits. He often talked of things he'd learned or done growing up, and I was an eager audience.

But my father believed the Bible was the "Inspired Word of God" and that by carefully following lineage and counting the begats, one could *prove* that the Earth had been created about six thousand years ago. So, no dinosaurs. But he'd also just acknowledged them. *He'd seen the evidence.*

I knew I was toying with my father's logic, but I wanted to see if he would ever notice the disparity between what he believed and what he knew. He never did — or at least, not to me; his belief system was about as flexible as cast iron.

The spirit of the lord!

My father had once played saxophone in the orchestra of the Angelus Temple for Aimee Semple McPherson, a rather famous Bible-thumper. Since he was in the orchestra, he was looking over her shoulder while she preached. At some point in the proceedings, McPherson would give her personal blessing to anyone who came forward. Many were on crutches or disabled in some other way.

Ray said McPherson would pray over them, then (out of sight from the audience, but visible to the orchestra and choir), give them a quick shove in the solar plexus, staggering them back. The ones with crutches often fell over. "This," she proclaimed with a shout, "is the power of Almighty God!" My father saw this acted out over and over and described it with a chuckle. Thought it was terribly funny, how she fooled the rubes. Didn't change his mind one bit.

Old enough to shave?

Ironically, the initial seeds of religious scepticism came from my parents, who considered "the Catholics" terribly misguided in their adoration and apparent worship of Mary and their overly ornate churches. Too much gold and marble was their opinion. That and all the crucifixes. Their attitude raised the obvious issue that nobody seemed willing to deal with—that with some 10,000 religions on the planet, most of them affirming with great vigor that they and *they alone* were the One True Faith, it seemed reasonable to suppose that either:

A. There was a god, and for some unknown reason the religion my parents followed was the only one that knew the correct *version* of the truth. Which made all the other religions wrong, or

B. All the religions were right in one narrow and specific way—that there *was* some kind of god, but all these belief systems were just different interpretations of the same phenomenon. Perhaps it was like language. Earthlings have lots of different languages and even regional dialects and accents, but it works anyway—we all communicate. Or... *(cue ominous music)*

C. God was a myth and every religion was wrong, including the one my parents seemed to believe.

Even a kid who had only just figured out that there was more to reading than adventure stories could understand the choice I had. I didn't know anything about Occam's Razor back then, but I had a feel for what it said: The simplest explanation is usually correct. I decided that Option A was way too complicated. What were the odds of me being born into the only correct religion? Was I really *that* powerful?

Option B had too many moving parts, too many loose ends, and was altogether too self-serving. It felt like all these religions were just slightly different ways to frighten people into reaching for some universal talisman that would allow them to cheat death and stave off loneliness.

In that way, my language metaphor seemed spot on. People were using different religions in an attempt to communicate with the cosmos, and we didn't really know if there were any gods or not. *Hello? Anybody out there?* It seemed reasonable to have an open mind, but to believe something so complex based on nothing much more than the fact that my parents believed it was nuts. That much I knew.

I wasn't against religion per se; it was the magical thinking that bugged me. It sounded just like Æsop's Fables, but my parents acted as if there was an actual fox which had clearly attempted to eat a bunch of real grapes in a vineyard somewhere in Greece, and I didn't think that made a lot of sense (foxes don't eat grapes, sour or not, and they certainly don't talk to birds).

And my parents knew better, they really did. They just had this massive blind spot because of their personal history and the risk-to-benefit ratio. For them it was better to be safe than sorry. Plus, you know, peer pressure. Not believing kind of put you on the Island of Lost Toys with nobody to talk to. But as it was explained to me, the "better safe than sorry" logic didn't work either, because God would *know* you were just hedging a bet, which was like cheating, and wasn't allowed.

Coping with the vicissitudes of life is difficult, and letting go of worry can promote mental health: (id est, peace at last). Religious cults allow individuals to assign problems to a higher power, which removes the stress of personal responsibility as long as we conform to accepted dogma.

I didn't understand why we needed to have a god in the first place. What was the point? It implied we needed a parent, some sort of "sky daddy" to watch over us and keep us from doing harm to ourselves or to others. Except he wasn't doing a good job. Obviously. All I had to do was read about WWII. Perhaps he was off in some other part of the universe, watching over the squid aliens on Paradise Prime or something. Either that, or he enjoyed the pain of others. Some kind of cosmic schadenfreude. Either way, it didn't make much sense.

Religious cults argue that the belief in life after death and that magical beings live amongst us, judge us, and watch our every thought and action is not magical thinking. They think it's perfectly normal.

Edith and Ray had handed me a mixed message of epic proportions: believe whatever the Bible says with all its fairies and ghosts and streets of gold up in the clouds, but think for yourself and refuse to be indoctrinated into cults. The qualifier was that *their* cult wasn't one of the bad cults because it wasn't a cult at all, but rather the Way, the Truth, and the Life, and I'd be a fool to reject it. Embrace the dogma, think independently, and be your own man!

The crops failed. Again.

Religion started out as an explanation for the inexplicable when we didn't know how to do science. We didn't know any better, so what the heck. Let's invent some Egyptian, Greek, Roman (and later, Norse) gods to explain all this. And then it became a valuable tool to control the general population; to give them purpose, and to keep them obedient to authority. Why else have a pope or any organized religion unless power and structure were needed? And power and structure exist for no reason than to control (or help) the general population.

For the individual, it has always been insurance against the unthinkable horror of being buried alive. Which is what we all secretly fear, even though simple logic tells us it isn't. We are scared to death of death, primarily because we have no way to describe it and we fear what we don't understand, so we self-medicate with a "higher power."

I felt the chill of winter in my bones the day I realized it was all just an elaborate ruse we played on ourselves to make us think we could cheat death by "earning" eternal life.

I once asked a marketing guy I knew about the Publisher's Clearing House Sweepstakes, which involved a massive mailing once a year to sell magazine subscriptions. Why was there a sticker that had to be removed from one side of the mailer and placed on the other side? It seemed pointless.

He said it was to make people think they had "earned" the huge discounts being offered. That one tiny physical action brought the response rate up some 80%. Without it, the mailing would never have paid off. If you don't believe in Jesus, you won't get into heaven, so move the sticker.

The hard part for many is facing up to the reality of mortality. It is a wonderful idea that death is not the end. It's nice to think we'll meet our loved ones again in the sweet bye and bye, but it's a false comfort.

We devalue our one and only life by pretending that it is just a step in some eternal journey. By devaluing life we allow and encourage atrocities, like the activities of terrorists who believe fervently that by murdering innocents they will ascend to paradise and be awarded eternal bliss with seventy-two raisins (or virgins, depending on which translation of the Qu'ran one ascribes to). *I always wondered what the women got... Seventy-two cabana boys?* There is no real difference between an Islamic terrorist and a devout evangelical Christian except geography.

The Power of Prayer

The power of prayer is a belief system working as a self-reinforcing closed loop of emotion. If you believe, you will feel it, and because you feel it, you must believe it. Despite that, there is the matter of intentionality and living with purpose that comes into play. If I believe I can achieve something, it is far more possible for me to achieve it than if I don't. And in that, prayer becomes a form of meditation — a self-actualized attaboy system that can propel us forward. But everything else, including the direct result of prayer, is chance, coincidence, and the power of belief overcoming reality.

If prayer really worked, people who believed in it would heal faster, have better lives, and live longer. And they'd win more football games.

People will believe almost anything if they are in enough pain, and pain is an intrinsic part of the human condition so it gets a lot of attention. It just depends on what people turn to for solace. Some turn to religion, some to food, some turn to alcohol or drugs, some turn to conspiracy theories, and some just buckle down and work harder.

Religion admonishes us, "Do not even attempt to understand Biblical mysteries," and that "all will be revealed in the sweet by and by." But if we don't understand something, how are we supposed to believe it? "Take it on faith!" Why? "Because if you don't, you'll end up in a sea of flames! But if you do, you'll live forever in a wonderful place where every man will get seventy-two virgins." Or maybe it's raisins. (It's a mystery.)

This business about faith starts all the way back in Genesis. The Eden myth is the root of modern anti-intellectualism, a demand to cast aside our ability to reason and believe blatant nonsense for no reason other than we were told to do so. Eve was Prometheus, bringing enlightenment to mankind. Eve was a hero to all of mankind. Insecure men made her out to be a tool of the devil.

People believe what their parents believed for absolutely no reason other than their parents believed it. And in a general way, it makes sense to take direction from those who have survived longer than we have. And coming up with completely new solutions is a lot of work, and doubting our parents is not allowed when we're young and impressionable. Teenagers do it all the time, but by then they've already been imprinted. Like ducks. Let's just all go to church and make your mother happy.

They say great minds think alike. Well, ignorant minds think alike too, and if enough of them get together they form a mob, which is how lynchings and wars happen, and how dangerous politicians get elected. Money may be the root of all evil, but religion follows closely down the backstretch.

I read *The Source*, by James Michener, when I was a teenager, and I found it fascinating. It is a huge doorstop of an historical novel that reveals how it all might have raveled up out of almost nothing. In his book, Michener traces the history of the Jewish people, from prehistory to the present, via artifacts found during an archeological dig (or *tel*) of a fictitious city named Tel Makor (Makor means *source* in Hebrew).

Along the way, he explains how one of the Semitic religions might have arisen from nothing more than a tall stone in the center of a dusty village a very long time ago — a stone that people in pre-historic times erected and gathered round and assigned magical powers to for one reason or another.

But as the debris of the growing city cluttered the streets the stone became buried under an ever-thicker gathering of detritus, compacted by the hooves of donkeys and the feet of people, and was eventually lost to sight. But the rumor and fear of it remained. This stone of mystical power was assigned a tetragrammaton, written and read from right to left: יהוה or YHWH in the Latin script of modern English — and pronounced *Yahweh*.

Shamans evolved into priests to provide pomp and dignity. Strict rules for correct behavior to please the stone were established, and *voilà*, the ONE TRUE GOD was born.

On the other hand

Religion in America is a piece of cake as long as you stay in one of the main channels and don't go rocking the boat. All it takes is faith on a grand scale. And if you're wrong, what's the downside? Not much; you either live forever or you don't. And if you don't, you're no worse off. I'd be worried about all the boredom though. In heaven, I mean. *Eternity?*

I always thought the moment of "being saved" to be like falling in love while being given a medal by the community — at least in part because both involve unconditional acceptance. Plato once said, "Love is a serious mental disease." He may have been poking fun, but the heartache and euphoria of love aren't just a form of expression for those who are head-over-heels; it's been studied as if it were an actual illness to see what's going on. Science shows that those in love experience a kind of high similar to that caused by drugs such as heroin. The flood of ecstasy that comes with unconditional acceptance can be intoxicating, like a kind of rapture. No wonder True Believers are so fanatical; they think they're in love.

Despite all that, church fellowship can do wonderful things. It's handy to have a way to maintain hope during tough times; people make better decisions in a crisis when they can see a path forward. The camaraderie of a church group and the belief system that binds everyone together can help people cope with catastrophe and grief—a wonderful attribute as long as the reasons for gathering for fellowship under a religious umbrella don't transform overwhelming emotion into the kind of blind denial that says, "It's all part of God's Plan." or "Your mommy is an angel now, looking down on you from heaven." Or worse, the theocratic alliance between True Believers and politics.

And I am also not saying that churches, in their efforts to feed the hungry and help people gain access to better housing, clean water, and medicine are not doing a great job. Such efforts are wholesome and meaningful. Piety *can* be an ideal, a dream, a wish for unity and love everlasting, but that's not the pattern of most religions throughout history. Striving to enjoy a virtuous and loving life was never the problem.

We all seek reassurance and validation in our lives, and religion can provide that. As children, we get it from our parents, as adults we should be able to provide it for ourselves, but we also enjoy outside validation—in our job, the military, through sports, via art, in marriage and family, and with religion.

Parents get validation from helping their children, partially due to the "extension of self" we get from pushing our genes forward in time, and partly from mankind's perpetual mythic quest to live forever, if not personally, then through our children and grandchildren. My father's desire to have me take over the family business certainly fit within that framework, despite whatever imperfections and inadequacies I may have had. He was projecting himself into the future. My mother was also, given my love of books and education.

Positive beliefs can set up a self-fulfilling prophecy. We create what happens to us based on our own feelings of self-worth and whether we feel that our life is in harmony.

The success we earn and the harmony we feel confirms and strengthens our beliefs and the cycle repeats. When our belief is strong, we perform smarter, better, and with greater resilience, which creates energy in our lives. This is true everywhere: business, athletics, education, art, and personal relationships. Athletes hit their stride and enter the zone, artists get on a roll, salespeople get on a winning streak, and people all over… fall in love. With themselves, with each other, and with whatever brings them true happiness—including religion and charismatic leaders.

Religion is the artificial sweetener of life. It isn't real, but it works as if it were. It adds undeniable value by incorporating comfort and self-assurance into our lives. It creates the feeling of harmony we crave. And, if we truly believe the illusion, our feeling of harmony can be quite real. Disquietingly ethereal, but real.

Churches provide a sense of structure, belonging, and security for their parishioners—all those Sunday afternoons and church picnics do add up. It's no wonder that people find solace in religion, since that's one of its main functions.

> "And God shall wipe away all tears from their eyes; and there shall be no more death, neither sorrow, nor crying, neither shall there be any more pain: for the former things are passed away. " — *Revelation 21:4*

Black churches have provided a spiritual backbone throughout the South and the nation in our struggle for freedom and social change. The unending work for voting rights, desegregation, and justice was held together through very dark times because the people could come together, encourage one another, lift up their voices in song, and find unity in prayer and common cause. They don't seem to be subject to believing in conspiracy theories, perhaps because they've had to deal with real conspiracies all along from their own neighbors.

But religion also upholds the self-righteous for toeing an imaginary line. No need to worry about the guy you're bombing; he's most likely a heathen anyway; let some god sort them out after the smoke clears and we've won the war, or police action, or whatever the hell it was. It seemed to me that a lot of this was being driven by the glorification of organized religion, passed down from parent to child without any regard for common sense or empathy for the oppressed.

My argument was not so much with the everyday churchgoer who wanted nothing more than to live their life with as little pain (and as much joy) as possible, but with the concept of religion itself and the considerable harm it's caused down through the ages.

Without religion driving us, almost every war we've had on this planet would never have started. There would be no middle-east crisis, or issues over abortion. There might still be racism, but it would never have been cloaked in the white sheets of sainthood. Without religion, the Earth would still spin just fine, but we wouldn't have nuclear missiles waiting for two people somewhere to flip a switch, turn two keys, and push a button. Religion is not just bad and wrong; it is *very* bad and wrong. And all the good it does in this world cannot make up for all the harm. The war in Vietnam was just the latest manifestation of what we'd done to ourselves.

I was also struck by a growing realization that the United States might not be such a wonderful country after all. We might not have all the answers. Maybe—*just maybe*—we were being bullies, and not just with Vietnam. Maybe one thing *was* just like the other. Perhaps our nation was just like all those religions, proclaiming we were the ONE TRUE NATION, and just because we *said* we were the best at everything didn't mean we *were*. The maybes kept piling up, like the broken bodies of children nobody had planned for.

It reminded me of baby ducks and imprinting. Train a duckling young enough and it will follow anything—including the family dog, a cat, or an old pair of boots. That's how all the adults were acting, like ducks that had been imprinted on something at an early age and never bothered to rethink their philosophy. It wasn't turtles all the way down, it was ducks, and I seemed to be the only guy in the room who thought the ducks might not be quite right.

Wake up call

Starting in the mid-sixties, something different began to emerge during the morning service. Kids names (and the names of their parents) were being read from the pulpit all across the country. Our nation was at war, whether the politicians and generals wanted to acknowledge it or not.

They were calling it a "police action," as if it could be rebranded into something more palatable, like New Coke. Our church took down that massive cross at the front and did a complete redesign, with white doves and a swirly thing to symbolize hope and forgiveness. (Re-branding takes many forms.)

Our pastor wasn't just reading the names of the dead and wounded; he was also implying (sadly) that they had died in the line of duty. That going out into the jungle half a world away and getting shot to ribbons was regrettable, but somehow necessary and appropriate—somehow noble. That may have comforted grieving families who needed a reason for their pain and loss, but it made no sense to guys like me who had no choice in the matter.

Getting killed for no reason wasn't noble, and reading the names of dead and wounded children during the service every Sunday made our moral choices very real. I knew some of those names, and those kids were gone. Wiped out. No promise of heaven could bring back the sound of car doors slammed on a summer day or the slap of running feet.

Draft age was eighteen and by the time you were trained to hunt and kill the Viet Cong you were nineteen, still just a child, but armed to the teeth, and one of the most dangerous animals on the planet. *Lord of the Flies,* anyone?

Somewhere along the line my brain put this mangled mishmash of religion, patriotism, and death together, and I woke up with a jerk. I realized our church was fronting for the enemy. There was a battle raging between logic and wishful thinking, and every Sunday I was putting myself right smack dab behind enemy lines. I continued to attend for a short period while I mulled this over, but one Sunday I'd had enough. That day after church I had it out with my parents.

The Voice

Edith was the powerhouse in our family, no question. Ray held his own, but Edith was a force beyond all reckoning—partly because she'd had to help raise all her younger sisters in a hardscrabble environment, partly because she'd been running herd on a half-dozen border kids frothy with teenage energy, and partly because she was a brilliant fourth grade schoolteacher with a district-wide reputation as a strict disciplinarian. Old Lady Robertson they called her, and they weren't kidding.

Edith had a certain tone that came up from time to time when she was truly on the edge. She didn't use it often, but when she did, the Earth stood still. My brother called it "The Voice." The Voice couldn't be used casually: didn't work that way. It was something that arose like the personification of an ancient prophet from the very depths, and only when life itself was teetering on anarchy. Edith had it, Glen had it (I had heard him use it), and I evidently had it too, because that Sunday afternoon I wielded it for the first time. Like a sledgehammer.

There is nothing quite so powerful as a teenager driven by righteous anger, and I was furious. I had been thinking long and hard about the war, my opposition to it, and the hypocrisy of our government. And now our church was defending it. I slammed into my thesis with every bit of who I was, and The Voice did all the talking. I stood there with my knuckles white and the mantle of righteous truth upon my shoulders, and my parents saw me for who I'd become. And they changed.

The Bible had it both ways: slay the Amalekites, but turn the other cheek. I'm guessing our pastor had to Sophie's Choice it. You do or you don't; can't have it both ways. That Sunday morning, with doves and hearts up behind him on the wall, he preached the straight government line, admonishing teenagers and parents alike to "obey established authority," citing ancient scripture to drive home the message of blind obedience:

> "Let every soul be subject unto the higher powers. For there is no power but of God: the powers that be are ordained of God." — *Romans 13:1*

> "Obey them that have the rule over you, and submit yourselves: for they watch for your souls, as they that must give account, that they may do it with joy, and not with grief, for that is unprofitable for you." — *Hebrews 13:17*

It's in the Bible, which is the Word of God, so God told us to do it. We had to do it because it came from God, etc., etc.

My parents were conflicted. On the one hand was their minister saying to follow the Official Rule Book (actually, the Old Testament), while their brains were telling them something quite different. And then there was their last kid, Jonathan the First, saying he didn't want any part of it.

Almost every parent in America was hearing support for the war directly from the pulpit, and some at least—probably most—thinking their youngsters should pay better attention. Because it was the Bible. It's God's Word. You must all obey. It's called Faith. *You'll burn in hell, kid. Do as they say and pick up your gun; it's your sacred duty to kill commies.* Nobody said this out loud of course, and I may have been reading a lot into the atmosphere of the times, but it all rhymed with orange, which was the agent they put in charge. Bob Dylan even wrote a song, *With God on Our Side*, which spelled out the baffling codependence between religion and man's inhumanity to man.

Identity politics

It was confusing, since my father identified as a Republican, which seemed to be the party of the Old Testament: stern and unforgiving. Edith kept her own counsel but told me in later years that she had kept her mouth shut for the sake of her marriage. Her side of the family belonged mostly to the Society of Friends (Quakers), who did not believe in war.

I saw the terms *Republican* and *religious* as interchangeable with *conservative*, and that didn't make sense when I looked at who my parents were, day-to-day.

Perhaps Ray was only conservative in the money sense, given that he had been an accountant and was in business, and maybe he divorced himself from the other issues. He took care of everyone at work and was certainly willing to take a hit on profits if somebody needed help. If a vendor undercharged, he pointed it out and paid the difference, just as I did in later years (surprising a few people in the process, including the IRS). That example was held up to me time after time, and it seemed to have nothing to do with being a Republican or a conservative. It was about living the Golden Rule.

Due to their example and what I had gathered through all my reading and music, plus what was on the news every night, I was slowly coming to grips with an important issue. People like my parents, who cared about the greater good but didn't exhibit the smug superiority of white privilege, were not conservatives at all, because their thoughts and actions just didn't fit the description. Suddenly the world made more sense.

My parents taught me that the primary goal of business was to provide a decent living wage for staff and family and to do so with honor and fair dealings. Profits came later, if at all. That was Edith and Ray Robertson, soup to nuts. Making a profit wasn't ignored, but it wasn't the main goal. Ray didn't say it directly, but his whole life was based on it. It's how he taught me to be when I took over the business. Save your nickles and dimes, treat everyone with respect, do nothing rash, but bet the entire farm when you have to. And none of that squared readily with the war in Vietnam, which clearly caused widespread destruction and death with no discernible benefit to anyone, least of all the Vietnamese people.

The draft was a huge issue. The army needed warm bodies who could carry a rifle to drop into the jungle so our politicians and generals could win their pissing contest against this tiny little country in Southeast Asia where everyone worked in a rice paddy or on a fishing boat. No one could explain why we were in the war (other than some vague and rambling thesis concerning the threat of godless communism and the domino effect), and I was being told that killing under orders in war wasn't really murder because it was war and everyone had to do their duty, and somehow that made exploding people okay.

At first, I just played my music louder and escaped into more books. Which was pretty much what a lot of other guys my age were doing. But there is a tough terrier strain in both sides of my family that somehow decanted its wisdom and folly into me until it finally emerged. Another kid might have held his yap shut and just listened to his music, but I stood resolute. I started reading more difficult books and asking myself tougher questions, particularly about the war, the concept of religion, and the history of World War II.

Not that being contrary is a bad thing necessarily. To a certain extent I grew up on the stuff, but I didn't want my ideas to be tainted by intellectual arrogance or blind assumption. It was important for my conclusions to be clean and simple, and my ideals to be based on logic.

Some ideas seemed obvious, and I wrote them down to keep my focus. These concepts later formed the nucleus of my thesis when it came time for me to present my beliefs to the FBI. The Commandments According to Jonathan seemed cogent and reasonable enough at the time.

- Individual morality always supersedes legal and religious authority: do the right thing as you know it. That doesn't mean breaking the law left and right, but the Golden Rule is a good place to start. You have to pick your battles or you'll never get anywhere, but you don't just follow orders and do whatever you're told, either.

- Intentional killing is always murder, and as we value our own lives, murder is wrong, even when state-sanctioned in a time of war. With the following exception: that under direct attack, everyone has the right to defend life and country any way they can.

I knew society agreed with me on at least some of this due to the Nuremberg Trials. I had read one of the court transcripts as part of my self-education project. You could end up in prison for following orders you believed immoral; it was in our own Military Code of Justice. It still is. I looked that up too because I wanted to know if I could use it to argue my case.

The law states that U.S. soldiers are not allowed to follow unlawful orders (one of the lessons we got out of World War II). The president could order SEAL Team Six to assassinate a political rival, but if they did so, they'd all hang for it.

If there is a process, use the process. Civil disobedience was a well-honored course of action and respected by everyone but the authorities it inconvenienced. I read up on that as well, primarily because of people like Bertrand Russell (who had done his best to intervene during the Cuban Missile Crisis, and had been a conscientious objector during WWI), Dr. King, and Joan

Baez, whom I'd met in Oakland. Joan Baez was a huge influence on my life, particularly during this period. She showed the world by example that beating people up didn't make you right. It made you a bully.

At the same time, I wasn't the bleeding heart liberal that some people thought you had to be in order to object to war. I wasn't clear about everything, but I didn't think human life was *sacred* in some way. I really didn't. I was perfectly willing to defend my country, I just didn't think it was right to shoot people or set them on fire because some politician wanted to prove he had enough testosterone in his veins. I also didn't think it was right to make somebody else do it. Murder by proxy is still murder.

The bigger picture was also coming into focus. Vietnam in toto may not have been our ally, but if they "went communist" they weren't going to invade the United States, either. I also suspected that whether they went communist or not wasn't really going to destroy our way of life and that the possibility of a domino effect was probably not a good reason to kill well over a million people. Completely different from World War II, when Germany and its allies had the power, resources, and stated intention of making the world over as a fascist state with death camps for anyone they didn't like.

The symphony of violence

War was an easy way to make a ton of money: one massive transfer of wealth from taxpayer pockets into the coffers of companies such as Northrop Grumman, Boeing, and Bell Textron. A lot of that tax money subsequently found its way into the re-election campaigns of politicians who voted to increase military spending. The situation was incredibly self-serving and self-perpetuating, but also perfectly legal. We spent $19,847 per minute for fourteen years to kill people we didn't even know.

Raytheon, Boeing, Lockheed Martin, Dow Chemical, and such companies were and are America's Merchants of Death. Their kill ratios played out a symphony of violence to a well-ensconced choir of greed, arrogance, and indifferent cruelty. It was all about power and money, with politicians pushing the agenda on their behalf. In my opinion, Dwight Eisenhower was the last intellectually honest and truly decent conservative to hold office as President of the United States.

> "In the councils of government, we must guard against the acquisition of unwarranted influence, whether sought or unsought, by the *military-industrial complex*. The potential for the disastrous rise of misplaced power exists and will persist."   – *President Dwight D. Eisenhower*
> Farewell Address to the nation

The penultimate irony

Another part of this puzzle (which appeared to be lost on all the so-called adults) was that girls didn't get drafted. It was as if every girl was a proxy for Mary, mother of Jesus, and the thought of her carrying a backpack, a string of grenades on her belt, and an M16 whilst slogging her virgin self through a rice paddy with a joint hanging out the side of her mouth couldn't be borne. Do your duty and die for love of country. Men only, of course. The discrimination against women and their right to bear arms was a side issue that only added to the hypocrisy. Women my age were not happy about it at all, and said so.

I wasn't likely to see combat. Heck, I could type sixty words a minute, so — another irony my brother pointed out — I probably would have been filling out forms in some office at Long Binh Post for the upper brass. Or fixing typewriters. Nevertheless, the government didn't have the right to use me as its murder weapon, and I was willing to spend an unknown number of years in durance vile to make my point.

So many times we hear the phrase, "Well, there are two sides to every story." And that's often the case. But really — are there two sides to an issue when one side is using force or deception? I decided I would always be correct to oppose bullies and liars. There really was no middle ground, no "two sides" to the issue. It was just a quick way to deflect, like saying there are two sides to the Holocaust or reasons other than racism and slavery for the Civil War.

Making what you do justify the way you do it is an easy solution. It makes it all better. No need to think about it any harder than that, there are two sides, and we've justified what we're doing with the glory of what we're going to accomplish. If you object, well, that makes you the bad guy. Projection is a time-honored defense mechanism for bullies. Call the other guy a bully first so people can't identify what's really going on.

The ultimate irony

I was against the draft and the war, but I was also resentful of the way some parents kept their kids out of it. Sometimes it was an issue of privilege—power, money, or connections. If having money meant you didn't have to put on a uniform, it was not only unfair but dangerous. It wasn't lost on me that any *free* democracy needs to use some kind of plan if they are to have a military with enough independent thinkers to call a halt to things if something goes horribly wrong.

In my opinion, bad behavior is often excused by circumstance, particularly in the military and police, which have a built-in bias to self-forgive, ignore their own issues, and move on. It takes more courage to put a gun down than to pick one up. Patience and a commitment to rational thinking are needed to make negotiation the primary tool. If all you've got are gung-ho yes men, that's just a loaded gun waiting to go off.

There is an old saying that anyone who really wants power shouldn't get it. It's generally applied to police, military, and high office. Switzerland understands that. Whether it's the military or helping the poor or working with the police or fire department, *everyone* serves—rich and poor, no excuses—unless they are truly, absolutely disabled. Bone spurs? Okay, here's your office. Sit here; you get to work in social services. They even have jobs for people of conscience such as myself. Everybody does their bit.

I have no problem with the Swiss because they don't believe in wars of aggression and they treat everyone the same. You don't end up with an army full of military fanatics who think flamethrowers and land mines are a good thing because, "They get the job done."

Getting the job done is beside the point if what you're doing is despicable. Eisenhower had it right all along.

Ode to Yellow Line

Q "You say you're a conscientious objector?"

A "Yes," I said, staring into the mirror. "That's right."

Q "Why?"

A "Because it's wrong to kill," I replied. I was pacing the floor in my three-piece suit. "Because it's murder."

Q "Who says it's murder?"

A "I do." I said. I whirled to face him. "And millions of other people agree with me. What, you think it's *okay* to murder people? That's something that *works* for you?"

I was playing both parts to a house of one—Perry Mason *vs.* Clarence Darrow to me: the man in the mirror—arguing one side and then the other like opposing lawyers having a go at the ethics of war.

The living room in our house on Englewood Avenue had a huge mirror covering the wall above our couch (probably Edith's idea of how to make a small house look bigger). That mirror became a silent witness to my struggle. It was my primary tool for gauging my presentation as I pitted logic and philosophy in an epic battle against the momentum of history and legal doctrine. I was winning of course, but just barely.

With all the passion a teenager could generate, I strode up and down in front of that mirror for two days, reasoning both sides of my wretched little equation. I spoke for and against my own beliefs and logic, imagining I was in a wood-paneled courtroom in downtown San José.

I wanted to come within striking distance of the truth, and this was my way of doing it. By acting out this little thought experiment, I was able to compose my arguments. I had to know my own truth without hesitation and without question. I had to know it cold, yet also convey the intensity of my convictions.

Repetition creates familiarity and competence, even mastery with good coaching. Well, I didn't have a coach, but in every other way, I was like an athlete preparing for his one shot at the Olympics. I was hoping to develop an ability to function under the pressure I expected to face in a courtroom. I knew my own capabilities (or lack thereof) and was worried I would be overpowered under rapid questioning by a competent lawyer.

I'd been selling business machines to local firms for several years, so I could talk easily enough with business owners, but I wasn't particularly glib outside that setting. I could speak passionately about the quality of Olympia typewriters and driving English sports cars with élan, but not much else. For me, there was only one solution: practice, practice, practice.

By repeating my thesis over and over in different ways and by hitting every issue I could think of, I wanted to make myself as competent as I could. We always remember the bright snappy things we should have said long afterward, but my freedom was on the line. I had to be prepared.

So I there I was, working the room. The guy in the mirror wouldn't let up, but I didn't expect him to.

Q "It's your patriotic duty. This is war. You have to defend your country."

A "The United States is not at war. War has not been declared. That requires an Act of Congress." *Say it better.* "The United States has not declared war, and no one has declared war on us." *That's not relevant to him, get to the point.*

"How dare you say I'm not a patriot? It is my patriotic duty to do the correct thing; to help steer my country in the right direction. To save us from the generals and the politicians who are completely wrong. Patriotism has nothing to do with killing people, and everybody knows it, including you, sir." *I'm a pompous little twerp, aren't I? Spouting off like I'm so high, mighty, and wise. I sound like a fool three times over. Crap. This isn't going to win me any points.*

Q "In the military, you are defending your country. That's what our military does."

A   "No. No, that isn't true in this case. They don't want me to defend the United States." *Say it better.* "They want me to attack another country. Vietnam is not the United States."

Q   "We're fighting communism."

A   "We aren't at war and communism isn't a country." *Say it better, but keep to the point.* "And I don't think this is about communism anyway. It's about a bunch of politicians and generals who want to be right no matter what, supported by some idea we're always right even when we're wrong."

Q   "What if the Viet Cong tried to kill your sister?"

A   "My sister? *My sister?* If the Viet Cong came to Los Gatos to hurt my sister, I would fight to protect her, of course I would. But no one is trying to kill my sister." *Keep talking.* "Or anyone else in the United States for that matter. It's wrong to attack people who haven't attacked us. We're setting people on fire over there. Burning them alive. Everyone's seen the photos." *I turned to stare into the eyes of the man in the mirror.* "We are being a bully. Worse than a bully. We're committing war crimes. It's in the news. Hell, you've even got Walter Cronkite telling you that you're wrong."

Q   "So it was wrong to attack Germany in World War II?"

A   "This isn't about Germany, it's about Vietnam."

Q   "Please answer the question."

A   "Germany attacked England, which was the same as attacking us."

Q   "So it's okay to defend England, but not Vietnam?"

A   "That isn't the issue."

Q   "Why not?"

A   "Because at one time we *were* English. We were a part of the British Empire. It was like defending our own parents. We didn't come from Vietnam and we aren't allies. We have no business fighting some other country's civil war just to prop up a corrupt government—a fake democracy." *Stick to the main reason.* "If Germany had defeated England, they would have been coming after us next. But that isn't the case here. The real issue is that it's just plain wrong to kill people who aren't attacking us. It's wrong and I won't do it."

That was just the start of my mock trial because I kept working the problem with more questions, pacing back and forth in our living room while repeating myself with do-overs and anything new I could think of to throw at that mirror.

I was convinced that an emotional argument without intellectual rigor would get me nowhere. If you don't believe in your cause people wonder why you're fighting for it, and a collectively raised eyebrow would doom me just as surely as anything I might or might not say. But if I didn't have logic on my side, I would be doomed from the start.

If I had learned anything from my brief time on Earth, it was that there are times when you have to take off your glasses, put on your cape, and stride out of the phone booth with purpose. At the same time, being a prig about it would get me absolutely nowhere. I was a Teddy Roosevelt man at heart; speak softly, but carry an internally consistent philosophy. When I got that letter from the Selective Service telling me to present myself at the San José bus terminal for a *one-way ticket* to the Oakland Induction Center, I knew it was all coming down to the wire. The singular shit-storm of my young life was about to descend, and I had work to do.

If I was going to prison, I wanted to make certain the bastards who sent me there knew they'd been in a fight, damn it. This would be my one chance to be heard, my one chance to get it right before I took the stand. I wanted my words to stick in their craw and force them to look hard at their own beliefs and assumptions, whatever they might be.

I knew that wasn't likely to happen, but I had to give it my best shot. Conscientious objectors were something to be swept out the door, and introspection on the part of the judge and prosecutor really wasn't part of the equation. But I needed to fight the fight even if it proved futile in the end. Losing wasn't the worst that could happen. Standing up for my own convictions was paramount. I was not going quietly into that gray cellblock for lack of gumption or inability to say my piece properly.

Stand and don't fight

Aside from the clarification I got through my mirror exercise, one particular idea came to me that helped tremendously: that what I was doing was patriotic, and that I was really just defending my country. Not by carrying arms, but by refusing to do so.

I realized that everybody and his Aunt Martha saw it the other way, but voicing the argument *out loud* during my homemade courtroom drama made me realize the truth of it. Our country had gone over a cliff and only moral outrage could drag it back. The irony was bittersweet: that if I was willing to sit in some prison for five years and give up any expectation of a normal future, that made me more hero than coward. Thinking of it that way made a huge difference, and bolstered my resolve.

But in the meantime, I kept at it. Like a gymnast who had come too far to tumble out, I was going for the gold. Anything less would have been catastrophically bad, and I knew that my answers had to be virtually automatic and decidedly firm.

Did I think my argument would stand up in court? I really didn't know. I wanted to blow them away with my earnest and irrefutable logic, but there was certainly a part of me that said I was just fooling myself on a grand scale to think I wasn't going to prison.

This wasn't Jimmy Stewart shouting "I will not yield!" in *Mr. Smith Goes to Washington,* just a teenager trying to work through a massive moral issue. The situation may have confused my parents, but to their credit, they listened — carefully. When the United States entered World War II, there hadn't been any question of who the bad guys were or what we had to do.

My parents' church held itself up as the arbiter of right and wrong in an imperfect world, but preached obedience to lawful authority instead of one's conscience, sanctioning the killing of soldiers and Vietnamese alike instead of peaceful coexistence? My parents couldn't justify that kind of contradiction.

My father set up an appointment with some lawyer in San José and talked me into going, but the meeting was pointless. A legal out wasn't what I wanted. Not that there was one; this guy was talking Magic Beans. It was obvious to my father and me what that lawyer was all about. His fingernails were too perfectly manicured — with clear polish! His face had too few wrinkles for his age, and he had a deep tan in the dead of winter, making him look unnatural and waxy, as if he had a mortician on retainer to make him presentable to the living. He had *wrong answer* written right across his forehead. We got out of there as quickly as we could and never spoke of it again.

I did not know until much later that there wouldn't be a trial as I thought of it, since the courts were really only looking at one thing, and it was a yes or no question. Did I break the Selective Service Act or not? *Why* I broke it wasn't the issue. The whole question of morality and how decisions might have been reached through internal struggle over years of introspection and evaluation never came up in court documents. You either did it or you didn't, and that was it.

Who to believe?

My parents were intelligent people. They read books and magazines and ran businesses. They didn't get out much except to work and church and didn't take a newspaper, but they did watch Walter Cronkite's nightly news broadcast on television. They knew he wasn't lying. And Cronkite agreed with their son, who was a decent enough kid (I didn't get into too much trouble). The cognitive dissonance finally became unsupportable. Church and government officials saying one thing, but their son saying it was wrong, and Cronkite on the nightly news showing them just how wrong it was — in living color. Thank goodness for a free press.

Nixon came in after LBJ, and despite his concern for the poor, I thought him smarmy. His impeachment hearings a few years later proved beyond the shadow of a doubt the amount of tricky-dickery going on and how shallow people can get when money and power are at stake. The blatant lying when the truth was right there in front of us.

It wouldn't be until 1971 when the Pentagon Papers were leaked to the press that we'd learn how each successive president had lied to the nation. It wasn't until 1972 when the Watergate scandal backfired in Nixon's face that we'd see how low one president could go. I was on my own, with nothing in the public record I could point to. My argument was based on what I'd learned, what I'd been taught, and what I'd decided on my own. A big advantage actually, due to the organic nature of my message; I hadn't just copied it from somebody else.

Edith and Ray didn't say much about it, but their thinking did change. Ray had been a Republican all his life, and thought it was just like Kiwanis; if you were in business, that was the club you joined. And it made sense. Conservatives talked a good game when it came to not spending over our income or exceeding our ability to repay the national debt, but it was starting to ring like a cracked bell when the government kept spending so much on the war.

Edith, Ray, and I had changed during those years. It was a difficult time. My parents and I had conversations about all of this—so many conversations. They were concerned, both for me and for themselves. Their world was shifting, and they didn't much like it; Vietnam was not World War II, and they knew it. I dragged them into the greater conversation because of my age and the belief system they had instilled in me. *Do what is right, no matter what.* Well, that particular chicken had come home to roost, and I was the egg it hatched.

It didn't make my parents any happier, but they understood who I was becoming and why, and they supported me to that end. They were trying to be good parents while they were being told by their minister and the government that their son was some kind of traitor. A coward. A fool. Parents all over the United States were struggling with the same issues. I was lucky Edith and Ray didn't have closed minds, for that made all the difference. I began to realize that political thought wasn't two-sided, but a broad spectrum, with an entire rainbow of nuance. But for me it narrowed down to a matter of independent thought *vs.* blind obedience.

Assembling all the parts

Prison or war. Such a decision was out of my parents' control. They could argue, cajole, entreat, and even threaten, but that life or death decision was really up to the one person with the least life experience: me.

In my letter, I told the Selective Service that I refused to murder anyone except if the United States was directly attacked on our own soil, in which case I would fight shoulder to shoulder to defend my country. They had an existing category that they could have used: 1H - *Registrant not currently subject to processing for induction or alternative service.*

But the government at that time was treating all conscientious objectors as situational liars on a fast track to prison unless they belonged to the Society of Friends, Mennonites, Jehovah's Witnesses, or the Amish, all of whom were routinely given CO status because their belief systems were so adamantly against violence in any form. Nothing was automatic, but if they made a strong case and had their church elders back them up, they were usually exempted. I wasn't one of those. Religion was the only litmus test for COs, and I didn't pass. My parents were Baptists. The wrong kind of church.

Irony of ironies, Nixon himself professed to be a Quaker, yet continued the war and made it worse. In his case, the clothes did *not* make the man. Nixon evidently put on his religion the way most people put on their pants. Situational morality in the Oval Office. Wow.

Mistaken identity

When I arrived at the Oakland Induction Center, the people at the front counter didn't understand who I was or why I was there. The facility was housed in a massive, anonymous-looking building on Clay Street. After looking over my paperwork, the people behind the counter seemed to think I was an attorney *representing* Jonathan Robertson. Their mistake was understandable. I didn't much look the part of a draftee. I told them I was there to refuse conscription. It took a bit of explaining, but they finally understood.

I was a twenty-year-old kid wearing a dark gray business suit, complete with vest, white shirt, and maroon tie. It was the only armor I had. Hey, I sold business machines for a living, and to a great extent, that's who I was. But I was also nobody's fool. That suit spoke quietly, but it spoke volumes, and it didn't mince my message. It made me stand out from everyone else, and to my mind gave me a hell of a lot more purpose than if I had been wearing a T-shirt and jeans like every other guy in the building. I could have been in that O. Henry story, *Clothes Make the Man* when I walked in looking my finest. The people in charge treated me with respect, at least in part based on my clothing. But more importantly, I became the person I needed to be in that hour.

The Group W Bench

I looked around. There were hundreds of kids in that big main room — all going through the basic physical before being inducted into the Army. The room had a tall ceiling and partitions all around the walls like a trade show, except there were medical doctors in every booth, each specializing in a particular exam. Guys kept filing in and joining the line as the busses kept arriving — day after day and week after week — from all over Northern California. Everyone got undressed down to their skivvies, then carried their clothing with them in a long line that snaked in and around all the different booths where doctors in white coats were testing for hearing, vision, blood pressure, basic intelligence, and so on. The dull roar of conversation filled the building.

There were kids who didn't know how to stand in a line for any length of time without fidgeting themselves into a decline, kids who stoically endured the indignities suffered upon them, and other kids who had to go through the whole ordeal without any underwear because they'd forgotten to put on underpants that morning. They probably forgot their toothbrushes, too. It was a strange reality to face — to be decanted into a mass of humanity and herded like cattle past a long row of workaday doctors. As I stood at the counter explaining who I was, this conga line of teenagers snaked behind me like disoriented robots. I couldn't tell if they cared what was happening to them or not.

Legally, every guy getting processed into the Army in 1970 was a child. Couldn't vote and couldn't own property. Couldn't even get married without mommy and daddy's say so. The government was doing its very best to award the red badge of courage to *children*. If anyone accepted that as normal, then they sure weren't thinking straight, and everybody knew it. After a few years of hearing from way too many pissed-off parents, Congress finally ratified the 26th Amendment in July 1971 and lowered the voting age from 21 to 18. This then became the new *age of majority* in most states. As far as the government was concerned, we were now all adults, putting the kibosh on all those parents.

My issue wasn't with anyone who went into the Army; almost no one wanted to be there. Most draftees probably hadn't thought it out enough to make a real decision. I had friends who fought in Vietnam. No, my argument was with the generals and politicians. They were the ones ordering up all the body bags while threatening kids with prison time in order to herd them into an abattoir eight thousand miles away.

The number of people objecting to the war was growing. Many of us had shown up at anti-war demonstrations. We knew what we knew, and we were no longer willing to kowtow so quickly to the toxic male jingoism selling us down the river.

Moment of truth

After I'd explained who I was to the women at the front counter and they finally understood the situation, confusion was replaced by resolve. One of the ladies told me in a nice way to wait where I was, and a moment later two soldiers came out. They ushered me through a doorway into a side room. It was much smaller, and out of sight from all the draftees being processed in the main hall.

Six or seven very official-looking soldiers filed in, with ribbons and badges and crisp-looking uniforms.

I was told to stand right behind a piece of yellow tape on the floor. One soldier pointed it out. The floor was just nondescript linoleum of uncertain vintage, but it was also thin ice over a swiftly flowing river that led to prison and a dark, uncertain future. When I was standing where they wanted me, they all lined up about six feet in front of me and put on their service caps. The air felt heavy and serious, but snow was blowing all around me and I was very far from shore. The ice was starting to crack.

If this was about intimidation, it worked really well. I was just a skinny kid with a head full of ideas, but those ideas were more important than how scared I was, standing there on the ice. I resolved myself, fixing my mind on the people who had gone before, the people I admired for making a similar stand. I was surprised to find that my parents fell into that category.

An older guy with gold braid and a clipboard was there to administer the oath of enlistment, and the rest were present as witnesses for the inevitable court case to follow — and coincidentally, to frighten the hell out of the misguided schmuck standing in front of them. I suddenly understood the reason for this second, smaller room. No witnesses, no moral support, and no one getting any bright ideas to do the same thing.

This isolated room must have been standard procedure. Shield the other kids from anything that might give them second thoughts. Keep them ignorant and compliant until they're on the bus for boot camp. I heard an echo of my brother's voice: *Dangerous information upsets the balance of power; don't release it into the wild or we'll all reap the whirlwind.*

Except for the uniforms and the studied look on their faces, the men I was facing could have been me. They weren't much older. They had families and hopes and listened to music just as I did. They weren't much different except for the choices they'd made and which side of the yellow tape they were standing on. A character-defining choice. *We were just following orders.* The distance between Nuremberg and Leavenworth has always been just one transformational step of independent thought from the room in which we stood.

I knew about the yellow tape. Stepping over the yellow tape would take me into the Army, and if you stepped into the Army... *Abandon hope, all ye who enter here.* With my heart pounding and reminding myself why I was there and why I was not going to step forward, I stiffened my legs. I stiffened everything. I stood as still as I could.

I was wearing my uniform and they were wearing theirs. All except for that one guy with the paperwork; he was a little different. He was an officer; it showed in his age and uniform, given the number of ribbons on his chest. But I was able to identify with him too. I could have been any one of these guys in a few more years, given different circumstances.

In times of trouble we develop our own courage out of whatever works. I was there for a reason: as a witness for freedom, common sense, and to stop a war. I was shaking inside, truly frightened. But as I stood there, I kept thinking that I was doing my bit; I was contributing. And I knew it was going to cost me.

The United States of America was killing people for no reason other than ideological fear (of communism), patriotic momentum, and toxic machismo. *We're right, we're Americans, Americans are always right, and besides, a bunch of little gooks in black pajamas can't possibly win against Northrop Grumman and the United States Army.*

As I stood there in that silent room, it felt like I was facing a firing squad aimed at my brain. They didn't want me to think, they wanted me to kill or be killed. I was nervous as hell and shaking inside. The air tasted metallic—*how did I get to this point? Maybe I could be that guy who works in the prison library and goes around with the cart and hands out books...*

I was directed to raise my right hand and repeat the oath of enlistment as it was read aloud, and then to step across the yellow tape on the floor. I heard the ice crackle under my feet. One of the soldiers read the oath. I didn't raise my right hand or repeat the words. I stood very still. The soldiers stared at me. The ice continued to crack, a star of fissures scattering from beneath my shoes.

What I was doing felt unreal and a little horrifying. This moment would mean losing years of my life with no hope of carrying anything from it but the knowledge that I'd struck a blow for sanity and stood up for my convictions. Some people would hate me and think me a coward. The blood was pounding in my ears.

They waited a minute in case I wanted to change my mind. I wasn't dumb; I figured this "stage wait" was based on some statistical model that allowed sixty seconds for peer pressure and abject fear to peak in the heart of a frightened kid. Once again, the ritual was repeated. And, once again, I stood my ground. I was committed. My goose, as they say, was cooked.

The ice broke and I was falling through, plunging down into the icy waters and swift current below. The soldiers kept staring at me; I had changed myself into something different, something wild and strange, even though they must have seen this transformation many times before.

The soldiers relaxed and became regular guys again, despite their uniforms. They told me to go home, that the FBI would contact me in due time. I walked right over that yellow tape and left. Forty-five minutes was all it took, start to finish. And for a while, that was it, but the current had me; I was in its grip. *Great.* Now I get to go to prison.

Leaves of grass

I'd already been to the FBI field office at the Pruneyard Towers in Campbell. I explained my position, and I was glad I'd practiced at home, because the experience was intimidating. They listened to my presentation, but couldn't give me a timeline or court date. Of course they couldn't—the courts and the FBI were overwhelmed. Nearly a half-million men refused to register or report for induction. Many deserted right from boot camp. Some just took off for Canada.

Many of the kids who enlisted, once they were beyond basic training and in-country with their boots on the ground, shifted their thinking. The vast majority of kids my age—both boys and girls—thought the Vietnam War was immoral and wanted it stopped. Most went because they felt it was their duty to their country, then desperately wanted out after discovering what that duty entailed. I knew one person who committed suicide. A mass revolt was in progress and despite my feelings of isolation, I was right in the thick of it.

The courts were backlogged, and the government was promoting lawyers into judges as quickly as possible. Our court system was a little like "Lucy, the conveyor belt, and the chocolates," trying to put all of us through the legal process and into prison. After Oakland, I was left waiting for what I assumed would be a sentence of five years at some minimum security facility out in the middle of California, picking beets perhaps, or artichokes in season, but unlike "I Love Lucy," the sound of laughter would not accompany me into my cell each night.

This had to have been a nightmare for my parents. I was expected to take over the family business so my father could retire. How would they be able to handle it if I were in prison? My father could have kept it going for several more years, but he was already in his sixties, had endured a hell of a lot during his lifetime, and was weary.

But Edith and Ray didn't try to dissuade me. Parents all across America were coming to grips with this new reality, that if their children were expected to die in battle they also had the right to make their own decisions.

The courage to act

My path forward was not well defined. I had been writing poetry and short pieces of intellectual exploration for some time. I was also attempting to paint, first with acrylics, and then with oil. My efforts were as expected at first, tedious and dull, but I persevered against what I perceived as a decided lack of talent. I desperately wanted to respect myself for something more compelling and complex than an ability to sell typewriters and office supplies, a fate that loomed before me like a drawn-out train wreck of mediocrity.

To become a writer, an artist, a songwriter perhaps — a man of parts who created books and paintings with uncombed hair and wild abandon — that was the glue that held body and soul together. To be like any one of the writers of all those books I read. To create works of art like Turner or Van Gogh. Perhaps if I'd been a genius it might have been different, but I wasn't that. Smart, yes. Some talent, perhaps. But talent isn't always enough, no matter how earnestly we push and struggle. The tide of life is strong, and I had enough self-awareness to know there wasn't enough of the good stuff inside me to make my dreams come true in the real world.

It was a very long and draw out heartbreak, really. I had to give up on who and what I dreamed of and pick another, less interesting route—knowing that what I truly wanted was just beyond my grasp. I lived my impotence every day, like a bad memory that kept nagging at me, mocking me, and making me feel like less of a human being. My high hopes began to mock me with the knowledge of my own selfish interests. This awareness of my own inadequacy followed me around and I shared it with no one. It was embarrassing. I was no fool; I had talent. It just wasn't enough to carve a life out of thin air. I had to change the dream.

Affecting this decision was that old saying, "It's ten percent inspiration, but ninety percent perspiration." Which might or might not be true as far as I could tell. I did find out over time that the percentages weren't as important as the intent of the message; diligence pays off if there is talent in front of it, and talent can grow over time. But how quickly? I knew I wasn't going to art school, and YouTube hadn't been invented yet. If art was to be my life, I couldn't afford to be a dilettante. Art didn't pay enough soon enough unless I could get really good at something or find some sort of niche within a wider school. I wanted to follow the path blazed by people such as Bertrand Russell, who had taken his life to a much higher level.

My commitment to my parents was strong, but I didn't want to lose myself in the process of being their son. Or what would have been worse to my mind, to end up living a kind of half-life as an unknown artist, dependent on the goodwill of some lucky woman (to be named later), living out my life on wishful thinking and increasingly smaller portions of the good kind of ice cream.

In the meantime, President Nixon had just ordered the U.S. Army to invade Cambodia, widening the war into an entirely new country that had never even been part of the conversation.

As if in counterpoint, the number one song at that time was Simon and Garfunkel's *Bridge Over Troubled Water:* a hymn of sustenance and encouragement just when we needed it most. Perhaps more on point was a very different song: *I-Feel-Like-I'm-Fixin'-to-Die Rag* by Country Joe and the Fish, which immediately became an anthem for the Vietnam War.

In May, National Guard troops were called to Ohio's Kent State University to suppress a student peace rally in protest of our invasion of Cambodia. They fired tear gas and advanced with bayonets fixed. Somebody fired their rifle, and then the bullets began to fly and students fell in their tracks. The Kent State Massacre (as it came to be known) brought everything to a screaming halt as parents watched their children being gunned down on television. Everything changed.

The mood of the nation was suddenly in flux, but guys like me were still going to prison every day. I had written my letter to the Selective Service, I'd refused induction at the Oakland Induction Center, and now I was just waiting on the FBI.

Wild idea

Go to war or go to prison. It was the summer of 1970, and I was miserable. My life was about to be ruined no matter what I did, and I had plans to ruin it further. I had already refused my high school diploma, and now I had a hankering to go to prison for five years and lose my right to vote or hold public office forever. Great thinking, right? *That's it, Jonny – drive the nails deeper.*

The Vietnam War was out of control and the body bags were piling up. The U.S. Army was this monstrous sandworm, sucking all of us down. I had taken a stand to stop this star-spangled madness, but the courts were packed, and I was left drumming my fingers. I was left waiting for a court date, knowing my trial would most likely lead to a five-year prison sentence. I felt useless and alone. And that's when it hit me: to see the world (or a part of it, at least), by motorcycle.

It seemed that what I was fighting for, the freedom to make my own choices and defend myself from fools, was very abstract. I was living in a kind of philosophical bubble, disconnected from the real world. It might be a good idea to go out and see what I was fighting for: to take a trip into the heartland, travel right on through, and witness everything for myself: sunshine on my shoulders and grit in my teeth—that sort of thing.

The tension had been building for some time due to my own struggles, but now it was becoming insufferable. Tired as I was of my own conversation, my own thoughts, and the narrowing scope of my life, it became important to see rivers and mountains and new places with my own eyes. At first, it was just an idea, then it became a dream.

From early high school on, I had been working to bootstrap myself into a greater existence, but now I felt blocked, trapped. All those books I was reading, all the music I listened to—there was more to life than what I had, and I wanted it. Not for money or social reasons, but for an undefined motive that touched on exploration and self-respect.

Glen had once told me that I was the only person he knew who did pure thought for its own sake. I wanted to have that tone for the rest of my life and I wanted to put it to some use. If I couldn't be an artist, perhaps I could be that. I was carving my own life from driftwood and rocks I found lying about in plain view. Not well, as I didn't have the dexterity yet, but I was making an effort. And if Glen respected me for it, that was good enough to go along with.

This trip would be part of that effort in its own way, like a painting or a novel, but created in the moment, and experienced just as it happened. One massive push to express who I could be without the overlay of fear and rebellion that had been dogging me for these past few years. It was time to bang the drum. I wanted to try my hand at experiential art without thought or plan, an expression of angst, joy, and grandeur on the largest canvas of all: life and life only.

To go or not to go? Making the decision to actually leave the comfort of ongoing inertia seemed impossible. Protesting the draft hadn't been easy, but it had been clear-cut; it was a moral decision for which I'd been preparing a long time. This held no such consequences. It had no such history. It seemed that my life had become the Hamlet-Ophelia dichotomy writ small. Was I to remain passive and frustrated, or act on my intentions despite the consequences? I was a kid on a mission, belittled by doubt. And then Suzy came up with her own, homemade intervention.

Push comes to shove

I was living with my brother Glen and his wife Sue in the Willow Glen area of San José at that time. I was not the best company then; there didn't seem to be anything I could do about my standoff with the military, and it rankled like hell. I kept talking about taking a trip, going off on a motorcycle, wandering the highways and byways, because anything like that seemed so romantic and impossible, yet irresistibly wonderful and free. I made myself ridiculous, with Glen and Sue as silent witness.

We were sitting at the coffee table in the living room; Sue was on the couch. I had been wondering (yet again) why I felt so lost when Suzy perked up.

"I have something I want to say," she said. She was sitting on the couch, a scotch in one hand, a cigarette in the other. I looked at her. Glen looked at her. Sue put her book down, crushed out her cigarette in that orange glass ashtray they had, and looked down for a moment as if marshaling her thoughts.

Glen and I just looked up at her. Sue commonly makes pronouncements when she stands up. Or rather, she stands up, says what's on her mind, and then heads into the kitchen. Like tossing a verbal grenade into the room, then walking out; it's kind of how she is, so that's what I expected.

"Jon," she said, "Dear Jon. You've been sitting here day after day complaining about your situation, saying that you'd like to take off on a motorcycle or whatever, but you're not doing anything about it. And I love you dearly, you know that, but..." And here she paused. "But I want you out of the house. Really. I'm kicking you out. I'm sorry, but that's it."

My heart skipped a beat. I looked from Sue over to Glen; this was more than a little strange. Sue never acted like this; it wasn't her way. Glen looked at me over his glasses; he didn't know any more than I did. *Oh shit.* I'd seen this movie before. I've *been* in this movie before.

Sue said, "I'm giving you notice; I'm giving you a month or whatever it takes, but I want you out. I'm sorry. I love you, you know that, but you have to get out and either go on your motorcycle trip or do whatever you want to do, but you have to leave. Now. Or maybe not now, but very soon, and I absolutely mean it. I'm dead serious. You can't just mope around; it's getting ridiculous. I'm tired of you sitting here, waiting for the damn FBI to show up."

And in that heart-stopping moment, I realized that I could stay or leave, accept her challenge or not. The room fell silent. It was like the last scene in *Casablanca* after Bogart's hill of beans speech with all that fog. I looked at Glen, he looked at Suzy, and Suzy looked at me. *The engines were revving up.*

"Okay," I said, "I'll go." Simple, earth-shaking words.

In my life I have had one absolutely scary great adventure that took the kind of courage we've all read about in books. And Sue was the one who got me to stare into the mist and take that first step. She overcame her own reticence and fought for me when I didn't know how to fight for myself.

My mother had got me to love reading, an endless internal adventure. My father had taught me to appreciate quality and precision. My brother had shared his ability to think critically. But it was Suzy who thwacked me upside the head and got me to get off my ass and do something in the real world. Instead of gray cement and razor wire, I found an open road that ran flat out into the unknown.

The Wet Shoe Journals
9,847 Miles by Motorcycle

Kickstart 181
- Day 1 Campbell, CA ~ Gentlemen, start your engines 193
- 2 Jackson, CA ~ Settling in 206
- 3-4 Lake Tahoe, CA ~ Camp Miller 207
- 5 Lassen Nat'l Park, CA ~ Siskiyou primæval 212
- 6 Central Point, OR ~ Mel's Diner 217
- 7 Burns, OR ~ How to pitch a tent in a monsoon 223
- 8 Boise, ID ~ Shunned by Chevron, Giant water fountain 231
- 9 Arco, ID ~ Only hippie in the Midwest 238
- 10-12 Yellowstone Nat'l Park, WY ~ Lynn's mom, Dodging bison 243
- 13 Grand Tetons Nat'l Park, WY ~ America, Love it or Leave It ... 253
- 14 Riding the I-90, SD ~ Arapaho, Cheyenne, and Dakota 254
- 15-16 Wind Cave National Park, SD ~ Wind Cave, Helmets stolen ... 255
- 17 Rapid City, SD ~ Wall Drug, Baby sharks 257
- 18 Sioux Falls, SD ~ Camping on cement, Bathroom huddle 261
- 19 Jackson, MN ~ Falling down, Lineman's basement digs 263
- 20 Madison, WI ~ A night behind bars 269
- 21-22 Elmhurst, IL ~ Chicago crash | Neefe rescue, The Girl in Blue .. 273
- 23 Coldwater, MI ~ Homeless shelter 283
- 24 Canada & Buffalo, NY ~ Overnight at the Isralows 285
- 25 Syracuse, NY ~ Story, song, sleep at Syracuse University 289
- 26 Boston, MA ~ Sleeping on broken glass & dugout cops 292
- 27 Riding I-95 into Maine ~ Toes to the briny 294
- 28-34 New Haven, CT ~ Jim Miller, Missing girl, Boogie Woogie 297
- 35 New York, NY ~ Kazoo concert, Empire State Building 302
- 36 New Haven, CT ~ Rainy day women & blues 308
- 37 New London, CT ~ Smuggled into a women's dorm 308
- 38 Amherst, MA ~ Frat house roof girls 309
- 39 Stamford, CT ~ Hampshire College 309
- 40-44 Watkins Glen, NY ~ United States Grand Prix 312
- 45 Cleveland, OH ~ Broken chain, Refused service again 321
- 46 Route 66 into Missouri ~ 572 miles in 7 hours at 81 mph 326
- 47 Tulsa, OK ~ Sleet, black ice, and the Water Absorption Ratio ... 329
- 48 Oklahoma City, OK ~ Hobbies, Inc. 331
- 49-50 Route 66 through the New Mexico & Arizona deserts 335
- 51-52 Sand City, Los Gatos & Willow Glen, CA ~ Home 338

Map & Legend 348

Kickstart

Once I'd made the decision to go, everything fell into place. I had to polish up and sell my car, a Triumph GT6, so I could purchase a lightly used Honda CL350 motorcycle, outfit it, and have enough funds to get me down the road. It took three weeks to get ready. I left the bulk of my money at home so my father could wire funds when I needed cash.

I had been riding for several years, but only smaller bikes. I'd learned to ride when my cousin David and I rented a couple of small motorcycles and rode them around a parking lot near his home in Mill Valley, California. I think I was sixteen at the time, and a learner's permit was good enough.

Later, I had a 90cc Suzuki, which had been given to me as a basket case. Literally, a box of parts, an engine that wouldn't start (the piston rings were shot), and a rolling frame. I rebuilt the bike, then rode on side streets and down in the creek bed when I lived with Glen and Sue; their house in Willow Glen backed up to Los Gatos Creek. The Honda had almost four times the engine size and power, and about twice the frame weight of that little Suzuki.

Until this point, I'd never gone beyond the local neighborhood by motorcycle. This was a real leap for me, and the more I thought about an extended journey without a specific goal, the more I got to thinking how empty the open road might feel, traversing the never-never map of America's red, blue, and gray lines.

Riding partner

Couching my idea in snappy terms (adventure, finding what's out there, what have you got to lose?), I got in touch with a friend I'd not seen in a number of years and talked him into going with me. Tom Duncan had been attending San Diego

State University, but was open to the idea. He had a job waiting for him a few months later, and the timing seemed right.

Tom Duncan conformed, as nearly as a human being could, to the definition of a straight line with a brain. From boyhood, he had grown like a weed, till he gave people the idea that if he stood still, you might miss him entirely. But he rarely stood still, and when he spoke, it usually meant something. Often enough, he was funny in an obscure, dryly observational way, which made him handy to have around.

Kid stuff

I met Tom in the seventh grade at R.J. Fisher middle school. We both happened to take drafting from Mr. Greewall, we were both interested in Formula 1 racing and European — that is to say — *real* sports cars, and we hit it off.

Our prime focus was on European cars built between WWII and the late 1960s — mostly English. Roadsters with two seats, a canvas top, manual gearbox, and plastic side curtains.

Triumph, MG, Austin Healey, Jaguar, Morgan, Lotus, Aston Martin, Ferrari. Most of these were way too rich for my teenage budget, but I managed to buy a (Bugeye) Austin Healey Sprite as my second car. Tom soon had a newer version by the same marque: the Sprite Mk.II. We shared our enthusiasm for driving, and took pride in our discernment and appreciation for that sort of engineering and design.

Tom lived up on Oak Grove Avenue. It's one of the streets off of College, where it goes up into the hills below the Sacred Heart Novitiate. Tom and I used to go hiking up along the Los Gatos flume behind his house. The flume was a large half-pipe covered with boards, making a wooden walkway that snaked along the wall of the canyon created by Los Gatos Creek, carrying water down from Lexington Reservoir. There were sheer drops of a hundred feet or more in various places. It was visible to anyone driving along Highway 17 as a line along the cliff face.

Tom once told me that in the silence of the night he sometimes heard car accidents from across the creek on 17. The noise came from near the Cats Restaurant. It was dangerous getting back onto the Santa Cruz highway after dinner.

"I could hear the screech of cars braking, and then sometimes the crump when they hit and the sound of a hubcap rolling. And then, five minutes later, I would hear the sirens." Tom learned to sleep with his radio on.

Tom had a sharp eye for the kind of detail most people paid little attention to, which would help him become an award-winning photographer later in life. He asked questions and made wry, often funny observations. There was often a small bemused chuckle when he spoke. When a line had been crossed or some ridiculous behavior was under discussion, there it was.

That I had initiated the trip was an odd reversal for the two of us. Tom was a natural instigator, always ready to get out and do things. I was often buried in a book somewhere, dreaming of being a writer or an artist. But this time was different. We had not seen each other or spoken much during the second half of our high school years, mainly because I hadn't been at school all that much. When I called Tom to invite him on this trip, it was two years after *that*.

The passing of time had made little difference. We each knew who we were and what we stood for. I was also pretty sure from our days with sports cars and learning how to drive that our mutual trust and friendship would come right back. We were a bit fuzzier perhaps, and not as buttoned-down, but probably closer in temperament than we had been in grade school.

I had never shared my deep dive into folk music and literature or my resistance to the war with anyone other than family, and yet Tom seemed familiar with much of what I'd been studying and what I was striving towards. We were on the same page of the same book, and that made a huge difference.

By the beginning of 1970, I had draft number 83. Tom told me later that he had 296 — the highest number called that year was 215. My number was up. His wasn't. It was random, like which rifle has the real bullet, but we both knew the score.

At speed

Tom and I studied car magazines and became familiar with race car drivers such as Jim Clark, Dan Gurney, Jackie Stewart,

Ken Miles, Graham Hill, and John Surtees. We read accounts of Grand Prix, Gran Turismo, and sports car races, which took us lap-by-lap through spilled oil, race team politics, and design characteristics. We went together and with others to sports car races at Laguna Seca, within driving distance down along the California coast near Monterey. But neither of us had been to a Formula 1 event or a GT race like the 12 Hours of Sebring or the 24 Heures du Mans, with its legendary Mulsanne Straight.

We were not particularly interested in NASCAR or oval-track racing such as the Indy 500, since such events favored a heavy foot over driving skill, and cubic inches over engineering.

Tom and I were both learning to drive, and we wanted to know how to drive *quick*. Quick (as opposed to quickly) means braking and down-shifting into turns, clipping the apex, and powering out with the pedal floored. It means reacting in the moment and leaving nothing to chance. It means driving with deliberation and grace, and out-driving other, more powerful cars in less capable hands.

Tom and I got a few books such as *The Art and Technique of Driving* by Pat Moss and Erik Carlsson, which showed us with text and photos how to heel-and-toe, how to double-clutch, how to measure the curve ahead with our eyes, looking for the apex (always watching for wet leaves of course, which could easily send us flying off into history), and how to perform a controlled four-wheel drift. I even learned the art of the hand-brake turn, not that I ever used it.

By practicing over and over, we hoped to translate such techniques into muscle memory and instinctive ability. The Japanese have a word for it: *kaizen*, constant and never-ending improvement. We knew that if we focused everything we had on each skill, we could do everything just a bit better each time and improve our technique.

It took excellent reflexes, hand-eye coordination, inner-ear sensitivity (to measure momentum, positive and negative acceleration, and centripetal force), plus a good sense of distance and timing. Judgement and courage underpinned everything, and a bit of self-humor didn't hurt. Getting frustrated just meant we weren't learning from our mistakes. Much of what we were doing could be developed, but some of it was innate.

I learned how to drift through corners in a little area of interconnected streets near our house. The streets had just been repaved by putting a hot tar slurry down on top of the existing tarmac, then fine gravel on top. The cars driving along pressed the gravel into the tar and made the surface firm. That was the theory of it, but there was more than enough gravel and the road crew hadn't cleaned up the extra yet when I discovered this new playground.

I drove my Bugeye over and over through those streets. I slid around and through that neighborhood for several days, developing my skills. All very fun and exciting for a sixteen-year-old kid. Went through a brand-new set of Perelli soft-compound tires that year.

Tom and I chased each other through the hills of Los Gatos, frightening half the population into an early decline. We aspired to greatness, and we wanted to drive as well as could be done — with brio and élan. There was joy in mastery. Being that alive and the best we could be.

There were moments that tested our mettle, to show us what we had inside. Sustained concentration, grace under pressure, and the ability to measure distance and speed without thinking. Those were the hallmarks we strove for. Each of us found out in our own way whether we could take in all the various bits of information at once, from our car, the road, the traffic pattern, the weather and surface conditions, and translate all of that into decisive action.

With Tom, it was up on Reservoir Road in his Sprite Mk. II with his friend Bill Potter as passenger when (at speed) they suddenly came upon a garbage truck blocking the road. Tom calmly powered through a gap between the truck and the canyon wall with nothing to spare.

"I was able to gestalt the moment, including our lives. There was enough room, and I punched it without emotion. It was then that I knew."

With me it happened rather memorably on the Pacific Coast Highway. With cliffs going up to the sky on my right and all the way down to the ocean and rocks on my left, I suddenly had to slalom across traffic and all the way over to the wrong side apron for just long enough to avoid a head-on with some idiot who hadn't looked long enough before attempting to pass. I didn't think. I just did.

About motorcycles

Tom Rodgers, one of Tom's friends on Oak Grove Avenue, owned a Honda 305 Superhawk, which helped Tom decide on that model. Rodgers helped Tom purchase the bike, and since Tom had never ridden a motorcycle (and didn't have a license), he rode it back to the house in Campbell for him.

Tom had just a few days to learn. At that time in California, a simple two-part test was required to get your license endorsed with M/C in fine print, at which point you were grandfathered in as a licensed rider for the rest of your life. There was a written test with ten rather obvious, common-sense questions, and then a riding test out in the DMV parking lot.

After Tom bought his bike (which I had to ride home for him), he practiced for a few days, then took the test and got his license updated. Our bikes were not large, but easy to ride. Both had been previously owned but were still in very good condition with not more than a couple of years on them. They were modern bikes in that they had electric starters, but sadly, no fuel gauges. We used our odometers as a guide, but often peeked inside the tank to make sure. While standing, we would jostle our bikes left and right to get the gas to slosh a bit so we could see how much was left.

Motorcycles at that time were classified into five groups: street bikes, cruisers, choppers, dirt bikes, and café racers (in the order of popularity at the time). There is more variety now than in 1970, but the general classifications are quite similar.

Street bikes are made for regular street and freeway riding. Larger than scooters and smaller than cruisers, they are general-purpose bikes and the most common in use. They come in two varieties. Standard bikes are geared and tuned for general all-around motoring and are designed for an upright riding position, with larger gas tanks, lower gearing, and exhaust pipes tucked low under the bike on either side. Street scramblers have the same riding position, but rev higher at the same speed, have higher exhaust pipes (along one side), accelerate quicker, and are not as comfortable for distance riding due to the higher pitch and vibration. They weigh in at about half that of a large cruising bike, such as a Harley.

Touring and cruisers are for long-distance riding and are easier on the lower back, which can take a pounding on long rides. They include Harley-Davidson, BMW, Triumph, Moto Guzzi, and the touring class Hondas, Yamahas, and Suzukis. They weigh between seven and nine hundred pounds, including windshields and saddlebags. I rode a 1978 Harley Electra-Glide once. Like a pig on ice. Well, perhaps not that bad, but in order to manhandle it properly, I would have needed another ten inches in height, two hundred pounds in net weight, and the upper body strength of a far more robust individual. So, not qualified. I learned to never ride a bike I couldn't get back up at night in a rainstorm.

Choppers are custom-modified cruisers, usually Harleys, and quite distinctive. They usually have extended forks to keep the steering straight at high speed, but that also makes them difficult to maneuver in parking lots and campgrounds where a tight turning radius is imperative. Think of the film, *Easy Rider*.

Dirt bikes are just what they sound like: off-road trail bikes with distinctively high mudguards and minimal sound dampening. They often have two-stroke engines, which rev higher and faster.

Café racers are lightweight, powerful street bikes of a casual coolness that mimic racing motorcycles. They are optimized for quick handling and bursts of high speed. Visualize Tom Cruise being chased by bad guys.

Tom and I rode regular street bikes. Tom's was a black Honda 305 Superhawk, and I rode a blue Honda CL350. They were popular street bikes of that era. The 350 was able to travel 130 miles on 2.4 gallons and weighed 328 pounds without rider. The Superhawk was able to travel 230 miles on 3.6 gallons and weighed 350 pounds. Both had turn signals and electric starters (in addition to the kickstarter), but no fuel gauges, windscreens, or radios.

Honda 305 Superhawk ~ 350 lbs.

Honda CL350 Scrambler ~ 328 lbs.

Riding regular street bikes instead of much larger cruisers contributed greatly to the texture and safety of our journey. Larger motorcycles would have provided more comfort with windscreens and dampening of vibration through sheer mass, but we wouldn't have been able to pick them up again when we had to, at least not on our own. Cruisers aren't very nimble, either. Dodging cars and negotiating tight corners was an issue for both of us on several occasions. Just getting through a parking lot can be daunting, and we weren't always on paved roads with easy turning points and clear lines of sight.

We also would have been treated differently by the people we met (and by the police). Our bikes were non-threatening because they were common as dirt, inexpensive to own, and everyone knew they weren't that difficult to ride. And as odd as this may sound, we were given a measure of respect for the distance we traveled the further we were from California, at least in part because of our unassuming street bikes. We were barn-storming America on Hondas, and we looked the part. People didn't have to guess much about who we really were, which takes fear out of the equation. In all those ways, our mid-sized street bikes were perfect for the journey.

Parlance

It's a minor thing, but you don't drive a motorcycle; you *ride* it. You never sit *on* a motorcycle, you sit a motorcycle. It's just like with a horse. You sit a horse; you don't sit *on* it, and you don't drive one either. Motorcycles are often referred to as bikes. Probably from motorbike out of bike from bicycle, but who knows the derivation—the words are interchangeable.

Riding

With the wind in your face and the sun on your back, motorcycles can be a wonderful and exhilarating adventure. You're in the world and of the world, and everything is immediate. You aren't in a big metal box with cushion-soft tires, air conditioning, and power steering; you're riding a far more spirited machine. You don't just ride on top of a motorcycle; you embrace it with your body. Such a melding of man and metal becomes an extension of your thinking. You steer a motorcycle almost unconsciously, as much with your body as with your arms and hands, leaning into every curve as you come upon it.

Twist the throttle and suddenly the flesh | metal unit you've become snaps with instant acceleration. The power-to-weight ratio is much closer to that of a Formula 1 car than that Chevy or Toyota blocking your lane, and you are far more nimble. You can whip around corners, shoot through and past the sluggish automobiles that surround you, and ride on to glory.

There is not much to do on a motorbike but stay in control and observe the world you're passing through. There were no rider-to-rider radios built into helmets at the time of our trip, and no cell phones. If one of us wanted to pull over, it meant hand signals—sometimes frantic ones! It also meant we were always vulnerable. We couldn't call for help if something went wrong. And one of us couldn't ride off in a huff. It was two for one and one for both, all the time.

As Tom put it years later, "What we were doing was incredibly dangerous. No cell phones, no radios. The fact that there were two of us was great, but if one of us went down and the rider in front didn't notice how empty his rear-view mirror had become...."

You ponder all sorts of things while riding: your life up to that point, your life going forward, what the next town will look like, that guy you're traveling with, and the imaginary road map of where you might be going, floating forever in your head. And these thoughts aren't always concrete and discrete or even identifiable, but rather amorphous clouds of contemplation that overlap in multiple ways and pop in and out of existence as you buzz along.

And then there's rain

Riding in the rain is treacherous beyond all imagination, and anxiety goes to a whole new level. Snow or sleet is worse. The same goes for swimming out into the ocean when sharks are in the water. It might be okay... then again, it might not. Just like the sharks, rain has no sympathy.

There is always a film of oil on the road, feathering out to the edges, and you only have two tires. Rain makes that oil as slick as teflon. If you lose it, you don't spin off the road, you crash off the road. If there is a bump you become airborne. You go down *hard*, and somehow it hurts far worse because of how cold you are.

It's risky to change direction or speed in the rain. Sudden movements, slinky weaving, and hard breaking don't work; all that kind of riding is deadly. Riding in the dry is one thing, and on the open road without traffic on a good day, you can enjoy the heat of the sun from a blue sky, the view, and the wind. But riding through rain, snow, hail, or sleet isn't like that. You smell the rain, and you can feel it hitting your body, and you even get the grandeur of nature because you're immersed in it. But that's where it ends. On a scale of one to ten, your attention level gets pegged at ten and stays there, because that's how you get to stay alive.

Rain is unavoidable on an extended trip with no planned stops. So you ride through it, but you ride slower than you normally would, and you're always searching down the road for problems. Inexperienced riders often get into trouble because they just haven't survived enough mistakes to know what trouble looks like before it's too late. Without riding experience, you have no riding wisdom—no muscle memory to get you out of trouble quickly.

On the other hand, there's death

Because you can get killed. Death is right there, always. Messing up on a motorcycle is not the same as messing up in a car. If you have an accident, you are twenty-five times more likely to die, and injury is axiomatic. The pavement is right there under your feet, like a belt-sander of death. Although you'd never understand the peril without having had some real riding experience, because after you know the controls and have had some practice, it seems effortless. But one wrong move and you merge your DNA firmly with the road's, which is why you wear a helmet with a Snell Foundation rating, dress in robust clothing, and ride as defensively as possible.

You are in control of a machine with a power-to-weight ratio far beyond what most people have ever experienced. The smell of hot metal and rubber, the resistance of the brake lever, the slam of power that jolts the bike forward, all combine into an amalgam of flesh, metal, noise, wind, and vibration.

Riding a motorcycle is unique unto itself and unknowable to the outside world. In that bubble of energy and time, you are truly invincible, no matter your failings. You are the lightning bearer—and you are doomed. If you ride long enough something very bad is almost certain to happen. Motorcycles are a solitary endeavor, and the experience enhances life *and* death in a singular way.

Prep work

We had racks behind our seats and backpacks with aluminum hiking frames attached with bungee cords to hold all our food, extra clothing, and cooking gear. We each had a down sleeping bag in a stuff sack, which we strapped to our front suspension or at the small of our backs. Tom had a blue two-man tent, which he usually strapped to his front forks. Bell helmets with visors, jackets and jeans, hiking boots, padded riding gloves, and Buck hunting knives on our belts. We wore scarves around our faces, tied like a bandanna at the back of the neck; they kept the bugs out and warmed our faces when the wind was cold or freezing. I had an old plaid scarf my brother had used when he went to school in Chicago, sort of tan in color. Still have it. Tom fashioned his out of white cloth.

The way we were

We looked scruffy but sincere, and to most eyes, benign. We might have been more comfortable with flight suits from army surplus or full leathers, but they would have been difficult to take on and off and might have changed first impressions. As it was, we looked like anybody's brother or son—in need of a hot shower perhaps, but nothing to be worried about.

Tom had an inexpensive acoustic guitar strapped on top of everything else behind him on the bike, (sound hole up, neck pointing back), into which he put his innumerable gum wrappers, which I thought casually irreverent. Near Yellowstone, we got two bumper-stickers and pasted them on either side of the soundbox—visible as we rode. *One said America, Love It or Leave It,* and the other said *I'm Proud To Be An American.* Riding through semi-hostile territory, we thought it might be advantageous to assume native coloration.

Safety affected our route as well. We purposefully did not travel through the Deep South because we had very real concerns. If you weren't local and something went wrong or there was a misunderstanding, it could get very bad, very fast. We probably would have been just fine, but accidents happen, and even one failure to communicate could have been catastrophic. So, first rule in life: don't poke at it.

Tim Schenk was a friend of ours from school whose family had a small house in Campbell. Tom had been staying with Tim after hearing from me and coming up from San Diego. I had started living there as well just prior to the start of our trip. So, it was Tim's driveway we rode from that first morning: Butch and Sundance on a couple of Hondas.

August 23, 1970 was a bright, sunshiny day, as good as any other. We were ready to go. We had no idea what we were getting into, but we were going to do it anyway. I took the leap, trusting the net would appear beneath me.

The Wet Shoe Journals
9,847 Miles by Motorcycle

Day 1   Sunday, August 23, 1970 – Campbell, California

"Ready?"

Tom looked up and gave a nod. I pulled the bungee cord tighter and hooked it, then got back on my bike. We had checked our packs for the last time. I put on my helmet, threaded the strap, and snugged it. This was it. We started our motorcycles with a raspy rumble, snicked into first gear, and accelerated away. Just two guys on a couple of Hondas.

The freeway was the quickest way out of town, traveling north across the foothills toward the city of Pleasanton. Our initial goal was to visit Tom's mother, then go northeast, up to a property near Jackson where we could stay. The ride was uneventful and somewhat tedious, coping with freeway traffic and iffy drivers. Sunday was a good day to start: fewer cars. Tom was new to riding, and I was aware of that. I kept him in sight as best I could during that first day. It was a bright day.

On a motorcycle, you're immersed in life and everything is louder, brighter, quicker, and ridiculously dangerous. You pay attention to small things. Traffic and noise and vibration and road signs are everywhere, but so is solitude. You're very much alone in your thoughts: King of the World, flying through like some Norse god. That's what it felt like that day in August.

Alive and kicking, screaming—being me, myself, and I for the first time in a long time. The summer air was perfect and the edge of the unknown filled me up. I saw everything, felt everything. Our best moments happen when we stretch ourselves to the limit of what we can accomplish. That was me in the moment, with a deep satisfaction for riding along the edge of my own tomorrow, reckless with life..

The pavement was right beneath our feet, a gigantic belt sander made of rocks and tar and the flickety-flick of that blurry white line to our left. The road's texture hummed through the frame of our bikes as we polished out the minutes and miles, from coarse to smooth, then back to coarse, with sporadic rocks and debris for the occasional bump and thrill.

That first hour was a jumble inside. Feet hot and shoulders tight. Ski gloves shock-absorbed my arms from some of the hammering, but the dull roar of it still got through.

The draft board, the FBI, Tom riding behind me, doing his best to be a friend. *What had I talked him into? Oh hell, he can take care of himself.* I had a vague notion of America's Midwest out in front of us somewhere. *How far will we get?*

The emptiness and cornfields of my imagination stretched out into a fuzzy middle distance until skyscrapers suddenly loomed up in New York City like one of those Hallmark popup cards with a million tiny little windows and millions of people in grey suits going to and fro. And maybe a woman in a bright orange scarf or a kid in a wheelchair. Throw in a couple of Great Lakes and a few prickly pear cacti down in Texas, and that's all I knew. Oh, and a baleful shark—hungry, and cruising the coast of Florida with impassive eyes. *What the hell was I doing?*

The road was a promise—of hope, of renewal, of redemption and truth. I was excited and horrified by my own actions, but I was doing it anyway. *Shit, they could all go to hell. I had to get out and clear my head.* My world was a box so tight and full of doubt I could hardly breathe. *What if we die out here, or get maimed? Well, I wouldn't have to go to prison. Ha ha, Jon. Laugh it up.*

Tom had called his mom before we left, so she knew we were on our way. June. Her name was June. Pleasanton wasn't far. A good first stage. We found it, found the right street. Click went our kickstands in her driveway, and I was feeling proud of myself for having gotten us this far without falling off or smacking into something. Two teenage girls came running out to greet us. Oh god... women. I kind of knew it, but hadn't thought it through—that half the people on the planet were women and I'd have to deal with them at some point, since that was part of the trip too. Gorgeous, perfect in their humanity and grace and happiness, Cinda and Debbie were Tom's cousins from New Mexico.

The gravel crunched under my feet. Tom looked surprised to see them. Tan slacks and bright blouses and sharp eyes full of mischief. June Duncan, wearing a green dress, was right behind them. I had no idea what she thought of this trip; Tom was a pretty independent guy, but she was still his mom. By the time we got seated at the kitchen table, the girls were spilling out with questions.

"Where will you go?" asked Cinda. Her clear blue eyes looked from me to Tom. Now, there was a question without a good answer. One of many, perhaps.

I excused myself and jogged out to the bikes to snatch a map off the tank. This was getting very real, very fast. I came back, flattened the map to the table, and pushed it in front of Tom.

"We're riding east right now," Tom said, putting his finger on the map. But we're heading for Lake Tahoe." The girls were excited and leaned in to look. Cinda tucked a curl behind her ear. Mrs. Duncan put a plate of ham and cheese sandwiches on the table. I wasn't hungry, but you never know. I took one. I would be the quiet one, as always.

"You'll be camping?" Cinda glanced up at Tom.

"We've got sleeping bags," said Tom. "And a tent."

"Where to next?" asked her sister, looking from Tom to me. "I mean, where after Lake Tahoe?"

"North at first, and up into Oregon," I said. "Then east." Not so quiet. I stood with my feet apart with my hands on the back of a kitchen chair, ready for anything. The questions were harmless, but made me nervous. I didn't like sewing up the future. Tom followed the blue line with his finger, up and to the right, then stopped near Idaho. *Was that Idaho?* Northeast of where we were, anyway.

"After that, we're not sure," said Tom.

"We might get tired and come home," I said. *Good for me, I said something. Two things, actually. I was on a roll.*

"Or get lost in the badlands," said Tom. *True. We might die.*

"Or turn outlaw. Could go either way," I said. *Hey, I made a joke.* Tom's cousins just looked at me like I was a houseplant or something. Interesting, perhaps, but not something they'd considered before. But now it was different; I was a talking houseplant and capable of thought. Maybe I wasn't a houseplant at all, but this enigmatic guy who thought out loud from time to time and rode a motorcycle and fought windmills and stuff. Maybe I could be interesting.

"Or maybe we'll keep on riding," I added. They were lovely. And very real. He'd never mentioned cousins. Of course, I never mentioned mine either, and I had lots. It wasn't something we did. Who talks about cousins?

"Have you been planning this for a while?" asked Cinda, ignoring our back and forth. She glanced up at me and tucked that one curl back again. She looked up at Tom, but Tom was looking at me. *Time for better answers.* Holy crap, this felt like a sinkhole. I cleared my throat. I hadn't wanted to get into all the reasons and convolutedness of my life. The conversation felt risky, like getting married to someone you'd just met. If I spoke, that was like pouring cement. The whole trip was about rejecting the cement, hating the cement, breaking the cement up with a jackhammer.

"I had to do something," I said. *There it was.* Mrs. Duncan, the girls, Tom—everybody looked at me. The room got quiet. "I'm fighting the draft. I've been waiting for a court date and got the idea of doing this. To see something of the country. Before I run out of time. Before going to prison."

Short statements strung the words of my life like colored beads, small and round and plain and dangerous. I felt like a fool, like some pompous idiot. I felt like Frodo, just setting out, or maybe Huckleberry Finn on his raft. But that was backwards; I'd already been to the Cracks of Doom—that had been the yellow tape and Oakland. I'd already tossed my life into the volcano. It felt surreal, yet plain and simple.

That was it—my big speech. My voice was straight and light, but I didn't *feel* light, saying it out loud. *Shit.* I had barely told Tom this stuff, let alone anyone else, and I felt off balance, just blurting it out. Nothing to explain who I really was or why. Tom said nothing. Mrs. Duncan looked stunned. Tom would have to be my validation here: the fact that we rode together.

"How do you know you're going to prison?" asked Debbie, concerned. "Have you seen a lawyer?"

"Everybody goes to prison," I said. "I'm fighting the government. I refused. I stood there in that room while they read the thing and I refused. I think I'm going to prison." The certainty of it was right behind me all the time now, a quiet predator keeping tabs. A backpack at full weight.

"Well, I hope you don't," said Mrs. Duncan. She smiled at me. So she was in favor. No objections, anyway. Tom didn't look worried.

"How long will you be gone?" asked Debbie.

"I've got a job interview at Sugar Bowl in late October," said Tom. "Ski resort. So that gives me a couple of months."

Everybody looked at everybody, but I didn't say anything else. I'd poured enough cement for one afternoon. Actually, it was fine. I was full of potential, on the edge of something bright and dangerous. It felt good. I was okay with it.

Lunch over, we went back outside, our boots rattling the pebbles in the driveway. It was a gorgeous afternoon. We still had miles to go and started saying our goodbyes. Cinda stood ten feet away and took a picture of us next to the bikes with her Instamatic. *Click.* "You can stay at our place if you ever get to Albuquerque," she said. So somewhere there is a photo of us on that day, of what they'd witnessed.

Gloves on, zippers up. Tom and I leaned down to turn our petcocks to the *on* position, and started our engines. We adjusted helmets and threaded straps through D-rings under chins as Mrs. Duncan and the girls watched.

"That's right," shouted Debbie. "You'll be welcome. I'm sure Mom and Dad would put you up, and we can show you around. You can see the sights!"

Everybody waved.

One last look at Tom's family standing there, and I toggled first gear with the toe of my boot: *clunk*. Trees threw dappled shadows on both sides of the street. We eased our clutches out and bumped over the lip of the drive, crunching into the street. And then we were gone, moving through the air like two acrobats on metal horses.

Our visit had been a callback to earlier times whenever Mrs. Duncan called her son "Tommy." It was her way of showing affection, and I remembered that tone, that voice, that habit of being. It was always present between them whenever she spoke his name. *I shifted into third.* And somehow I had always felt included. Not directly, but as Tom's friend. It's funny how families can have different cultures, like different parts of the country. In my family, everyone was on a first-name basis. Edith and Ray were my parents, so that's what I called them, what I'd always called them, even as a child. *Stoplight. Waiting. Back into first, release the clutch and brake, signal, turning right, heading for the freeway. Follow the big green signs.*

I'd been to Tom's house often enough in the 60s. Tom and I used to watch *The Man from U.N.C.L.E.* and similar fare on their living room floor. *I snicked it into second gear, then third, Tom right behind me.* On our stomachs with couch pillows and Super Dupers, which was a concoction we used to make by stirring a packet of unsweetened Grape Kool-Aid (enough to make one gallon of regular Kool-Aid or choke a small child to tears), along with a half-cup of sugar over cracked ice and water in a tall glass. *Up the ramp and onto the freeway, fifth gear and staying in the right lane, Tom steady in the mirror.* Mrs. Duncan always gave us those long soda fountain spoons for our Super Dupers.

California freeways sometimes weave through and around large cities like sailor's knots, with road signs on top of road signs. Riding through the asphalt entanglements was a nightmare, but ended once we got out of the Bay Area. Traffic was less congested and there was more room for us to ride. It was wonderful to get off the interstate and start traveling through the texture of smaller towns and farmland.

After our visit with Mrs. Duncan and Tom's cousins, we rode east through Livermore, then northeast on Route 50, past Tracy, and into Manteca on Route 99. A cattle truck trundled by, with its very large smell of very large animals. *Whew.* I could see right through it, see the shapes of the cows between the slats. On its way to Stockton probably, in addition to all the usual suspects: the Toyotas and Chevies, plus every Ford truck with a gun rack that ever carried a bale of hay. We buzzed along.

This was wine- and table-grape farmland, hot and dusty, where Cesar Chávez had helped lift thousands of field hands out of abject poverty with his union. I remembered the boycott. It had been in the newspapers, and everyone got behind it. Supporting the braceros was the right thing to do. We just didn't eat grapes for four years.

Route 99 went into and through the city of Manteca. The highway curved right to go straight into the middle of town on city streets, then came to a full stop and took a hard left at the traffic light—red, yellow, green. Then down a few more blocks, and right again with a windbreak of dusty trees before widening back into a regular highway, like an elongated stair step, or chicane. It was one of those highways that slowed down, turned into a street, and went right through the middle of town, keeping their main drag alive.

It was the commercial street of any small town at that time, lined with a jumble of low-rise buildings, their pastel façades weathered by time. The storefronts were as individual as people. Most looked happy enough, with some more tired than others. Cars rumbled the asphalt, pedestrians walked the sidewalk. The sun beat down, casting short shadows on sidewalks where people got in and out of parked cars, in and out of buildings. It was a scene of quiet routine, the heartbeat of a community pulsing steadily through its day.

I glanced from one side of the street to the other as we rode. My family owned an office supply store in a downtown much like this one, so it was a place I understood. I'd dressed the windows and stocked the shelves. I'd rung up sales and carried out the trash. We passed a Mode O'Day dress shop: pastel and upbeat. Then Sunshine Alley bowling, with four large diamonds as a grand design over the entrance, as if it were wearing a giant argyle sweater. It seemed odd to have a bowling alley right downtown. Then the Manteca barber shop with a bright yellow sign. A tired-looking letter R was tipped sideways, about to fall off onto the sidewalk. The El Rey theater was showing a western: *Monte Walsh,* starring Lee Marvin.

Over all of this was something else that declared beyond any doubt we were in the middle of agricultural California; the Manteca Feedlot by Spreckels Sugar. It gave off the rich odor of endless manure and a reminder that life wasn't perfect.

I pulled into a Shell station by the traffic light, Tom right behind me. Four gas pumps, and I rolled to the last one, near the building, and shut down my bike. I dismounted and set the kickstand next to a slick of black oil. Tom walked his bike to the pump behind mine. His Superhawk had a larger tank, so I was often first to pull over.

We took off our helmets and looked around. The day was warm and held the smell of raw gasoline and exhaust, with enough eau de hot rubber and old farm truck (along with the unseen but ever-present feedlot), to give the still air a strong aroma to mark this place and time.

Between the constant sound and vibration of our motorcycles and the insulation of our helmets, everything external to our own thoughts was naturally muted while we rode, but with the bikes shut down and standing there, all the sounds native to this corner of the universe filled the air—small gravel movements, the metallic clanks and tinks associated with filling stations: engine noises and tires crunching, the murmur of voices, the sudden bright *ting* of a dropped tool, and the classic double-ding of another truck rolling in for a fill-up.

"We've got another hour before we reach Jackson," I said. "Then a twenty minute ride after that. You doing okay?"

"I'm fine." Tom looked over his glasses at me and made Expression #3: annoyance.

"What?"

"Drivers are idiots."

"Yep. Did you see that guy in the red Ford—talking with his hands? I try to stay out of their way."

An attendant turned on the pumps for us with that special key they always carried. We glanced around the station while fueling our bikes. Tom turned and gave me a wry smile.

"You could do that."

"Do what?"

"Be a gas station attendant." Tom pointed to a sign that read "Help Wanted" in the station window.

"You're kidding."

"No—you'd be great." Tom looked at me and grinned. "You could run around with that little key and make people happy all day."

Tom continued, sizing up the customers with humor. "At some point, they'd notice your zeal, and you'd get promoted."

"Promoted to what?"

"Station Manager."

"Station Manager?" This was getting ridiculous.

"Yep. And all your friends would show up looking for a discount."

"I don't think so." I acted horribly offended.

"You wouldn't give them a discount?"

"Why should I? I'm in this to make money."

"Well, how about people from back home? Would you give them a discount?"

"Of course not."

"Family?"

"No way." I puffed out my chest and looked at Tom with mock disdain. "Are you kidding? Family pays extra."

"They might have driven a very long way."

"No discounts. Totally against it." I waved my right hand down and away. "It would erode the profit margin and decay the corporate structure."

"So now you're a corporation?"

"Of course. Gold seal and everything. I'd still be humble, of course." I shuffled my feet and looked over my glasses. And there I was, on the cover of *Fill Em Up Monthly*.

"But no discounts?"

"Nope."

"Well then, I don't think you should take the job."

"Well then, I guess I won't."

"Or get promoted."

"Probably not."

"We'll just have to keep riding."

It was a big issue whether I'd end up working at our family's office supply store, probably running it someday. Tom's lighthearted joke that I might work for a gas station wasn't that far off the mark. It bothered me, not knowing what else I would do for the rest of my life. What I hungered for: to become an artist or writer—didn't seem probable given my spectacular lack of talent up to that point, and selling business machines held no sparkle as yet. Everything was up in the air, and the only things I had control over was my attitude and this trip. That Tom and I could make each other laugh was a good thing. It took the edge off.

It was two o'clock or so, and the place was busy. One car up on a rack and another had its battery being charged. Cars and trucks and middle-aged men in jeans coming and going. A lady in a bright orange dress went into the station. The attendant came around again, and we dug in our pockets for money.

After paying, we nosed a path between the cars and people, scrunched over the curb, and turned left at the light. Two blocks later we finished the Manteca chicane and accelerated back onto the open road. We headed north towards Stockton, where we would exit Route 99 onto 88, traveling northeast. I was hungry for mountains and pine trees and redwood forests, and northeast would take us there.

We were crossing the width of the huge agricultural valley that runs north to south down the middle of California—between the Pacific Coast Range and the Sierra Nevada. It would be nothing but flat roads and farmland until we got to the far side. Telephone poles, barns with fading paint, and side roads that doubled as long driveways. I saw a sign for custom hay baling, whatever that was. Maybe they put a big wire bow on it.

The small towns always looked older, and the buildings varied a lot, like Norman Rockwell paintings that had seen better days. Victorian homes with front porches and picket fences sat right next to locksmiths and grocery stores. The big supermarkets, strip malls, and mile upon mile of tract homes lined up like anonymous dominos hadn't yet blurred everything into ticky-tacky. The world we moved through was a product of the 1940s and 50s in many respects, so everywhere we went still carried its own personality. Land was cheap, friendship dear, and life had more texture. Not good texture necessarily, but a lot more of it.

I pushed thoughts about the war and my personal predicament as far from my mind as I could as we rode. I was trying to live life in the present, feeling that I needed a rest from the drudgery of such thoughts. My brief explanation at lunch with Tom's family had been a hard reminder. I knew it would come up again, but for the trip to work the way I wanted, I had to let all that stuff go. Somehow, I had to lift myself into the act of being alive without thinking about it. Like not thinking about a giraffe, I suppose. The giraffe was there and would always be there, but having it on my bike with me wasn't a good idea.

Every stop gave us a chance to stretch our legs, then share whatever thoughts we had about where we'd been and where we were headed. And fill our tanks, of course. Some stations had a few candy bars on the counter and there was usually a soda machine next to the window where you pay, but no regular food or drink. The 7-11 franchise was brand new, so convenience stores were almost non-existent. We stopped at grocery stores, which probably looked odd to the locals, since we were wearing heavy clothing and carrying helmets, but we always came out with the staples we needed. We didn't have much room in our packs, hence our reliance on eggs, canned stew, and sandwiches. Sometimes a couple of apples or bananas.

There wasn't much of a breeze, other than what we created for ourselves as we forced a passage through the air, but it carried with it the scent of wherever we were. When cattle trucks rattled by, there was a stark reminder of beef on the hoof with that earthy scent of manure, animal sweat, and hay. It wasn't a bad smell necessarily, unless we got too close, and then it could be overwhelming.

We were motoring along with me in front, our gear strapped to the backs and fronts of our bikes. The genial afternoon was at its ripest. It was one of those crisp, bracing days, and I felt at my peak: bright-eyed and bushy-tailed.

Country roads are best for riding, no matter where you are. State highways like Route 88 were okay, but there was always more traffic with a major destination ahead like Lake Tahoe, and the cars bunched up sometimes because of logging trucks.

We followed 88 into and through the small city of Jackson, where half the gold pulled from the Mother Lode had been discovered. It was home to two of the deepest mines on the planet. This rich California history was the reason my parents bought land in the area. Ray was always reading up on the gold miners and ghost towns of the Old West. I think he liked the idea of wearing khaki and squatting next to some river, panning for gold—about to hit it rich. We even had our own gold pans. And Edith taught California History to her fourth-graders. All this stuff became part of me over time. I knew more about John Sutter and his famous creek and millrace than was strictly necessary, but it was lodged in my brain and that was that.

A few miles out of Jackson, we turned onto the Pine Grove–Volcano Road and followed its winding curves through pine trees and fading sunlight to my parents' property. It was coming on early dusk when we got to the wire gate with its large round wooden posts (like sawed-off telephone poles). I'd dug the holes and painted them with creosote as a fourth-grader, helping my father. The gate was in-line with and part of the barbed-wire fence that encircled the property.

I popped the padlock with my Master 2035 key, then closed the wire gate and relocked it once we got our bikes through. We followed the dirt road to cross the weed-covered field my parents liked to call a meadow and finally shut our bikes down on the far side of their Magnolia double-wide trailer at about 6:30. We'd been on the road eight hours, with an hour for lunch.

The mood was anticlimactic. We hadn't seen or done anything in particular other than visit Tom's mother and his two cousins from Albuquerque, but we were on the road, which was something. And we'd made our first destination. Pine trees all around.

"Well, we haven't died yet."

"And nothing broke."

We decided to consider it our introduction to riding. So that was good. And the ranch, as our family called it, was a haven after our first day.

The property consisted of twenty-plus acres of ponderosa and sugar pines, creek alder, and scrub oak, along with a wide variety of other trees and plant life. A ridge ran along the far side and a ravine with a seasonal creek at the bottom that had one spot deep enough to swim in during the spring runoff. I once found part of a stone wall on the far side of the creek — almost completely buried in forest debris — which we wistfully conjured into the last remnants of a gold miner's cabin from the mid-nineteenth century.

There was a huge bramble of blackberry bushes down there as well — large enough to fill a living room. Edith made jam one year and blew her eyebrows off when the propane stove exploded (it was match-lit and she'd gone through several before getting it to ignite). We were able to save the jam, which turned out to be excellent — hardly any glass.

My parents purchased the raw land in 1961 and added the mobile home with a screened-in porch a few years later, putting it at the back end of that field so it wouldn't be visible from the road. Ray and I put up a four-strand barbed-wire fence around the property a few years later, which was interesting work, going wherever the surveyor's stakes took us. I lost control of the roll of barbed wire on a steep slope once and we watched it go bouncing and plunging down into the ravine. Pain in the neck to wind it back up again too, with all the leaves and twigs and stuff caught on the barbs. Thank goodness for leather gloves.

My father wanted a complete change from his everyday business routine, and we drove up there often enough, mostly during the summer. Aside from exploring the land via hour-long hikes and plinking with my brother's old single-shot .22 rifle, there wasn't much to do except read and enjoy the quiet. Edith made sure there were plenty of *Reader's Digest* magazines and books and ancient copies of *National Geographic,* as well as a half-dozen novels: Agatha Christie and the like.

"I lost that red lantern," said Tom. We were getting our sleeping bags and packs off the bikes.

"What lantern?" I asked. I was busy with a bungee cord that wasn't coming loose.

"It was red."

"A red lantern?" Now I was working on my sleeping bag.

"The small one I had hanging off the back." Tom gave a good yank and hoicked his pack up and off the bike.

"Nope," I said. "Don't remember it." I looked up. He wasn't even there. Tom was clumping up the steps to the sun porch. I had brought along an aluminum Boy Scout kit that held a frying pan, a small pot with a lid, and a drinking cup, all nested together: our mess kit. I was trying to pull it out for dinner. That, and a can of Dinty Moore stew—the one with the lumberjack's seal of approval, a giant thumbprint on the top of the can. Plus forks and the can opener. And maybe napkins. Hey, I'd thought ahead.

The light was starting to dim into evening. I knew that can of stew was in there somewhere, and with my hand rummaging through the contents, I played the image of each item as I searched with my fingers. Socks, flip-flop sandals, underwear, second pair of jeans, can opener (okay, I'll need that), a half-carton of eggs, more socks, and some smaller items, like an envelope with some spare cash, a notepad, a small plastic box I'd brought along for some reason, my journal, the pen I used to write in the journal, another pair of socks, and so on.

Finally, I found the shape and size of a Dinty Moore can. Well, hello there! *We'll eat like kings.*

Tom had brought a compact Sterno stove and already had it out. By the time we finished our can of stew, it was night. We unrolled our sleeping bags on the porch and went to bed. It had been a decent ride, about 150 miles.

Doesn't sound like much for eight hours on the road, but it was our first long ride. Despite my experience with motorcycles, in some ways this was as new to me as it was to Tom. Lying flat on my back that night to let the stiffness unwind was great. I listened to the crickets chirping and started to fall asleep thinking about Tom's red lantern. I shuffled through mental images to see if I had one or two that included it swinging from the back of his bike, but then a question came to me.

"What job are you trying to get?" I asked.

"What?" Tom was still awake.

"Your interview. What's the job?"

"Shop manager."

"Where?"

"The ski shop, right below the first lift. At Sugar Bowl."

"You worked at Wildcat Sports Shop, right?"

"Back home, yeah. On Main Street. St. Clair and I ran the ski department."

"So, world-class ski runs and no lift fees."

"Not exactly. Doctor's orders. I mean, there are no lift fees, but I'm not supposed to ski."

This was new news. *"You can't ski?"*

"Just cross-country. Doctor said I could really screw myself up if I stayed with downhill. Loose joints and a bad knee."

"Well, hell." I remembered something about it. His shoulder, anyway.

Flashback: We had been staying at Tim Schenk's house in Campbell before we left on the trip, and one night I got a rude awakening—*something was wrong.*

"Jon, wake up!"

"What?" We shared a room. Suddenly I wasn't asleep. The house was dark, and dead quiet. "What is it?"

"Come over here, okay?"

Now I really wasn't asleep. It was the middle of the night. "Why?"

"Just get over here." His voice was terse. *Click.* He turned on his bedside lamp and sat up, facing the wall. I came over, curious and still waking up. He was holding his left arm at a strange angle, away from his body.

"Just hold my arm," he said. "It's come out again."

What the hell? I gripped his left arm with both hands.

"Easy," he said. "Now, hold on. I'm going to pull."

I did, and he did. He pulled away as I held onto his arm. Something happened: I felt it.

"Now raise it. Lift my arm."

I did that, slowly and carefully. By the time I'd figured out what was going on, Tom was gripping his left wrist in his right hand.

"Okay, I've got it. You can let go."

He moved his left arm with his right in an odd semi-circle while I watched. It must have worked. He was massaging his shoulder.

"It's okay now," he said. "Go back to bed."

When I mentioned it the next morning, he didn't remember any of it.

"Must have done it in my sleep," he said.

Day 2   Monday, August 24 – Jackson, California

We repacked the bikes, checked our oil, and got going after a quick breakfast of eggs, no bacon. I'd forgotten to bring any, and cooking eggs in a dry aluminum pan wasn't a lot of fun to clean up. Another lesson.

We were riding through forested land, with pine trees on both sides of the road. It was our second day out, alive, vibrant, and real. Our bikes rumbled beneath us and the cool wind whistled. I felt just right. The air is colder at higher elevations because of the lower air pressure (fewer molecules banging about to keep us warm). We went back to Pine Grove to turn left and continue along. The road was beautiful, with sweeping curves, trees everywhere, and a mixture of shade, light, and dappled views of green and brown, and then our view would open up to sudden distance and far mountains. The world had never seemed this close or real from inside a car.

I hadn't known how it would work out or how well we might get along. I still didn't know, really, but I was thinking about it as we travelled that second day. It was a calculated guess, but I was content. The answer to that would undoubtedly work itself out in the days and miles ahead.

The idea of travel by motorcycle was also going well. I had learned on a much smaller bike, which is far more about staying out of trouble and upright than anything else. These were serious mid-sized motorcycles, and riding them allowed us to become part of the world we were in: sky, clouds, cars on either side, the smell of the land, and pine trees. We were traveling out of wherever we'd been and hurtling into our future at a mile-eating clip. The belt sander kept moving.

We had climbed well up into the Sierra Nevada mountains at this point. I looked across at the soon-to-be Kirkwood Ski area as we passed it about thirty miles out from Lake Tahoe. The whole mountain was under construction, with yellow bulldozers and trucks moving about like Matchbox toys on the mountainside. Kirkwood had a natural alpine meadow at the base, and I could see the scars of newly created ski runs snaking down the mountain. I noticed one of those metal road signs with the elevation: 7,800 feet. There were more than a dozen ski resorts near the Tahoe Basin — some quite famous, like Heavenly Valley and Sugar Bowl.

We changed roads without knowing, from Route 88 to 89, and our last run carried us due north to the resort city of South Lake Tahoe, which consisted of real estate offices, restaurants, and hotels quite near the lake. The smell of summer and pine trees mixed with heat and bright images. When we stopped, I noticed the heat shield on my exhaust pipes rattling, under my left leg. It was cracked, and a screw was missing.

Tom took us on a mission to find a friend of his, Jim Miller, who was on vacation with his family at the lake. They had a tradition of staying at the same cabin every year. Apparently, several other families did this as well. They all went on vacation during the same two weeks and stayed in the same group of cabins. Over the years, these families created their own culture by spending time together. It was similar to the dynamic within a cluster of sports fans who hold season tickets and sit in the same seats every game, swapping stories and cookies year after year. It was interesting and different, the trade-off probably being the variety you wouldn't get versus the comfort of always knowing where you'd be going — plus friendships you'd make, and always having someone to go boating and to the casinos with.

Tom finally hunted them down, and we spent some time with Jim and his brother, Will, who played the banjo (rather well, actually). We learned later that Jim played the piano. So, music lessons early on for the two Miller boys, I guess.

Tom lost one lens of his dark glasses in the wind; it flew out as he was riding around the lake area. Oddly, I had brought a spare lens of almost the same size and shape, but I had forgotten all about it until I was going through my pack. He was able to use it and kept it in place for the rest of the trip with some black electrician's tape, which made him look somewhat odd and a little piratical.

Sitting at the picnic table, Will and Tom got into a discussion about teaching techniques. Tom seemed to be focused on process while Will maintained that interaction was secondary, that the lecture method was more efficient.

"My mother is a teacher," I interjected. "Fourth grade. She keeps her students active because she knows they learn best while doing something."

Will gave me a blank stare as if I'd come down from the moon with information about some new kind of green cheese, then continued preaching from his ivory tower. Tom had a better understanding of what worked. Rote learning and droning lectures had their place in some situations, but trying to learn using that method was so difficult and time-consuming that everybody I knew considered it a form of torture. People learn by doing stuff, not by memorizing. I had thought everybody knew that. Well, I guess not.

After a while, we walked down to the shoreline with Jim and watched the people on the sand and messing about in the water. There were a couple of speedboats at this end of the lake throwing up small rooster tails of water, plus the occasional waterskier trying to stay upright. The water was Tahoe blue.

The sky was an azure canvas, brushed with wisps of cotton-white clouds, infinite and flawless. And then I felt a chill.

I wasn't party to whatever triggered his reaction, but Tom was starting to feel unwelcome, remarked sotto voce that we had overstayed. Or it might have been that a couple of guys taking off on motorcycles wasn't something Mr. and Mrs. Miller cared for and finally spoke up. In any case, we put our sleeping bags outside on the ground and slept next to Will and Jim. There was a soft murmur of voices in the distance as darkness deepened into night. Somewhere, a screen door opened with that scratchy hinge sound, paused, and banged shut. And then nothing but the quiet, the stars above, and in the quiet distance, the soft lapping of waves against the sand.

Day 3   Tuesday, August 25 – Lake Tahoe, California

The day came early, since we'd slept outside. After trying to make sense of our hair and getting some breakfast, we played Tom's guitar, then rode over to Meeks Bay Resort. Jim wanted to show us his catamaran—a boat constructed of a blue canvas deck stretched across four-inch aluminum tubes, with two pontoons and a lanteen sail. He showed it to us proudly, said it was a dream to sail around the lake. Tom had misplaced his regular glasses, so I don't know how much he could appreciate Jim's bright blue water-strider. It looked like an elegant blend of form, function, and girl-appeal. Not something to weather a storm perhaps, but the perfect toy for a rich kid vacationing at a California lake in summer.

We ran a few errands (and found Tom's glasses back at camp), and Tom got a topological map of the Tahoe Desolation Valley area, thinking he'd like to go exploring there at some point. We rode around in our shirtsleeves looking at girls. Even when the temperature hit ninety-five degrees, it didn't seem oppressively hot. Low humidity and the distraction of natural beauty.

I had stayed at Camp Richardson for a whole week once when I was fifteen, with my cousin David and his family on their vacation. It was a perfect time to be alive. David and I would crawl out of our sleeping bags before dawn and trek down to the lake while it was still quite dark, then fall back asleep on the sand until we were aroused by the sun. After a bit people started putting up umbrellas and laying out their beach towels and summer reading.

Mothers, fathers, children playing in the sand were summer texture. Girls close to our age were an exotic mystery to be solved, and I watched for them surreptitiously throughout the day, my eagle eyes scanning the sand and searching the water. We had a face mask and fins to share, and we went to the water and back over the *hot hot hot* sand. No responsibilities, no homework, and no supervision. I even started smoking my pipe. We were innocent as rain and full of ourselves in paradise.

Tom and I had been to Lake Tahoe any number of times in the past, but never like this, riding around the lake and experiencing it for what it was, a beautiful place in time that lived for hot summer days or winter ski trips. Everything smelled like pine needles and barbecue, and everyone wore sandals. Station wagons, picnic tables, wet bathing suits, and beer. Comic books, ice cream bars, paperback books, and suntan lotion. Boats at full throttle on crystal-blue water. A child's cry, a mother's voice, three young girls chattering and smiling, walking back from the shoreline. Two guys on motorcycles, riding slowly past the campground and down to the lake, just looking around before heading off to never-never land. It was the Indian summer of a nation made of ice cream.

We left the Miller family at four o'clock and stayed at a wide spot on a side road near a family by the name of Smith. They had a camper and told us they stayed there every year.

Tom had a blue tent that he brought with him, strapped across the front forks of his bike. We set it up for the first time that night. Once it was up, we had to figure out how to fit everything inside: packs, sleeping bags (unrolled), helmets, plus the two of us. It took some maneuvering and odd contortions, but we figured it out. Jackets and jeans for pillows, we listened to the quiet sounds of the night.

"How's your back?"

"Tired."

"We should stop more often."
"And all that friggin' sun."
"Yes."
"Night."
"Night."

"An occasional car would crunch it's way past us on the road, and then nothing.

Day 4   Wednesday, August 26 – Lake Tahoe, California

It was midday before we got back on the road, continuing up Route 89 on the California side. (The California-Nevada border runs through the middle of the lake, with an obtuse angle at the center.)

The road hugs the edge in places and moves away in others for some 70 miles over three hours of riding, creating a moving flick-flick-flick slide show of Ponderosa and sugar pines with their chunky yellow bark, then blue lake and sky through a gap and tall trees again and rocks, then another gap with more lake and sky through your semi-private tunnel of trees, then trees and sky again as you glide like silk through glimpses of sunlight and dappled shade with the lake always there, like an old friend, winking at you from time to time.

Route 89 turned west near Tahoe City at the top end of the lake, then north again. This area was home to several major ski resorts and a lot of minor ones, and we passed the entrance signs for Homewood, Alpine Meadows, and Olympic Valley. Not too far away were Sugar Bowl, Boreal, and Northstar. In a heavy winter these places were packed with skiers.

That reminded me: we'd forgotten to buy another pair of gloves. As part of our riding gear, we both wore ski gloves, which were leather and heavily insulated. Gloves help with the cold, but also windburn, sunburn, bugs, and the occasional rock that might be tossed up by a passing truck. Tom had lost his somewhere while riding around the lake, which was a nuisance — not so much then, but it would be later when we hit cold weather. We should have bought a pair while we were still at Lake Tahoe.

Noticing a sign to a public campground, we turned off the highway and scrambled up two miles of dirt road to a man-made lake which looked stagnant. This was nothing like Lake Tahoe. Along the way, I lost an air mattress, a spare clutch lever, and one swim fin from the roughness of the road. Tom's habit of losing stuff seemed to be rubbing off on me. I only found out these things were missing because I had corded the swim fins and air mattress to the top of my pack and only one fin was still there. And, not unlike shoes, swim fins travel in pairs. We stayed at the lake. Terrible place: spindly trees, a bush or two, and maybe a bit of grass. And mosquitoes. Later that night, Tom spoke into the darkness of our tent.

"What's with a spare clutch lever?"

"Not sure. It came with the bike."

"I wonder if that means anything."

"Does it have to mean something?"

"Maybe. We can look for it on the road out."

"How's your back holding up?" I turned to look at him. Useless of course, in the dark.

"It's okay. Tired is all."

"Okay."

Day 5   Thursday, August 27 — Lassen National Park, California

In the morning, we motored slowly back down the road, our eyes sweeping back and forth in front of our bikes till we managed to find the items I'd lost coming in, one after the other, lying there in the dirt. Over time, we learned that just piling things higher in layers on the back of a bike and then trying to hold everything together with a complex system of interconnecting bungee cords was not the best way to transport loose items. How we got five whole days into the trip without figuring this out I have no idea.

We got back onto the main highway heading north. We had decided to ride in the general direction of Central Point, a town of 4,000 people in Oregon. I'd known a family who had moved there from Los Gatos, and I thought it would be nice to see them again. Their mother had taken care of me after school for kindergarten and first grade. I remember plain peanut butter sandwiches, which I never understood. I guess she thought grape jelly might be bad for kids. Too much sugar or something. On the other hand, welding our mouths shut might have had an additional benefit: tranquil afternoons.

I got a kick in the pants at one point from an unexpected bump. I'm sure Tom got it too. Experienced riders know that dark patches in the center of a lane are an indication of oil. Such splotches only show up at a sharp rise or dip, where oil droplets have been jolted loose from car motors. They're an averaging of all the droplets left by all the cars and trucks ever to come that way — a thin film of automotive DNA — and darkest toward the middle. Tom and I never rode in the center of a lane; we didn't want that oil making our tires slippery.

We rode up 89, to the small town of Truckee. We stopped at the bug inspection station at the Truckee River Bridge — a big barn-like building made of aluminum — where we became part of a line of vehicles. They asked us if we were carrying any fruits or vegetables, then waved us through. California had to protect its crops, and foreign insects were not allowed. It seemed odd that this station wasn't right on the border, but I figured it wasn't necessary; it was only important that they be on every main route into the state, and prior to any major divisions in the highway. They weren't looking for fruit smugglers in trench coats and dark glasses, but tourists who might be carrying an unwanted hitchhiker or two in their picnic basket.

We continued through Plumas National Forest to Lassen Volcanic National Park. We got into the park and rode slowly through the campground at Manzanita Lake, snagging site 28 on Loop A for $2. I remembered staying in that campground at least once on a family vacation. We had always gone up into the gold country with the small teardrop trailer, and the national park system was part of our usual route.

There were pine trees and lots of other bushes and trees in the wooded areas, but mostly manzanita in the campground itself. They are spindly things with a thin red bark that peels continually in small curly flakes. They always look as if they're unsure whether they want to be proper trees or merely overgrown bushes. An endearing quality, oddly enough, if only because it's so strange. Manzanita grows all over the place at 8,000 feet, which was roughly how far we'd climbed.

It was still early, so we rode over to Bumpass Hell, which is a major hot springs area. The place was named after Kendall Bumpass, who stumbled into it in the late 1800s while hiking. It was named Bumpass Hell because he broke through the thin crust into boiling acidic water and burned his foot on his first visit. When he returned to camp and the guys asked him where he'd been, he said, "Boys, I have been in Hell." One could argue that it should have been named Bumpass's Hell, but I'm guessing his buddies weren't sticklers for grammar.

There's a boardwalk through the area to keep all the tourists from falling in and clogging up the works, and we read the storyboard signs explaining objects of interest along the way. Steam rose from boiling pools and vents, and mud pots bubbled like the witches' cauldrons in Macbeth. The entire area was a painter's pallet, with turquoise water deepening to blue the farther into the water you gazed. Purple, gold, and chocolate browns contrasted with tan, zinc white, saffron, and teal. The mud pots were the color of Cadbury chocolate, with steam bubbles the size of softballs popping and splattering at irregular intervals.

All quite colorful and smelling strongly of sulphur and whatnot. Kendall Bumpass had been accurate in his description; it was a hellish-looking landscape. Lassen hadn't erupted since 1915, although Mount St. Helens, about 700 miles north in the same Cascade Range, would do so in a rather spectacular fashion in 2008.

A helmet is cumbersome in warm weather at slow speeds, particularly when you're turning your head from side to side, trying to take everything in. It was the only time on the trip we had our helmets and didn't wear them. At that time, helmets weren't required in California, and that privilege extended to all the other states as well for riders with a California license, whether those states had helmet laws or not. Kind of an odd situation. Different laws for different states. Turn right at a red light in New York City and see where it lands you.

We were riding through the park to get the lay of the land and during one straight bit of road Tom tried resting his feet up on his sleeping bag where it was strapped to his front forks, à la chopper. His stance looked idiotic because his feet were too high, so he gave it up. That was before someone in a dark blue Chevy almost clipped us, passing way too close.

It was the heart-stopping swerve of something ten times our weight and size—like a charging rhinoceros and twice as stupid. Too fast and too close. It was the third time that day, and the uncaring arrogance pissed him off. He shot up next to the car and kicked it with his right boot, thumping the rear fender. His bike wavered, but stayed upright. *What the hell?*

The scene played out right in front of me. I braced myself for locked brakes and the screech of tires, with car doors slamming and people getting out to yell at each other in the middle of the road and curse our mangled bodies twisted in broken shapes on the pavement. The driver kept going, as did we. I'm sure he got the message. I'd seen Tom angry before, but jeeze...

I think car drivers see motorcycles kinda sort of, but don't pay much attention because we're not a threat. Compared to us, they're in a Sherman tank. Casual danger, indifferent destruction, statistics galore. Or at least, that's my theory.

We mailed our first postcards from Lassen: Tom to his mom, mine to mine. "Made it this far. Wished I hadn't brought the swim fins or mask. They're taking up room. Walked around Manzanita Lake, then back to camp. Lots of girls." Not terribly communicative, but it told them we were still alive, and my parents knew the lake; we'd been there before.

Our motorcycles parked at a campsite looked odd to me. I had been walking around the loop, getting a feel for the area. Then I came upon our site. No car, no trailer, no big tent; our spot didn't look like much. It looked, I don't know—*wimpy*, as if we weren't really camping. All the other campsites had tents and lawn chairs and various containers sitting out. I tried to remember that Tom and I were doing something quite different. After all, we were steely-eyed, clear-thinking men with determined chins. Sort of, anyway.

There was a film at the amphitheater that evening, so Tom and I decided to attend, in tune with the whole Camping in America spirit of the place, despite our underdeveloped campsite. We followed the path and the signs, scuffing our feet in the pine needles and brown dirt.

There was a semi-circle of benches made of logs split in half, flat side up. Everyone sat where they wanted, in twos and threes, slowly filling up the place. We got a forty-minute ranger talk explaining the features and history of the Lassen volcano and why we shouldn't walk into a fumerole. It was dark at the end, and we were part of a procession of clumsy fireflies as the gleam of flashlights bobbed and wandered back to individual campsites.

This wasn't the forest primæval exactly, but it was close, particularly in the dark. A kind of peaceful wariness came over me as we walked back. There was always something beyond the next tree, some unknown quality just out of sight. Stop all the clocks; throw away the lists; we were on our own with no one in charge but us and the wild places of the heart. Who knew what creatures had padded between these trees over the centuries? A timeless calm was at the center of it, mysterious yet tangible. We had a grand dinner: stew with potatoes, then sat staring at the fire. After the occasional pop and flare, it finally burned down to embers after we stopped adding wood.

I could just hear people talking quietly in the distance. And then a car drove by. And then nothing but the small, soft sounds of evening. I put away the marshmallows and dinner gear, and we threw our packs inside the tent. Neither of us said much until we were inside, settled, and buttoned down. The ground was lumpy, but I dug in and it was okay.

"Most beautiful car?"

"Ferrari 275 GTB."

"Jaguar D-Type or Lotus 49."

"Best taillight assembly?"

"The Cortina. Simple and perfect."

"Most interesting car?"

"Blower Bentley. Or the Isetta. Also the MGTD."

"Lotus Super 7."

"Didn't Bill Potter have a chain-driven Honda?"

"An S600. Now, that was a truly weird car."

"Most interesting engine: BRM H-16. I have a book about it with a record of it revving. Incredible."

"Best carburetor?"

"Weber."

"DCOE. Dual throat."

"Well, of course. Form follows function."

"Night."

And in the darkness surrounding our campsite, manzanita trees went on with their meaning in life, patiently sloughing off their weird red bark.

Day 6   Friday, August 28 – Central Point, Oregon

Tom got into a conversation with some girls after breakfast and wasn't set on leaving, but I felt the urge to keep moving. I wanted more miles between me and what I was facing.

I was starting to get a kind of nervous energy. I'd noticed it before we left Tahoe, and it was coming on me again. There was an urgency, a need to get on with it. I felt driven to get past the beginning and into the substance of whatever this was. I felt that if I didn't get past familiar surroundings, something might happen to us and I'd wind up back home again without having accomplished a damn thing.

Oregon was different. We were 175 miles beyond Day 5, and there was a decided change, both in the feel of the road beneath our tires and the landscape. We were coming down out of the Siskiyou Mountains, a coastal range that crosses from northern California into Oregon. The mountain pass we traversed was foggy and dream-like: a forest of mature redwoods. The highway itself was beautiful, smooth, and black, with clean edges and new-looking signs. Oregon was gorgeous.

One or two cars flitted by, going the other way, as quiet as owls. There was no litter. Curve after curve opened up to more and more trees, tall and mysterious, edging a forest as deep and quiet as the ocean. One long curve flattened into a very clean stretch of road, all downhill, several miles at least, like a path through the wilderness, paved in black, with a dotted center line and wide shoulders to define it. They couldn't have said, "Welcome to Oregon!" any better.

Suddenly Tom flew by me travelling at a shuddering blur, and then he was gone, far ahead, still flying, dwindling into the mist. The wind of his passage was just a flitter of sound.

I thought about it for three seconds, then cranked the throttle, set my mouth, and hunkered down. I was already in fifth gear, so there was no kick in the pants, but the acceleration was there and kept climbing: I still had more juice. The needle kept going up the dial, but it was jiggling so much I couldn't read it properly — I could barely read the numbers.

This long cut through the trees was a green wall on either side as the tachometer continued to climb and the engine rose from a roar to a wail to a high-pitched whine. Everything was a shudder and blur and incredibly fast. I could taste the death, the copper, rubber, crash and tumble, the grinding jumble of parts and life and bones sliding down the road, but elation welled up so strong, so alive in that drawn-out wink of time, and *BAM*, there was Tom, right in front of me, cruising easy and maybe wondering where the hell I was and *BAM*, I passed him at a zillion miles an hour.

Speedometers invariably read high (faster than reality), so they are really just a guide. So, when I say I passed him at a zillion miles an hour, understand that the hammering I took from the road and air pressure against the front of my body and the blurring of my eyesight, the horror and elation in my heart as I raced toward certain death only made it *seem* like a zillion. Probably not, though; my bike wasn't geared that high.

We both pulled into a rest area at the end of that furious ride, came to a halt in one of the parking spaces, and shut down. The fog was thick and silent. We got off the bikes to stretch and limber up and let our jangling systems get back to normal. The bikes creaked as the metal cooled. We pulled off our helmets and scarves and stood in the silence. The forest was like a cathedral, but without all the superstition and magical thinking. The quiet enveloped us with wonder.

"Well, that was certainly interesting," said Tom. There was that chuckle in his voice. He was looking back toward the beginning of our long descent.

"I've never opened it up like that before," I said.

"Check your speed?"

"Hard to tell. The needle was bouncing all over."

Tom was pointing at my face and laughing. "There are eyeball prints on your glasses. *Excellent!*"

I took them off and laughed. "Okay, you're right. You?"

Tom had taken his glasses off. "Nope. Mine are clean."

There were clear imprints of my eyes (including the lashes), on the inside of each lens: mute witness to raw energy and wind pressure. Tom and I looked around in the silence. There were no people, no cars, no trucks coming down the grade.

"They say you're only fully alive when you're inches from death."

"Who says it?"

"Oh, you know... they." I waved a hand in a vague circular motion. "Them." I glanced at Tom. "It's the kind of thing Hemingway would have said."

"Well, we were close to death."

"And I certainly do feel alive."

"Yeah, but do you feel close to Hemingway?"

"Not particularly."

"Me neither."

It was just the road, the two of us, and the forest. The Siskiyou Mountains were reserved, brooding and ancient, and we were smack in the middle of it, cracking feeble jokes. The road was a veneer of civilization, a modern slice through primæval land. Glancing sideways at that wall of Douglas-fir, ponderosa pine, and redwoods hinted of bears and mountain lions, deer, and streams with trout. Bracken crackled underfoot, and branches whipped back, closing in behind you the further you went until you'd be lost forever unless you were wearing moccasins and knew what the hell you were doing.

Running on momentum is a deadly killer. All of us go back and forth from job, to work, to that party at Bob's house, to our annual trip to Disneyland or the beach or that mountain cabin. It blurs into khaki with a few sweet memories embedded like chocolate chips in a Tollhouse cookie. What Tom and I were doing was something quite different. We were coming closer to the trees and the wild things than we knew. We were edging into the wonder of the natural world. Joking aside, the world around us was edging in.

This trip was turning out to be far more than a break from our regular lives. The difference was there. It was scary and invigorating. We thought of the morning air as crisp instead of cold, which was a marker for all the other differences. Once out of California, we weren't visiting the road, we were part of it. We didn't talk about it, but it was how we considered things. It was how we were with each other and with people we met. We spoke less and said more.

Since everything was all one big shift, that also meant everything we knew was wide open for change. We were beholden only to ourselves, and that felt amazing, at least to me. I could be anybody I wanted. We trusted each other, we had nothing to live up to, and no one to impress. It was a very real freedom, something I'd never thought about or experienced before except perhaps as a child, and not even then, really. The closest I could remember was that summer I spent with my cousin David, girl-watching and smoking my pipe at Lake Tahoe.

The bikes had cooled down a lot by the time we saddled up again. We travelled northwest, down out of the mountains, stopping in Medford, then continued north to Central Point. Gas stations always had a city map taped to one of their windows for handy reference, and I had an address.

We soon located the family who'd taken care of me after school as a child. Awkward and alien in our riding clothes and boots, and holding our helmets like odd buckets, we knocked on their door. I'm sure it was at least a little bizarre for Helen Kettleman to find me at her door. I had phoned ahead, but still — some kid she knew fifteen years ago?

I'd known I was pushing the boundaries showing up, but I'd wanted to see one last friendly face before turning east. Kind of an iffy anchor, but an anchor nevertheless. Polite as strangers, we talked with Mr. and Mrs. Kellerman in their living room while we waited for their kids to come home from a football game. Their eldest son, Ron, was on the team. Martha (wow), her baby Michael, and Sally, the youngest. I gave Ron my swim fins, thinking he might find a use for them, and made an effort not to call him by his childhood nickname: *Ron-Ron*.

Tom and I weren't quite sure what to do with ourselves that evening. I was glad of the helmet; it gave me something to do with my hands. Based on our interaction so far, it seemed that trying to create any more conversation would probably turn into a series of awkward pauses over a long evening of silence.

We asked the kids where the local hot spot was and ended up riding back to downtown Central Point in search of a drive-in restaurant—*Mel's Diner*—which we found easily enough due to all the cars and activity in the parking lot. Mel's had some tables inside, but most of their burgers and fries were served at a couple of windows, then everybody went back to their car to eat, with lots of chatting along the way.

We pulled in and found a spot near the entrance. The place was busy. We got a couple of large Cokes so it wouldn't look like we were just watching everyone—which of course we were. Central Point culture included jacked-up cars, girls with beehive hairdos, and two cops in a patrol car just waiting for something to happen. *American Graffiti* wouldn't be released until 1973, but it was right there in front of us: the 1950 zeitgeist encapsulated better than we could have imagined it.

After watching all the action for a while, I looked at Tom over my glasses and pursed my lips.

He laughed, looking around. "We're in a time warp."

"Yeah, but *we* can ride out of it."

"I'm not sure they can." Tom nodded toward all the cars.

"You ever see anything like this?" I had finished my Coke and was busy chewing ice.

"Only on TV. It feels like—I dunno—1955. I think we grew up lucky," said Tom. "We didn't have to deal with it."

We could see some of the kids staring at us from time to time, especially when a car drove right past. We were like two wasps at a picnic.

"Maybe. But we'll have to blend-in better if we run into much more of this."

Tom rolled his eyes. "Right. Like we could blend. This is like an old movie. Black and white. And we're in color. "

I grinned and nodded. "We need better camouflage."

We people-watched for a while longer, then put our cups in the trash and saddled up. It had been a splash of cold water in the face for both of us, and we thought about it as we crunched gravel getting out of the parking lot. It was as if we'd been transported back to when our older brothers and sisters were in high school and Elvis was still relevant. This was not familiar country, nor did it seem particularly safe, despite my tenuous link to the Kellermans.

I had been telling people the reason for this trip had been to see something of America before the Men in Black came to take me away, and there it was: a slice of the good old USA, cherry Cokes and all. This was America, no doubt about it, and it was weird to think of people living like this. Most of us do our best with what we have, whether we're from Central Point or Silicon Valley, but having the right fuel is important if the rocket's going to go up instead of sideways.

I also wondered what these kids thought about the war. They must have had opinions. I suspected their thoughts were quite different from mine. Most of them probably bought into the publicity and anti-communist propaganda. Not every individual, but as a community. They probably thought of it like World War II, where everyone had their duty to perform, and if you died, you died. Protesters like myself were probably dismissed as cowards. Or idiots. People who didn't understand the price of freedom.

That night we set up the tent in the Kellermans' backyard on some sheets of cardboard for insulation (the grass was wet), then shoved everything inside. We wrote in our journals that night by flashlight, and caught up on yesterday's entry as well.

As we were going to sleep, I kept thinking about the kids at the diner. And then I said it out loud:

"What will they do with their lives?" There was a long stage wait, and I didn't know at first if Tom was thinking about it or if he'd gone to sleep. He finally spoke up.

"Some version of what their parents did, probably."

Our disembodied voices were odd in the darkness.

"I guess, but it's not obvious. What jobs?"

"There are jobs."

"Some will move, I suppose. Find some other life. Kids go off to college or the army, then settle someplace else. The Kellermans came from Los Gatos." I was thinking about their house, back when peanut butter sandwiches were everything.

"Well, it's quieter here."

"But it feels more dangerous, like you could turn a corner and suddenly everything could turn horrible. A hunting accident, or an upset homeowner, or you'd be shunned by your neighbors at church."

"Especially for anybody who doesn't fit in. Like us. We bring danger wherever we go." We'd stumbled into a segment of the world that lived and breathed differently. Silicon Valley was light years away.

"Like the two of us are from a different planet."

"Yep. That we are."

"They probably bake pies and stuff."

"And hunt deer."

"Probably."

"You ever do that?"

"Went fishing once. On a houseboat."

"Catch anything?"

"Yep. A whole bunch of perch. I hated it. We were under a big tree at the edge of the lake. Or maybe it was sunfish."

"Well, there you go."

We were undiscovered countries, our opinions and inner thoughts brought out and tested against the night. Ninety percent of the inner gears and pulleys are disclosed only over a matter of years, but if you want to get to know someone, do something together. Do enough stuff and you either hate each other or form a bond, because whatever you have inside will eventually come out.

Day 7   Saturday, August 29 – Burns, Oregon

We said goodbye to Central Point and rode 290 miles to Burns, Oregon. 140 west to 395 north to 20 going east. It was our seventh day on the road. Sunny and warm when we started, but getting colder. We took various local roads through farm country, which was a matter of map work since we had to watch for critical turnoffs to make sure we didn't get sided into some desolate no-man's-land.

We'd taken to riding with paper maps wrapped in plastic, taped to our tanks in front of us so we didn't have to fiddle with them. All we had to do was glance down. When we needed details or a possible route change, we pulled off to the side and got studious. By this time, we'd settled into a riding pattern: Tom front left, myself back right, with the dark center of the road between us. Twenty feet apart most of the time.

It was during this ride that I began to feel the freedom of the open road ahead—a sense of autonomy that had been so elusive. The weight of thought, with all my questions and partial answers that had been pushing down on me started to lift. I felt lighter. Experience was beginning to eclipse anxiety. The weight was shifting.

In my life there are places where something happened. And then there are all the other places. On this road, with the sky growing darker and more ominous as we hummed our way toward the far gathering point where it met the land, I was suddenly in the quick and thick of it. This was one of those places, one of those moments. Tom and I were raw, tangled up in life, but breaking free to be whoever we wanted. This first long push toward Idaho and points east was a moment I could taste, like copper on the tongue. It was happening and I knew it was happening. Things were starting to get real.

Turning east and simply riding was something new, just as choosing to go on the trip in the first place had been new. But this first ride east was cementing how I was going to be in the world with action over ideals, a shifting of gears without words. It was scary, joyful, and unknowable. It was more than getting out of town. We were riding into our own history, and as the road disappeared behind us, it also opened up in front like a ribbon of black that led to compound probabilities.

The sky was ominously dark. We were coming into rain through the Harney Basin, a wide desert-like depression that extended up into Oregon from Nevada. It wasn't much of a basin up here, but flattened out to high desert at about 4,000 feet. It looked a desolate, dreary area. East Oregon had been much different. We'd been motoring along under cloudy skies for some time, but what was out in front looked darkly ominous. Riding into what might be heavy rain was unsettling. On our last gas stop prior to Burns, it came up.

"Ever ride in the rain?" asked Tom. We were in a filling station, next to the pumps.

"Nope," I said. "Not under something like that." We were both looking east. The clouds had become a dark ceiling, angry and close. I fumbled with my wallet, pulling out a couple of dollars. Gas cost $1.72 a gallon. Minimum pay for honest work was $1.45 an hour. Gas wasn't cheap.

"Just do the best we can, I guess," said Tom. He was screwing his gas cap back on. "We'll ride slower when we get into it."

"Yes, but we'll have to find some place to stay."

Tom got on his bike and reached down to fire up the engine. "Doesn't feel like vacationland anymore."

We didn't know what we were facing or what kind of shelter we might find. We heard lightning crack as we left the station, and then the boom, but didn't see it. The wind was picking up, but still no rain. Only that strange heaviness in the air, and then sudden strong gusts as we rode. I could hear it and sense the whump of pressure on my body and the bike.

Our vision was sharper and the world had less contrast, as if we were part of a Turner painting, only darker, with less crimson or yellow. And left unfinished too, as if Turner himself had put down his pallet and brush and abandoned our world to get a sandwich.

Our motorcycles gleamed in the sullen light as we vibrated along. There were occasional trees off to the side. Scrub brush clumped the base of the barbed-wire fencing that paralleled the road on both sides, thin lines of perspective that went on forever, just as the road did, pulling the two of us, the road, and the entire landscape toward the far horizon.

It hadn't started to rain by the time we reached Burns, but the air was heavy with it. Tom noticed a white Alfa Romeo 2600 coupe when we got into town. It seemed out of place here, like its owner drove and drove from some place far more exotic and then just parked it on the street. People out here didn't care for foreign cars, leaning more toward Ford and Chevy pickups.

Foreign cars are foreign, for one thing, and expensive to fix, since the parts aren't readily available — there weren't many dealerships — and definitely not practical. You can't carry a standard family in a sports car, and bales of hay don't fit in the back. Not even Toyota or Volkswagen had made any sales out here. It was more on the East and West Coasts and the big cities in between where people owned sports or foreign cars, which is why this lonely little Alfa stood out. Foreign cars were luxury items, and the people in this part of the country were practical folks who didn't spend a lot of money on things that didn't increase productivity.

This was even more evidence that we were anomalies in this place and time because we loved sports cars, loved to drive them and work on them, and appreciated the unique experience of owning them. For us, putting good money into an exotic automobile was not extravagant, but rather a sign of personality and good taste, like saving up to buy original art or paying attention to proper grammar. The farther we traveled, the more we realized how culturally different we were.

There weren't any motorcycles around either, or very few. We drew blank stares from people on the street. This was cattle and potato country for the most part, and we were headed right toward Idaho, which was a land filled with potato farmers, if bags of Ore-Ida Tater Tots hadn't been lying to me all these years. If there were any motorcycles in this part of the world, there was a fair distance between them. Dirt bikes more likely, or three-wheelers. Used in leu of horses for rounding up cows or checking fences.

A movie was about to start at the local drive-in, so we took a gamble on it. Thinking about something completely different seemed refreshing. It was John Wayne as Rooster Cogburn, in *True Grit*. The entrance to the drive-in was deep in loose sand for some reason. I was trying to navigate at very low speed, and the front tire sank right into the sand. I lost my balance and went down, but a man ran over to help pull the bike back up.

That's one thing we often found: total strangers quick to help in awkward moments. It didn't matter where we were or what it was, but when a person was struggling, some people naturally jumped in to help.

Tom and I got to an empty spot and parked the bikes sideways to watch the movie. John Wayne was his usual colorful self and his swaggering personality almost carried the film, but many of the actors were miscast and the plot was just silly. I hate movies where the characters don't behave like real people. Sprinkles of rain during the end credits galvanized us. We put on our helmets, saddled up, and got ourselves out of there as quickly as we could.

Motorcycles can be awkward in traffic or bad weather, but they're like magic for quick maneuvering. We scrambled out of our spot and snaked a path through the traffic emerging from the drive-in. The glow of our instruments measured the darkness, and rain was starting to splatter down. Tom and I turned onto the main road and motored through town, searching left and right for any kind of shelter.

There was an abandoned grocery store on our left, across the street. It had a flat awning over the entrance, perfect for two riders caught in the rain. Tom went for it and I followed. We crossed the parking lot and got underneath the awning just as the rain started coming down in earnest. We shut down our bikes and watched.

The rain was really coming down now. In buckets, like the sky opened up. The sound of it came through our helmets like white noise as we waited. Tom still didn't have any gloves.

His hands were white blotches on the ends of his arms in the gloom, and then he put them in his pockets. Cold blotches. I don't know why I didn't think to lend him one of mine. We could have ridden with one glove each. *No brains.*

Sitting on a motorcycle under a cement awning with a curtain of rain on three sides wasn't much fun, but it was better than being in it. We waited some more. There was a weird balance going on. Safe and relatively dry where we were under our awning, but we couldn't pitch our tent on cement. Plus, the locals wouldn't like it. It wouldn't be safe. We had to get beyond the town. Burns was about 3,000 people; it wouldn't be too far. Maybe a mile or two out and we'd find the same sort of grazing or farmland we'd been riding through. We kept our helmets on, which meant we had to shout just to talk.

"WHAT DO YOU THINK?"
"FIFTEEN MINUTES"
"THEN GO FOR BROKE?"
"RIGHT"
"THEN CRASH TWENTY MILES OUT?"
"SURE"
"OKAY"

The rain was really whipping down. Riding in this wouldn't be easy, it certainly wouldn't be fun, and it frightened the hell out of me — particularly since it was now pitch black and we'd be finding our way on just our headlights. But after a time — *presto-chango* — the downpour became a light steady rain, quiet by recent standards, then slacked off to a drizzle.

We looked at each other, nodded, and grumbled our engines back to life. This main street stayed straight as we left downtown; it was actually the highway we wanted. The drizzle turned back into rain. One odd twist in the road at the far end of town, and we were soon motoring carefully along through the black of night beyond the Burns city limit.

I could feel every beat of my heart. Every drop of rain. The unevenness of the roadway beneath my tires. Five miles out, the rain and wind came back hard.

Blackness all around, no separation between Earth and sky. We were riding through a whipping downpour. It was like a monsoon. The running fence on both sides of the road gave us direction. Sometimes I could see the dotted white stripe in the center of the roadway and sometimes not. The rain sparkled in the beams of our headlights like a shower of diamonds in front of us. Tumbleweeds crossed right in front of us — suddenly in our headlights and then gone, bounding and spinning into darkness across the highway.

Our jeans were soaked, our shoes and socks were squishy. I wasn't sure about my fingers, which meant they were numb. I was hoping I could operate the clutch and brake. Outrunning this deluge wasn't working, and we had to stop. What we were doing was horribly dangerous, and we knew it. The night had become a trial by elements, which exhaustion sometimes wins.

We finally found a rest area about twenty miles outside of Burns and pulled into the parking lot to take a look. Neither of us were in the mood for an accident out in the middle of nowhere. There was not much more than the slap and hiss of water hitting everywhere, and the black and silver glare from our headlights. It wasn't a campground. It was a place where people stopped because they had to. It was all dark shapes and harsh lights. Everything was blurry and wet from the constant downpour, but we didn't care. We were like all the other people who came here; we just had to stop.

The rain kept whipping rain into our faces with a kind of swivel action, and heavy gusts were trying to topple us over. We managed to get across the parking lot to a concrete blockhouse — ostensibly a bathroom — a last resort perhaps for the truly desperate. Looking at its stolid existence out here next to Desolation Road, it didn't take much to imagine the oily odors that permeated its cement. I'd seen bathrooms like it before.

Tom and I didn't need to speak. We both knew that ugly building was our best protection from the wind, even if sleeping behind it in our two-man tent wasn't exactly gracious living. Mother Nature felt like she might go all CATEGORY ONE on us later in the night, and we couldn't take chances. And we had to be close to that bathroom; if things really turned south, we'd hide inside and breathe through our mouths until the storm died down.

In case you've ever had a hankering to pitch a two-man tent in a crazy-ass storm outside of Burns, Oregon, let me tell you how it's done. First, you have to locate a really desolate stretch of road. Make sure it's night, and in the middle of the local monsoon season. The rain has to be coming at you sideways to get the full effect. None of that wimpy stuff you get back home; this is East Oregon, with sagebrush plains and craggy mountain ranges. The sort of place where Mother Nature cracks her knuckles and narrows her eyes when she sees a couple of Hondas coming down the pike. Anyway, it's raining, you're exhausted, and you need a break. You can barely think straight. That's the condition we were in when we pulled into that roadside attraction Oregon calls a Rest Area.

Ignitions off: **Vroom-*ticka-ticka-ticka***. Now for the fun part. Tom started undoing bungee cords to get at the tent while I stomped around in the dark to find a place without too many rocks. We were acting mechanically and methodically at this point. We did the first logical thing and then the next and then the next because that's how it works. If we did enough logical things, we'd get to sleep in a tent tonight instead of huddling on the cold tile floor of a public restroom reeking of urine.

It was pitch black and my flashlight wasn't much, but I smoothed things out as best I could, kicking away the debris with my head down while the wind and rain battered the two of us. There was one large rock I had to move by hand, but I got it out of there.

The slap-*flap*-slap of the tent whipping back and forth made it difficult. Tom had it from his end — or at least one corner — and I was pulling from the other side, but it was slippery and the wind kept grabbing it. My feet slipped on the muddy grass and I banged my knee when I fell. What we had was a rather large and ungainly kite disguised as a two-man tent that clearly wanted to sail off into the night.

"We have to weigh it down," I yelled. "Hold on!" I ran to the bikes, pulled my pack off, then ran back, throwing it inside the tent. The rain pelted us from all directions as Tom and I tried to lay it out, but that tent was like a living thing. We each grabbed a handful of support rods and went to work, step-by-step, as best we could.

Long rods went into short rods and short rods into long rods, then one end in the corner, then fed through the loops — *did I skip one?* I bent these multi-stage rods like Robin Hood pulling an English longbow. Somehow we had to get the ends into that X-socket thingy at the top. This went on for days, and then suddenly everything fit. It all worked, and we were standing next to a proper, happy-looking tent. We didn't bother with the tent stakes, figuring it would either stay up or collapse, but with both of us inside, along with all our stuff, it probably wasn't going to blow away.

We threw everything inside. Sleeping bags: *check*. Backpacks: *check*. Guitar: *check*. Helmets: *check*. Two exhausted guys, soaked to the skin, crawling in after: *check*.

"Your knee."

"Crap. Sorry."

"That towel dry?"

"You get it next."

"Effing nightmare..."

The wind whistled through the rigging, flapping the blue nylon as we arranged everything to fit. Our stuff usually went to the back of the tent. We were finally in our sleeping bags, our heads resting on our folded pants and inside-out jackets, and ten seconds later we were falling asleep.

"Shit."

"What?"

"Is the flap closed?"

"Yes."

"All the way?"

"Yes."

Evidence suggested otherwise.

"I hear a drip."

"A drip?"

"Yeah, I heard a drip."

"I think it's closed."

"Are you sure?"

"I'll get it."

"Okay."

"Wait. Did you empty the guitar?"

"Yeah, sort of. It's still has some gum wrappers."

"Okay then."

"G'night."

"Tom?"

"Yeah?"

"Happy Labor Day."

"What?"

"I saw it on a newspaper. Thought you'd want to know."

Day 8   Sunday, August 30 – Boise, Idaho

Tom and I woke up to blue skies with white clouds and a Triumph 650 traveler in the parking lot working on his bike.

"The clutch is acting up," he said. He was tall, with brown hair. Friendly enough, wearing jeans and cowboy boots, with one of those quilted vests. He had a black Triumph. A classic English motorbike. At 650 cc, quite a bit larger than ours.

"Could be a couple of issues," he said.

His clutch might have had oil on its surface, which would have made it fail to grip. The throw-out bearing might have been going out, or it might have been as simple as the cable from his clutch being too tight, a simple adjustment if that's what it was.

Tom hunkered down next to his bike and spent some time trying to help while I studied the map. Although his bike still wasn't perfect when we left, he was able to shift, which meant he could ride. We packed up and continued east, toward the Rocky Mountains and Yellowstone. We had a couple of burgers with fries and Cokes at a gas station-diner combination: good eats. When we wandered back out into the sunshine the guy with the Triumph 650 had caught up with us and was back to working on his bike. We said our greetings, got on our bikes, and headed out.

Tom and I had started to get on each other's nerves for some reason, so I tactfully moved things along. Getting on my bike and putting on my helmet was like a little clue. If he didn't get that message, clue #2 was to start my engine. Clue #3 was to run my bike up to the road and wait.

We had two things going for us. We had a solid history, and if either of us wasn't quite up to par, we had a workable solution: stop talking and ride. I suppose that when two men with personalities the size of Mt. Whitney live in close association there are bound to be occasional issues, but everything lost its edge and fell away over time. Although we rode together, we were usually ten or twenty feet apart and alone with our thoughts. Plenty of space to sort things through and get over ourselves if that's what we needed to do.

With the rain behind us, I began enjoying the ride again. I was living in the moment and able to take everything in. I was starting to breathe the freedom I'd been looking for. The day got warmer, and the hot sun made the road shimmer in the distance from refraction. The air tasted like summer from the fields we buzzed past, deep green with plants waiting for the final harvest. Dirt roads went off at right angles, straight as arrows into the distance. *Who lived at the end of that?* Sometimes we'd see a mailbox or a tractor in a field, a farmhouse, or a barn. Maybe a silo with a cluster of buildings.

We had bacon and eggs almost every morning. First the bacon, then two eggs, and as soon as they had been frying—for about 30 seconds—we'd put a bit of water in the lid, turn it over into the pan, then leave it for a bit. The water turned to steam, condensed on the eggs, and poached the tops so we didn't have to turn them—a near impossibility with that small aluminum mess kit.

We bought six eggs at a time when we could and a full dozen when we had to, and whoever had enough room to stuff them into his pack would carry them. They never broke, and didn't have time to go bad because we each ate three eggs every day for breakfast while we were on the open road. Despite our inert posture on the bikes, we were burning up the calories. A lot of energy went into keeping us warm when the sun wasn't visible. Plus, you know, all that vibration.

It was like sitting on a gasoline-powered weight-reduction machine, except we didn't lose weight, we gained it. Or at least, I did. Our bodies compensated to protect us from the weather and vibration by adding a layer of fat—that was my theory, anyway. I had weighed myself at 145 pounds before we left. Even before we hit Yellowstone, I had gained 10 pounds and kept that bit of extra for the entire trip. I've heard people say appetite increases on camping trips, and I have to agree. I happened to step on a scale one or two times after we got back—just out of curiosity—and those extra 10 pounds were gone in not more than a week. It was as if I'd done some strange on-the-road science experiment without knowing it.

We stopped at grocery stores along our route to purchase supplies, and when we hit the Midwest I was shocked at the low cost of a dozen eggs: only 34¢. A dozen eggs back in California sold for about 60¢. I had never noticed the price of eggs in particular before; I hadn't had to. But I was suddenly very aware that the cost of staying alive in Iowa (for instance) was radically different from what I was used to.

That idea stayed with me as we traveled, and it came to me that land was probably cheaper, making houses less expensive because the cost of labor would be lower. And everything would be, all down the line, except for a new car (or pickup truck, given where we were riding). A car made in Detroit cost the same to build, whether it was sold in New York, Florida, or Idaho, except for transportation costs of course, but that wasn't much. As we rode, I ruminated on this, and it seemed to me that cars (or trucks) would be considered very expensive, relatively speaking, for someone living in the Midwest. I didn't have any conclusions, other than the cost of something was only proportionate to income if it were made or grown locally, like a house perhaps, or eggs.

All across the Midwest we ran into Native American place names. Everywhere and everything was named with a different language. From Pocatello to Sioux Falls, from the Dakotas through Illinois, Mississippi, Oklahoma, Texas, and beyond, we were riding through lands that had once belonged to people with a very different way of life.

The ghosts of the Cherokee, Apache, Navajo, Cheyenne, Iroquois, and Sioux were all around us. Hell, they'd named almost every lake, mountain, river, state, and major city in the country. Our maps had the reservations marked with dotted lines. As two guys from California, we were used to Spanish locations and names. We'd grown up with them. It was subliminal during the trip, but the knowledge that we were in someone else's living room couldn't be denied. All we had to do was look at our map to know that we were interlopers.

I also had a history of listening to folk music, including the songs of Buffy Saint Marie, who wrote *My Country 'Tis of Thy People Your Dying*, and I'd read about the Trail of Tears, so I had some idea. But to be suddenly right there in the middle of where so many had died for no reason other than greed was creepy, even at a distance of so many years.

We made a habit of stopping for gas about every hundred miles, my bike being the limiting factor because of its small tank and higher gearing. On this day we stopped at a Chevron station that was right in the middle of nowhere. Road, then this one gas station, then a lot more road. We always filled our own tanks, although an attendant would have to come around with a special key to turn on whichever pump we were going to use.

In this case, there were no other cars, and the place looked deserted. We tried the pumps and they worked, so we fueled up. No one came to take our money, which was unusual. We went over to the station, but it was locked. We knocked on the door, but no one was there. Maybe it was only one guy, and he was in the bathroom?

We weren't sure what to do. We went back to our bikes to confer. Then, when we looked back at the station, we saw two guys peeking out at us from inside the office window. Tom waved his money in the air to indicate that we wanted to pay. They wouldn't come out. We could still see them, there in the window, watching us. It was bizarre.

"Let's leave the money on top of the pump."

"I need another twenty cents."

"Got it. Okay."

"Close enough."

We put our dollar bills on the pump with the change on top, then shouted and pantomimed with exaggerated arm movements and finger pointing to show what we were doing.

"WE'RE ... LEAVING ... THE ... MONEY ... HERE!"

After we'd done our bit for plain dealing, we saddled up and started the bikes, took a last look at the two guys staring at us from inside that filling station, and motored back onto the highway. My main concern was getting hassled for theft, even though we'd paid. We had no receipt, and who knew what those two guys were going to do? Would we be riding along a half-hour from now and get pulled over with lights and sirens? But nothing happened. We thought about it during the ride, then talked it over at the next stop. Tom thought it was all very amusing.

"Never thought of myself as scary," he said. He was grinning, and it was infectious. "Do I *look* scary?"

I shook my head and laughed. "I wonder what they were thinking? We're on *Hondas,* not Harleys."

Tom straightened his back. "Well, we haven't shaved since we left home." He gave me a rueful look and laughed. "And we do look a bit worse for wear."

"I don't think we look *that* bad," I said.

"Strange," said Tom. "Very strange."

Tom was laughing at the absurdity of it the next time we stopped for a rest. "Do we really look that bad?"

"Maybe we smell funny," I said.

Tom looked me up and down. "It must be you."

"I don't think so. If it's either of us, it's probably you."

"Hey," laughed Tom, "I'm reasonably clean."

"Oh yeah? When was the last time you took a shower?"

"I'm not sure."

"See. People can tell. We can't tell because we're used to it, but everybody else can."

"We have an aura?"

"Damn right we do. Like bad apples. And getting riper by the minute."

"Like cheese?"

"Or wine. I think wine is the better analogy."

"Maybe we could bottle it when we get back home. Call it *Eau de Motorcycle*."

"Right. We'll make millions."

We entered Idaho en route to Boise and stopped at a lake that had a strange water spout some fifty feet offshore: a single stream of water shooting far up into the air. The water formed a tall arc, falling back into the water. We stopped to rest and read the large sign they had erected at the site:

YOUR TAX DOLLARS AT WORK
BUILT BY THE STATE OF IDAHO
U.S. ARMY CORPS OF ENGINEERS
ALL THE USUAL FINE PRINT, PEOPLE IN CHARGE, STATE OFFICIALS
BLAH, BLAH, BLAH,
BLAH, BLAH, BLAH,
START DATE • DATE OF COMPLETION

"Idaho is quite proud of their lake," said Tom. His humor was so dry at times you could strike a match on it.

"Well, yeah. Wouldn't you be? That's an exceptional arc of water." I laughed. "Goes up high enough."

"But what's it for?"

I re-read the sign for clues. "Maybe something broke."

"Think it's aerating the water?"

"Sure," I said. "So the fish don't die."

"Right," Tom replied. "Because they stocked it with fish. Then the fish died. No plants to make oxygen, right?"

"Except for the algae."

"Then they restocked the lake."

"And built the fountain to restock the oxygen."

"It's what I would have done."

"Do you really think that single stream of water could aerate the whole lake?"

Tom shrugged. "Maybe it has *religious* significance. Think about it. People come from all over Idaho to worship at the Great Fountain. Kind of like the Great Pumpkin, but wet."

"Either that or something broke."

"Maybe it's a sign."

"Or a warning."

Tom restarted his bike. "Let's look for a campsite."

We found one with a few empty sites and stayed there for the night, fighting off mosquitoes the size of small bats.

If you've never tried camping near a lake that just sort of sits there (well, except for its giant water fountain), I can tell you the procedure. After pulling in and finding your campsite, you unpack and set things out for dinner on the picnic table. Everything seems nice enough, and you set up your tent. After walking around a bit, you stroll out to the lake and throw rocks in a desultory manner and talk about that stupid water fountain and how soon before you get to Boise. If it's hot enough, you take a dip in some cutoffs you happened to have, then dry off by walking around. You sit at the picnic table and stare at a map and think about the fact that you've had your first bath in a week in questionable lake water.

As the afternoon wears on, you become more popular with the mosquitoes, slapping your neck or arm from time to time as you try to eat dinner and they try to eat theirs. When afternoon turns to evening and you've washed all the smashed bug parts off your body, and after you've said everything you can think of about the Army Corps of Engineers and their weird sense of humor, you crawl into your little blue tent and do your best to get to sleep.

The mosquitoes hang about, betting amongst themselves which one of you is going to emerge, and give a complete miss to perfectly good campers with lots of red corpuscles not that far away. Occasionally, a particularly evil specimen will work its way into your canvas castle through some microscopic opening you absolutely never will find, and whine at your ears with unrestrained glee until you finally scooch down into the bag and try to sleep on just a limited amount of oxygen. Great fun.

Day 9   Monday, August 31 – Arco, Idaho

We were well on our way at this point in our journey. We had no final destination except back home once we'd gone far enough, and our only time constraint was that job interview Tom had in a couple of months. I may have had a vague notion of walking a beach on the Atlantic Ocean only to say we'd done it, but nothing more than that. We were in the common center of rural America and fine with it. Nobody was bothering us, we weren't getting sick or overtired, our lower backs were holding up okay (sometimes an issue when riding day after day), and that constantly moving sand belt beneath our feet was grinding up the miles toward a far horizon.

We rotated our socks every day and washed them in bathroom sinks (or lakes, more recently) along with our underwear when and where we could. This experience was quite horrible at times since public restrooms across America are not uniformly maintained in the pristine condition one might expect. Forget about it, we took a vote and decided. Nor do they all have that sweet, freshly sanitized look or the scent of spring daisies on a new day. We did the best we could with available resources. Tom and I usually had several pairs of dry socks in our packs and one or two freshly washed pairs tucked under a bungee cord across the back of our bikes, drying in the wind. Everything else took a beating.

We were getting used to riding longer distances and for being with each other over an extended period. Fortunately, we had time to be alone with our thoughts, and I'm sure that helped. We stopped to rest and say a few words about every hundred miles or so, but we were about five to ten yards apart for most of the trip. Tom and I had met in seventh grade over mutual interests: design, music, sports cars, and motor racing.

The two of us were concerned with the world we wished to inhabit and in the way we did things. It was an attitude that included style and grace and knowledge, but we also knew when to get out the big hammer and bash away. Those times made our laughter strong and joyful, in part because we had something that didn't depend on words.

My thoughts wandered as we rode, and I thought about the war from time to time. Kids just like me, dying in rice paddies a million miles from home. Couldn't help thinking about it, although I tried not to. I was doing my best to live in the moment, just as life came at me instead of in the past or the future. I'd done a lot of that lately. The future would come soon enough. I thought about those kids who'd died at Kent State, gunned down by their own National Guard troops, their parents wondering what the hell had happened. All I would have to do for five years would be to sit in a cell, pick beets during the day, eat cafeteria food, and drum my fingers. Maybe read a couple of thousand books. And maybe I'd have to fight Bubba. It wasn't death.

We were riding two to three hundred miles a day with four to six stops. Enough to tire us out, but not enough to exhaust us. These were new and different lands: flat country with trees and curvy roads or farmland with nothing but crop rows that seemed to run clear off into the horizon — and all of it empty of life. We were the only living boys on a road to nowhere.

A strange vulnerability came upon me the farther we traveled into the flat, featureless areas of farmland. It was so *empty*. There were hardly any trees and not much shade. There were no hills and hardly any houses. Only mile upon mile of dusty green crops, with our plain straight road cutting through the middle of it. We were riding toward the Rocky Mountains, and it was as true on this side as it would be on the other.

Occasionally, we came across a massive grain silo with faded lettering on the side, proclaiming what company or cooperative it belonged to. There were few cars or trucks from either direction. Part of that was the roads we traveled. This part of America had main roads and side roads, and that was it. There were no freeways as we thought of them in California. There was often not much of a breeze either, merely the two of us buzzing right along. I suddenly realized what was bothering me and mentioned it the next time we stopped.

"The ocean," I said.

"What?"

"I miss the ocean."

Tom looked around. We were at the side of this long stretch of road, the bikes creaking as they cooled. They always did when we stopped. Ordinarily we couldn't hear it because of everything going on all around, especially traffic. Today there wasn't much ambient sound, and the occasional *ping* was noticeable. Metal changing shape.

"I do too," said Tom. He'd had to think about it. We'd both grown up on the West Coast, only twenty or so miles over the

Santa Cruz Mountains from the beach and the Pacific Coast Highway that threads along the coastline. We'd both been to the beach often enough and to various places along the coast. It was a very real part of our inner landscape.

"Feels weird with nothing at our backs."

"Like something could be coming up on us from behind."

There were places out here you could look all around in a circle and not see a single bump. Not a tree, a hill, a house, or even a mountain far off in the distance. We were right smack dab in the middle of the whole continent with nothing but nothing in every direction. Our isolation was like a wall we'd slammed into. It was strange to realize that growing up near the coast had provided a sense of something solid, that it had seemed protective in some weird way, but that's how it was.

It had been like having an edge to the puzzle of who we were, and the rest of the pieces could fill in as we went along. Out here the pieces had been tossed into a jumble, without anything to call our own. There was just us and our bikes and our intent. Tom unscrewed his gas cap, stood higher off the seat with his feet flat on the ground, and rocked his bike to slosh it, peering into the tank. "I think I've got another hundred miles."

I did the same. "I've got fifty."

We peered at the maps taped to our tanks, fingers tracing red and blue lines.

"Craters of the Moon National Park," said Tom.

"Okay," I said. "Craters it is." We started our engines, looked back along the road for traffic, then spun bits of dirt and pea gravel behind us getting back onto the highway.

We took a dirt road into Stanley and Sun Valley, then southeast to the small town of Arco (Pop. 1,244). The visitor center in the middle of town was a stone building with the old Niels Bohr atomic model as a badge of honor at the top of the sign.

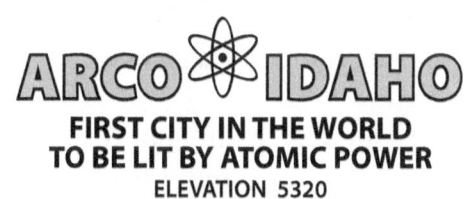

**FIRST CITY IN THE WORLD
TO BE LIT BY ATOMIC POWER**
ELEVATION 5320

A breeder reactor had been built for the military about eighteen miles southeast of Arco, but it blew up after twelve years in a nuclear accident lasting all of 4 milliseconds in 1961. There was a small cement graveyard for the three men who were there at the time.

It was in the town of Arco where we came across a young guy who really didn't match his surroundings. We were parking our bikes to stretch our legs when we spotted him. He was 16 or 17, with brown hair, running towards us, cutting across the street. Skinny, and wearing some kind of fringed vest and bellbottom jeans with red paisley inserts that looked hand sewn. Classic hippie garb like that seen in the Haight-Ashbury area of San Francisco during the mid-60s.

He came running across the street as we were setting our kickstands, ecstatic and bubbling over with questions that came out all in a rush, tumbling over each other like puppies.

"**HELLO!**" – *From clear across the street.*

"**HELLO!**" – *Now on the move and waving his arms.*

"Wait! Don't go! *WAIT!* I want to talk to you!" – *He's crossing the street at a half-run to intercept us.*

"Who are you guys?" – *Now he's right in front of us and we realize too late that we should have escaped while we still could.*

"You guys from the Bay Area? Can you tell me what it's like in San Francisco?" – *He walked clear around us without stopping with the questions and must have seen our license plates.*

"Do you play that guitar? Do you play any folk music?" – *He'd also noticed the guitar.*

And why were we in his town, and did we know any hippies, and that he was "the only hippie in the Midwest," and how far had we come? How long had we been on the road?

I don't know if Tom or I had said one word during this stream of consciousness, but when he finally ran out of breath or questions (or both) we talked with him. He bemoaned his cultural isolation "surrounded by farmers" and his fate to be "stuck in this town."

We felt sorry for him but didn't know what to say. He was concerned about his situation, and we wondered if he would ever get the courage to up and leave someday since that was what he wanted. He certainly stood out from his surroundings — far more than we did, and yet he'd spotted us as sympathetic characters right off.

The melody of our journey was traversing a richer weave than we had thought, growing bolder, finding moments worth pausing over, creating unexpected ripples to make us pause, yet tug us into motion at the same time — allowing us to forget unfinished business and roads not taken. It was the first time we understood where we were and who we were, that the road was now home, and that the people we met became part of us as we passed through their lives.

Some were traveling like us, and others were part of the fabric of where they lived. Everyone was friendly, which was a relief. I don't know what we would have done had we met with serious antagonism.

This hippie without a country was so glad to see kindred spirits it almost hurt, and it made me think how lucky we were to have grown up in a place where strangeness is usually considered a personality quirk or an indication of character. Not that we thought about it that much, but our otherness was becoming ever more noticeable as the miles added up.

As we pushed beyond the Rocky Mountains and into the Midwest, we knew we looked different to most locals, what with our worn clothing, wind-burnt skin, and bug-dotted motorcycles. And of course, our California plates. I started to get a feeling from talking to people that being from the West Coast gave us a certain aura, a cachet we would not have had otherwise. Not so much anything people said, but you could see the Golden Gate Bridge and the Hollywood Sign reflecting in their eyes when they said it: "Oh, you're from California..."

We camped at Craters of the Moon National Monument on Highway 26. Hit a ton of rain getting there, which came down without warning.

"You get the tent, I'll get the packs."

Getting into our tent, out of our wet clothes, and into our sleeping bags was horrible; we were drenched.

Day 10   Tuesday, Sept. 1 – Yellowstone, Wyoming

It wasn't until morning that we were able to see where we'd camped. The ground looked dark gray and black, all the way out to the horizon. It was a strange reality to wake up to.

Craters of the Moon was a charcoal drawing of desolation, as if we were Hobbits on motorcycles in search of Smaug's great treasure. But there was no treasure; in real life there rarely is.

Just miles of grey lava that had flowed out in tubes like corduroy from 25 long-extinct cinder cone volcanos. All about 2,100 years ago. A desolate area. No trees, no life to speak of. We were just a couple of riders from California huddling for warmth in America's Midwest, staring around us at a strange place consisting of nothing more than unending gray rock and the occasional bit of sagebrush, somewhere along the Snake River Plain.

Leaving Craters of the Moon, we cut across one corner of Montana to get to Yellowstone National Park in Wyoming. We could see the Grand Tetons in the distance, a part of the Rocky Mountains going north into Canada.

As we traveled into the mountains, the sunshine and sweet warm air met us like a high wave. I looked across the plain to the soaring heights, rocky, enormous, hazy in the daylight. We were riding out of desolation into majesty. There was just flat prairie and then—spectacular in the far distance—a line of jagged gray mountain peaks with snow that never melted.

We stopped at a diner that catered to cowboys and farmers, and there was a jukebox, so we played Peter, Paul &Mary, Donovan, and the Beatles to goose some contemporary culture into the place.

"You think anyone here would listen to the Beatles unless some stranger played it?"

"Probably not. Maybe some kids."

"Or Donovan?"

"Why have it on the jukebox?"

"Maybe the jukebox company decides the music."

We left after paying and got back on our bikes, feeling quite subversive. Helmets on and D-rings snugged, we rumbled up and jounced over the lip of the exit, motoring back up to speed. We were now riding at a higher elevation. The air was cool and crisp. There were patches of pine trees between areas of grassland as we went over Targhee Pass. 7,000 foot elevation.

We made it into West Yellowstone, Montana, and stopped at a Texaco station to fill our tanks. As we filled up, I glanced around at this village gateway to the park. Many of the buildings were modeled on a simple A-frame architecture that emulated those I'd seen throughout the National Park Service: ranger stations, natural history museums, and the like. Except for a few small signs and a couple of buildings that looked as if they'd been added later, the look of the town made me feel as if I was already inside the park, but not as thick with trees as California.

The main drag was also the entrance road, and although the various shops were mostly retail, the uniformity of the coloring, building materials, and architecture muted everything into a gentle acclimation, an introduction to camping and the natural wonders not too far away. The scent of pine forests and dirt. Car doors slamming and local grocery stores. Folding maps. Kids in shorts and t-shirts. Station wagons with camping gear strapped to the roof.

The buildings had round log joists painted dark reddish-brown and roof lines — usually of dull brown or bright metal — steep enough for new snow to slide right off when winter set in. Rock walls with old white mortar the first three feet, then wood from there up. The entire town had been built to blend into the forest. Every business had wooden signage. You had to be able to tell where the barbershop was and which building housed sporting goods, but even the graphics were subdued. Well, most of it.

The Texaco Star, red on white, branded the station where we'd stopped as if to proclaim that all things crude came out of Houston or Dallas, bright and shiny against the natural and subdued browns and greens of the rest of the town. *Ding ding,* another car pulled in. While I was busy checking tire pressure and getting a quart of oil, Tom got into a conversation with one of the attendants. He told me about it later.

"If I were an artist, I could paint everything down to the smallest detail: his sandy hair, his lined face and blue eyes sizing me up. Everything about him spelled regret. He was envious of us for being on our trip but couldn't bring himself to do the same. He had resigned himself: stuck in his job, his choices, and his life.

"Until that point, I'd been thinking of the trip as a holiday—nothing more than an extended road-trip with a friend. But listening to that gas station attendant changed it for me. Our trip became an adventure; something more than a road trip. During the silence of riding protracted distances, you get to wondering. You watch the clouds and understand the road, but something more is going on as well. Change happens in subtle ways, and sometimes it sneaks up on you.

"Growing up, you occasionally become aware of how *not* to have your life turn out, and (hopefully) live your life with good, educated choices. Sometimes you experience something directly or see something happening to others and vow to not let it happen to you. That gas station attendant's conversation, situation, body language, environment—everything about him spoke to an epiphany that not only clarified what *not* to do with your life, but also seemed to confirm that what we were doing was the right thing."

After leaving the gas station, we took Highway 191. We were now in forested land—tall pine trees on both sides of the road. 191 led us to the Yellowstone West Entrance, which is still in Montana, although the park itself lies almost entirely within Wyoming—just a short ride away. Tom and I rode up to the ticket office in the middle of the roadway, and took our helmets off.

The ranger looked down at us from his window. "Regular pass or Golden Eagle?" He was wearing the khaki livery with the badges, even to that flat-brimmed ranger hat. He looked me in the eye. He wasn't smiling.

"What's the difference?" I was closest to the window.

"Regular pass gets you in for seven days if that's all you're staying, but that fee covers only one of you. The Golden Eagle Pass is still seven days, but covers two motorcycles at any of the national parks for a full year. It costs a little more."

"Golden Eagle?" I said, glancing over at Tom.

Tom raised his eyebrows and looked over his glasses at me: *Mr. Noncommittal*. He was saying it was my money.

I looked back at the ranger in the window. "Golden Eagle."

Not that we had specific plans, but you never know. And we might find ourselves at another national park at some point.

The entrance road ran thirty miles and took us directly into Wyoming. We met sleet about ten miles in. It was sudden, cold, and icy. We didn't know what it was at first, but the road was turning white. Hail was bouncing off our tanks like gravel, not something to ride through. Tom spotted a culvert that ran under the road. The shoulder wasn't too steep, so we were able to ride our bikes off the road and then down to the stream. There was hardly any water, and the pipe was large enough for us to stand inside. We parked the bikes near the entrance to the culvert—the ground was hard enough to support our kickstands—and listened to the hail bouncing off our bikes with an irregular tap-tap-tapping.

"Jeez, this is cold," said Tom. He was shivering. He still didn't have gloves, and it had caught up with him. He was hugging himself with his hands in his armpits. We were both stamping our feet to increase circulation and create warmth.

We had started putting used newspapers inside our pants and jackets back in Idaho to fight the cold. I had read it was something men did during the Depression when they were living on the streets in winter. There were always one or two used newspapers at diners. We'd grab what we could and put them in our packs for when we might need them. Turns out you can put up with hot or cold weather a lot easier when your body core is okay. And they made for local reading, which was entertaining. So, double-duty.

When the hail stopped the ground was white with it, like snow, but granular and icy. We finally ventured out into the silence, wary of the hail starting up again, our boots crunching footprints in the thin white blanket. We didn't want to sleep in that culvert, so we fired up our bikes again and continued on into Yellowstone.

The hail hadn't fallen as heavily in Camp Madison, which is where we decided to stay. We chose a site next to a couple from Santa Barbara: Marti and Max. We also met two girls, Cindy and Marsha, who came over later to say hello. The action of pitching our tent warmed us, or perhaps it was knowing we had a place to sleep, but we settled down once we had a campsite. It was our anchor in the moment. We were the friendly motorcycle guys, camping between those three pine trees at #106. Yep, that was us.

We wandered around the campground that afternoon, saying hi to people and getting to know our neighbors. The dirt road wound through the trees, and everyone got their own bit of privacy and sense of the forest as a living presence.

We met sixteen-year-old Lynn near the entrance. A brown-eyed girl with a shy smile and dirty blonde hair, she walked back with us and we talked of this and that going around the loop. Her father was a captain in the Marine Corps, and she was camping with her mom, who was having coffee when we came around to their site.

She offered, and we all had a cup. Even Tom, which surprised me. If anything, he usually stuck with hot chocolate. We sat with them for a while. Their campfire was going, and it crackled and burned and turned to embers as we talked. Every once in a while one of us would put another stick on the fire.

I remember the woman's eyes and the deep emotions. It was unusual for us to talk with someone who was affected so directly by the war. Most people kept it to themselves. Her voice washed over me. Alone with her daughter, camping out to get away, trying to change the conversation in her head. Jeans and a white blouse, dark eyes and her hair tied up in a bun the way women do when they haven't got time for it.

I tried to understand how she coped to get by. So isolated. They call it collateral damage like it meant nothing. It meant a hell of a lot to her, trying to hold it together.

"I get letters," she said. "But we can't talk like we used to. How can I explain everything Lynn is going through at school? How can he explain what it's like for him out there, with what he has to do?" She sat in her lawn chair, leaning forward, holding her coffee mug with both hands and staring into the flames.

Her face was a journal of life, and her eyes closed from time to time as if in memory of distant issues before shaking it off. She glanced this way and that, off into the trees and then back again before locking onto Tom or myself in tired defiance.

Tom and I could only listen. Sharon and her daughter hadn't done a damn thing, yet they were trapped in the whirlwind of war. They stood to lose a lot and could only hope things would fall their way. And none of it was of their own doing or in their control. If they were lucky, he would come back in one piece, but common knowledge said nobody really did.

Vietnam had become such a hot topic it was difficult to talk about. And when the opinion of the country turned, the soldiers got a huge share of the blame, which should never have happened. Many thought of themselves as patriots.

The war was a jigsaw puzzle on everyone's kitchen table, with an edge over here and a corner and part of the sky over there, but still not whole. The concept was amorphous, with too many pieces. A lot more time would have to pass before any of us would be able to put it together.

Later on, Tom and I hiked down to the amphitheater with our flashlights for a Ranger Talk. About fifty of us sat on benches made of half-logs among the redwood trees to hear a program describing the features of the park. As the ranger explained it to us, the Yellowstone Supervolcano had erupted every 600,000 years or so for several million years, but was completely unpredictable. The next eruption could make life very unpleasant. Kind of odd to think of camping on top of a ticking time bomb. It was quite dark by the time the park rangers wrapped it up and we used our flashlights to get back to our site.

When we got back, I thought to make a fire. I used my Buck knife to shave bark from several logs given to us by three guys from Washington D.C. They were camping nearby. Where they got the logs, I had no idea.

That was one of the things about camping; people sharing resources back and forth. You need some wood? Well, we've got extra. Out of marshmallows? Have some of ours. It was spontaneous camaraderie that led to conversations and unguarded smiles. We were all in it together. Looking up, I could see stars between the treetops.

The idea that the average guy doesn't take enough time to appreciate nature certainly applied to me. I seem to have spent a good part of my life — probably too much — either reading, thinking, or creating enough space to do so. Doesn't mean I don't love nature, because I do. I just never ordinarily took the time to immerse myself in the Tao of the outer world except for my parents' annual vacation trips when I was a kid, and now, on this trip, during small moments like this.

I was just sitting by the campfire, whittling on a manzanita stick I'd picked up back at Lassen and stuck in my pack. Nothing fancy. I was working it over with my Buck knife, scraping off all the little twigs and rounding the ends of it, making it into a sort of baton, I suppose, and I had no idea why. It was something to do. The fire snapped from time to time.

Tom had gone off on a walk around the loop, probably talking to people, seeing everything with quick glances. He noticed more than I did most of the time. But now, in the quiet of the evening, with that half-dark settling in, I seemed very aware of my surroundings: the hard feel of the log under my butt, how my jacket felt across my shoulders, the pine trees around the camping area, and the mystery spaces between them and the wooded areas farther off.

During the day the scents and small sounds of the natural world get lost in the scuffle of life, but the stillness of the night brings them out. I could taste the wood smoke and the green of the trees in the air. Someone zipped up a tent. A car crunched gravel, rolling quietly through the loop, looking for an empty spot.

I was sitting on a log in front of a fire, whittling on a piece of wood, but I was also in the middle of a great, ancient forest, despite the veneer of civilization the National Park Service provided. Our bikes gleamed by reflected firelight just ten feet away. Our little blue tent, darkening into the background. Our fire pit — nothing more than a circle of rocks really, filled with old ashes and burning wood — had been used by any number of people over the years. And yet, in this moment, it seemed unique unto itself. I thought about Sharon and her daughter, and what they were going through. I wondered about all the little families with their private concerns, like mine, dealing with so much uncertainty and doubt.

The fire, the forest, and even our bikes (evidence of our journey to get here) were mute witness, along with myself, just sitting on a log, thinking about it, being with it in the moment. The fire popped and a spark flew into the air. This was the language of a world I didn't inhabit often, but I was immersed in it now. It was a little unexpected, but certainly welcome.

In the tent that night when Tom told me all about the guy he'd met at the filling station in West Yellowstone and his life of frustration and regret, I was reminded of that Help Wanted sign back in Manteca. Suddenly his joke turned serious as I contemplated by own future. Did I really want to sell business machines and office supplies with some kind of assured future, or did I want to be a writer, dependent on a skill I might not have? Maybe I should be a park ranger and tramp the forest. Did Tom want to work in a ski shack forever? We both knew we didn't want to be the gas station attendant in West Yellowstone, despondent and frustrated.

Day 11   Wednesday, Sept. 2 – Yellowstone, Wyoming

"Eggs again?"
"You know that's all we've got."
"I was thinking waffles."
"Well, maybe when we find a diner you can have waffles."
"With hot syrup?"
"Sure."
"Most diners just have cold syrup."
"I'm sure we can ask. Maybe they can heat it."
"Why would anyone pour cold syrup on a hot waffle?"
"I agree. It's a crime no one should be subjected to."

We went into West Yellowstone to do laundry and take showers, but going back to the park we hit serious rain, which was near freezing. Tom was still without gloves and wasn't happy about it. We were both on the lean side and handled heat better than cold. I'm not sure what the wind-chill factor is on motorcycle handlebars, but I'm afraid Tom's hands got like blocks of ice since they had to be right out there to control his bike. The cold shot right up his arms to his back and torso, making his whole body sensitive to what we were going through. He stamped his feet and tried to warm his hands with his breath whenever he could, then walked around with them jammed into his pockets, trying to get some relief.

En route to our campsite, we stopped to talk with a couple who had come over from Belgium to work in a research department for the University of Washington in Seattle. They offered us coffee, and we spent some time by their campfire.

Meeting strangers, talking to people on the road was certainly different. Some people have a persona they use with new people, and I found myself trying to decipher who they really were from conversation and body language. The dynamics were elusive. Sometimes people found us interesting, but other times we were dismissed with short sentences and eyes that slid away.

Tom and I were from California, and that could change things as well. California was for America what America was for the rest of the world—a land of riches and opportunity. When we sat down with strangers, we sometimes got the pressure of their eyes, assessing us and measuring the look of us against their own notions.

California conjured up bright images of redwood groves and the Pacific Ocean, the Golden Gate Bridge, and Hollywood. We were from the land of hippies, psychedelic drugs, and smog. That wasn't who we were, but it formed a backdrop and probably made us a bit more interesting than we really were.

It was getting dark and starting to drizzle, so we headed back to our site and the shelter of our tent. We munched out on pretzels and sugar wafers with milk. We had been reading Peter Fonda's interview in *Playboy*. The film *Easy Rider* had been released in theaters the previous year and turned counterculture grit into a kind of aspirational chic. We were nothing like the main characters, but may have been perceived as safer versions by some of the people we encountered.

Cindy and Marsha, two girls we'd come across the previous day, came over, but we were snuggled up in our sleeping bags. We'd gotten soaked while riding in the rain (our clothes were drying at the back of the tent).

Day 12   Thursday, Sept. 3 – Yellowstone, Wyoming

Fully dressed, we talked with Marsha and Cindy again and rode them into town on our bikes. Tom was impressed with Marsha and would gladly have spent more time with her. We said our goodbyes, and they left with their parents. *C'est la vie.*

We took a ride to see Old Faithful geyser and stopped at a few of the hot spots along the way. The geyser areas are colorful but desolate for the most part: fumaroles with hot gases, boiling and steaming hot springs, geysers, and mud pots. So, our eyes met turquoise, crimson, and milk chocolate mud bubbles, but no green pine trees, no bushes, no forest floor, and no forest, except on mountain slopes in the distance—which only sharpens the sounds: the cry of a solitary bird, the murmur of campers in small clusters along the paths, the shuffle of our shoes on the hot dirt.

All quite dry and desolate until we arrived at the geyser itself. Old Faithful had gathered quite a bit of infrastructure around it over the years, including an inn and a lodge, along with parking and plenty of signage. Everything named after Old Faithful, of course.

My bike ran out of gas on the way, but I had packed a red anodized aluminum bottle of spare fuel, untouched until now. I emptied it into the tank. Like an idiot, I forgot to zip my pack closed and lost my canister somewhere along the road. Both our motorcycles had built-in fuel reserves we accessed by moving the fuel petcock in the opposite direction. That red bottle had been our emergency backup.

Riding back to camp, we noticed several cars parked along the shoulder. People were getting out, shading their eyes, and gazing at a herd of bison in the meadow to our left. Sightseeing. That is, the people were sightseeing, not the bison. (Although the bison might have been sightseeing too, observing the strange apes in metal boxes who came to gibber and point.) We stopped to look, Tom farther ahead, up near some cars.

The bison is the largest living land animal native to North America, and capable of putting on serious speed when the mood strikes. Close up, they're about the size of a small truck, but weigh twice as much. This herd was about fifty yards away and meandering toward the road. As they got closer, the lead bison started moving faster and with purpose, heading toward the one place with a noticeable gap in the line of cars. A gap with me sitting — with my motor off — right in the middle of it.

Now, if I remember the manual correctly (How to Avoid Getting Killed Whilst Traversing National Parks by Motorcycle), one of the very first lessons was: *Never get in the way of super large animals trying to cross the road.*

I get it. Bison are stunning, single-minded creatures that are wonderful for photography, but not much fun up close. And they can move: 35 mph at a lumbering gallop.

At first, that lead bison was merely walking. Then he picked up the pace as he determined his final route. The herd began to move faster to keep up, all heading toward me. I couldn't really see what speed they were traveling, since they were headed in my direction.

Thud... Thud... Thud... Thud...

Again, he picked up the pace. Watching this unfold, I realized they weren't likely to change course. That huge lead bull was snorting, trotting faster, heading straight at me. Somehow, I fumbled my key into the ignition and twisted.

The engine cranked over and over, but wouldn't start. And wouldn't start. And wouldn't start. *Oh shit — have I flooded it?*

Thud. Thud. Thud. Thumpety-thud. Thud. Thud.

That bull with the entire herd thundering right behind him was getting a hell of a lot closer.

Pound! Pound! Pound! Pound! Pound! Pound! Pound! Pound!

The engine finally caught with a roar, and I got the bike into gear — *clunk*. Now I was on instinct and adrenaline and *getting the hell out of there.*

I'd never "popped a wheelie" in my life, but I did it then. The bike jolted, the front wheel came off the ground, and I'm standing on the pegs, desperately trying to keep the front end from flipping me over backward. The rear tire is screaming, burning rubber for the first time in its life, and for one horrible heartbeat the bike doesn't even move. I'm just poised like a monument to stupidity. Then the front end comes down and I'm a cruise missile. *Supersonic.* And *bam!* — I'm right up to Tom and slamming on the brakes, trying not to go all sideways, trying not to hit his bike, trying to stay upright. And then it was over. *Holy crap.*

Everybody was clapping and grinning at me and pointing. I'm feeling stupid and proud at the same time, mostly because I'm still alive and no longer in the path of all those hooves, but also because Tom can't stop laughing. *"Excellent!"*

And I'm shaking to pieces inside.

Over my shoulder, I see a blur of brown crossing the road, dust rising from their massive, thundering bodies. I feel the pounding of their hooves through the pavement, up my legs, through the air hitting my chest and the pounding in my ears. And no, they didn't turn; they didn't even blink.

I needed a few minutes to calm the inner man. At some point, the bison were all grazing on the far side, heads down, oblivious to everything. They had moved on with their lives, as did we. We stopped and talked with Max and Marti on our way back to our campsite, and decided to give them the rest of our marshmallows.

Day 13   Friday, Sept. 4 – Grand Tetons, Wyoming

We broke camp at Madison campground along with Max and Marti. It turned out they were heading in the same direction we were, out of Yellowstone and toward the Grand Tetons.

Tom and I stopped at a place with the odd name of *Cat Hat Eat Resort* and got bumper stickers that we pasted onto Tom's guitar: one side proclaimed "America, Love It or Leave It," and the other was "I'm Proud To Be An American." These glaring epithets promoted ignorance, intolerance, and saccharine simplicity: perfect camouflage for a couple of guys from California who couldn't afford to get into trouble with any of the locals. That guitar with those two idiotic stickers became our cloaking device.

We also got some polished rocks just because they looked interesting and you never know when you might need some polished rocks...

We noticed an ever-increasing number of signs for a place called "Wall Drug" in addition to those puckish Burma Shave signs that were ubiquitous throughout the American West. Each one had a spirited limerick painted on consecutive signboards about twenty feet apart.

Each limerick was unique, had no punctuation whatsoever, and we'd all sort of grown up with them. I only had a nebulous idea what the Burma Shave company actually did, but they had one heck of an advertising department.

We came across a guy named Jim Valentine working on his red MGA TWIN CAM and tried to help him out for part of a day. His plugs and carbs were messed up, probably because the altitude at 6,800 feet was not providing enough oxygen for the grade of fuel he had in his tank. He was traveling east for his first year at Harvard and told us to look him up if we ever got that far. He was a nice guy.

It rained again. We met four people from Ohio when we finally pulled over that night. They had a large bonfire going, which was unusual. Entire logs. We asked why they made such a huge fire. "It's cold," said one guy. Maybe they had a truck tucked away somewhere to carry such logs. We got dry at their fire and talked for a bit, then set up our own tent.

There was always more safety in numbers, plus the comfort of camping next to people with whom we'd had some real contact. If we talked to anyone long enough to call it a conversation, they became a friend, and got treated as such.

Day 14   Saturday, Sept. 5 – I-90, S. Dakota

We lost track of Max and Marti somewhere along the way. The morning was rainy, but we got bacon and eggs from our neighbors, which made for a terrific breakfast on our Boy Scout frying pan. We needed it, considering we would be traveling about 400 miles that day. We broke camp and left the Tetons, riding Interstate 90. I-90 runs over 3,000 miles, from Seattle to Boston, and it took us into South Dakota that day. *Rocky Raccoon* by the Beatles was playing in my head during this entire ride, although I couldn't remember all the words, which was irritating. Tom started singing it and then I couldn't get rid of it.

We were riding across one of the largest prairies in the world. Land historic to nomadic tribes such as the Arapaho, Cheyenne, Pawnee, and of course, the Dakota. Miles of bluestem wheatgrass everywhere we looked.

The plains weren't all that flat. There were slight swells and waves in the grass. And the wind made it ripple, even with just a light breeze. I squinted — past the long straight road crossing ours up ahead, past a barn on that same road off to the right, which might be massive, but looked like a red smudge from my perspective, and on into the distance even as we glided across this flat universe, like ships on a sea of grass. Home at one time to millions of bison.

Day 15   Sunday, Sept. 6 – Wind Cave, S. Dakota

We found Wind Cave, South Dakota, which is both a town *and* a cave, with 149 miles of subterranean passages. We caught some rain coming into Wind Cave National Park and set up camp on top of a hill. This was flat country for the most part, and we found ourselves riding towards a beautiful rainbow coming back from town with supplies.

We had entered into the land of shot up road signs some time ago, but this part of the country was particularly perforated. Mailboxes and road signs had both shiny and rusty bullet holes (the shiny ones being more recently acquired). Anything flat, stationary, and made of metal was a target, and if a sign didn't have a bullet hole, it quickly found one. Since every truck had a rack and a rifle against the back window, it was easy to see how those with high spirits and nothing better to do might pull over to take potshots at the authority such signs represented. *50 MPH, eh? Right. Take that!* Some signs got so shot up they fell right off the post to the tune of *Don't Fence Me In*.

We were almost completely out of cash. I had sold my car to finance the trip and had been concerned, even with traveler's cheques, that something really bad might happen—like getting robbed, or losing the money somehow—and had left the rest of my funds with my parents. Life savings, as it were.

Whenever funds got low, I always called home a few days before we'd run out, giving my best guess as to where we'd be the following day. I'd collect the cash and ride on. That worked most of the time, but occasionally—like right then—I hadn't timed it right. Plus, there always had to be a Western Union office within easy riding distance. I phoned Ray to send more money, which he was able to do the next day.

We had enough money for the cave tour and learned about the cave's formation and structure. It's one of the longest and most complex "maze" caves in the world, known for its calcium boxwork formations, which looked like a mass of geometric webbing made of mineral deposits. It wasn't rocket science or *Persistence of Memory*, but it was interesting and certainly something different from just riding the range.

When we got out of the tour and blinking in the sunlight, we realized we had made a huge mistake. Why we didn't lock the helmets to our motorcycles I have no idea, but they were gone. We'd been robbed. Harley riders never lock their helmets, but Honda riders must. It's a cultural thing and stupid as the day is long.

Getting back to camp, we cleaned and polished the bikes. The front part of the heat shield was now really cracked and vibrating right next to my left ankle, so I bent it back and forth until it snapped from metal fatigue. Wind Cave National Park had hardly any campers, and it was spooky. Riding without helmets was good for a change, since it was warm enough. Dinner consisted of good old Dinty Moore. Again. The sky was a Turner sunset that night, crimson and gold.

Day 16   Monday, Sept. 7 – Wind Cave, S. Dakota

We didn't do much, and stayed in town during the day. It seemed safer there than at the campground, because at least there were people around. There is nothing emptier than an empty campground. A place where people are expected to be but aren't. It was Labor Day, so the post office was closed. We promised the park ranger to mail $2 for our campsite fee.

"Tom?"

"Yeah?"

"Happy Labor Day."

"Go to sleep."

"Okay."

Day 17   Tuesday, Sept. 8 – Rapid City, S. Dakota

We left Wind Cave and rode on to Rapid City to get the cash I'd asked my father to wire via Western Union. Tom got two letters, one from his mom and one from Terry Flynn. Terry was one of Tom's long-time friends and wing-woman for parties. She and Tom were very close in high school, and she went to college at U.C. Berkeley. Her nickname "Leaf" came from a Halloween party where her costume was a bush made up of paper "leaves."

We rode into the town of Wall, and encountered Wall Drug Store, a composite of consecutive but disparate buildings with all the adjoining walls knocked down to create one long tunnel of a building. It probably started as a local drugstore, but the owners kept buying and occupying successive storefronts and hooking them together until it became one long emporium of homespun Americana, jackalopes and all.

Other than that one storefront, which went store-to-store-to-store for an entire city block, there wasn't much there but a gas station, supported by all the tourists visiting Wall Drug and its amazing mile of American hucksterism. Tom got himself a Mexican vest and finally ran out of money, which we knew was going to happen at some point. For a couple of days after that, he made telling me to pay for things into a running joke, which he thought hugely funny. I was fine with it but squared the charade with my famous mock grimace and eye roll.

Wall Drug was certainly an iconic place. Crammed full of Americana, it reminded me of those roadside attractions we used to see on vacation. Reptile exhibits, teepee motels, and Jurassic theme parks all had that same feel, born out of hardscrabble entrepreneurship, cheap land, and an endless supply of bored tourists traveling en masse along the interstate highway system. The inside was akin to a narrow mall or galleria, with everything from shooting galleries to photo booths and all kinds of merchandise in between. And everything imaginable with their logo emblazoned on it in Green Bay Packer green and yellow, in variations of a western font they'd picked up along the way.

WALL DRUG

The place had a carnival atmosphere more like a boardwalk than a store, and if you were hungry, everything from buffalo burgers to homemade donuts. I had no idea if they were still a pharmacy anymore. The jackalopes seemed to have consumed everything normal years ago.

They had every conceivable trinket and tourist knickknack you could imagine. A hand-thrown pottery coffee cup emblazoned with "A Gift from Stratford Upon Avon" is the best model I can think of. Smokey the Bear thermometers, pencil erasers, and music boxes. I used to have a stuffed Smokey the Bear with blue pants when I was little. When I wound him up he spoke in a gruff voice, "Remember... Only YOU Can Prevent Forest Fires." My thinking ran away with me.

"Hey, guys! Where you from?"

We had somehow picked up a small contingent of teenage girls in our wanderings from the "Genuine Petrified Wood" display over to the "Knives Engraved with Religious Verses" section. They seemed to think we were pretty special. Must have been our uniforms.

"California," Tom said, striking a nonchalant pose.

I cocked an eyebrow and gave him a look. He didn't fool me at all.

"That's a long way," came a voice from within the group. Two brunettes and a blonde, cute as a row of buttons. Their faces were fresh, their eyes were clear, and all three were looking up at us. This was new territory.

The girls were far too young for us, but it doesn't hurt to be polite. I glanced back at Tom, but I couldn't tell if he was having similar thoughts. *On vacation with their parents?*

"You girls on vacation?" I asked. I had picked up a Smokey the Bear thermometer, and it became a useful prop, holding it in my hands and inspecting it for authenticity.

"Yeah. We're with our parents," replied one of the brunettes. Blue, pink, and green T-shirts made them look like teenage jelly beans. Bright and very cute. Tom looked over his glasses at me and raised an eyebrow, which was his super-secret method of telling me something.

I wiggled both eyebrows right back, which meant I saw his eyebrow and raised him one. This was quite a hand we'd drawn, and I wasn't certain how to play it—whether we should raise, stand pat, or fold. Were we going to allow ourselves to be picked up like this? It felt a little out of hand.

I had a flash image of parents circling just offshore, and the two of us standing there with our helmets, road-warrior jeans, and wind-burned faces. *Motorcycle riders.*

All three girls were watching us, going from me to Tom and back with shy, luminous eyes—dangerous as hell. I was sure they saw our interchange of meaningful looks. They were doing something risky, but all the people milling around them was a safety net. What could happen in the middle of Wall Drug with all those jackalopes standing guard?

"Where are you guys from?" I asked. "I mean, are you all together?" I was looking at their faces, being polite, wondering why I'd asked the question. We had to get out of there, but I was curious.

"Idaho," said the blonde girl. "We're from Idaho." She was gazing straight into my eyes in a speculative way like she was the spoon and I was the chocolate pudding.

I consulted Tom once more in the language of the eyebrows. I raised one of mine. He raised one of his.

"We've gotta go," I said, putting the thermometer back on the display case. *Sorry, Smokey.*

"Nice to meet you," said Tom, polite as ever.

I started hustling toward the door and Tom came after. We glanced back just before going out the door. They waved, and we sort of waved, and then we were out the door. *Whew!*

I don't think either of us had been approached like that before. Kind of thrilling, really. Like swimming with baby sharks. Back on the bikes, we scrunched gravel out the parking lot and motored away.

The road we were on did double-duty as the Main Street of every small town along our route, so after leaving Wall, we traveled through the center of similar (but not nearly as colorful) townships such as Wasta (pop. 127), Kadoka (pop. 815), Murdo (pop. 865), and Draper (pop. 200). We stopped in a few places, to stretch, pause, and look around at the buildings and local fauna. Whenever I went to put my left foot down, I kept catching my pants on the raw end of my heat shield. Irritating.

In one such town, we noticed a local movie house on the main drag. It had a version of art nouveau architecture with an open-air lobby in front to keep the customers dry whenever it rained (or snowed, more likely), very much like our own theater back home. Tom looked at me, I looked at Tom; we shrugged our shoulders and went to the movies.

Once inside, the only thing missing was the **BILL MANDER FOREIGN CARS** clock, which should have been up on the far left wall, glowing blue, next to the screen. Which it would have been had we been in Los Gatos. We watched *Battle of Britain*, which had (appropriately enough) an all-English, tight-lipped cast. It felt strange going from middle America into an aerial battle over England and Germany for a couple of hours, then back to the streets of South Dakota. It was also odd that we were fighting a war overseas with nothing touching us here except the coffins that came home. Like watching a war movie.

We walked out at 11:00 P.M. and *wham*, we were almost blown over. We had to dance a bit and bend into the wind to keep upright! Our bikes were at the curb and still standing, fortunately. We mounted up and rode s-l-o-w-l-y out of town at a remarkable tilt to windward, leaning into the wind and battling heavy gusts.

The road turned, and suddenly that heavy wind was at our backs. We were coasting along like clipper ships sailing before the wind, using only enough throttle to keep the engines ticking over and to make sure we could pull power if we needed it.

We finally found a picnic ground about thirty miles out, at Badlands National Park. Not a fun place to camp. The wind came at us hard and threatened to push our bikes over as soon as we stopped. There were a few spindly trees, all of them bent over and whipping around. Tom and I pitched our tent on the leeward side of a cement block public restroom, the only building within a hundred miles. We decided that all the cement-block restrooms scattered here and there around the country served two purposes. The obvious one, obviously, but also to provide emergency shelter for poorly-equipped campers who didn't want to die out in the middle of nowhere.

While our tent flapped and billowed like the mainsail of a ship rounding the Horn in a high gale, we had dinner, such as it was. Good thing it was simple; we couldn't cook anything in the tent. We shared a Milky Way. Eating a candy bar slowly takes concentration and commitment, but neither of us had any idea quite how much, nor the techniques that could be employed until we saw how far we were able to stretch out such a meal. And it wasn't like we were trying hard. We each had half a candy bar. It constituted our entire evening, and we treated it as such — with deliberation.

"You're paying for this, right?"

"Yeah, but you're covering the tip."

"Very funny."

Day 18   Wednesday, Sept. 9 – Sioux Falls, S. Dakota

We found both sunshine and sleet on I-90 to Sioux Falls and stopped at a rundown campground, the kind you see on the outskirts of towns and cities all over. It was bare ground, a few picnic tables, and "trailer facilities," which meant that people were dumping raw sewage about fifty feet from where we were going to camp. Every once in a while we'd get a whiff. Not much, but just enough to remind us we were Camping

On Cement (or pretty close to it), and we would have been better off not to push that extra fifty miles.

The rain hit hard and fast as we sat down to dinner at one of the picnic tables, and we were suddenly very busy trying to keep everything from being blown away. There were bits of white all over and we figured it for hail. This was more than just rain. We moved quickly. Threw our packs under the table, grabbed our sleeping bags and the guitar, and ran like hell for the bathrooms.

We found a roof, such as it was, inside the cinder block bathroom provided by the management. It had been built sometime in the distant past, and, as with so many of these necessary but indelicate facilities, it seemed permeated by the fug of the years. Although the wind had come in briskly when we'd opened the door, the atmosphere remained quite distinctive; the air was heavy with the scent of vacationers-in-transit, last year's urinal cakes, and too many layers of disinfectant.

We were somewhat surprised to find several other would-be campers inside: two guys, and a girl with quiet eyes and a slow smile. We spent an hour or so huddled in blankets and damp sleeping bags on the floor without knowing when the rain or wind would stop. When you ride motorcycles across North America in the autumn, you can count on getting wet at least part of the time — it's in the by-laws. Tom and I acknowledged that, but still, that restroom was pretty ripe.

Our huddle-mates gave us a tuna sandwich and a joint, which we never smoked, but accepted. The tuna added variety, but the joint would have been an extra layer above and beyond all reason — although it would have masked much of the ambient odor of that room, had we lit it up. We ate the sandwich later that night and it was a welcome change from our rather unimaginative peanut butter and honey | local-diner hamburger | bacon and egg diet we had going up to that point. The tuna was good.

We all hunkered down in that evil-smelling restroom under a bare yellow light bulb. Our newfound friends had managed to save some peanut butter sandwiches from the rain (yes, just peanut butter and bread), so we munched out on those while waiting for the rain to slacken.

"Wichita," said the girl. She stood at the entrance to one of the stalls, one hand on the doorframe, the other in her pocket. Levis and a green parka. "We're *from* Wichita," she said to clarify. She wore a small gold watch on her right wrist, the one in her pocket. *Sister? Lover? Cousin?* She was left handed.

"California," said Tom.

"The Bay Area," I added. "Near San Francisco." Making everything crystal clear, like we were from one of the outer moons and not specifying might be discourteous and gauche.

"Where are you headed?" she asked.

"East Coast," Tom replied. "New York maybe. You?"

"Just camping," said one of the guys. "A vacation. You two on motorcycles?"

"Yeah," said Tom. "Not so good in the rain, though."

I decided the girl was pretty. She sounded bright.

"These mosquitoes. Amazing!" said the second guy, speaking up for the first time. "Huge."

Gallywompers were buzzing around the light bulb in its wire cage on the ceiling They looked like giant mosquitoes sizing us up. We'd been glancing up at them from time to time, like rabbits wary of hawks. Tom commented that they had the same lean and hungry look as the mosquitoes we'd encountered back at that lake in Idaho.

I didn't volunteer any personal reasons for being on the road and Tom stayed mum. "Road trip" was all we said. Despite the brilliance of our repartee, the time passed slowly as we waited for the weather to abate. But that was okay. It meant we were all normal people who could share peanut butter sandwiches and a joint (even if we didn't smoke it). The conversation finally petered out along with the rain, and the five of us emerged from that foul cocoon like prisoners released into the main yard, going back to our two camps to deal with the damage.

The storm couldn't have lasted more than an hour, but back in our little corner of heaven there was an inch of water in Tom's drinking cup. We also didn't have to get extra water to wash the plates; the hail had scoured them clean. Our tent was blown halfway to the creek. It was muddy, and I guess we were lucky the cottonwoods and dense bushes along the edge had snagged it before going all the way into the water.

Tom and I spent the next twenty minutes resetting everything. Our alternative was that Lysol-smelling restroom, buddy-buddy with the gallywompers and mosquitoes, slapping ourselves to sleep.

Day 19   Thursday, Sept. 10 – Jackson, Minnesota

We had our usual breakfast of bacon and eggs using the Boy Scout kit and Tom's ridiculously tiny Sterno stove.

"Mmmm, good!"

"Damn straight."

"Delicious!"

"I think the fresh air makes all the difference, don't you?"

"Yeah, that and the cement."

"Your turn to wash."

"Okay, but you have to dry."

We'd been riding without helmets since they'd been lifted off our bikes at Wind Cave. People had directed us to Kmarts and other stores along the way, but after perusing their selection of brain buckets, we had held off in the hope of finding something that would genuinely protect us. We rode into Sioux Falls, a fair-sized city, and found what we'd been searching for at a motorcycle shop: a Bell 500TX and a Bell Magnum, $33 and $30, respectively. That seemed expensive.

Wearing our new helmets, we traveled east toward Jackson, Minnesota, about two hours away. Jackson was about the size of our hometown of Los Gatos and I-90 ran right by it. Hunger led us off the main highway and through the downtown. Which is when I crashed. Well, I didn't crash exactly, I fell over. At a stoplight coming into Jackson. I will explain.

Given that my bike was a "scrambler" model, the exhaust pipes were tucked up high along the left side. This meant that when I sat the bike, my left leg was right next to the pipes—and very hot metal could touch the inside of my leg. So there was a perforated shield between the pipes and my leg to protect me. I've talked about it.

This shield had developed a small crack early on, becoming worse the farther we rode. It had been rattling, and finally bugged me enough that I had just snapped it off back at Wind Cave, five days before. What was left had a rough edge and my pants would catch when the wind ballooned my pant leg up over it. Which it frequently did.

Whenever I came to a stop and put my left leg out to support the bike, this snagged pant leg (with very little effort) stopped my left foot from reaching the ground. During such moments, those last six inches made all the difference.

I was always left with nothing to support the bike except sheer balance, which doesn't work for more than a heartbeat or two when 550 pounds of machinery and rider are at a dead stop (although I had made a few very spirited attempts). Ever since I had broken the heat shield, I'd had to fight like a madman to get my left leg out and down. And I'd always managed it just in time. If you ask why I didn't just tie up my pant leg with a piece of twine or get a bicycle clip, well I did. Later. Naturally, Tom thought the whole thing highly amusing. I'd be struggling heroically, I'd manage somehow not to fall over, and after a few seconds, there it was. *"Excellent!"*

At that moment, on that day, at that stoplight in Jackson, Minnesota, it happened again. With my forward motion at zero, my pant leg caught, my horizontal motion increased from imperceptible to rapid, and I toppled, stage left, all the way down.

I say "toppled" only because I can't find a word that properly describes such a dramatic fall from grace. One moment I was upright, all merry and bright; the next I was sideways, a sort of macédoine of arms, legs, and muttering steel.

My progress from the normal upright, in-control position (and self-appointed king of all I surveyed), to that of a sprawling intertwist of hot metal and bruised ego did not happen in stages. Oh no. Planting my left foot firmly in the air, I slowly and majestically collapsed into an attention-grabbing heap of embarrassment. Right at that first stoplight, I came to rest with a calamitous crunch. My clutch lever skittered away.

And I heard someone, myself perhaps, or the voice in my head, muttering quietly, "Jon, you perfect idiot." in a voice that reached right through the cacophony of my inglorious descent with the immediate impact of chagrin, softened just a tad by the sublime humor of it all. If you ever need to find true humility, fall over on a motorcycle at a complete stop in the middle of the street, surrounded by onlookers.

For a moment there was nothing but stunned silence and blank stares from people who turned to look.

It was one of those world-stopping moments we've all experienced when the space-time continuum gets spaghettified into a stream of clarity that lasts forever in a split second, and I saw the insignificance and vanity of life's struggle. Well, overall. And then good old fight or flight kicked in, reanimating my arms and legs and the good old frontal lobe. I realized the need to carry on, and energy once again coursed through my body.

A guy about our age — one of the many casual witnesses to my ignoble experience came over and helped wrestle my bike into the upright position and over to the curb.

When we got out of the way of traffic and over to the curb, I could feel Tom's laughter like a tangible thing between us, tying us together: "Well, now you've really broken it in!"

When we'd all stopped looking worried and I'd brushed myself off, the guy who had rushed over to help introduced himself as Myron. And after all the explaining we always went through about what we were doing, riding through the middle of North America with California plates, Myron invited us to a party. He assured us there would be *women*. And probably, if they could raise the cash, *liquor*. Myron added that we could spend the night if it was all right with his roommate.

Tom looked at me and I looked at Tom; two minds with but a single thought. We weren't interested in liquor, but we would need a place to sleep that night, so why not? Besides, I had that clutch lever to replace.

Did I mention clutch levers? Without a clutch lever, I would be stuck in first or second gear and reduced to a ridiculous caricature of myself until I could fix it. We were traveling to Beloit via La Crosse and Madison, and shifting any kind of gearbox without a clutch is virtually impossible. The gears don't care much for it either. Fortunately, I had an extra clutch lever in my pack, another source of fodder for Tom's amusement.

Fun fact: Years later, when I finally sold the bike, an extra clutch lever went with it. It became fixed in my mind that an extra clutch lever and that bike were somehow inseparably linked.

Anyway, that's how it happened that we pushed and shoved my battered beast over to Myron's place on a sunny afternoon in September.

His home was a windowless basement in the back of a clapboard house with a burnt-out rhododendron hedge along the side. Cement steps with an iron railing descending into darkness: cement floor, ceiling, walls, cement everything. Exposed pipes and posters of rock stars. Early post-high school Bohemia at its best. As soon as we parked our bikes, I got busy replacing the clutch lever with the spare I'd been carrying. Lucky me.

And then there were the residents. There was John, tall and skinny, with dark hair and eyes. Myron (our nominal host), had been in the Army and wanted to be a lineman. He was going to a trade school to learn how to construct and maintain power and telephone lines, the main or perhaps only industry in the town of Jackson. Tom figured that Myron had listened to *Wichita Lineman,* found sustenance in Glen Campbell's song, and had decided to walk that image into a career. Myron had offered his lodgings to us, and that was a link we would always understand and be grateful for, even if our life goals were different.

The evening became brutal in this lineman's basement digs as it deepened into night: people came, people left. There was beer and small talk with no describable thread of continuity other than, "What Has Happened?" and "Why Are You Doing It?" and "Where Are You Headed Next?" Questions that were asked and answered with each new person who showed up.

This, evidently, was the party. Unexpectedly dull and spontaneously depressing, the evening plodded on without end. We were instant celebrities for people who admired us for what we were doing, yet seemed oblivious to the notion that they were capable of doing the same. It was as though we had descended from Mars.

The inertia of our lives cuts a groove that gets deeper with time. It keeps going but doesn't always get better. Each step into the future is a threshold crossed, but it's often the same doorway. Change is the unknown country. It forces us to learn new ways of being, which is like a new woolen shirt—itchy if you're not used to it. Staying home certainly would have been easier, but it's the wrenching changes that form character, not the groove we're in. The groove of life had apparently claimed Myron and John for her own.

Tom and I carried the weight of our own history with us, but the choices we made—both to take this trip and while on it—were revolutionary in a way. We had stepped across a threshold into that *what-if* country where outcomes couldn't be controlled. That was the way of it; our choices were adding up, layer upon layer. I think that for John and Myron, the change we represented was foreign, exotic, and perhaps dangerous in an undefined way.

The final catastrophe occurred later in the gloom of night as we were staring up into the nest of water pipes that formed a sort of Mondrian collage of gray shadows and lines on their ceiling like a map of life.

Tom and I were in our sleeping bags on the hard concrete floor, merely observing, just being in the moment. We were doing our best to remain uncritical and to experience the culture of it all. And culture there was. It seemed like hours, but it must have been less than one. John and Myron started shouting back and forth in the darkness all the strange and terrible oaths they knew—all the swear words and curses and foul language that their age and wisdom had decreed were to be used upon such an occasion. I won't go into the great variety, repetitions, and innovations of their cursing, but the performance was epic.

It was all just sheer lunacy, but we didn't say a word. The four of us were about the same age, but we didn't think or act the same. Getting drunk (if drunk they were) and screaming (to the point of hoarseness) random obscenities and curses for about an hour into the darkness of the night with guests in the same room displayed a social dynamic difficult to understand. It was full volume Tourette and delivered without a word of warning. It was truly bizarre; we'd never heard anything like it. They kept this up until I wondered if Tom and I should try to leave. Would their verbal madness lead to other behaviors? Would they get up and start dancing about and slash the air with kitchen knives, or was this the extent of it?

Curses flew up into the night air like bats taking wing from the hollow of their mouths, bounced off the walls and ceiling in confusion, fluttering around that small basement room in wailing crashes of torment, lost vision, lost birthright, lost America.

It trailed off into the night as Myron and John wound down, the shouts becoming less frequent, the curses not as loud, until the four of us eventually slept, each of us taking with him whatever thoughts remained prior to our last nod and slumber.

In later years, I remembered the motorcycle trip in bright and graying patches, but that night of shouted obscenities stood out in stark contrast to everything else. I remember the basement, the water pipes, the lineman's dream, and the curses that filled that small cement room and made it theirs. For that is what I think they were doing. Despite their frustrations, they weren't really angry. I believe our presence was something that triggered them to curse the darkness. Because we were doing something special, something different. It must have been terribly important for them to be special and different as well.

If that cement room was their cell, it was also their home. Perhaps for that reason, it had to be branded and initialed and carved into something that the two sunburnt strangers who had come amongst them could not alter. Perhaps for that reason, the screams were real.

Day 20   Friday, Sept. 11 – Madison, Wisconsin

We used their stove to cook our eggs, and after breakfast, had to sneak out so the landlady wouldn't see us. It had been bizarre as hell, and we wanted to get out of there as fast as we could without being downright rude. Our eyes adjusted to the early light at the top of the cement stairway; the railing was cold and damp. Tom and I left quietly. We walked our bikes down the crunching gravel that ran the length of the driveway, lit up our metal chariots of freedom, and quietly motored out into the street that morning, in search of clutch levers and the rest of whatever else we came for.

We rode 35 miles to the small town of Fairmont, where I purchased yet another clutch lever. (At this point, it was painfully obvious I should never ride without a spare.) We also got some silicon lubricant in a spray can for our chains, which had taken a beating. The bikes were quieter after that. It took another six hours of solid riding to enter Wisconsin at La Crosse, on the other side of the Mississippi River bridge.

It was a wet gray afternoon. The Mississippi River bridge was made entirely of metal, suitable for melting tires in the summer and slippery as hell in the rain. Idiots. Oh, it had holes in the metal roadway to keep the water from building up, but it didn't help with traction when you've only got two small patches of rubber connecting you to the road. That black water down there was the Mississippi River. You don't play games with the Mississippi River.

We waved the cars to pass us on the left as we walked our bikes across. "Let 'em go around," was our motto. When you build a bridge with a roadway that provides no traction whatsoever over one of the largest rivers in the known world, people can wait if a couple of guys choose not to go sliding right over the edge at that moment. And there were guard rails—we could see them—but what of it? Logic has nothing to do with taking a 70-foot plunge into a strong current of freezing water while riding a 400-pound anti-floatation device.

La Crosse is located on a prairie flanked by tall bluffs at the meeting of the Mississippi and Black rivers. French explorers named it for the game Native Americans played. As soon as we were over that stupid bridge, Tom and I rode into and through the city itself. We traversed 190 subsequent miles until we got into Madison at 9:45 that evening, dead tired. It was rainy and dark, and the water had trickled down our backs, up our sleeves, and soaked our socks. We had ridden 430 miles in one day. We were able to ride longer stretches now as seasoned travelers.

Back home in the Bay Area, the cities and towns all blurred into each other such that you couldn't tell where one community ended and the next began, but in the Midwest, the landscape was quite different. Empty interstates were punctuated at discrete intervals by towns and cities, with farmland in-between.

Again I had misjudged the timing, and we were broke. We had 47¢ between us. Which was enough to initiate a phone call to my parents if I reversed the charges, but not enough for a meal unless we settled for splitting a candy bar. So I phoned Ray and Edith (in the dead of night, their time) to wire another $200 of my savings to Western Union the next day.

Whenever I heard Edith or Ray's voice on one of these long-distance calls, I was reminded of the thin connection between myself and home — that twisted braid of colored wires that hung from pole to pole, ran underground, then up again to junction boxes and beyond, stretching across prairies and mountains, around lakes, through towns and cities, then finally arriving at our home in Los Gatos. And I wondered what they wondered about when they got my call. Did they see me as I really was, huddled into some pay phone with Tom sitting his bike not far away, staring at the traffic as we spoke about money and Western Union offices and if I was keeping safe?

In the evening, Tom and I went looking for an address I had for Nicki Bailey and her brother Phillip. I had it in my mind that I might find them on our travels. They were from France but spoke fluent English. Nicki was older than me, and I was older than Phillip. They stayed with our family when I was in kindergarten. They were the last of our boarders.

I still remembered a few things about them. Phillip had issues when he first came to us, and seemed completely mute, but Nicki assured us he could talk. After a day of this, Edith lifted him onto our television cabinet, which was built of solid oak and was four feet high. She then told him he wasn't getting down until he asked. Eventually, he did, and spoke well enough after that. Although they had a soft accent, I never heard either of them speak a single word of French during the year they stayed with us.

The address was out of date. We didn't know what to do with ourselves, since it was so late at night. We were in the middle of an unfamiliar city and didn't have enough money for lodging. Plus, we had to overnight in the city to pick up the cash in the morning. And then I noticed a Madison police officer parked on the street. I waved my arm for Tom to follow. We pulled up to the driver-side window, and I motioned to the officer that I wanted to talk to him. Giving the two of us an appraising and wary look, he rolled down his window.

"We're stuck," I said. "We've run out of money and need a place to stay, but only for tonight. We have money coming tomorrow, Western Union, but they're closed right now." The officer thought for a second before replying.

"You can stay at the station," he said.

"What do you mean?" I asked.

"We'll put you up as lodgers," he replied. "We can do that. Doesn't cost anything, and you'll be safe."

"Can you take us there?" I asked.

"Follow me," he said.

Tom had been listening to this entire exchange, and when the police car pulled out, we followed him.

The police station was four or five blocks away. There were two officers behind the booking counter. The guy who brought us in explained our story, and they booked us as "guests" into the jail. They took our packs and helmets and put them behind the counter, then had us take off our belts and put them, along with what we had in our pockets, into a couple of large envelopes, which they stashed somewhere after writing our names on the outside.

While they were checking us in, we used what was left of our 47¢ to buy some candy from a vending machine. One of the officers took us upstairs to a large rectangular room and locked us into separate cells. It was all cement and steel and gray paint. There was one window, high up at the far end, with bars but no glass, and ten cells, side-to-side against the two long walls. Each bed had a thin mattress with a green army blanket. Every cell had a metal toilet. All very neat and tidy and clean.

Neither of us had been inside a jail before, and we had mixed emotions. In one way, this was an intriguing stop, but for me it was a stark glimpse into the future. As I lay on my bed with my one thin blanket, thoughts came at me ruthless and hard: *This is it, kid. This is what you asked for. This is the next five years of your life when we get back home. What if there's nothing to read? What if you can't get along and end up in trouble all the time? What if there's some huge guy named Bubba who likes you too much?*

It was a grim reality. I'd seen jail cells in the movies, but this was different. I was now on the inside looking out. The cell door had clanged shut. The key had turned. The guard had walked away. This was what my life was going to be.

There were kids just like me in prison all over America; some had been in there for years. Land of the Free, putting philosophers in jail for their beliefs. Because I hadn't committed any crime. Not to my way of thinking. I hadn't stolen a car or killed a man. That was what prison was for: people who did bad things to other people. But I was doing just the opposite. Later that night:

"So this is what it's like."

"Jail. Yeah. Kind of echoey."

"It's all the cement."

"I'd hate to have to live here."

"Yep."

"Not a lot of books."

"Not much television."

"Only you to talk to."

"Well, they gave us blankets."

"True..."

Tom was pissed off that they'd booked us into jail as if we'd done something wrong. In his journal the next day, Tom wrote: *Got out of jail. SHIT!!! I had no idea the cops were actually going to book us.* So yeah, he felt betrayed. On the other hand, we had a relatively warm, dry place to sleep, and over time we came to see it as just another part of the trip.

All the little minnows were swimming right into the government net. They were being harvested. All but me and a few others who refused to swim in that direction. *Hell no, we won't go.* But there were nets everywhere, and no matter which way we swam it was going to be bad. What kind of criminals would I be in prison with? Murderers? Rapists? That night I dreamt of strange men with tattoos. One guy kept cracking his knuckles.

Later in the night, Tom woke up to a commotion downstairs and overheard a booking. Someone had been stabbed, and they brought in a suspect. He must have been put into one of the other cells, but I wasn't aware of it, and we didn't see him in the morning when we left. Tom told me about it later.

Day 21   Saturday, Sept. 12 – Elmhurst, Illinois

We fetched our packs in the morning, one of the officers hoisting them from behind the booking counter while we stuffed our wallets and keys back in our pockets and threaded our belts. We thanked the officers who were there and said goodbye.

We pushed open the door of the police station and went out into very bright sunshine. Tom and I strapped our packs back onto our bikes, put on our helmets, and then took off. I glanced back as we left the parking lot. Plain as salt it was on the outside, perfunctory and intimidating on the inside. And then—way later—maybe 200 miles down the road, I remembered having that joint in my pack from the Wichita campers. What if they'd had us empty our stuff out?

We picked up $200 at the Western Union office when it opened and then got back onto I-90. This was Illinois. There are several really big lakes in the middle of the United States left over from the last ice age, and we were coming up on the first of these, which was in the super-colossal class. We had a choice. Either go around Lake Michigan or go across it by ferry. It was $30 per bike to take the ferry, and that would have been $60 out of our $200 to get across, leaving us with only $120. That didn't seem right. So we went around. I mean, what if we wanted to see a show later, in New York or something?

Around Lake Michigan we went, but we were coming up on Chicago. Again, did we go through it or around it? Anyone in their right mind with that choice would go around; it's an immense city. My older brother Glen had battled snow and ice to attend college here.

Two years before Tom and I arrived, the Chicago police had used their nightsticks to beat the hell out of a lot of students and senior citizens out in the streets, protesting the war during the Democratic National Convention. They broke arms, legs, and faces, beating young and old alike: the police riots of 1968. Whimsical me, I thought we'd ride through the downtown to see what it looked like — to see what my brother's eyes had seen.

Chicago is the largest rail center in the United States, with more railroad traffic than any other city in the world. All that cattle and wheat started going to market back in the 1800s, and there were many places where railroad tracks and city streets crossed each other; they couldn't have built enough overpasses to keep them apart. One of the largest and most poorly built of this unholy marriage of macadam and steel was waiting for us.

Tom and I were spinning along an eight-lane highway in the rain as evening turned to night, and the sun threw finger-like streams of sunset, lighting the chromium cars ahead with sharp glints of orange, red, and yellow. The traffic was dense and had us boxed in. Everyone was speeding into Chicago like a massively segmented machine of rolling, rushing metal. The highway bent to the right and decanted us into a six-lane city street, making all of us — cars, motorcycles, and heavy trucks — hurtle toward shining rails of cold, wet indifference.

Whoever had paved the street had filled the spaces between the railroad tracks with additional rails, spacing them about four inches apart. This left a *rail-slot-rail-slot* corduroy pattern of wet steel right across seventy feet of roadway at an oblique angle. The tracks were flush with the tarmac, but there was a gap next to each rail for the railroad wheel flanges to extend below ground level. While this didn't bother the cars — which had tires eight or ten inches wide that ran right over them with nothing more than a thumpety-thumpety-thump and done, but it gaped large enough to devour any unsuspecting motorcycle tire. If the tracks had been at 90° it wouldn't have been an issue; it would have been tricky in the rain, but we could have ridden right over them.

It was almost dark. There were cars and trucks all around us. Did I mention it was raining? Headlights dazzled through the raindrops with everyone jockeying for position going into Turn 1. A moment of nothing, then *wham!* The night was split by a flash of chrome and black and the sound of slithering rubber as instinct and panic kicked in. The handlebars twisted violently out of my hands and everything was lost in a screech of metal slamming pavement, and sliding, twisting, sliding, with steel rails and huge tires and horns blaring and headlights.

I had been riding point—front left. The bike fell hard and out of control, dragging me with it. Tom crashed right behind. We watched in strange detachment bumping along, our faces inches from the pavement and steel as we skittered and spun violently in the rain, our helmets *bam! bam! bam!* across the rails.

My bike slides to a stop. My left leg is pinned. I'm struggling to pull myself free. Tons of metal loom all around, desperately avoiding us, braking frantically into the turn. A truck driver with quick hands and eyes shuddered to a stop and blocked traffic, a bit sideways behind us.

And then I'm up. I've got the bike up. I'm walking it to the side. Next thing I know, Tom and I are standing at the edge of that highway to hell. Bruised, but not broken. My steering is all out of whack and my long-suffering clutch lever has taken another hit. Tom is jumping up and down in the rain, laughing like a crazy person and screaming into the night sky: *"I'M NOT DEAD! I'M NOT DEAD! I'M NOT DEAD!"*

And then *splosh!* Water came up in a wave through the air and drenched us head to foot, launched by a truck going through a pothole the size of Lake Michigan. At least it felt like Lake Michigan. And in that split second, without any previous training, we became the two wettest guys in Chicago.

"Are you okay?"

"Yeah, I think so. Are you okay?"

"Well, I guess."

"Shit."

"Damn, my steering is shot."

"Can you walk?"

"Yeah, I think so. Can you?"

"I think so."

"Crap, let's get out of here."

The Chicago police drove up while we were gingerly testing our arms and fingers and legs to figure out if everything still worked. The patrol car slowed to a crawl, played its near spotlight on us for a few heartbeats, then sped up and was gone. If we'd been dead, he might have had to stop and write a report. Welcome to Chicago!

We saw a sign about a block away — *International House of Pancakes* — and pushed our bikes in that direction. A coffee for me and hot chocolate for Tom as we tried to stop shaking.

"Our bikes are messed up."

"Yeah, they pretty much are."

"It's raining."

"I noticed."

"It's night."

"And we don't know anybody."

"Shit."

"On the other hand, we didn't die."

"True."

"Incredible skill on our part, of course. Not dying."

"Right."

"Any ideas?"

Cars and trucks whizzed by in the wet. We had arrived at the largest city in the Midwest and we knew exactly no one. Chicago was still the hog butcher, the toolmaker, the wheat stacker, and the nation's freight handler that Carl Sandburg spoke of fifty years ago, but it was a complete mystery to the two of us. All we knew were those gleaming rails that had caught us and slammed us to the ground.

Then I remembered something Edith had mentioned before we left: "If you ever get in a real jam, call a church. You never know. They might help."

There was a pay phone over by the entrance. It had one of those massive six-inch thick phone books they have in big cities, attached with a chain. I looked under "Places of Worship" in the Yellow Pages. There was a church that might be near the restaurant, and I dialed the number. Bingo, somebody answered the phone. It turned out to be a young minister named Bob Weigel, working late on his sermon. I explained our situation and asked if we could *please, please, please* camp out on his lawn for the night. There was a pause while he thought about it.

"I don't think that would be so good. You see, tomorrow is Sunday."

Hadn't thought of that. We hadn't been keeping track of each day. Wednesday and Sunday look about the same on the road. Then he said to hold where we were and stay near the phone. He would try to get us some help and call us back. It took a few minutes.

"I've sent someone to get you," he said. "He'll take care of you. Look for an old Volkswagen bug. That'll be Neefe."

And sure enough, twenty minutes later, a gray Volkswagen of indeterminate vintage drove up, and a tall, middle-aged man got out. We'd been waiting near the entrance, under a flat canopy. He stared hard and steady for what seemed like a while, then said, "Follow me."

So we did, with both of us trying to work our bikes the best we could, given their condition. It was still raining.

James Neefe was a deacon in the local First Baptist Church. Fortunately for us, he kept to regular streets and drove slowly. We limped along, following his lights street by street through the rain until we reached his house in Elmhurst, a suburb of Chicago. The house loomed large when we rode up. Two storey, yellow clapboard, front lawn, picket fence, and very tall trees in the median completed the picture.

He waved us right up the driveway and into his garage. We motored inside, parked, and glanced around as the bikes cooled off in the darkness. There was a serious workbench, a drill press, and a lot of other tools. His garage was a machine shop. It was unreal being brought in out of the cold gray city of Chicago on a single phone call, but Tom and I were taking life as it came.

An engineer for Sylvania, Mr. Neefe often worked from home—hence his shop. He was an inventor of sorts, one of those guys who come up with the ideas and solutions that Sylvania — and by extension, America — needed to stay in business. His house wasn't fancy, but it was large, at least compared to what we were used to, and it wasn't more than twenty years old.

Mrs. Neefe greeted us as soon as we came in the back door. All four of us sat at their kitchen table, and Tom and I gave our benefactors a bare outline of who we were and what had happened. I was careful to say nothing about my fight with the Selective Service and the FBI. I had no idea what these people were like and emotions could run pretty high where the war was concerned. This was no time to get cute.

We were ushered through the kitchen to a hallway and downstairs to their furnished basement, where Mrs. Neefe had made up a convertible sofa with fresh sheets. Tom and I didn't shower, since it was late and the rest of the house was asleep, but said our goodnights and crawled into that delicious bed. We slept like a couple of rocks.

Day 22   Sunday, Sept. 13 – Elmhurst, Illinois

Tom was up first and tying his boots when I opened my eyes. Everyone but Mrs. Neefe had gone to early church. She showed us to an upstairs bathroom we could use and gave us some towels. Getting showered and clean felt glorious, particularly after the banging around we'd had. Soap and soft towels! Mrs. Neefe had put out some of her husband's old clothes in case we needed something, but we had a clean set in our packs. We got dressed and Tom checked the guitar. He shook it out over the bathroom sink and fished the gum wrappers out so it could dry. Wonder of wonders, it wasn't broken. Or warped, for that matter. Mrs. Neefe put what we'd been wearing into the wash and then made breakfast for us.

We got to know Mrs. Neefe as we dove into her bacon and eggs, buttered toast and jam, and orange juice and milk. We were at the kitchen table, and conversing with a nice middle-aged woman we'd only met a few hours ago.

"Those eggs okay?" she asked. She was fussing around the stove. She had brown hair, brown eyes, and a friendly smile.

Tom and I were trying to appreciate the food she'd already put on the table.

"The eggs are great," replied Tom, reaching for the jam.

"So is the orange juice," I said. "And the toast." We should have been sick of bacon and eggs, but this was different.

"So, you boys are going across the country." Mrs. Neefe turned to put her back against the sink and looked at the two of us. "You're riding motorcycles?"

"Right," I said. "We started in California."

"Where are you heading?"

"Not sure yet," I said. "I'd like to make it to the East Coast before heading back. We *were* going to go through downtown Chicago, but that didn't work out."

I could see the rain through the window behind Mrs. Neefe, and the wind was whipping the trees. I was glad to be inside, but still wary. I didn't want to say too much until we knew these people better. I took another bite of toast.

"I've got a friend going to school on the East Coast," said Tom. "He's told us to visit and he'd put us up for a few days in the dorms if we got that far." Tom looked over and said *Jim Miller* as an aside.

"Well, you showed up at the right time," said Mrs. Neefe. She was wiping her hands on a dishtowel. "We're having a family reunion later today. You'll get to meet everybody."

We met the five Neefe girls when they came home from church: Lisa, Karen, Nancy, Susan, and Mary (ages 10 to 19).

"Five daughters!" Tom said once we were alone. "Can you believe it?"

"And they took us in."

"Well, you saw how he sized us up."

"I guess we looked okay."

"I dunno," said Tom. "Do I look safe to you?" He grinned at me and stood tall, as if he were up for an award.

I shook my head. "You're just lucky I was with you to even things out."

It was one o'clock when the rest of the family came over: uncles and aunts and cousins. I couldn't keep track of all the names. It was pot-luck and everybody brought something. As unexpected guests, we kind of stood out—like "Show and Tell" day at school.

"Where are you from?"

"Where are you going?"

"Why are you doing this?"

"Sounds dangerous."

"When did you leave home?"

Some of these questions were from the girls, who wanted to know more about us.

"Are you going to college?"

"Do you have any brothers or sisters?"

"Any girlfriends?"

"Have the two of you always been friends?"

"Did you grow up together?"

"Have you always lived in the same town?"

One of the younger girls—I think her name was Karen—noticed two baby squirrels on the front lawn and brought them into the house in a cardboard box, all excited. "Look, I think they fell out of their nest!"

They looked like drowned rats, but they were still breathing. The wind and rain had been ripping through the trees that the night and they must have fallen out of their nest. Susan and Nancy ran to get some bath towels out of an upstairs closet and put them in the clothes dryer to get warm. It didn't take long before the girls had those two squirrels swaddled in warm towels. As recently rescued ourselves, Tom and I could relate.

Lisa and Karen—the two youngest—took turns nursing them with paper towels dipped in warm milk. It was touch and go for a while, but they opened their eyes after a bit. And then Mr. Neefe remembered that one of his neighbors was a vet. The neighbor came over and took charge. He said the squirrels would likely survive.

Mr. Neefe found time in-between everything else to work on our bikes. He fixed all the broken and twisted bits in his workshop and we were very glad he got them back into ridable condition. It would have been far more difficult attempting to realign our forks and reform bent parts out on the road.

Two baby squirrels rescued. Two strangers and their motorcycles revived. It was the kind of family they were.

That evening, the three older girls invited us to a youth event at the church. We bundled into their car and Mary drove. We walked into a large event room, with a volleyball net set up in the middle. Some kids were already batting a ball back and forth when we came in. Mary started introducing us to several of their friends.

"This is Jon and Tom," Mary said. "They're from California."

"They're friends of the family," Nancy went on.

"They're headed east," said Susan. "On motorcycles."

The girls were talking about us as if we were some kind of treasure they'd found, or a discovery they were eager to share.

"They were attacked by a herd of buffalo," said Nancy. "In Yellowstone," she added. She turned to ask me, "It was Yellowstone?"

"Well, not attacked..." I tried to explain, but couldn't for Tom's quick laughter.

"You should have seen his face." said Tom. "All those buffalo wanted to cross the road, which went right through the meadow. Jon was on his bike, right in the middle, completely exposed. He took off like a rocket getting out of there."

We ended up playing volleyball for their youth group. They split us up, perhaps thinking we carried unknown abilities. There were social dynamics at play. There was one kid in a purple sweater who was about to become president of the youth group. He was quite the jerk, ordering everyone about as if he owned the place. There's always one guy, isn't there? After the game, there was some pretty good cake and punch. It was nice.

At that church social, there was an impossibly beautiful girl named Ellen. She wore a blue dress. I took to calling her *The Girl in Blue* when speaking of her to Tom, as if she were in a painting by Gainsborough. There was an inner stillness about her, a serenity, that set her apart and made her almost irresistible as far as Tom was concerned. Ellen knew her own mind. There were no odd corners that didn't fit. Her steady gaze held Tom's while they talked, and he was a goner. *Almost.*

"If she'd been just a few years older," Tom told me later, "I would have waited for her to grow up. I would have stayed in Chicago and let you go on alone. I would have waited years."

"You would have ditched me? Thank you so *very* much." I didn't know whether to believe him, but Tom was a hopeless romantic running true to form—all systems go all the time. And Ellen was indeed a spectacular human being, at least in part because she didn't realize it herself.

Getting back to the house, I phoned my parents and Tom got in touch with his mom. We glossed over the whole railroad tracks from hell episode and just explained that we'd met some nice people and were staying with them until the rain let up. And then we watched a television program with the girls. Pure luxury. It elevated normal into wonderful.

Twenty-two days on the road doesn't sound like a lot, but the contrast of being accepted into family life with hot and cold running water, regular conversation in their living room, hot showers, and some regular TV was dramatic. Later that evening, we fooled around on their acoustic guitar. It hadn't been played for a while. We showed the girls how to string and tune it, which was something. They invited us to stay one more night, and we graciously accepted, having nowhere else to go.

Day 23   Monday, Sept. 14 – Coldwater, Michigan

We left Elmhurst at noon, sorry to leave. But before we left, Tom and I and Mr. Neefe were all standing in his kitchen, trying to say goodbye. We were hesitating, and Mr. Neefe was just standing there, and then he held up his hand.

"I know what you're trying to say," he said. "You're trying to thank me, but you don't know how. And you can't—at least not directly. But one day—who knows when—you're going to come across someone who needs help. When that day comes is when you thank me—by giving them the help they need."

Years later, I remembered what he said, and it occurred to me that by becoming a foster parent and then a guardian, I'd passed it on. Probably also in other ways. I know Tom did as well. So there you go.

We left some of the polished rocks we'd gotten back in South Dakota as presents for the Neefe family—well, it was what we had. Tom got a visor for his helmet. Visors snap on, so installation is pretty simple. Both of us thought helmets without visors look like bowling balls and rather idiotic. We took a mad dash through Chicago to get out of the city and found ourselves on our first toll road, which was a new experience for both of us: 35¢ each. Tom noticed a driver taking our picture, which was certainly novel. This happened more than once. I'm sure we had an "of the road" look by that point. Highway 12 was more rain.

We stopped at a hamburger joint for lunch and filled our bikes at the gas station next door. Distracted by the accident and subsequent stay with the Neefe family, I hadn't thought to ask my father to wire any more funds. It was hard to believe we were low on cash again. We were talking to the station attendant and asking him what options we might find, since we were no longer in an area where we could just pitch our tent. He told us about a mission about 90 miles away in Sheridan, Illinois that took in people who needed a place to stay—a homeless shelter.

We were almost run down by some idiot driver trying to pass too close, and Tom gave his fender a solid kick as he went by. This was the second time he'd done that. I'm going, *Shit, Tom, don't piss off a car! They're big and heavy and made of metal and often driven by idiots.* But we made it to the city of Sheridan unscathed and found the Coldwater shelter. To gain admittance, we had to verify our indigence by having the police certify our lack of funds, so we did.

When we made it back to the shelter, a young man showed us to our rooms. It wasn't like any of the Spanish missions back in California. Those had been made of adobe, with heavy dark beams, reddish tile rooves, and a bell tower. This place looked more like a brick apartment complex with a cafeteria. And it wasn't a church so much as a place to house and feed people down on their luck. It's mission.

The place reminded me of a lesson my parents had tried to teach me when I was about eight years old. One fine day, Edith and Ray took me to downtown San José and parked right across the street from the San José Rescue Mission, an industrial-looking building with a big sign over the door:

JESUS SAVES

As we sat in the car, my parents pointed to the men who were standing around. "Those men," said my parents, "those men never graduated from high school. They don't have jobs or families. Most of them *drink*. Their lives are *broken*. We don't want you to end up like that. But you *will* end up like that if you don't buckle down and study and apply yourself and graduate from high school. Because if you don't graduate from high school, you won't be able to go to college. And if you don't go to college, you'll end up a *failure*, just like those men." Then, with me on the edge of a precipice and looking down into nothingness, we drove home and never spoke of it again.

This was their bright idea of a preemptive strike against the Forces of Ignorance, I suppose. I was *very* impressed. Scared the shit out of me, because I was obviously on the road to perdition and my parents were introducing me to the concept of *future conditional guilt*. Up to that point in my short life, guilt or innocence had always been about something in the past.

I had not known it was possible to project guilt into the future, and that's what they were talking about: a future conditional consequence for possible violations which had not yet happened. Such was my parents' level of expectation—that I would understand such concepts and be able to act on them.

The reverse side of that coin was less obvious, but just as valid. That if I could find a purpose higher than the one Edith and Ray were presenting to me: education through lecture and rote memorization (which is what school represented, as far as I was concerned), I might be able to avoid the guilt because guilt was always predicated upon failure. No failure, no guilt.

The usual assumption is that societal norms are correct and that the proper course of action is to follow the herd. I didn't care about the herd because I was busy rejecting the herd. I hated the herd. I assumed my path was awkward and skewed and different, and that trying to fit in was not a good answer for me. I assumed right, but it would take me years to find that out.

And now here I was, in a homeless shelter, remembering. Tom and I ate dinner and caught up with our journals before turning in for the night. Free room and board to cover a temporary need as far as we were concerned, but perhaps more desperate lodging for everyone else.

Day 24 Tuesday, Sept. 15 – Canada & Buffalo, New York

Detroit was over 300 miles away. We got there in about six hours and crossed into Canada. Customs asked us if we had anything to declare and determined that we were only passing through. I'd forgotten all about that joint I had in my pack. We rode northeast between two of the Great Lakes on Highway 401. Lakes Huron and Erie.

There was no direct sunlight but instead a strange luminosity pervaded the landscape, accentuating the greens and yellows of the fields, and painted them in stark relief against that plain overcast sky and the black road we muttered along.

It was along that road we discovered you can't park motorcycles at fast-food restaurants—surprise! Perhaps it was a city ordinance, but we tried to stop at an A&W drive-in—until we saw the signs warning us off. We got to Buffalo, New York via Niagara Falls—another 250 miles. U.S. Customs asked Tom if there was anything in the *trunk* while staring directly at his motorcycle—*ha ha!* Because that's undoubtedly what his little rule book said to ask. Rote ignorance with a uniform in charge of other people's lives. Incredible. It had been a marathon ride that day, about six hundred miles.

I tried to find Nicki and Phillip Bailey in Buffalo at yet one more address Edith had given me over the phone. We got local directions at a gas station; the attendant consulting a street map he had taped to the window of the station. After wiping his hands with a station rag, he pointed with an oily finger. He said we were close, that it was near the downtown area, and gave us some basic directions.

Tom and I rode around a bit until we located the address. It was on a tree-lined street in an old brownstone neighborhood, and lights were coming on behind many of the windows. An upstairs brick walkup. We parked next to the curb as the shadows merged and dusk gave way to night.

Tom stayed with the bikes while I went up to see if anyone was home. There was some business with an intercom, pushing buttons and such. I explained our mission to the man who answered. He listened patiently, then said he didn't remember the name Bailey, but might have an address somewhere. I explained how it was just the two of us and he buzzed me in and said to come on up—he was on the third floor.

I got the tall wooden door open and held it for Tom until we both got inside the building. There was a hall next to a long straight staircase going up into shadows. It was like something out of a Raymond Chandler novel. There were six flights and six landings to get to the apartment. Everything looked dark and worn. There was old oak everywhere, and the landings had a 1920s geometrical inlay. Fancy, but old, with the polish of living on every wall and step.

We eventually reached the top landing and a man opened the door just as we got to it. He looked us over, then let us in. He was maybe ten years older than us, with dark hair. He asked us to wait in his living room while he looked for the address. We gingerly stepped in. A woman came in from a side room and said, "Hi. I'm Edie."

We introduced ourselves all around. Eric and Edie Isralow asked us where we were from.

"California," I said. "We're on a trip."

"I can see that much by your helmets and the look of you." Edie was smiling. "How long have you been on the road?"

"About three weeks," said Tom.

"Vacation?"

"Sort of," I said. "Actually, I was waiting to hear from the FBI." That sounded weird. I looked from Eric to Edie. "I'm a conscientious objector, and the courts are taking forever. Not enough judges to handle the load or something. I wanted to see the country before they put me away. Tom decided to keep me company."

"Good for you," said Edie.

I'm not sure why I blurted all that out. I had a number of reasons for not talking much about the war or my opposition to it during the trip, so I always tried to keep it short and to the point. But these seemed like nice people. The kind of people who wouldn't judge me.

"I better look for that address," said Eric. He went into the kitchen. We could hear rummaging through drawers while we continued talking with his wife. Edie and her husband were easy to get along with. They were both professors at SUNY Buffalo, and after we'd explained who we were, they invited us to dinner and to stay for the night. Eric managed to find an address up in Maine, but didn't have a name to go with it.

Eric and his wife were pretty open, given that we were strangers out of nowhere. The Neefe family had taken us in because we'd asked for help, but this was far more tenuous. It made me wonder about the boundaries we keep; why some people are more giving than others. I envied people who were that brave, who could see beyond their own lives with such grace. It had something to do with upbringing and experience. Tom was already there. He had the ability to put himself aside and ask leading questions, prompting response after response until he knew a person.

The Isralows shared their dinner with us and asked about our trip. We explained where we'd been and what we'd seen so far, talking into the evening. Since they seemed interested, I talked about my stand against the war. I'd stated my case briefly at the Neefes in Chicago, and I was getting better at it, but it was still a struggle. It was important to say it for what it was, which meant being careful with my words. Eric and his wife were the first people I knew for certain agreed with Tom and I about the war.

They had a remarkable collection of vinyl records, including a lot of jazz and rock albums, indexed in box after box lined up against one wall, as if their inner lives were larger than their apartment and they couldn't fit it all in.

I took the opportunity to get rid of that joint I'd been carrying by flushing it when I used their bathroom. Tom and I unrolled our sleeping bags and slept on their living room carpet. The curtains covering the big window were backlit by the full moon. Good people.

Years later, Tom and I found out who's floor we'd slept on that night. Eric *Dr. Rock* Isralow, rock music historian, moved to San Francisco two years after we met him and became a well-known radio personality. It was at the University of Buffalo where a student first called him "Dr. Rock" due to his wide knowledge of music.

He was such a unique individual that several writers used him as a template for fictional characters. He wrote a weekly column in the 1980s for the *San Francisco Examiner*, in which he connected musical themes of the day with rock history—putting everything in context. Tom also worked for the *Examiner* during that period, but they never met.

We never did find Nicki and Phillip. They may still be living up in Maine somewhere with a distant memory of a family who had an obnoxious kid they stayed with when they were young. It seems odd to lose people like that. My inner "shoulds" told me one thing, but reality intervened.

Day 25   Wednesday, Sept. 16 – Syracuse, New York

We left early the next morning. Edie gave us orange juice and toast, which was evidently their standard breakfast. It was dawn when we said our goodbyes, waving up at the building, then starting our bikes and motoring slowly down the street.

We were soon back on I-90, exiting Buffalo and heading toward Syracuse, above the Finger Lakes area of Upstate New York. Occasional farmland alternated with a wall of trees that towered on either side: beech, dogwood, maple, and sycamore. The trees became splashes of color with the autumn. Orange, gold, and bright yellow were scattered amongst the darker evergreens, with the occasional red maple looking like an explosion of scarlet paint.

We'd see farmland and then be riding through storybook forest again. This was a huge change from the built-up landscape of commercial buildings, highway signs, and cement on our route from Chicago to Detroit. Riding through farmland in the Midwest, it had been flat and, to a certain extent, featureless. If we saw any trees, they were planted next to long driveways and far off houses as a windbreak. But here the trees were wild and massive on both sides, and dense as any mythic forest I'd ever imagined. It was the promise of deer and bear and branches creaking, squirrels chattering, leaves rustling, wind whistling around trunks, birds singing, insects churring and the rustle of hidden animals.

We arrived in Syracuse later that day after a four-hour ride. We didn't want to spend $4 each at the YMCA, so we rode over to the university to see if there was something going on. There was one building lit up, an open door with yellow light spilling out, and students moving about. We rode our bikes right up near the building, parked, and strolled in. It was the student union. For the first time in 4,000 miles, we heard one of Bob Dylan's songs and we suddenly felt home again.

It was a large room. There were plenty of tables, and people our age were talking, snacking, and studying. We walked in carrying our helmets and looking around. It wasn't more than a minute or two before a couple of guys approached us. Marty and Peter wanted to know all about us. We were used to it by now, and in this environment, with these people, and to the musical poetry of *It Takes a Lot to Laugh, It Takes a Train to Cry*, we were certainly up for it.

Within a short time, we were at the center of a small cluster of students who wanted to know everything. Somebody ran out to get a look at our bikes and came back to announce that we had California plates — and a guitar! And so we became even more interesting.

When Tom and I met people for the first time, we had no idea what their background was or what they believed. They might have recently come back from the war or had a brother or sister still over there and might not appreciate some random guy spouting off about the government being out of control. But this group was different. We were accepted, and I had no problem speaking my mind.

Road-weary with our scruffy looks and California plates, we were coming to the realization that we could have walked onto any college campus and started a decent conversation. All by themselves, our motorcycles opened doors we hadn't thought were there. Marty and Peter asked us to stay in their dorm room—which included free meals and advice on where to stash our bikes where they'd be safe. Quite a difference from a night in jail or asking for tent-space on a church lawn.

We could have saved some money had we designed the trip to hit college towns one after the other. Not easy to do except along the East Coast, but free was free no matter how far apart the colleges were. Our trip started to take on a different tone.

And none of this would have worked if we'd been riding Harley-Davidsons. The Hondas were key. Honda's advertising slogan at the time was: *You meet the nicest people on a Honda.* Well, they were right. The Honda | Harley dichotomy was an unbridgeable cultural divide. Harleys meant either rough language and bar fights, or a retired dentist attempting to fulfill a lifelong dream. Riding a Honda meant you played acoustic guitar and knew who Jack Kerouac was. Or something like that, anyway. (These things never were an exact science.)

Marty and Peter took us up to their dorm room for the night. Peter was a sophomore and played a good Fender twelve-string, which seemed quite different since I had always thought Fender only made Stratocasters. Our new friends showed us where to park the bikes, out of sight between a large hedge and the dormitory wall.

That night I asked to use their television and flipped channels looking for a news station. Tom and I were sitting on the carpet, hugging our knees in Upstate New York, watching a completely different take on what was happening in the world. It was a Canadian TV station, operating out of Ontario, just over the border.

That news program showcased not only our small slice of the world, but most of the planet's state of affairs. It quickly became obvious to me that American TV news was a watered-down version of world events, and focused almost exclusively on the United States. It was like I'd had nothing but American cheese all my life and then accidentally wandered into a specialty shop with shelves full of Gruyere, Camembert, Roquefort, Provolone, and hundreds of others, all waiting to be tasted. It was slap-your-forehead kind of stuff. What did the rest of the world think about the war and our part in it, I wondered? What else was I not being told?

I was struck by how isolated we'd been in Los Gatos, relying on television news and newspapers. The details didn't matter. It was the range of information that was so startling. There was news from Canada, Australia, and Brazil, and something about France. Twenty-seven people were killed in the African nation of Mali when a railroad bridge over a river collapsed. I would never have known about any of it by watching our local stations in the middle of California, even by watching Walter Cronkite. His focus was still on the United States or anything that impacted us. Did I need to know any of this? Probably not, but it seemed odd that I was so completely blind to it. I felt ignorant and untutored.

It looked to me like our news was being mashed and sieved into a single flavor. Keep the natives ignorant; keep the natives happy; they have no reason to worry about Bangladesh. Or anything else. It was as if America was a religion, in and of itself. Some weird mixture of capitalism and jingoistic patriotism, with corn-on-the-cob and apple pie on the side.

Day 26   Thursday, Sept. 17 – Boston, Massachusetts

The guys snuck us down to a breakfast of eggs, sausage, hash browns, and cantaloupe in the mess hall before we said our goodbye, retrieved our bikes, loaded everything back on, and zoomed off, heading for Boston.

You would think we'd be used to rain by this time, but no. Back on our old friend I-90, we were bummed out by a light rain. It was a five-hour ride to Boston, including pit stops — over 320 miles altogether, at an average 64 mph. We were tooling along, mile upon mile, pulling 70 with the flow of traffic on the interstate.

Tom and I soon located Harvard University and made an effort to find Valentine—the guy with the MGA TWIN CAM who we'd met back at West Yellowstone. We asked at the main office, but no luck. We ate dinner at a small diner, and Tom wasn't quite right afterward. Up to that point, we'd both had excellent health. There had been a touch of sunburn, occasional fatigue, and some irritability because of circumstances, but nothing of real concern. Now one of us was feeling rocky. We had to find somewhere to spend the night. We asked a couple of people, and someone suggested a park and gave us directions, but we couldn't find it. Instead, we found a high school baseball park and stayed there. Well, for part of the night.

Like all baseball parks, there was an outfield, a baseball diamond, and two dugouts, one on either side of home plate. City streets were all around, and tall multi-story apartments overlooked center field. Boston was a large city. It was raining. We took a chance.

We decided on the nearest dugout, which had some broken glass on the floor. Desperate times. Whoever had built the ballpark had made the dugouts out of concrete, twenty feet from end to end. There were narrow wooden benches against the back wall and a corrugated metal roof. We kicked the broken glass away as best we could, got our sleeping bags out, and crawled in. The rain fell even harder and we fell asleep to its pounding rattle.

Someone must have seen our bikes parked by the dugout. Probably from the apartments. I woke up looking up at three very large and stolid-looking policemen looming over us, their flashlights shining in my eyes. They wore black raincoats, uniform caps, and gold badges, all dripping with rainwater. They kept playing their flashlights around the dugout—on our faces, the sleeping bags, out to our bikes, and then back to us.

"What are you boys doing here?" asked one of the cops.

"Well, we couldn't find a place to stay, so..." I was up on one elbow. I'd never had the police shining flashlights in my face before, and this was a strange city. I glanced over at Tom, to see how he was doing.

"You can't stay here," another cop said aggressively, as if we'd said we could. He was shining his light down on Tom, who was awake by this time and looking up at our visitors.

"Look, officer. We had to get out of the rain," said Tom.

"Well, you can't stay here," repeated the first cop. "You'll have to get out. Go on, get going."

"Give us a minute," I said. I held up my hand to block the light from my eyes and waited. They finally stepped back a pace and stopped shining their flashlights in our eyes.

We were exhausted from the ride and Tom had been feeling sick to his stomach. The policemen weren't rough with us, but they were intimidating as hell. I guess that was the point. We had to do a lot of explaining before they let us go. It gave us a taste of what some people have to go through every day.

Day 27   Friday, Sept. 18 – Portland, Maine

It was dark and very early as we slowly rode out of Boston, heading north. Tom was feeling better and able to push on. We took Interstate 95 up into Maine. It was a wet ride. Very wet. The road degraded over the distance. Cracks in the pavement were larger, there were more rough areas, and the road was broken like nothing we were used to. With all the potholes merging into one, the hard surface was almost gone. At times we were trying to spin through mud, which made the bikes squirrely as hell. Our tires threw muddy splotches of water up around us.

It was a terrible ride, dangerous and grueling. When you're trying your best to stay upright, it's almost impossible to keep your eye on anything but the cars and the road. You simply ride as straight as you can and stay as far away from other drivers as possible. Finally the rain slacked off and we could see a bit. The road got better as well, so it must have just been a bad patch. We were following the coastline, heading up toward Portland.

Tom was in front when the trees disappeared on our right. Grey skies and the Atlantic Ocean all the way to the horizon. There was nothing but cold-looking water and a dark edge, far away. We found a place and parked. I got off my bike and walked over to the guardrail, looking around. I could smell the ocean, that tang of seaweed, wet sand, and vague summer days. I unbuckled my helmet, removed it, felt the cool air. There was a short pebble beach, then waves breaking and retreating. The shoreline curved around to a point. I looked back.

"I'm going down. Want to?"

"No. You go." Tom laughed. "I'll stay here. I want to be able to say I got within twenty feet of it but didn't go the distance."

I swung myself over the railing and walked down to the water. Another wave crashed, ran up the beach, and splashed my boots. I'd could say I'd done it. I looked back up at the road. Tom was still just sitting there. The moment felt like a bookend. Which made the Pacific into the other end of it, with all the stuff we'd seen and done for the bulk of life in-between.

I gazed around the countryside as we rode south, a patchwork of colors: autumnal browns, coppers and golds, all fading into the distance. There was a peacefulness, but also a sleeping power; I could imagine the brutal force of this place tossed by a winter storm coming in off the Atlantic.

We found a cabin for $6, which got us out of the rain, and gave us a chance to dry out. Dinner and hot showers had us back to human again.

Day 28   Saturday, Sept. 19 – New Haven, Connecticut

Our foray into Maine had been all about trying to find Nicki and Phillip's mother, Janine Bailey. It was a last-ditch effort and we finally gave up. So we turned around and rode south, and made it (dry) into New Haven. Tom's friend Jim Miller, who we had last seen at Lake Tahoe, had been accepted into Yale. By the time we got to the East Coast, he was already enrolled. This was great for us—instant lodgings.

We got in rather late but found Jim's dorm room. We asked around and connected with a couple of his friends, Steve and Mike Lewis, from New York City and Cleveland, Ohio, respectively. They showed us where we could stash our bikes in a back parking area without getting a ticket or having them stolen. They'd been rather conspicuous right next to the dorm. Then they took us in for the night so we wouldn't have to wait in the hallway for Jim to come home. We borrowed a mattress from

Bobby, in the dorm next door. I stayed in to recuperate, but Tom went out to a Poco country-rock concert with Jim.

Day 29   Sunday, Sept. 20 – New Haven, Connecticut

We wandered on and off-campus with Mike after breakfast. Jim showed up and took us around, wearing his white cowboy hat. We ended up going to a well-appointed restaurant called Olivia's on Chapel Street for dinner. We were enjoying the lack of vibration and noise off the bikes. When you've been riding day after day like we had, the constant drumming becomes a part of you. The sudden lack of air pressure, vibration, and buffeting when you stop is strange, and contributes to a weird isolation, as if you're leaning into something that isn't there but should be.

It was a big advantage that we knew Jim. He was a connection, a brass tack on the map to which we could attach the far end of the thread that held the world in place. Later that night we caught up on our journals back at Jim's dorm, rewriting in places we'd been skimpy with while on the road.

Founded in 1701, Yale University contained multiple colleges and schools, but the architecture was modern. I had been expecting ivy-covered brick, but found slab cement and glass. This was the frame for the picture we would find ourselves looking out of for the next week or so.

Day 30   Monday, Sept. 21 – New Haven, Connecticut

We audited two of Jim's classes: Biochem and Art History. Vincent Scully, Ph.D. was Jim's art history professor. I found out later that he had been voted "favorite professor" by Yale's student body multiple times, and I understood why. The class was engrossing and quite different. We sat next to Jim along with several hundred other students in a bowl-shaped auditorium while this Professor Scully lectured with a slide projector, pointing to features in the various photos and drawings he put up on the screen.

He spent the next hour linking seemingly disparate events, like James Burke would do later on *Connections* for PBS, turning history into a detective story. Scully described a web of life through architecture, and everyone followed his threads avidly, myself as much as anyone. I was completely engaged. Scully reminded me of myself, selling Olympia typewriters. He had that same passion and sense of purpose.

That lecture was a journey of discovery, from artist to canvas to political climate to sculpture to patron back to artist, from city to city and beyond. He was so animated, full of energy and life and love of art. There was a standing ovation when he finished. Scully looked drained from the effort as if he'd just run the Boston Marathon. He slumped against the podium during the applause. I looked at Jim. He smiled and said, "Every time."

Biochem was biochem, and unlike Scully's Art History class, not much to write home about. I found the Yale bookstore and got a few books to read, including "The Great Divorce" by C.S. Lewis and "Man's Search for Meaning" by Viktor Frankl.

Tom met a girl from California — Annette Lander. "Simply beautiful," he said. I never met her, but Tom's concept of female beauty is fairly accurate and not entirely limited to a girl's profile, so I believed him. He spent the rest of the day copying music into the back of his journal so he would have the lyrics while playing the guitar.

I spent the day in a book or two and found myself riding a rather preachy bus (speaking metaphorically, of course) taking a bunch of strange characters to heaven or to hell. An unrewarding book. Lewis had a habit of heavy-handed symbolism and allegory, which I can forgive when his story is strong, but *The Great Divorce* is a book you have to plow through with your head down. I fared much better with my second choice. Frankl I'd read before, but wanted to revisit.

The memory of Professor Scully standing at the head of that art history class stayed with me. I've witnessed six truly outstanding teachers completely caught up in their craft over the years. Scully was one of them.

Day 31   Tuesday, Sept. 22 – New Haven, Connecticut

We had to move our bikes because someone was worried about where we'd parked. We hadn't secreted them away quite as well as we'd thought. It turned out okay, because we were introduced to a friend of one of Jim's dorm buddies named Andy. He lived five miles out of town and offered to keep them safe since he wasn't really using his garage at that time.

When we got back, I started perusing some of my other books. Tom met a girl named Cherry. In his words, "Very nice." So, not True Love. He also bought a book on French, evidently intending to learn the language or at least some of it. Maybe Cherry was studying French, and he was going to wow her with his *savoir faire*. I was glad Tom didn't end up with her though, because her name conjured up memories of chocolate-coated cherries flavored with almond extract. Not quite *ma chèrie amour*. We both did things like that: try out new ideas or skills to see what it was like and whether we might be any good at it.

It was like trying on a new suit. You tried it on, walked around in it, then decided it was too stiff or it didn't fit across the shoulders. You might get it altered, but if that didn't work, you took it off and picked out a new one. Maybe you preferred the black hoodie with tan pants and green tennies. Maybe you didn't. At least it was different from what everyone else was wearing.

All our friends were doing something similar. That is to say, different. Working in stained glass, creating beds with headboards of inlaid wood stained in an intricate pattern, or writing. Everyone was trying something new, and mostly creative.

Many of these enthusiasms became hobbies or personality traits over time, and that was fine. But some of our friends were creating serious art forms that teetered at the edge of greatness. The internet changed everything and represented huge possibilities for anyone attempting to make a living at their craft. But it was still in its infancy, and the tools were crude. Learning to make websites to advertise artwork became a common and frustrating task for the more ambitious among us.

Tom took flying lessons once, tried the violin, and got deep into photography—deep enough to teach it. He was already working his own darkroom at the house in Campbell before we left; there were strips of film hanging from a clothesline and chemical tubs in a spare room. I was writing and learning to paint, and had made a few art pieces out of wood and marble. Some things stick and some don't, but you have to make repeated forays into the void or nothing ever happens.

Day 32   Wednesday, Sept. 23 – New Haven, Connecticut

We got breakfast, read a bit, then wandered around some more. It was nice to read books again instead of magazines. They gave me a feeling of accomplishment, that my true texture had not been subsumed by the trip itself.

Jim played piano (magnificently), and he somehow managed to purchase a used upright. Where he got it, I have no idea. It appeared one day on a delivery truck outside the dorms. Jim had been waiting for it, and Tom and I were immediately pressed along with an impromptu gang of five or six guys to push, pull, cajole, and wrestle the heavy thing all the way up and into Jim's room. It was old, dark brown, scarred up, and felt like eight hundred pounds.

Just getting it in the front door was a major issue. There was Jim at the far end, Tom and myself in the middle, and a couple of beefy-looking guys picking up the rear. I tried putting my hands as far under the keyboard as possible and lifting with my forearms, which was more than a little awkward and rather painful, so I silently muttered screw it, and used the front edge.

We hoisted it up over the threshold, then heaved it one step at a time to the first landing. And then we rested. And then we turned it on the landing. It was one flight of stairs after another with two landings in-between, banging into walls during the second landing turn (we were getting careless), scraping the bannister at one point, and upending the thing when we had to until we finally found ourselves on Jim's floor. One more effort and we got it down the hallway to his room. Fortunately, the hallway was wide enough that we were able to turn it into the doorway without a problem, and I was thin enough to skinny through the ten-inch gap to help at the far end.

It was quite an operation, getting Jim's piano up all those stairs and turning it around on every landing. All without serious damage, of course. It already carried the scars and weathering that all such pianos bear. Endless afternoons, the marks of common life scrawled into its dark wood and the echo of some poor kid banging out scales and "March of the Space Cadets" for a hopeful mom listening from the kitchen, praying the music would never end.

Once it was in his room, Jim immediately sat down and banged out a fast boogie-woogie. He never did say where the piano came from. He could switch from classical to rock to whatever, without regard to protocol and without losing a beat. Tom and I sang with some of Jim's friends as he played Dylan and some others. Which sounds so much like Iowa in the 1940s, but it was fine.

Tom kept meeting girls. I'm not sure how he managed it, but he saw Anne again after the piano move. Again? It was a slow day and still humid. We walked around a lot, sightseeing on foot.

Tom said he felt positively lonely and wanted to be alone for a while. Personal maintenance. I bought several magazines: The New Yorker, Playboy, and Car & Driver. I played around on the guitar after fishing out the last of Tom's gum wrappers through the sound hole and between the strings. Other than moving the piano upstairs earlier in the day, there wasn't much going on. It was the middle of the week, and people came and went to classes. We only audited the two, so we ended up just knocking about for much of the time.

Day 33   Thursday, Sept. 24 – New Haven, Connecticut

We wrote in our journals. I wrapped the books I'd finished for mailing home. They were too bulky to carry. Tom was walking around after breakfast and noticed a girl who reminded him of Kathy Alcott, a girl he knew from back home. We wrote a few letters and cleaned up the room a bit.

Being in one place without a plan was starting to affect us. We couldn't stay with Jim for much longer anyway, so we talked about moving on, perhaps leaving next Monday, when Jim would be back to class and into his regular routine. That would put us into action instead of merely hanging around Jim's campus. We had been so used to calling the shots on this trip that waiting for Jim to spend time with us didn't sit well. It was time to change the program.

It was dark; we were lying in our sleeping bags, and I was wide awake, working on an idea I'd had on my mind. I thought Tom might be awake also, so I put my thoughts out into the darkness.

"So. What do you think would happen if the government gave everyone a guaranteed income?" I said. Maybe I'd write a paper on it. It was often how I resolved such questions, with all the back and forth of it, figuring it out.

"Everybody?" *Evidently awake.*

"Maybe only people who make less than a certain amount. And it could be scaled, too, like income tax. But in reverse."

"So who would qualify, and how much would they get?"

"Well, let's say... for someone making less than $1,000 a month, it might be $500 a month."

"That's a lot of money."

"It's a drop in the bucket compared to the war."

"Okay, so your idea is to make sure everybody can pay their rent and buy food?"

"Right. No more homeless people wandering around."

"Some people would hate it. They'd call it communistic or something."

"I'm trying to follow the money, to see if it could become self-sustaining or drain us dry. Where does the money go?"

"If I got an extra $500 every month, that money could end up in a lot of different directions. My rent of course, the grocery store, the phone company, and a bunch of other people."

"Which they would pay taxes on. Then spend the rest in a lot of different ways and maybe save whatever's left."

"Well, savings would go up."

"Not at first, but yeah—later."

"And collection agencies would go out of business."

"There's probably some kind of cycle, like a weather pattern when rain falls. It waters the plants, fills lakes and rivers, evaporates to make clouds again, and then comes down someplace completely different."

"Negative cash flow."

"What?"

"The hard part would be negative cash flow for the government and an increase in the national debt."

"Not if we stopped the war."

"Well yeah, but the soldiers and gun companies would see a drop."

"The soldiers would be fine. They don't want to be over there anyway. And I have no sympathy for the people who make guns and bombs. Let them make something else for a change. Instead of wasting our money on bullets, we'd be helping people create an actual life."

"What about inflation?"

"Okay, prices would go up, but then I think it might level off. After a year or so. But the people at the bottom who are normally effected most would be okay. The difference would be no more poverty, and guys like us would have a cushion so we could go to college without sweating the details so much. A lot more people going to college would mean better conversations, better thinking, and better jobs. And the lower-skilled jobs would have to pay more, because there would be fewer uneducated people to work them."

"Maybe it should be keyed to inflation."

"Okay. Well, artists wouldn't have to get a job right away to keep from starving. That's how Michelangelo and those guys survived. Most of them were supported by patrons."

"And if single mothers could raise their kids and feed them properly, those kids would be safer and less likely to turn to drugs or crime, right?"

"Right. Plus they wouldn't have to, even after leaving home. So we'd have less crime. Maybe a lot less. That's huge. Fewer kids in foster care, fewer drug addicts, less despair."

"Which means the government would need less money to fight crime, and taxes could go lower."

"Republicans would love that."

"Everybody would love that."

"No more welfare. This would replace it. Like a safety net for everyone. And no stigma; we'd all be lifted up."

"What could go wrong?"

"Wages would improve at the low end, so companies like McDonalds would have to pay more to get people to take fast-food jobs. That would lower their profits for a few months until all the fast-food chains and diners adjusted their prices."

"Which would add to inflation."

"Probably. But a lot of people would be a hell of a lot better off. Those diners would get more business, too."

"But wouldn't everything just rise to a new level and be the same after a while?"

"Like all boats rising on the tide?"

"Yeah."

"But a lot of boats aren't even floating right now. At least they'd have something under the keel instead of plain rock."

"And we'd all be better educated after a few years."

"And education means freedom. Which means better jobs. And the bookstores would thrive because of fewer non-readers. Quite a few, really. A lot of people can't read."

"But overall?"

"Overall, we'd be a lot better off and getting rid of welfare would help pay for it. Plus better conversations."

"Like this one, presumably."

"Well, yeah."

"Problem solved?"

"Problem solved."

Day 34   Friday, Sept. 25 – New Haven, Connecticut

Tom and I got up for an early walk and noticed a knot of people gathered at a small park. We went over to see what was going on. One of the people told us that a little girl had gone missing at the park or near it.

"Everybody spread out!" Somebody had taken charge. The park had a lot of mature trees with medium to high canopies, plus quite a bit of low and dense undergrowth. Oranges, reds, and green. There was a whole line of us, all across one end of the park, shuffling apart to make about ten feet between each person. Then somebody shouted, and we all started moving forward in measured steps.

Trees and bushes got in the way, but we reformed the line after looking around and under everything in our path. It was tedious work. Some shrubs and plants were dense thickets of growth, not trimmed in years.

Joining with twenty or thirty strangers to look for this missing child took me outside myself. I wasn't thinking about myself anymore, or even about Tom or the trip, or the war and my reaction to it. I was thinking about this little girl. I had no idea what she looked like and only a vague idea of her age, but now she was more important than anything else.

Her mom was at the far end of the park, surrounded by people, worried as hell. And here we were, working our way towards her, sometimes down on our hands and knees. I was pulling branches aside and occasionally crawling around on all fours, sometimes coming face to face with another searcher.

Inverting my focus like this was certainly different. It had been happening more and more, like with the Marine Corps captain's wife in Yellowstone and the Neefe family in Chicago. It wasn't what I'd expected, but it was a main reason for the trip: to get me out of myself. Tom and I found out later that she'd been located. She'd only wandered away.

After getting back to the college, we waited until 3:00 to meet Ruth Connell, a friend of Jim's who came over from Vassar. Ruth's visit was about spending time with Jim, so we made ourselves scarce and went for another walk. Tom bought an air mattress and carried it back, having become tired of going to bed with not much under him but a half-thickness of sleeping bag and the bottom tarp of our blue tent. Wood or cement flooring was worse than grass. The dorm rooms we encountered didn't always have carpets, and despite the comfort of having a solid roof over our heads, our bodies were rebelling from too many nights on hard surfaces.

Day 35   Saturday, Sept. 26 – New York, New York

Tom and I really wanted to see New York City, and Jim and Ruth were up for it. So, the four of us hitchhiked into New

York and became true sightseers. We were wandering the city of grit and promise so many had emigrated to, a place of myth and heartbreak almost more American than America herself.

Greenwich Village, including the Chelsea Hotel, where Bob Dylan wrote *Sad-eyed Lady of Lowlands* and Joan Baez would immortalize in *Diamonds and Rust: check.*

Grand Central Station: *check.*

From Grand Central, we rode the subway to the junction of Broadway, Seventh Avenue and 42nd Street, pressed in amongst more people than we'd seen since college. Times Square: *check.*

The New York Times, *check.* Bastion of democracy and purveyor of "All the News That's Fit to Print." A thrill ran through me as I gazed across the street and saw that famous masthead over their doorway for the first time. Their imprimatur in black and white meant something meaningful beyond the commonality of life. The New York Times was like Shakespeare, always there. Forthright and dependable, no matter what.

And then it came to me. *Holy shit. I am finally free.* Thank god no one can see inside my head. If they could, they'd think I was desperate and delusional. The four of us walk down the unfamiliar streets of New York—Tom and I like aliens in our weathered clothing—just walking like normal people among the stream of sidewalk humanity.

This is it: the real world.

New York.

My bedroom growing up had stacks of books by authors like Thomas Wolfe and Saul Bellow, as well as every singer-songwriter I ever heard of. Creative genius flourished in New York City or been published from there or wrote about it as if the texture of it was a map of their heart, a secret key to the meaning of being alive in the real world. I imagined Janis Ian, perched on the edge of her roof at seventeen, surveying the streets below and wringing her heart out in words and music even I could understand. I didn't know what I wanted to do or be, but I knew I wanted to grok all of it and maybe—just maybe—be able to use that secret key.

And now, here I stand, on a busy street, amidst the legendary beings known as New Yorkers. They can probably smell my awe, my fascination, my alien status. I want with all my heart to have already lived here my whole life. Actually no: I want my origin planted, like a three-legged Colossus of Rhodes, spanning the continent plus one ocean. One metaphorical foot in New York, another in England (the land of Shakespeare and Tolkien), and the third — my only real origin — back home in Los Gatos, rooted in reality, safety, and possible mediocrity.

I try to imagine what it would be like to live here in the grime, beauty, and competition. I imagine myself as a New Yorker, emerging from my brownstone walkup, going down to the coffeeshop to work on my novel for a while. Then taking the subway to Central Park, where I people-watch and make notes. On my way back I pick up a few staples — French bread, a bottle of Beaujolais, a couple of apples, a small round of brie and fresh ground coffee for my own machine — all fuel for the creative engine my mind | body construct has become. And back to work again, late into the night, burning bright with the fever of creation, tearing the page in my righteous attempts, living on pure energy perhaps, hungry for better ways to nail everything to the page and canvas.

We ate at a restaurant advertising "frappés," pronounced with two syllables for some odd reason, like it was a French import that nobody knew what to do with.

"Do you mean *fra-pay?*" is what people asked us with a puzzled look when we asked for a milkshake.

Tom: "No, we mean milkshakes."

Waiter: "Two frappés."

Me: "No. Two milkshakes, not whatever it is you're saying."

Waiter: "I don't understand."

Me: "Look. Just go into the kitchen. Get two tall glasses and fill them to the top with chocolate ice cream, but don't smoosh it down. Then fill all the crevices with fresh whole milk until it comes near the top of the glass. Add two long spoons and bring them out. Don't use a machine to mix it. No whipped cream, no cherry on top. We'll do the rest, okay?"

We'd run into this issue on a couple of occasions once we'd crossed into New England. These "frappés" tasted exactly like a milkshake, had the same consistency as a milkshake, and no, they didn't have any crushed ice or coffee. Just milk and ice cream. Confusion reigned until we came to the realization that somebody somewhere with a bit of gumption had decided to make their menu *très magnifique* with a highfalutin name for something anyone could concoct in their own kitchen with two ingredients and a tall glass. And then every restaurant along the Eastern Seaboard did the same. *Et voilà.*

New York City was all neon signs and cement-gray buildings, shiny with rectangles going all the way up to where stockbrokers and book editors lived on cigarettes and coffee and roast beef sandwiches. J.Smith was furiously importing from Turkey, Belgium, and Argentina, making deals that would show up a week later in the warehouse of A.Jones, across the hall. I imagined impresarios lining up plays for Broadway, off Broadway, around the corner from Broadway, and sometimes Teaneck, New Jersey. You could get a crook in your neck in this city just by looking up. So we all took the Empire State Building express elevator for a completely different view.

"Whatcha gonna do when we get up there?" Ruth giggled. "Spit off the top?"

Jim gave her a look, "That's from a movie."

Ruth made a face, "So?"

The elevator rumbled on and on until we disembarked onto the 86th Floor Observation Deck. The city was reduced to one particular view of the world as we walked around outside, looking to see if any of the coin-operated binoculars had any life left in them, and hooking our fingers in the wire barrier that kept people from leaping off. I could see the Brooklyn Bridge, Central Park, most of Manhattan, the Hudson River, and the Statue of Liberty.

How easy to become jaded about this city of cities, having experienced it in so many movies and books, but I wasn't blasé at a thousand feet up. Hearing the distant sounds of the city and breathing the tang from the East River, I gazed over the edge to the streets and buildings below.

This was where The New York Times published, where the Museum of Modern Art and the Frick Collection held sway.

Somewhere down there was the Met, home to *La Bohème*, *Aida*, and *Carmen*. The wind whistled around the building, reminding me how precarious my life was at that moment.

We hitched a ride back to where our motorcycles had been stored — Jim knew the way — and then rode two-up back to New Haven. An errant car nearly sideswiped Tom and Jim, and they barely got out of the way. *No, Tom didn't kick the car.* Motorcycles are nimble, but with both a rider *and* a passenger, they can be sluggish, with much of their natural agility gone. These were not country roads, and these were not huge bikes.

We went to a mixer with Jim and Ruth and met a girl named Tina Menzella. She and Tom got along well. The mixer turned into a party, with singing and music. Jim produced a couple of kazoos, and he and Tom ended up giving an impromptu performance, playing the Jimi Hendrix version of *The Star Spangled Banner* at Woodstock, with bombs falling down on Vietnam like rain. American hypocrisy made manifest by its own national anthem, slaughtering people by the thousands.

<u>Day 36   Sunday, Sept. 27 – New Haven, Connecticut</u>

The rain came back, so we stayed in the dorms all day. I fooled around on the piano a bit and plinked out some of Jim's sheet music. It was a quiet day. Ruth left. Tom walked Tina to the bus, and she left. This meant Tom wasn't a bright penny that evening. We got to talking about our itinerary, where we wanted to go, and what else we wanted to see before leaving the Eastern Seaboard.

Staying in one place like this was becoming like an endless game of solitaire. If I'd thought more about it, we might have gone to Washington D.C. for a couple of days to see the Capitol Building and the Smithsonian. We were in the general vicinity — only 300 miles away. Oh well, no brains.

<u>Day 37   Monday, Sept. 28 – New London, Connecticut</u>

We got back on our bikes and went downtown to get new strings for the guitar. The world had started to sound muffled for some reason, and I thought I might be having problems with my hearing. It might have been the cumulative effects of riding something as noisy as a motorcycle rather than a sudden defect in my hearing. Or I was going mad. One or the other. In any case, the hearing place wasn't open. We rode back, ate, assembled our materials and repacked the bikes, then said goodbye to Jim. It took forever to get going: we'd gotten a tad rusty during all those lazy afternoons.

We left New Haven with the intention of going to Watkins Glen, the site of a major race in upstate New York, just south of the Finger Lakes. After a short ride on Interstate 95, we got as far as Connecticut College in New London, where Tom's new friend Tina was going to school. It was a private liberal arts college for women. We met two women in the Art Complex and talked with them for a while — sculptors, both of them. Later we went to see the Streisand movie, *On A Clear Day You Can See Forever*, which had been released just a few months earlier. Streisand was genuinely funny, but I had no affinity for the French singer — Yves Montand — who played opposite her. He seemed out of his element and Streisand was a far better actor.

Tina and her roommate asked us to stay the night and smuggled us up the stairs. In their eyes, we were exciting and a bit dangerous — but in a good way. The kind of guys you wanted to have known in your past, but not the kind to marry. That's how it felt, anyway. Tom was kind of out of it. He said seeing Tina again was strange for some reason and wished we hadn't stopped. Oh well. We slept alone on Tina's dorm room floor, and she begged couch-time in someone else's room.

Day 38   Tuesday, Sept. 29 – Amherst, Massachusetts

Tina smuggled us down to the cafeteria in the morning. We sat down to breakfast amid an ocean of college women. There were lots of sidelong glances. It was great.

We continued on to Amherst, Massachusetts. It should have been just a three-hour ride, but we got bogged down in traffic. Tom looked up some friends from high school: Larry Dardide and Doug and John Cody, who had evidently invited us to stay overnight at their frat house, an older two-storey home with a couple of large trees in front.

No giant Greek letters painted on the outside of the house when we arrived, but it was the correct address. A little run down, but okay for an older home. We met all the kids who were there at that particular hour of the day, and there were a couple of desultory conversations in the kitchen and living room. Things became more lively after four girls showed up. They left but came back again later. Tom said he thought they were interested in finding one or more connections (perhaps they'd made a beer or condom run). Tom wanted to fraternize the hell out of the situation, but I was less interested.

Competing for girls with some sort of fumbled sex in mind was completely out of character for me, and as the evening drew on, I wandered around, looking for some private place to park myself, away from all the chatter. I finally found a perfect spot upstairs, and ensconced myself in one of two comfortable old armchairs in a small sitting area, near a dormer window.

I had my pack with me and got out one of the books I'd purchased back at the student bookstore at Yale. As my perusal of the back cover had promised, it was a particularly juicy one, full of head-scratching symbolism. I was soon absorbed.

I had been reading for some time, when I heard an odd sound. I glanced up to see Tom — grimacing at me through the window. Scared the shit out of me, and I tried to do the sitting high jump. He was saying something and tugging at the window. He finally got it open, and stuck his head in, a bit sideways, evidently kneeling on the roof of the porch. Tom looked at me owlishly, like a disembodied head.

"Come on out."

"Why?"

"It's a party out here."

"On the roof?"

"Yes, on the roof. There are people out here."

"I'm reading."

"Well, stop reading."

"Why?"

"There are naked chicks out here, man!" *Trust Tom to find naked girls on a frat house roof in the dark.*

"I don't think so. You go ahead. Don't fall off."

Tom gave me a blank look, then shrugged and closed the window. What Tom may not have realized was that my personality was still in the proving drawer and my internal timer wasn't set to go off for about another year.

Anyone who's ever baked bread knows that the dough has to rise — sometimes twice — prior to going in the oven. This stage is called the *proof* because it *proves* the yeast is working. Cute, eh? A longer, slower proof makes for a more flavorful bread. Think sourdough from San Francisco, which has to be proved for two whole *days*. Shove that same dough into the oven right after mixing and you end up with a dense, tasteless loaf that nobody wants, not even your mother.

The whole idea of trying to hoist my ego up onto that roof was beyond pointless, and I knew it. It was a recipe for personal disaster. I'd been in college for a couple of years and had gone on a number of dates, but I'd spent less than two years in high school, having educated myself at the library and local parks instead. I listened to music primarily to understand the *lyrics* for crying out loud, attempting to figure out how Shakespeare overlapped with Bob Dylan through Ezra Pound via James Joyce (with a side order of Allen Ginsberg). So going out on that roof would have been rushing the process by a lot.

I like to think that by keeping the process at a controlled rate (except for the occasional social rebellion or motorcycle trip, of course), I ended up creating a more intriguing Jonathan, full of all the little nooks and crannies that bright women love to discover. The longer the prove, the better the loaf. I was the son of a baker, after all.

I was ready to save the country from idiots, but I didn't need to be falling off a second-story roof with some girl, no matter what she might or might not be wearing. We stayed the night and nobody fell off of anything.

Day 39   Wednesday, Sept. 30 – Stamford, Connecticut

We rode over to Hampshire College, also in Amherst. We toured the place. It was unorthodox, but with good vibes. Tom talked with Jerry Heibling, a photography professor, and we had lunch with him and some of his students. These were good people: they had brains and motivation. Tom taught photography at San Francisco State University later in his career, so an idea may have been planted during that conversation.

Spent the whole day wandering the campus getting information and looking at brochures. It was an experimental college; not the usual mission or curriculum. No SAT or ACT requirements, no letter grades, no application fee, and only about 1,000 students. Hampshire could have worked for either of us.

We traveled from there to Stamford, Connecticut. It was wet, with a wind chill at 50 degrees (even lower on a motorcycle), then called it quits for the day. We spent the night in a field just outside of town, pitching our tent in the dark.

Day 40   Thursday, Oct. 1 – Watkins Glen, New York

"Hey, get up!"

That's what I woke up to. It was Tom's voice from somewhere outside the tent.

"Get up. This is great!"

Once I had scraped myself together enough to crawl out of the tent, I realized what had happened. There was a large apple tree right next to us. We hadn't seen it in the dark. It was one of many; we'd slept in somebody's orchard. The world smelled of earth and green leaves and new weeds and dew in the glaze of dawn. I was stomping around and rubbing my hands together when Tom tossed me an apple.

"Try one of these. And there are a lot more!" He was grinning, holding one, half-eaten.

Man, he was cheerful. I was still woozy from sleeping so hard. I tried a bite. It was an explosion of taste: crunchy and tart, green and new. What a way to wake up. Peering up into and between the branches and leaves we found a few more. We had them for breakfast before taking down the tent and repacking the bikes. I stuffed four of them into one of the side pockets of my pack. It was a perfect day, cloudless and still. There was peace in the air. The orchard had been a great place to sleep, off the road a bit and quiet.

Once packed, I sat my bike while Tom finished whatever he was fiddling with. I loved the trees, the twisted trunks and spindly branches, all the green leaves and apples like nuggets of color throughout. All with a carpet of green, with blue sky overhead (the dawn had turned to day). And then he was ready.

Our engines chugged into raucous life, clutches released, and we left that gnarled and sweet green apple orchard behind. We were on our way through upstate New York in search of Watkins Glen, a small town with a big claim to fame: the UNITED STATES GRAND PRIX, due to be held in a day or two.

FRUSTRATION
an agony in two acts

There were any number of exits in this part of the country, all common as dirt. Tom and I always signaled prior to an exit, and I, the great and mighty genius, took an exit I thought we'd agreed on. We'd been riding along, not a worry or a care. Peeling off the freeway, I watched in honest horror as Tom sailed right on past and out of sight. I was riding off to the right while he was keeping straight. Oblivious, probably. *Crap.* Now what? Did he see me drop away or not?

We hadn't planned for this. Better use the old Boy Scout method; stay put and try not to starve or get eaten until rescued. It was just an off-ramp. Roadway, signs, rocks, and bits of trash, but not a bear in sight. So, I probably wouldn't get eaten.

I pulled over at the stop sign, switched off, and began my long zen-like wait. The sun feels hotter when you're not moving. The bike creaked as it cooled. I looked around. Not much. One or two cars came down the ramp, stopped next to me, then left.

How many times had we gotten separated? Never. Brand new experience. Lucky me. But anything other than never was too often to be sitting by some stop sign with my partner on his way to Neverland. Probably twenty miles down the road by now. Probably looking for that exit we'd agreed on, thinking I was right behind him. Zen. A way of life for some.

As fate would have it, Tom *had* noticed I was missing, but that still meant ten miles out and ten miles back to find me. Our reunion was matter of fact. An acknowledgment. Tom came down the ramp, rode up next to me, stopped, and looked at me. I started my bike. Not one word. And off we went.

Then it happened again. *Damn.* Different exit. This time, the off ramp went down to an underpass. I came to a stop at the bottom, drumming mental fingers. I waited. And then I waited some more. Zen is like chicken soup, I decided. Good for the soul. Right? Right. I'd be a better person because of this.

Tom returned via our patented Great Circle Route about forty-five minutes later and came to rest some distance away. I wondered why, and then I got it. His bike had stalled. Now, that was funny! Tom got off, shoved his bike over with a horrible crash, and flung his helmet W—A—Y up in the air, screaming at the sky. Pissed doesn't describe it. Poor guy. Oh well. That was life. I started my bike, motored over, and helped him get his bike back up. We tried it again, this time with better results.

This was an emotional ordeal with far more weight than the silly mistake it might have been back home. We weren't back home. We were, in fact, 3,000 miles from home. And no one knew where we were. And whether we liked it or not, we were dependent on each other. So we were inseparable by choice, but also by necessity. Separation anxiety was quite real and rather unnerving. But, like everything else, we managed to survive it. Probably good for the blood or something.

After a rest and a brief review of our "signal strategy," we got back on the interstate and rode on. We hit intermittent rain but kept going. We fueled our bikes one last time, and eventually wandered our way into the town of Watkins Glen, sneaking up on it unawares. There were signs showing the route to the racetrack, so it wasn't difficult. We paid $15 each to enter the general camping area and pitched our tent near the track's "Big Bend," and next to a friendly-enough couple: newlyweds, as it turned out. We walked the course, which was wide open. By the time we got back to the tent, it was dark, so we went to bed. Tom wrote that he kept waking up to see if it was tomorrow.

For years Tom and I had followed driver ranking and lap-by-lap analysis of each race by reading magazines such as *Car & Driver*, *Road & Track*, and *Sports Car Graphic*. Neither of us had seen a Grand Prix race, although we had gone to sports car races at Laguna Seca, near Monterey down Highway 1, having grown up in the Bay Area. So this was a big deal. Huge.

Each country hosts only one Grand Prix race per year, and it's usually at the same track. At that time, the United States always held it at Watkins Glen, in the Finger Lakes region of upstate New York. Later, they switched it to Long Beach where I witnessed Emerson Fittipaldi driving yet again. But in the meantime, we had perfect timing. It was all Tom's doing. I'd had no idea when the race would be running until he brought it up.

Day 41   Friday, Oct. 2 – Watkins Glen, New York

We could hear the blip and growl of engines being tuned in the pits, but it was still early and there wasn't much else going on. This was the practice day before the actual race, and the cars weren't due to be on the track until 1:00. Tom had too much pent up energy, so he rode into town to get groceries. We had run out of peanut butter or something.

While Tom was off on errands, I read the Viktor Frankl book I'd picked up at Yale. Frankl was a psychologist, but he had written a handbook of practical philosophy. I was searching for better and more interesting ideas, since I thought they might help me complete the internal maps I used to navigate life. The road I was on – to prison – was scary as hell, and Frankl had survived the Nazi concentration camps.

I could hear the muted roar of exotic engines in the background as I dove headlong into Frankl's idea of what it meant to be human. I was snacking on raisins, trying to gain traction on his ideas. His book held critical clues that nested everything together. Big ideas sounded small until I paid close attention, when the map of my life fit together with a click.

Viktor Frankl believed that despite external circumstances and suffering, individuals still possessed an *inner* freedom to choose their attitudes and actions. This was a reminder of what I was doing, and that I was in good company. Frankl was my life coach during those months. I had chosen a difficult path and knew this trip would be my last hurrah – a last taste of freedom before the FBI and a razor wire reality closed in.

The stance I'd taken with the military was always there, floating like some massive thought balloon, barely tethered, and always trailing just behind me. Caring too much about an outcome I couldn't control seemed silly, and Frankl agreed. Picking at it seemed to get no results. Letting things gel for a bit often brought clarity. I was a part of something, but that something was very large, and I couldn't see to the top of it. It was usually at this point that I would read a book by someone like Frankl, Carl Rogers, or Rollo May, and get a real benefit. Not that I understood why at the time — that capstone would come later. But I knew it was important to explore.

"When we are no longer able to change a situation, we are challenged to change ourselves."   – *Viktor Frankl*

I stopped reading for a moment. I knew that Frankl and his family had been sent to Auschwitz. He had managed to survive, but wasn't able to control the circumstances of his life any more than I could. Although his situation was far more extreme, there was a parallel. He had found a kind of escape hatch by changing his attitude. Had I stumbled onto the same solution? Perhaps. Was I turning into a philosopher? No, but I was becoming *philosophical*.

Snacking on raisins while engrossed in why we search for meaning in our lives, I became aware of an insistent tapping on my shoulder, then a whisper about something or other. My mind held fragments of information, desperate to bring these bits of knowledge of something terribly important to my attention. Buzzing. There was a buzzing. I became aware of some kind of weird buzzing near my fingertips in the box, then buzzing at my fingers near my mouth and a curious soft buzzing on my lips and then... *bam!*

YELLOW JACKET!

Holy crap! Throw away the raisins, brushing at my face, flailing all over to get the damn buzzing thing away from me and out. Silence. Forget philosophy, maps, raisins, and everything else.

PAIN!

I got a fat lip and felt rather odd and self-conscious for the first day or so, but I got over it. It wasn't worth the energy and I couldn't change it anyway. (I did throw away the box of raisins.) Fortunately, the excitement of seeing a Grand Prix race for the first time overrode my emotions. I got on with it. Mental cartography would have to wait.

By 1:00, the cars were taking practice laps and Tom was back from his errands. We walked the track outside the safety barriers and in many places were actually able to walk right out onto the track. There weren't that many people yet, which seemed odd. It was a muted carnival of advertising and bright colors, especially near the pits and the grandstand.

Lotus, Ferrari, BRM, Castrol, McLaren, Dunlop, Brabham: iconic marques murmured their history in the wake of our memories as we made our way around to the pits. The roar and shriek of engines blipping to 10,000+ rpm, the smell of hot asphalt, hot oil, hot engines, plus all the people milling about... this was just prologue of course; the actual race was tomorrow.

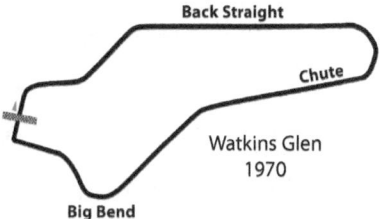

When we finally turned in that night, our minds were racing an endless circuit of speculation on what tomorrow would bring. This was Formula 1: the ultimate and most iconic automobile racing on the planet. The drivers and marques we'd followed for years would be racing at ten tenths, and we were here to experience it, fat lip and all.

Day 42   Saturday, Oct. 3 – Watkins Glen, New York

It rained a little; it hailed a little. This wasn't warm weather, and Tom thought he was catching a cold. He got up early and went into town on my bike, since it was a little better in the mud. It got stuck in third gear, but fixed itself, probably going over a hard bump. He got a letter from his mom but didn't get any food because there was a long line at the grocery store.

When Tom came back to camp the rain had turned much of the ground to mud, which is not fun to ride through: scary!

When the rear tire loses grip in very wet mud, the back end of the bike goes sideways and the rider has to compensate as best he can. Sometimes you wiggle all over the place getting out of it. Difficult to manage with four hundred pounds of bike. Tom said he felt like an idiot, squirreling all over the place.

We saw more practice. Jackie Ickx (Ferrari) got pole position. We set up camp close to the track with our bikes positioned so we'd have our own little viewing area in front of the tent, but Watkins Glen was crowded with race fans. So, we ended up getting out and pushing in with everybody else when the activities heated up. We were eating more peanut butter and honey sandwiches than ever. Cheap, easy, and fast.

Day 43   Sunday, Oct. 4 – Watkins Glen, New York

Finally: race day. The place was packed, but everyone was getting along, so it didn't seem overcrowded. We had bacon and eggs for breakfast. Tom walked the circuit again. The clouds couldn't make up their minds whether to rain or go away and kept to an intermittent drizzle.

Crimson and gold surrounded the racetrack in shades of Autumn. The rumble and high-pitched whine of very expensive works of art and science warming up assaulted our eardrums. The odors of burnt oil, hot metal, and hot asphalt hit us like a wave. We were within touching distance of Icarus in full flight: twenty-four drivers we'd read about in magazines.

We were two years too late to see Jim Clark drive for TEAM LOTUS; he had died in 1968 in Germany. At age 32, he had won more Grand Prix races (25) and achieved more Grand Prix pole positions (33) than any driver in history, including Fangio. We admired him tremendously.

Fourteen drivers would finish the race, and two would end up naked in the pits. Jack Brabham (Brabham) was running around with a huge false beard, mocking those who had called him the "old man" of F1 in recent conversation. The pages of our lives were coming to life all around us, in the vibrations, through our ears, and in the truest colors of the sport.

Graham Hill (Lotus) was easy to spot with his iconic blue, almost black helmet with white London Rowing Club markings. At forty-one, he was just a bit younger than Jack Brabham. I'd read about him for years. He had broken both legs and was nearly killed at The Glen in last year's Grand Prix, but he was declared fit for the race. If I was going to root for anyone, it would be him.

Tom made some sandwiches, took two cans of V8 Juice in his blue nylon stuff sack, and went hunting for a place to watch. His "good" place had been taken. So he wandered around trying to find out how he would be able to get in where he wasn't supposed to be — to no avail. He finally planted himself opposite the pits and stood for two hours, waiting for the start.

It was almost raining, but not quite. Finally, the national anthem. There were a few practice laps, but people seemed confused. Jackie Ickx (Ferrari) had pole position, with Jackie Stewart (Tyrrell-Ford) next to him. And then it was on. We watched from different positions.

I was secretly hoping Graham Hill would finish in the low numbers, but he had to drop out after a series of somewhat unusual events. He was driving a privately entered Lotus 72. I read later that he came into the pits on lap 30 with fuel leaking into his cockpit: a coupling had come loose under his seat. The pit crew fixed the leak and doused Hill with water because his overalls were soaked in fuel, then sent him back out.

A few laps later, Hill returned to ask for some dry overalls, since the high octane fuel was burning his skin. When he came in again to change clothes, his pit crew said they hadn't been able to find any fresh ones. But Hill noticed John Surtees, who had retired on the seventh lap, sitting on the wall kicking his heels, and asked to borrow his overalls and undergarments (everything had to be flame-proof).

The two former World Champions were stark naked in the pits as Hill was sprayed with water by his pit crew prior to putting on Surtees' clean clothes and returning to the track. He had to retire on lap seventy-two with a broken clutch. I can only presume that Surtees got his outfit back after everything was said and done!

Emerson Fittipaldi won the 1970 United States Grand Prix at Watkins Glen, driving for TEAM LOTUS. He had started from third position. It was his first Formula 1 victory, and the first ever for a Brazilian driver. Mexican driver Pedro Rodríguez came in second in a BRM, while Fittipaldi's teammate Reine Wisell of Sweden finished third.

Belgian driver Jackie Ickx finished fourth in his Ferrari 312B, having started from pole position before pitting to repair a broken fuel line, similar to what had happened to Graham Hill. Jochen Rindt became the first and only posthumous Formula 1 World Champion, having died earlier in the year.

I later read about what Fittipaldi said after the race. "I took the lead and, going over the finish line, I saw for the first time Colin [Chapman] jumping and throwing his hat, something I'd seen him do for Jim Clark and Graham Hill and Jochen Rindt, and I kept saying to myself, *He's doing that for me. I won the race. I won the US Grand Prix!* It was unbelievable."

It was his fourth Grand Prix race. Years later I was to witness Fittipaldi at the Long Beach Grand Prix, in an unbelievable display of concentration and mastery of craft as he spun out right beneath my position in the stands at high speed, downshifting and double-clutching from gear to gear to gear to gear until he was positioned correctly — still spinning at well over 100 mph — and then lighting it up, throwing up dirt and rocks as he fishtailed like a mad thing back onto the track under full power. Unbelievable skill and presence of mind.

Grand Prix racing is arguably the most demanding and elite of motorsports. It also seems like the most international; the drivers come from all over the world, and there is only one race per nation per year. There are only about thirty drivers in the world at any given time qualified to drive Formula 1. Usually a twisty track with at least one long straight, F1 races are the final word on speed, cornering ability, stamina, and mental capability and concentration.

We were lucky to get interested in F1 when the races were still as much driving ability as a test of the motorcar. You might call it the golden age of motor racing, where people like us could imagine driving one of those cars and doing well. That's how it started, with a small group of high-spirited sportsmen betting each other on who would arrive first at the next hotel.

Tom took it to the next level in later years. He became SCCA Club Racing Champion in a Formula Ford on similar tracks.

There was still a balance in Formula 1 in 1970. Nowadays, without one of the fastest cars — set up for that particular track on that particular day — it is very difficult to win. The sport is in transition: at some point Formula E will take over and it will be nothing but electric blurs of silent color flashing around the track instead of the rasping roar we heard that day. I think without the visceral impact and the "that could be me" aspect, the sport might become something of an intellectual exercise. The farther you are from something, the less it matters. Except astronomy and cosmology.

Tom met Jim and Ruth on lap 100 and walked around with them after the race. Everybody left quickly once the race was over. Tom used a public payphone to call a couple of friends, Greig St. Clair and Mary Crawler. He connected with Mary, but not Greig, who was probably at a ski equipment show.

Some idiots next door awoke us later that night making a lot of noise. It turned out okay though because the sky was light and we saw an amazing cloud formation, which looked like nothing we'd ever seen. It was large, oval, and well defined. There were no other clouds. Everyone who was up saw it. The phenomenon lasted quite a while, then flashed briefly and sped off at a high rate of speed. No, of course it didn't. It was a cloud. Pretty weird though.

Day 44   Monday, Oct. 5 – Watkins Glen, New York

We went back into town and Tom checked in at the post office. He got a letter from Leaf. He'd thought it might be there. He also called Greig St. Clair again. When Tom got off the phone and came out to the bikes where I was waiting, he said he had to get back by the 15th — just ten days away — to make arrangements for his work interview. We motored out slowly, taking mental snapshots of the people and all the small shops along the main street of Watkins Glen, then up to our regular cruising speed as we rode out of town.

The U.S. Grand Prix was the apogee of our trip. From that point on, we had one goal: home. The tenor of the trip shifted.

Not right away, but it was in the air and I think both of us could sense it. We got about 200 miles that day and stayed in an older rooming house with a bath.

Day 45   Tuesday, Oct. 6 – Cleveland, Ohio

The next day started fine: not too hot, and good weather for riding. We breezed right through Cleveland and heading for Akron. A moment before, I had been completely content, buzzing along without a care on my horizon. It was foolish of me to have expected such a state of things to last, for what is life but a series of unexpected corners, around which life lies in wait with something funny up its sleeve?

We were riding along as per usual when my engine suddenly rose into a banshee scream; the tachometer pegged itself hard over, and the bike lost all power. *Wonderful.* I released the throttle and coasted to the side of the road. The problem was apparent once I'd parked the bike and taken a look. I had arrived at one of those corners. The drive chain was hanging from the rear sprocket. I was lucky not to have lost it completely.

I stood on the shoulder and waited for Tom to notice my absence, find an exit, cross the road, find an entrance going the other way, backtrack beyond my living art piece: *Rider at Bay, with Motorcycle,* find another exit, cross the road, find another entrance going the way we had been before this had happened, and eventually come up behind me. Which he did. Then both of us squatted down next to my bike to inspect the damage.

"Broken chain."

"Yep."

"We'll have to get that fixed."

"I agree."

"You don't have a new chain in that pack of yours, do you?"

"No."

"You sure? You keep pulling things out of there."

"I'm sure."

"Then we'll have to find a dealership."

"I agree. Want to go back to Cleveland or on to Akron?"

"Cleveland is bigger."

"Yes, but Cleveland is behind us, and I had to travel some distance to find an off-ramp."

"Okay. Akron it is."

I was soon riding pillion behind Tom in search of a motorcycle dealership to locate a new drive chain, a few extra links so we could fit it to the correct tension, and a link breaker.

The drive chain on a motorcycle is like a bracelet or metal watchband; you add or subtract links to change the fit. Over years of riding a drive chain will stretch a bit, and there is a tensioning device, but it can only do so much before the amount of slack becomes too great. At that point, removing one or two links is the obvious fix. Also, with a used bike you never know what the previous owner did to it, and a brand new chain is always too long, requiring it to be fitted to the bike. I was lucky to have learned all this stuff several years earlier when I was rebuilding a small Suzuki.

We were able to find a shop and got the parts we needed. My bike (Angelina the Blue Wake, as I had named her), was still on her kickstand with all its luggage in the same spot when we got back. She looked lost all by her lonesome, with a busted chain and no purpose. We soon set about putting everything to rights, and it didn't take long to get going once we had the chain tightened correctly (with a bit of slack to keep everything from wearing to quickly).

Snick went our keys and roar went our engines. Up clacked the kickstands. A scattering of gravel squiveled us back on the road. Our next stop was the Western Union office in Akron, to pick up $50 I'd asked my father to wire the previous day. We got the money just a few minutes before they closed, then went looking for dinner. Easier said than done.

We stopped at a Howard Johnson's Restaurant (open 24 hours), walked in, and sat down at one of the tables, figuring we'd get a generic, albeit nourishing meal. We glanced at the menu and waited for someone to come take our order. Nobody came. We talked for a while and nobody came. We played with the spoons and tried to launch sugar packets at each other and nobody came. At this point we started looking around. The staff kept not coming to our table.

"What are they doing?" asked Tom.

"I have no idea. Don't they see us?" I'm leaning over the side of the booth to get a different perspective.

"That person's eating already, and we came in before him."

It was late, and the restaurant was half empty. I tried waving to one of the waitresses, but wasn't noticed. Or perhaps it was something else. Perhaps they were actively ignoring us. Seemed odd if they were. Tom waved. We waited some more. Time became tangible, like a lump of emotion in our throats.

We sat at that table for I don't know how long before we both finally figured it out; no one was coming. Not ever. So we grabbed our helmets, got out of the booth, and stepped up to the register. This was on a glass case with rows of gum and Lifesavers inside, a chrome toothpick dispenser and a bowl of mints on top, plus a spike full of receipts. And the register, with VISA and MasterCard stickers. Nobody came then, either.

Nobody would look at us. They were all focused intently on whatever they were doing. I turned and shrugged at Tom. The whole situation felt creepy and weird. Had we turned invisible? Did we grow tentacles we couldn't see? Signs pasted to our backs? After another minute or two, we walked out to the parking lot, helmets in hand. Our feelings were unsettled. Tom stopped. He was angry and so was I. "Do we really look that awful?" he asked.

"No," I said. "We don't."

"Well then, what's the deal?"

"First that gas station where they wouldn't take our cash."

"And now this. I know."

"It's gotta be the helmets."

Tom laughed into the night sky, "We're riding *Hondas!*"

We saddled up and roared off in search of some other restaurant that might still be open (and would serve us), but the experience grew upon me as we rode. It had been strange and degrading, as if there was something wrong with us that they could see and we couldn't. I thought long hard thoughts about racism, bigotry, fear of the unknown, and everything else that went bump in the night.

From that point on and for the rest of my life the music I listened to (poetry really, set to music) became more tangible. Songs were more gritty, the history more important. Something had shifted. The term "folk music" often conjures up images of hootenannies and guitars, but the music of our lives was more personal than that, more tangible, and it hit harder.

I already knew about Emmett Till and I had been a witness to the murder of Medgar Evers—all from music. I knew what had happened to young Carole Robertson on Birmingham Sunday. It wasn't the only music I listened to, but it certainly wasn't pop music. For anyone paying attention to the words, it was impossible not to draw conclusions, impossible not to feel the outrage and the pain.

Up to that point, I'd always thought of the United States as one massive extended family, with squabbles and quarrels and crazy uncle Eddie who spent all his money on boats for some reason. And some of this you only saw at family reunions or they lived too far away even for that, but this was different. Our experience in that restaurant broke the glass and pulled the handle. It became the tangible experience I needed to understand for myself and within myself what it was really like to be hated or feared, and then ostracized.

Sometimes it's important to reduce things down to basic principles: Good *vs.* Evil, Hate *vs.* Love, Joy *vs.* Despair. This wasn't Joy, and it clearly had never been Love. It crept up on me as we traveled that what we'd experienced was born out of the same mindset and social values that drove those politicians and generals to drop every American boy they could coerce into a uniform down into a jungle half-way around the planet. It was part and parcel of the same wayward machine.

But who really was to blame here? The waitresses rejected us, two motorcyclists holding their helmets who walked in out of nowhere late at night. It was the only explanation I could come up with: some kind of common and automatic fear and disapproval. Everybody on earth thinks they're blameless and puts it on the other guy, but what if *we* were the problem? Weird thoughts like this kept flying through my brain as we hammered out the miles.

When Tom and I were shunned at that gas station back in Idaho, we figured it for a one-off. It was just some weird thing that happened, and we soon dropped it from our thoughts. But now there were *two* points of reference, and that's all you need to define a line and plot a course. By the time of the second incident, you know how things are headed. It was quite a contrast from the Neefe family in Chicago, the Isralows of Buffalo, and all the people we shared marshmallows with across our campfire. Not as discernible perhaps to a couple of unseasoned guys from Los Gatos, but still.

And we might never have connected the dots except for that restaurant, which made us think back to the gas station and the two guys peering out from behind the window. This wasn't book learning, it was organic. It happened, and to me it was indicative of something badly broken.

I wondered at my own emotions and attitude. Which wasn't new; I often questioned myself and wondered how high I'd jumped to come up with such stuff. It was too easy. Like blaming people at the Howard Johnson's. It was simple to do because we'd been the ones who left hungry — Tom and I were the victims, right? It felt that way.

But if their fear was rational, then our presence caused it, even if unintentionally. Perhaps that area of Ohio had been *plagued* by a motorcycle gang and, at a quick glance, we looked the part. Maybe we happened to walk into the wrong place at the wrong time. We didn't know. It was all very iffy and problematic. *Except for three things.* We hadn't been riding choppers and anyone with half a brain could tell we didn't look the part. And we'd been polite. Scruffy perhaps, but well spoken.

I kept sifting through these ideas, searching for answers. And I kept coming back to Hattie Carroll, who had been working the bar one night at Baltimore's old Emerson Hotel in 1963. She hadn't been quick enough with the drinks for a man named William Zantzinger, whose cane whirled up through the air to come down crashing with a sickening thud. She died later that night and got one inch in the local paper. Zantzinger got a six-month sentence — *suspended* — and went on his way. The danger was lethal. The fear is real, and those who discount it are ignorant at best, enablers at worst.

We were riding through Indiana when I realized something else I'd been blind to. There was one major redeeming aspect to the U.S. Army. I hadn't noticed it because I hadn't thought about it, but our experience in the restaurant brought it into focus. People from all walks of life are thrown together higgledy-piggledy in the Army, just as they are in universities. Whether you were holed up together in a jungle somewhere, in a dorm in Boston, or a foul pit of a public restroom en route to Sioux Falls, we all shared a taste for peanut butter and we all had to clean the toilet once in a while. That is really how people get used to strangers and how racism ends with young adults—through the shared struggle and experience of relying on each other to achieve common goals.

But I couldn't square this with what I knew about the military, since the Army had a despicable reputation of racism in the ranks. I'd heard Sammy Davis Jr. tell of his experiences in the Army to Johnny Carson. What he described was almost unbelievably bad, and he said it was common practice. I had no reason not to believe it, and it underscored everything. Such thoughts flitted in and out as we rode, filling the empty night.

We pushed our envelope out to 500 miles in one day that took us to 2:00 A.M. the next morning, then pitched our tent behind a gas station, somewhere between Cloverdale and Terre Haute. As for the trip itself, we wanted to pick up the tempo. We were still on the wrong side of the continent and had two weeks to get back for Tom's interview. I also had a set of relatives to find (my mother was from Shawnee, Oklahoma), and we thought that might take a day or so. There were still other sights along our route, such as the Grand Canyon or Meteor Crater, but we were back in the groove and the belt sander was cranking.

The moon was half-full and sometimes obscured by scudding clouds. As we were settling down for the night, I mentioned my thoughts from the previous ride.

"I think that's why some people complain about schools like Berkeley and Yale as being radical," I said.

"Hotbeds of liberalism?" said Tom.

"Right."

"People at college get exposed to new ideas." Tom paused, thinking it through. "They listen to new music and talk to people they never would have met, similar to what we've been doing—away from their parents. Away from what they're used to. Away from what they know."

"That's how people learn to get creative if they aren't that way already."

"Plus, if you think about it... the kids who get away to college in the first place are self-starters. More motivated maybe. Rule breakers. Not all that interested in being told what to do. Not all of them, of course. There are a lot of frat boy idiots in the world."

"Enough to make a difference?"

"So far, yeah. But that's changing."

There wasn't much more after that under a waxing crescent moon in a dark tent in a field of weeds behind a gas station in Indiana. Crickets and dreams.

Day 46   Wednesday, Oct. 7 – Missouri

We were up two hours before dawn—way too early—and rode 572 miles during the next seven hours, which made for an average speed of 81 mph, even with fuel stops every hundred miles or so. Our throttles were wide open or near enough for that entire ride.

A change had come, bringing clear air and a thin layer of cloud that obscured the sun without diminishing the clarity and brilliance of the light. The road was a curious slate blue with none of the sparkle that sunlight usually brings after a rain, and it contrasted nicely with the light rock and dirt of the shoulder. The reds and golds of the trees lit up our world, and the fields presented a patchwork of yellows and browns, each field a different shade, separated by dirt roads with a running fence. It was stunningly beautiful countryside, and I just soaked it all in as we traveled along.

With the wind at our backs, we pushed the top end of both bikes, and rode from Indiana clear through Illinois and into

Missouri. Urgency had kicked in. We stopped for fuel just near the Missouri border. I'd been on reserve for fifteen minutes. A risky business.

Tom looked across his bike and laughed, "According to the map, we rode all the way through Illinois without touching the ground."

"You're kidding."

"Nope. One long ride. Our toes never touched pavement."

"We should call Guinness."

The sky was turning soft and darkening into purple as we rode into the evening. Uncertain of our surroundings, we rented a cabin for the night. Not so much a cabin as a small bungalow in a small row of identical bungalows. Gnats and midges were fooling about as we unpacked our bikes and hefted everything into the room. Nice, really. Blue stucco walls and two beds. It gave us a chance to shower and relax before dousing the lights.

"You know that exit we didn't take?"

"Which one?"

"The one going south."

"Oh. You mean the one going toward *the* South. The one headed right through Mississippi, Alabama, Florida..."

"Right. The one we said we'd never take, no matter what. What about it?"

"We could have been on our way to Key West."

"Sunny and warm..."

"Or New Orleans."

"Mardi Gras!"

"Is it that time of year?"

"Probably not."

"So, Key West."

"Scuba diving."

"Expensive."

"Well, somewhere else then."

"Key Largo. We ride around and look at girls."

"Okay. We take the causeway that connects all those little islands like beads on a string?"

"Sounds like fun. We'll get tanned and fit."

"We're already tanned and fit. Well, fit anyway. And it's the beginning of winter, we aren't going to get any more tanned than we already are."

"Cute girls and palm trees."

"Alligators and sinkholes."

"Sinkholes?"

"Yeah, I looked it up once. Houses, people, cars, idiot motorcyclists... Most of Florida sits on huge slabs of something called karst. Dangerous as hell. It dissolves and you get these huge holes opening up where your motorcycle or house used to be."

"We could sightsee around the boardwalks."

"You really want to see Key Largo?"

"No. Not really."

"Just as well not head south, then."

"I guess not."

"It was fun while it lasted."

We were getting punchy. An extended ride and only a few hours sleep the previous night. Crazy. *Key Largo*.

Day 47   Thursday, Oct. 8 – Tulsa, Oklahoma

It was one of those heavy, sultry mornings when Nature seems to be saying to herself "Now shall I or shall I not scare the pants off these guys with a hell of a thunderstorm?" But we decided to risk it.

We left our cozy blue bungalow refreshed and ready for life and almost immediately ran into a wall of rain. And then we were out of it. As soon as we could see straight, there was another one, coming up fast. The world became dim and uninviting. It was chattering cold. We stopped at a cafe to get dry, then got back on our bikes and rode to just outside Tulsa before the weather closed in. We were trying to get to Oklahoma City to find some distant cousins of mine named Barlow: two brothers who owned a wholesale toy and hobby business.

The sky had become more and more inky, and the odds on a thunderstorm shorter than ever, but we rode on. Then the rain came down harder. It had turned to sleet, and it froze to the road: *black ice*. We were trying to ride without sliding off into oblivion. I kept thinking, *As long as I keep riding in an absolutely straight line...*

We rode our swift chariots of steel and fumes and whipping canvas under the watchful eyes of barbed-wire fencing that ran beside us along the road and against a flat plain with cold thunder behind us and the flashing of our headlights slicing the rain. We paced ourselves into the night, pushing, always pushing against the driving wind and deluge that hit us and hit us as the storm came down upon us and our forms tore through it, black and wild upon the naked land. We rode on. It was only when there came a noise like fifty-seven trucks going over a wooden bridge that I knew looking for shelter would be a smarter way to spend the night. Rain was one thing; a gazillion volts of lightning melting us into the pavement was quite another.

We finally found a rest area with wet sleeping bags, wet clothes, wet everything. It was a difficult night.

Fun fact: Draining the guitar gave us a measure of what we'd recently been through. The sound hole is a bit under four inches across—that's a small target for a rain cloud one mile up. Of course, clouds hit you with everything they've got in the hope of making life unbearable, but still. We had been traveling at speed, so the rain or sleet would be coming at an angle (the higher the speed, the flatter the angle). But we had to slow down in heavy weather, which lessened the angle and filled the guitar quicker. The heavier the downpour and slower our speed, the more water we had to shake out at the end of the day.

Anyone with a mathematical bent could have calculated whether we were winning or losing our ongoing conflict with Mother Nature by using the time-honored formula for calculating the Water Absorption Index:

$$\mathbf{WAI} = (\mathbf{dpm} - \mathbf{s})(\pi r^2)\, \mathbf{t}$$

...where **dpm** was a measurement of drops per minute per square inch of the downpour we'd survived; **s** was our speed in miles per hour; πr^2 was a calculated value based on the area of the guitar's sound hole using **r** for the radius at a smidge more than four inches; and **t** being the amount of time in hours we had been attempting to escape that particular deluge. When the Water Absorption Index was less than the number of fingers on both hands, we were winning. Otherwise, not so much.

Another method for measuring our Water Absorption Index was the *Wringing of the Socks* ritual, usually performed to the tune of "Bringing in the Sheaves" (or "Bringing in the Sheep," depending on how one remembered it), and always performed at dusk. We never really measured with a bucket or anything, so we don't know how many gallons were involved, but if our socks had become particularly squishy, we knew that Mother Nature was grinning down on us with satisfaction.

Anyone standing in the rain outside our tent prior to lights out would have observed a pair of hands mysteriously emerge from the tent flap with a sock gripped between them. Then the *twist* and *twist* and *twist* to wring it out, whereupon the hands would withdraw. If our unknown observer were patient, the hands would come out yet again and perform this same ritual with another sock. There would be a brief intermission. Then a completely different pair of hands would emerge to twist socks three and four. This set of hands might even have used a different technique. I'm not sure, because I was never outside to observe while this ritual was being performed. Of course, this was somewhat predicated on how tight we'd tied the laces on our boots, the tire spray-back factor off the tarmac in front of us, and whether our socks had been completely dry when we'd put them on. Score one for Mother Nature. We didn't actually drown, so score one for us as well.

Day 48   Friday, Oct. 9 – Oklahoma City, Oklahoma

Oklahoma brooded under a grey sky. There had been rain in the night, and our bikes were still dripping. Presently, however, there appeared in the leaden haze a watery patch of blue: and through this crevice in the clouds the sun, diffidently at first but with gradually increasing confidence, peeped down on the two of us as we packed the tent and prepared to get underway. Stealing across the Earth, its rays reached Route 66 at the oblique angle of early morning, and created a ribbon of black and silver wending off into the distance.

A cop drove by and looked us over, but didn't stop to roust us. I wanted to wait in case he came back with coffee, hot chocolate, and croissants. But Tom, ever the skeptic, was doubtful, so we packed everything onto the bikes and took off. Our maps reminded us that huge sections of Oklahoma was now home to the Miccosukee Creek and Seminole nations (both having been relocated from Florida), Chickasaw, Coushatta, Thlopthlocco and Choctaw, Indian nations.

Some of these people had undoubtedly been native to the area, but many had been moved by the U.S. Army because other people wanted them out of the way. Even the Alibamu (the Alabama People) had been "settled" here. My mother always claimed to have Potawatomi blood in her veins, but I thought she was simply being contrary—her natural inclination.

Aristotle once said, "Men take on a particular quality based on a pattern of behavior." If so, America was a land of racist pirates and thieves, and although not necessarily worse than other countries and other people throughout history, not much better, either. Calling ourselves the "land of the free" seemed rather ironic to me, considering how we treated our own.

We weren't riding that far from Okemah, where Woody Guthrie grew up, southeast of Oklahoma City. I had listened to a lot of Woody's music, and was in fact acting out his most famous song, even as we rode. I'd always known of him, but got differing perspectives through folk singers like Pete Seeger and the Weavers. And then I got a whole new understanding of his importance when I learned of his influence on Bob Dylan's writing and their personal connection during his final days. It was through Woody Guthrie's writings that I got a more complete picture of what my people had gone through prior to the Dust Bowl years. A hardscrabble existence if there ever was one.

We stopped at a Howard Johnson's restaurant for lunch. Yes, another Howard Johnson's. Those orange-roofed restaurants were all over, and we didn't blame the company itself for what had happened before. We noticed a cute cheerleader having a sandwich. Tom swooned as per usual: *instant love*. I was getting used to these moments of his.

We rode into Oklahoma City, found their business: Hobbies Inc., and got the 50¢ Tour from the Barlow brothers, sons of my great aunt Ione. She was a colorful lady who lived near my parents for some unknown reason, because she was closer emotionally to her sons than to us. The brothers were surprised to see us, but very polite.

Hobbies Inc. consisted of a front office and a warehouse with steel racks full of toys, model trains, and art supplies. It was a wholesale business, not open to the public. We poked around through their inventory racks for a while, then asked what else might be interesting. They directed us to the Cowboy Museum nearby.

There were lariats with a history and spurs with a past, and faded photos of ancient cowpokes and chuck wagons and horses and Glidden's barbed wire, which had a white placard under it explaining how it had "Tamed the West." When we'd had our fill of history, we came out into the sunlight, blinked a few times, got back on our chariots of metal and fire, and continued along the Oklahoma Panhandle.

As we buzzed along Route 66 and watched the desolation of the land unfold, my mind wandered back to California. On Highway 1, going down to Monterey, there was an abandoned two-storey farmhouse off to the right and away from the road, right in the middle of a field. There were acres of low-growing crops, possibly lettuce or alfalfa, all around it. The house was solitary and abandoned on the one road we always drove to get to Carmel-by-the-Sea and points further south, like Big Sur or Laguna Seca. Every time I drove down the coast, I noticed it and wondered about the people who had lived there. What children had slammed those doors in their mad dash to play outside? Where were the flowers that once grew at the edge of their lawn? Who was the unknown family this farmland had belonged to?

Shear perfection can become boring, at least in part because it's all the same. Although beauty and symmetry might catch our eye initially, it is the imperfect we fall in love with because the flaws reveal character, a quality more important and lasting than beauty. They reveal the craftsman who created it, marking our passage through this world by the sincerity of the creator's hands and heart.

I've always loved older houses for that reason. They've been lived in. They carry the wear of life scarred upon them where feet have trod, hands have touched, and voices have been raised in anger and joy. A brand new house is antiseptic by comparison, and to my mind, feels like an institution—an anonymous building designed for anonymous people.

I want to hear the ghostly shouts in the hallway, the sound of a dropped book, the scent of bread coming out of an oven. All such life and living exists in memory, and older houses retain our patterns in the texture of their walls, in the creak of their floors, and that one doorknob that doesn't match any of the others. People are like that too. If you don't have any lines on your face, where have you been and what have you done?

That house on the road to points south looked to have been there since the 1920s or before, with its sagging front porch, broken gingerbread, iron widow's walk up on the roof, and all the paint faded to chalk. No trees, no pickup truck, no nothing. Not even a faint trace of driveway. Only that one house, alone and empty, with two upstairs windows like sad eyes gazing out on a world that had passed it by, leaving it to disintegrate with its history under the relentless California sun.

For years, there had been a gigantic sign midway between the house and the road:

FREE HOUSE

In smaller print was the reality of it: you'd have to move it to some other location. The land underneath wasn't part of the bargain, if bargain it was. The owner wanted to get rid of a liability and gain the acreage beneath it for planting crops. And have a contiguous field, probably, so he wouldn't have to always go around and around that house when he plowed and harvested.

Riding across Oklahoma reminded me of that house near Watsonville. The paint on all the houses in this area seemed just as faded, just as exhausted. The houses weren't empty, but they had that same look of old drama and lives played out. They didn't look like happy houses; they looked sad and unwanted and left behind, despite the families still living in them.

I had been told the story of how my mother's family had left what would soon be known as the Dust Bowl during the 1920s to start their own chicken ranch in California. Campbell Brookover converted the family's Model T Ford into a motorized covered wagon as other poor families had done, and they picked cotton and fruit to pay for food and gas as they went.

With both parents and all six children working the fields (Baby Aunt Dorothea would be born later, in California), they could pick over 1,000 pounds of cotton a day. The pay was 1¢ per pound. So, $10 a day divided by 8 workers. About 12¢ per hour per person for a ten-hour day. The youngest walked behind all the rest with a clothespin bag hung from her neck, picking up scraps of cotton that had fallen from tired fingers as the family worked the fields. It took them almost a full year to make their trek to Northern California.

As we rode through Oklahoma, New Mexico, and Arizona, I kept thinking about what my mother had done to survive, to make a better life. The stories Edith and Ray told me as a child hadn't impressed me when I was small; I considered them the wallpaper of life. I'd listened, I'd asked a few questions, and I'd remembered. But kids are kids, and nothing sticks until it becomes personal. Well, it was personal now. The memory of what it must have been like came up to re-ink their struggles in dust and hope as we rode past every farmhouse and small town. My existence was easy and privileged by comparison, and I knew it. I had always had more choices, including the one that had sent me riding clear across America in search of what I had no concrete name for.

As our tires spun our temporary mark upon the road, we were comforted that the thumping of our hearts and the grit in our souls meant we were alive and open to the beauty of the world, even though we hadn't done much to deserve it.

Days 49 - 50   Oct. 10-11 – New Mexico and Arizona

We rode Route 66 through the New Mexico and Arizona deserts, sleeping in our tent a little way off from the road, among rocks, dirt, and sagebrush, which grew all over. Sometimes a pinion pine, which looks more like a large bush than a tree. Snakes also, probably. And scorpions. And more rocks. And maybe a coyote or two, trotting along, not that far away.

We went right through Albuquerque where Tom's cousins Cinda and Debbie lived, but we forgot to visit when we finally made it into their neck of the woods. We fumbled that one. They'd seen us off, they'd been interested. It would have been nice to bookend our journey by visiting with them and sharing. But we didn't stop, and went on instead to Gallup, New Mexico, where my father had spent his youth.

I learned our family history in bits and pieces over the years; never in one gulp like reading a book. By all accounts, Ray's family was poor. Not dirt poor, but pretty close. They lived near Fort Wingate in Gallup, New Mexico, on Route 66. We rode right past the entrance.

My grandfather had worked for the railroad, and then as a government agent for the Navajo. He had some kind of stipend, but it couldn't have been much or Ray wouldn't have been working to support his sister and parents at such an early age. I don't know if my father was taught to do this or if he came up with it from his own precocious noggin, but as a young boy still running around in short pants, Raymond got the idea to repackage candy and sell it in smaller quantities to the servicemen on the Army base.

He would buy a bag of candy, along with a few smaller, empty bags at the general store, then divvy it up, the sum of which, when sold, doubled his money. Quite the young entrepreneur. Ray evidently made a strong impression with one of the soldiers, who took him into the barracks to meet the men. He introduced my father and explained that the kid was selling candy to support his family. He strongly encouraged all the guys to buy a bag from the cute kid.

This was Navajo, Hopi, Hualapai, and Apache land we were riding through, and about as inhospitable as you could imagine. The U.S. Government had settled the Native Americans on land nobody else wanted, both here and back in the Upper Midwest. Desert-like and barren as can be, this was not land anyone could thrive on unless they stumbled across a mineral resource no one could do without—as they had with oil in Oklahoma. People couldn't survive without a water source, so most of the towns and cities throughout the Southwest were strung like pearls along river channels.

We traveled through Flagstaff, Arizona, where my father had set himself up as an accountant at the ripe age of 17, having learned how to keep books from my grandfather. The car dealership and funeral parlor were his biggest accounts.

We rode right up to the mile-wide Barringer Meteor Crater in Arizona, but there was extensive fencing—the entire crater was on private land—and we thought the entrance fee was too much for not much more than a big dip in the ground. The crater was formed by an asteroid about 130 feet wide, making a gigantic hole and scaring all the locals, whoever they might have been, 50,000 years ago. I wanted to go up to the edge and look over, but we couldn't get near enough to try.

The weather was cool, but nothing like Oklahoma, thank goodness. We crossed the Colorado River almost without realizing it, near Needles, Arizona. The rainwater that would fill it during the winter and spring hadn't arrived in enough volume yet, so it wasn't all that impressive from the bridge.

We camped about fifty feet from the road once again. I can't say that the dirt or rocks had changed much since the last time we'd pitched our tent. We were at the edge of the Mojave Desert, named after a California tribe of fierce Native Americans living in and around the Needles area. The Aha Macav tribe, whose name had been garbled into "Mojave" (by settlers with too much wax in their ears), were quite distinctive because of the tattoos they had all over their bodies.

We finally pitched our tent next to a fence near the road. Tom had already gone in, but I stayed out on my own for a few minutes, drinking in the night air.

I stood there in the twilight, looking around at the scrub grass and cactus. The moon was full, and there was a slight breeze. The air carried a bite, a warning of winter. The once vibrant hues of the landscape had pulled back to a muted palette of dark grays. The evening chill seeped into my bones. It was a subtle reminder, as if my life lacked enough complexities, to practice patience. To keep pushing forward even when the world seemed determined to test my resolve.

Small winged creatures came at me, then darted away, and every once in a while a car or truck would whisper by on the road behind me.

This was one of those stolen moments, sometimes shared and sometimes not, found in the quiet solitude of introspection. In these pockets of serenity, a lightness descends. I pierced the veil of anxiety and glimpsed a future where the scattered pieces of my life coalesced into one complete person — the me I should be, the me I hoped to become.

The world I saw that evening accepted the encroaching winter, a testament to the cycle of life. It was resolute in the evening light, a silent encouragement to embrace the unknown with determination, just as surely as the seasons relentlessly turned. Perhaps this was the truest lesson — to find beauty in the uncertainty and live fully in the present, even when the grip of winter tightened around me.

The sky was vast overhead, with stars so clear against the blackness of the desert night (despite the moon's glare) that I felt more connected with the world and the universe than ever before. All my reading came home to me — the cosmology and astronomy and science history books I'd devoured over the years. Copernicus and Kepler had gazed at these stars also.

Everything fit. The trip, Tom, our blue tent, our bikes. Even my clothing had its place. I needed nothing but the moonlight, stars, and the air in my lungs. I was replete — an odd feeling for me. I was so used to making a huge effort, but this new way of being was a choice I'd made, at least for now. I was alive and that's all that mattered. It was a new glimpse at life and my place within it, and for once I savored it. Everything was quite real—almost surreal, like colors too bright and rocks too hard—I was *happy*.

"Hey, I cleaned out the guitar again."

"Noble of you."

"Certainly my man, certainly."

"Any eggs left for tomorrow?"

"But of course. And an apple."

"Right."

"Hope you get that job."

"Thanks. And good luck with the FBI."

We tried to sleep without disturbing any of the local rattlesnakes and scorpions. Fortunately, our tent had a four-inch lip and snake-proof zippers, which offered some solace.

Days 51 - 52   Oct. 12 - 13 – Sand City and Los Gatos, California

After traversing the rocky, sandy, hilly, flat, hot Mojave Desert, we got right into the middle of Southern California before deciding to take different routes on our final leg home. The moon was almost full again and visible as a pale gibbous disk during daylight hours. Tom was determined to get to that job interview at Sugar Bowl. He took the quickest route, over the Grapevine and up Interstate 5 to 152 to 101 to Los Gatos, then to Campbell to spend the night, drop off his bike and switch to his Volkswagen van, then finally charge on up to Sugar Bowl. He got the job.

As Tom told me later, "My trusty 305 Superhawk lasted just long enough to see me home. Riding slowly up North Santa Cruz Avenue and looking around at all the familiar Los Gatos shops and restaurants, I suddenly noticed the bike was noisy as hell. Everything felt loose, and the main drive sprocket was out of round, causing the bike to surge oddly.

"I was riding a bucket of bolts but hadn't realized that until it no longer mattered. During the trip that bike had to function, it had to get me to the next place and then the next, and it always did. But as soon I hit Los Gatos, my Superhawk was telling me in every way possible that it couldn't take it anymore."

After Tom left, I headed across to Highway 1: the Pacific Coast Highway. I was going home to face the FBI and a situation fraught with issues, and I wanted one last look at the ocean. Highway 1 is scenic as hell and curves right along the coast. Cliffs going up on my right and cliffs going down to the sea on my left, with the road snaking along like a ribbon between, and me on it. I was motoring quietly along, a hundred feet up, breathing clean sea air and basking in California sunshine.

I continued north, past Santa Barbara and along the coast towards San Simeon, with Hearst's Castle high up and out of sight. After an hour's ride and approaching Big Sur, I stopped at a wide spot, pulling onto the gravel and parked near the guardrail.

California did feel golden that afternoon. I took off my helmet and gloves and just sat the bike, taking a moment to gaze at the ocean, darkish blue with flecks of white.

I rotated off, scrunching the gravel-dirt soil with my boots, go to the back and pull out a Granny Smith apple from the backpack: the last bought food I had, and green as grass. The guard rail was there, so I perched myself on the galvanized edge of North America and munched away, thinking of nothing but the tart crunch of being there, that day, in that hour. I hadn't been that still since that night in the desert, and it was so quiet. Well, except for an occasional car whooshing behind me.

Seeing the Pacific again, I wished Tom could see it as I was, rather than riding up the dusty middle of California. One thing about Tom; he didn't chatter. He knew, as I did, that there are moments for silence. It felt strange being on my own again; our constant interaction, even in the quiet, had been a way of life.

The blue light ocean waves below and into the distance were a reminder to breathe again—that I and my chariot, my metal freedom chaser, were still alive and vital, perhaps more than we'd ever been. I was perhaps more real right then than I would be again. Perhaps.

Somehow, I knew it would be my life's job, no matter what, to make sure I tasted ocean air as clean as this—to not waste the rest of my life standing through an endless series of Chamber of Commerce mixers with a drink in one hand and an empty look on my face. I realized—and it came as a start—that I was past the whole prison thing. The trip, plus the writings of Viktor Frankl, had wrung it out of me. It would happen or not, but I could control neither. In the mean time, here was the great Pacific, laid out before me like a sheet of blued metal. And for some reason full of fish, which seemed odd.

The jumble of emotions I'd felt two months ago was gone, replaced by something akin to peace. I had set my life in motion and felt ready, whatever that might mean. The trip had been good and the timing perfect. I was fine with it. I hoped Tom was as well; this had been his adventure as much as mine. I threw my apple core over the cliff; time to go home.

I made one last stop to visit some friends who lived in Sand City, then continued on Highway 1 to Santa Cruz, and peeled off to take 17 over the Summit. Another twenty-five minutes of every curve threading into another through the redwoods, sunlight, and darkness, and I eventually came down out of the Santa Cruz Mountains. I was like an unknown, newborn thing riding the wind down that long straight that went through Los Gatos, then up toward Silicon Valley and San Francisco.

I soon passed the storied Cats Restaurant on my left and the old Lexington flume half-pipe snaking along the cliff on the far side of Los Gatos Creek to my right. I used to toss rocks off that flume. Some had pried up the boards and thrown them off. Somewhere on that forested mountain, in some secret, hidden place among the trees, was our town's only nudist colony. Lupin Lodge was a mythic place that held the stuff of teenage dreams. Every boy I knew had thought to sneak up there one day, but no one had done it.

I took that strange left-hand exit off the fast lane, and was soon motoring quietly into town, past the post office and our small downtown park. The largest redwood tree always blazed with lights at year's end in a tree lighting ceremony worthy of Hallmark, with horse-drawn carriages and people gathered together.

I finally came to rest at the first light, near the old Rexall Drug. Two storey brick, with a cylindrical corner and conical roof. Who had their offices up there? Whoever it was had a great view of the town park and the mountains behind the town. I waited. The light changed.

Rumbling along the main drag, I saw my own history in the texture of every storefront, the signs, the old theater with tired art deco and green tile. It was a Tuesday, and everybody was at work. And then Village Toys at the corner of Bean Avenue, and our family business to the left, with OFFICE SUPPLIES, ELNA SEWING MACHINES, and OLYMPIA TYPEWRITERS shouting from my father's somewhat inelegant signage.

The Place Funeral Home was right next door. A Victorian mansion with gingerbread and all the frills—what had once been somebody's dream house, with a brace of tall monkey puzzle trees on the front lawn, framing the entrance behind its elegant wrought iron fence. Then Arthur Mintz Photography and real estate offices and the side street where George Kane and the Times Observer lived. Then somebody upstairs trying to eke out a precarious living with guitar lessons and that diner I only ate at once in my whole life, and then I was at the next light.

This was downtown, but it was sharper, more real than I'd remembered. The edges were sharper and the colors were no longer slurred into the fog of common memory. I saw everything as if for the first time. Each tree, every building, and the wording on every sign was etched in details I'd always known, yet never noticed. It was still my alma mater, but different.

Turning onto Highway 9 at the light, I surprised myself. The thought struck me—it was rather a silly notion—that I didn't actually have anywhere to sleep that night. I'd been living with Tom at the Campbell house, but he'd gone north for the winter. I laughed into the wind. Wow. It was an unusual feeling.

I made my way back to my parents' house on Englewood where I'd grown up. The house with the huge hedge out front and the great mirror I'd argued my case into long ago. I had to tell Edith and Ray they could stop praying. Their idiot son had returned.

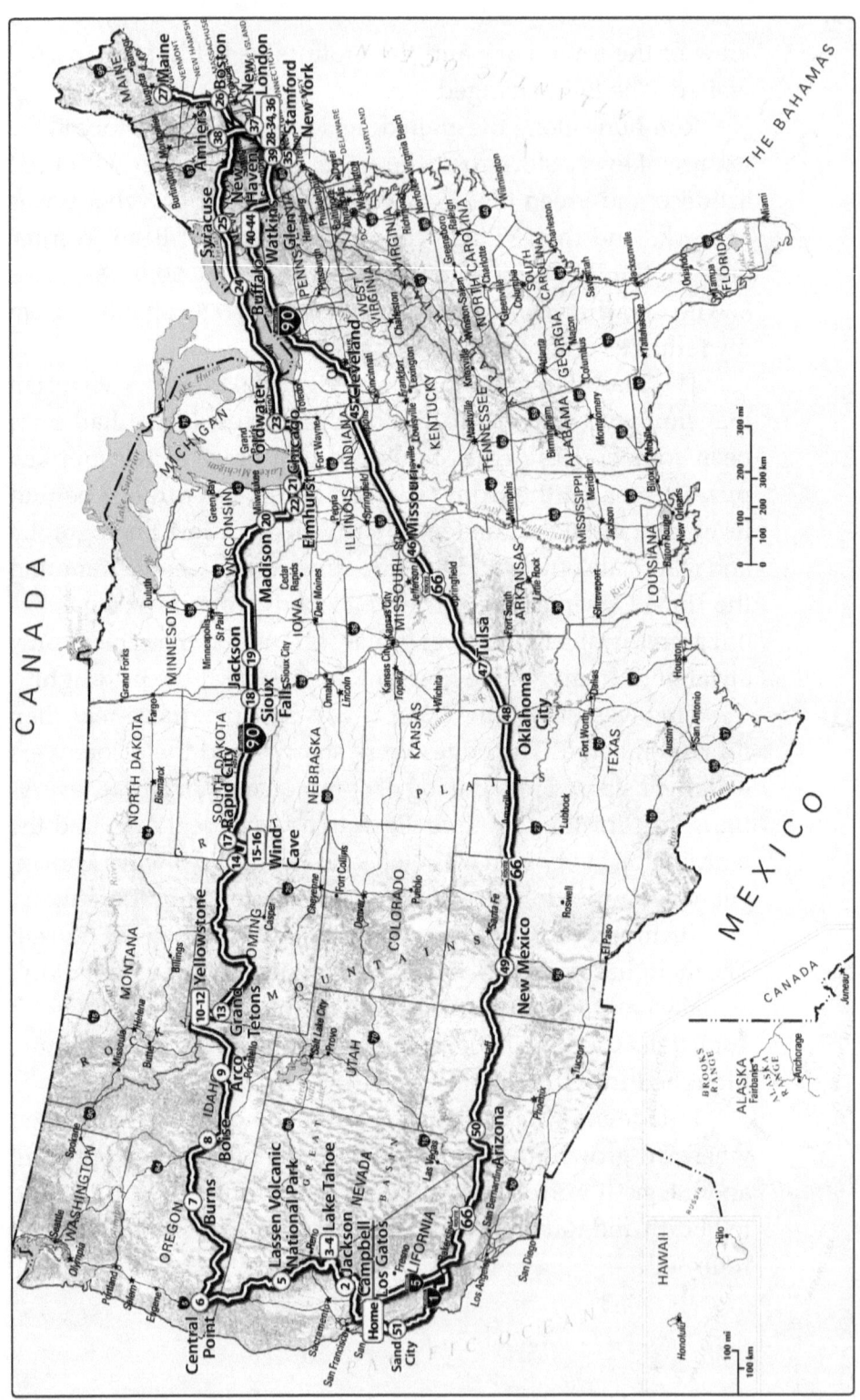

The Wet Shoe Journals ~ Map & Legend

1 Aug. 23 — Campbell, CA
2 Aug. 24 — Jackson, CA
3-4 Aug. 25-26 — Lake Tahoe, CA
5 Aug. 27 — Lassen Nat'l Park, CA
6 Aug. 28 — Central Point, OR
7 Aug. 29 — Burns, OR
8 Aug. 30 — Boise, ID
9 Aug. 31 — Arco, ID
10-12 Sept. 1-3 — Yellowstone Nat'l Park, WY
13 Sept. 4 — Grand Tetons Nat'l Park, WY
14 Sept. 5 — On I-90, S. Dakota
15-16 Sept. 6-7 — Wind Cave, SD
17 Sept. 8 — Rapid City, SD
18 Sept. 9 — Sioux Falls, SD
19 Sept. 10 — Jackson, MN
20 Sept. 11 — Madison, WI
21 Sept. 12 — Chicago, IL
22 Sept. 13 — Elmhurst, IL
23 Sept. 14 — Coldwater, MI
24 Sept. 15 — Canada & Buffalo, NY
25 Sept. 16 — Syracuse, NY
26 Sept. 17 — Boston, MA
27 Sept. 18 — On I-95 in Maine
28-34 Sept. 19-25 — New Haven, CT
35 Sept. 26 — New York, NY
36 Sept. 27 — New Haven, CT
37 Sept. 28 — New London, CT
38 Sept. 29 — Amherst, MA
39 Sept. 30 — Stamford, CT
40-44 Oct. 1-5 — Watkins Glen, NY
45 Oct. 6 — Cleveland, OH
46 Oct. 7 — On Route 66 in Missouri
47 Oct. 8 — Tulsa, OK
48 Oct. 9 — Oklahoma City, OK
49-50 Oct. 10 to 11 — On Route 66 through New Mexico and Arizona
51-52 Oct. 12 to 13 — Sand City, Los Gatos, and Willow Glen, CA

Rebel Without a Clue

Fifty Years Later

The trip brought Tom and me together again after having drifted apart since our early days of sports car enthusiasm. If you want to know somebody, if you want to make a friend or revive a friendship, you do stuff together — that's how it works. At least, that's how it worked for us. We got lucky.

We were fortunate in other ways as well. We survived to tell the tale; we learned from our experience, and our appreciation of life became more complex for having the audacity to travel through it with throttles wide open.

The farther Tom and I rode and the more issues we had to deal with, the stronger we got. We grew accustomed to pushing on regardless, which served us well in later years. Battling a tent in a rainstorm and persevering it into position isn't that much different from remodeling a commercial building or reinventing a business to survive in a changing world. The scale is different, but the creativity and moxie required to get the job done are similar.

Our lives were like those stock charts with all the little steps and dips and occasional plunges that nevertheless climb upward over the course of a lifetime. We didn't clip the apex of every situation, but we made our best effort. By practicing over and over, we translated whatever we had into better skills and more nuanced abilities, and did well for ourselves in the process.

When we returned, we stepped back into our lives. Tom went north to work in the ski industry for the winter; I found an apartment near downtown and went back to work. The 1970s were a crazy and wonderful time to be alive in Los Gatos. At the unripe age of twenty, I was soon managing our office supply company with a staff of six, right in the heart of town.

Artists and poets were everywhere. There was a grassroots renaissance in play, with education, individual freedom, and choices all around. Without realizing it, our parents had homesteaded our lives in a new and wonderful way.

The Hill

> "When we are young, we can imagine the most terrible and perfect things, for we ourselves are terrible and perfect. We see ourselves in what we dream. For a time, we retain that clarity of vision before graying into adulthood with its rounded imperfections and wise admonitions."
>
> *– Oscar Wilde*

Caught for a time between rebellion and responsibility, I became part of a salon of sorts, a small group of friends about the same age. Tom knew them and I knew Tom. Eventually, everybody knew everybody. We lived in high contrast: either madly in love or completely focused on our art; we had tons of power but very little traction. From the last years of high school until a few years into college, we lived for late-night conversations over coffee and cigarettes, ski trips, tinkering with our cars, folk music, rock music, weed, stained glass, woodworking, painting, strange poetry that meant nothing and everything, and whatever else caught our attention.

The moon was in the seventh house of the rising sun by the dock of the bay, and we were terribly serious, frenetically self-absorbed, and starved for a future that seemed just out of reach. Our colors were too bright, but it didn't matter. Our common ground was a place called The Hill; the chief instigator was a girl named Vicky, and our patron saint was her mother, Gloria.

Mrs. Morrill lived with her only daughter and two Siamese cats in a monster of a house on four acres of heavily forested land in the hills behind and above my family's office equipment and supply store. The first time I came to that ancient house, I was with Tom, picking up some friends for a ski trip to Sugar Bowl. I was truly awestruck. The house was gigantic. It was neither the House of Usher nor Blenheim Palace, but a kind of West Coast blending of the two. There were antiques everywhere. The place reeked of forgotten history, long-lost mystery, and magnificent obsession.

If I'd come of age in England or anywhere in Europe, I might not have been as impressed, but California was still in its salad days compared to the rest of the world, and large old houses filled with antiques and ancient memorabilia were unusual, and to my mind, a bit unreal. Part of what impressed me so much was the sheer number of marvelous artifacts that had been collected. Every wall and shelf contained something of interest, something of value. Every room held its share of memories.

Battleship grey with white trim, the house had been built with two great rooms—living and dining room—on either side of the front entrance, which had a black and white checked floor, like a giant chess board. There were two long hallways running through the middle of the house, both upstairs and down. Vicky's room was at the far end of the lower hall, behind the conservatory and living room, like a retreat.

Outside, there were gigantic oaks and deodar cedars and pine trees and tree ferns, and brick paths going through the gardens, and staghorn ferns in pots on the side of the house. When the house became quiet, there was an utter stillness about it, partly due to the sheer size of the property, but also because of the forest of trees that surrounded it.

Some of the interior walls were hollow, and thick enough to walk inside. Inexplicably, I once found garments hanging from a clothesline inside one of the walls, a practical use for so much unused space.

There was a six hundred pound beehive in a storeroom off the upstairs hallway that could never be removed. I saw it only once. It was strange and a little frightening. Alien, and otherworldly. It looked like a gigantic *brain*, six feet across. The bees had built it against the far wall of the closet, smooth and round on the outside, and off white in color. There were no bees in the room; the hive was only open to the outside through the wall. The bees got in and out through an opening, then flew inside the wall to a crack in the gable, from whence they escaped.

So the bees didn't leak into the house, but the hive *hummed*. On a summer day, if you looked way up at the front of the house, the left gable always looked a little fuzzy and out of focus because of all the bees flying around. Gloria said she'd hired beekeepers to remove them, but they just couldn't get it done. There was honeycomb inside the wall beneath the hive, and honey ran down sometimes during really hot days in the summertime. One of the beekeepers was able to harvest some of it once, long ago. He filled Mason jar after Mason jar.

One of the upstairs bedrooms was always referred to as the Ball Room—a crude pun, however accurate. There was a crack in one of the windows with a small bit of glass missing, which had been plugged with a pair of blue panties. Those panties had been stuck there for years, a mute testament to some poor girl's effort to stop the damn hole once and for all with whatever was handy as she sat there, naked and shivering.

On one wall of the living room (a room rarely used), there was a truly ancient manuscript—magnificently illuminated—of a Gregorian chant with square music notes *(neumes)* in a gold frame. I had to do a bit of research to figure out what kind of music it was, and in what century it might have been created). In that same room was a large portrait of a man in Elizabethan dress, painted in richly muted colors, said to have been created by a student of Raphael or some such. The heavy gilt frame was marred where a number had been scratched off—evidence perhaps that the painting had once been displayed in a museum.

There was slab marble, white with gray veins, on almost every horizontal surface in the house. Unanswered questions and permanently closed-off rooms. Victorian and Georgian furniture. The Red Room, with sheet music and musical instruments mounted on the deep red walls and a Wells Fargo rolltop in the far corner, complete with a bullet hole from some forgotten robbery. A hidden doorway from the Red Room in the far corner led to a sealed-off bedroom.

When you passed the Red Room going down the hall, the last door on the right was always shut. It was blocked from the inside. When Gloria and her ex-husband had been married, that had been their bedroom. Gloria sealed it after the divorce by pulling a chest of drawers across the doorway on the inside. You could see where the missing room was from the outside, looking at the back of the house: a ruined porch with broken steps overrun by vines, and dark windows with drapes pulled tight. From what I'd gleaned, everything was still there: the bed, the furniture, even their clothing. Gloria had just sealed it up.

Between Vicky's bedroom and the living room was a zink-floored conservatory with windows and its own glass roof, like a miniature hot house. It was plumbed for water and dripping over with green life, both real and plastic. (Vicky's mom loved plants, but she was also a practical woman.) There was a tiny doorway between Vicky's bedroom and the conservatory, providing a second exit in case of fire or some other dire emergency.

Just off the kitchen was a gigantic redwood burl table, held up by heavily carved piano legs. There was a full bar as well, with a counter made of burl from the same tree, and a black lacquered grand piano in the entry.

I had many conversations at that table over the years, ideas striding far and wide through fields of philosophy, metaphysics, and how to fleishhacker a ski. The burl itself provoked us, with all the whorls and edges layered inside one another, indeterminate and repeating, like the shell of a nautilus with its private Fibonacci sequence. Endless layers of Varathane magnified the depth—something you could get lost in just by staring too long (which some of us did, particularly when ripped).

Mrs. Morrill smoked three or four packs of unfiltered Lucky Strikes every day, and there were little silver sugar pots filled with sand all over the house. She used them as ashtrays, each with its own tiny forest of cigarette stumps. It was a bizarre effect: antique sugar pots with silver sconces, foliation, ribbon wreaths in high relief, and gadroon borders—and all of them sporting a ridiculous denial of elegance: cigarette butts unceremoniously snuffed out in white sand.

A Farberware coffee pot was forever perking away in the kitchen for anyone who wanted a cup, and there were perhaps ten or twenty cartons of Lucky Strikes in the walk-in pantry (Gloria really did not like to run out of cigarettes), along with three walls of canned goods, spices, and baking supplies. Lucky Strike was a brutal cigarette, and nobody touched her stash.

Young adults were always in and out of the house—for coffee and conversation at that massive burlwood table in the kitchen, a game of chess, or to watch Johnny Carson's *Tonight*

Show with Gloria in the Red Room. These conversations were of no particular type, but they were the language of our lives. We were exploring what it was to be alive and able to make adult decisions on our own hook.

We were about to change the world. Our parents had done what they could, but they had been shackled by their past. We were going beyond all that to set the future straight for all time because that's what you do when you're young and full of yourself and self-righteous and true. It was all very important and necessary. We were coming into our own, but we didn't think of ourselves that way. It was more instinct than knowledge, unvoiced and unknowable, yet built into our bones and sinews and the air we breathed. We were the Juliets and Hamlets, the Jay Gatsbys and Holly Golightlys of our age, damaged and struggling, finding our way through the maze.

Beyond the cotton wool and sharp edges of our parent's lives was a pattern we had discovered, that we were somehow connected to and through everything, that the entire planet was its own work of art, and that we were an intrinsic part of that art.

We discovered it was we ourselves who hammered and welded and infused it with how we were in the moment. Greig's stained glass installed into the kind of house we thought of when we read Tolkien, creating a space for Bill's jigsaw rope beds, and Cathee's incredible eggs—with art so delicate and real you could get lost in the story she'd told in the painting of them.

All of which existed in the real world all at once, with the righteous blast of some motorcycle mixing its rude roaring truth into Joan Baez singing her soul out with the effort of caring beyond anything imaginable, and all of *that* soaring into the bluest of daylight, spinning round and round and round like the bees at the top of the house, and then it was gone, pffft... and we left to meet up down at the Broken Egg.

That was the moment. It was the moment of our truth, our youth, and our madness.

Ski trips were organized in our imaginations, in the Wildcat Sports Shop on Main Street, and in Morrill's kitchen. And then, while working out logistics of who of us piles into which car, someone glances at you in the mirror behind the bar and it's yourself you see, a look into your own eyes, a glint of humor perhaps, a sardonic exaltation of life that we only glimpse but once and far away, just for one moment in the mirror, behind the bar at Vicky's house. And then, pffft... that too is gone.

As the years progressed, Gloria grew weary of putting up and taking down all the Christmas decorations, including the three huge trees she always had in the entrance hall. So one year she just left everything as it was. Christmas was year-round from that point on, growing a little worn around the edges, a little shabbier as the years went by.

Long after Victoria and I were no more, I continued to visit her mother from time to time, and the conversations were as natural as rain on a roof. Gloria and I would drink coffee and talk into the night about politics, art, and her gardening. I got her version of the world as I could never have witnessed it—particularly the FDR years during the New Deal—and she got my perspective on current events and business. The television was usually on Carson or the news, and we would speculate on why the world was the way it was. Gloria was not instrumental to my growing up, but she accepted me for who I was as an adult, which added to my confidence.

When I first came to that house on the hill, neither the house itself, my friends, nor I had faded. Our brightwork still shone and we were all in full sail. Despite, and perhaps because of all its ruination, that house and the people in it were the grandest things I'd ever known. The scars and tragic memories and lost hope only made it more so. I have a tapestry of photographs in my mind, a collage of recollections that includes my friends and all the events and Christmases and interesting cars and ski trips and people who gathered there before the fading—the laughter and the sadness. It was an age of innocence and reckoning. It was the way we were. I was hungry, and it was her world.

In the fading light of evening through giant childrenstory trees looms that great gray house, and a dark green MG with a bit of rope tied to the driver's door latch, waiting at the top of the drive.

A world in flux

During the 1970s, people started making sandals out of leather and wood and throwing pottery with new designs. We created surrealist paintings, wrote bad poetry, crafted art furniture, leaded stained glass, and sold what we could at craft fairs and small shops. We kept ourselves alive listening to music no one had heard before, had breakfast down at the Broken Egg, drank coffee and smoked cigarettes and weed until all hours, and were forever thinking, thinking, thinking.

We weren't chuckleheads. We listened to Grace Slick sing *White Rabbit* channeling Charles Dodgson via Lewis Carroll and amplified by Jefferson Airplane. And we knew *exactly* what she meant. We fed our minds as best we could—books, music, conversation, art—anything and everything to expand our universe. We read Colette, Brautigan, and Vonnegut, stood in awe before Turner's sunsets.

We learned to appreciate that women had been muttering a silent dirge throughout history—the refrain from Carly Simon's *You're So Vain*. Some of us got the complexity and implications better than others and wrestled with our inner mensch; tried to address it squarely, failed, lost sight of it, found it again, and tried harder. Others didn't.

Sometimes we drank too much. Sometimes we got lucky. Young blood and animal spirits. We played the Eastern game of *Go* on gridded boards, snapping our way through Saturday afternoons with lazy dust motes in the quiet air between us. When we could afford it, we stayed at little hostelries like C&M Rooms and skied the snow-covered mountains surrounding Lake Tahoe. In the pursuit of mystical ideals and the perfect song of life, some of us attempted to exist on air alone, or the casual kindness of tie-dyed strangers.

Some of us grew beards, became engineers, or started new companies with bizarre names that merged imaginary objects with wafers of glass and lines of code. We were riding the Marrakesh Express through a land of exploration. This time around it was incense and sitar music that built the topless towers of Ilium while our parents prayed for our salvation. We were full of ourselves, arrogant, and expected to win all the races. We were a nation of misfit toys who grew up on Howdy Doody, Disney Magic, and 31 Flavors of ice cream.

We watched Mary Tyler Moore shift the face of our humanity by showing us in fifteen years how a woman could thrive on her own terms in a modern society. She went from being Dick van Dyke's cute wife on one show (1961-66) to Mary Richards, single and plucky television producer in the next (1970-77). By doing so, she upended the moribund narrative that the woman's place was in the home tending to children and supporting a husband. And she did it with disarming charm and humor.

Candice Bergen as the character *Murphy Brown* (1988-98) took the idea of modern womanhood even further. The show was singled out by evangelicals with pious horror: she was a professional newscaster who prioritized her career, a single woman who controlled her own sex life, a single mother intentionally raising a child without a male partner. Oh, the humanity!

The New Age movement flowered in San Francisco, New York, Paris, and London, and weedy green shoots sprang up in between, including Los Gatos. We read *The Teachings of Don Juan* by Carlos Castaneda and *The Way of Zen* by Watts. *Siddhartha* by Hesse was in there as well, along with *The Lord of the Rings* by Tolkien. All part of the struggle to understand who we were and why and what we might do about it. Our parents could no longer shutter and contain our lives, fearful of what we might be learning. We learned it anyway.

We rediscovered the subjectivism of writers who had hobnobbed in Paris back in the early 1900s, like Scott Fitzgerald, James Joyce, and Gertrude Stein, but reinterpreted the spirit of their observations through the gonzo prism of Hunter S. Thompson, held like refractive glass before a sun too bright.

Los Gatos was green with trees and new money. A Ferrari dealership opened up on Main Street, where I'd purchased my Triumph GT6 from Ken Keegan, and our staff had grown to ten. The Good Earth restaurant sprang into existence down the block, and our staff was now fourteen. The Old Town artisan center opened up just a block over from our new, larger office supply store, and after a few years, I was working with a staff of eighteen.

There was money being made in Silicon Valley, and Los Gatos was just close enough to benefit as a bedroom community for all the movers and shakers. But this massive wealth and cultural influx did not happen everywhere. Farm communities just outside where I lived stayed much the same as those throughout most of the Midwest. There is only so much money to be made from lettuce and wheat or the work that brings them to harvest. Many people watched in a kind of sick horror as certain parts of the world became swept up by fancy houses, glamorous automobiles, and double Ristretto Venti half-soy nonfat decaf organic double-shot frappuccinos — as if we'd all started speaking French and wearing berets.

Rainy day women

As I began my life's work at the family business, girls with attitude who missed at nothing wove a quiet dance behind my eyes. I was young, full of beans, and impossibly disconnected. I found myself facing a labyrinth of contradictory and unstated social mores, scared to death of coming up short in this new age of reason. Love wasn't easy. Infinity might take awhile.

I had to be strong and stable, but only when appropriate, and not too much or I'd be a soulless idiot, but also vulnerable and emotional but not too much or respect would be gone — *zip* — just like that, and I'd be left alone in the dark forever.

I had to be independent and put-together, able to handle all of my own baloney without outside help, but also willing to open up and be dependent in exactly the idealized way they imagined I should, but not beyond that. Dark and brooding was good, but humor was critical. If I was mysteriously creative, that was even better.

It would help if I was funny and charming and entertaining and appealing and the kind of guy who would make every effort, but I couldn't come on too strong.

I had to make the first move, but only when they were ready and not a second sooner or I'd been seen as pushy. They could signal me when I was on the correct side of that line, but I had to read it with intelligence and *act* or risk being a disappointment. Or at least, it seemed that way.

This was in addition to the overarching dichotomy separating the sheep from the goats. A bit of danger was evidently attractive, but nobody with any sense expected Dangerous Dan McGrew to settle down, support a family, and help with the dishes. The guy who rode motorcycle might be exciting to date, but a girl didn't bring him home to meet mom and dad unless he was also stable, educated, well-spoken, and empathetic. And liked dogs. And didn't talk down to kids. Or, to paraphrase Meredith Willson, "And if she'd sometimes ponder what makes Shakespeare and Beethoven great… she I could love 'til I die."

I was looking for was someone who didn't have time for the drama and could remark from time to time in a way that let me know all the lights were on (sarcasm optional). As iron sharpens iron, I sought wit and mettle to push against. Interesting ideas are the primary reason for conversation; talking about events or people was just empty calories as far as I was concerned. Unlike the songwriter Billy Joel, who didn't want clever conversation (because he didn't want to work that hard), I did. Still do. And I never understood people who don't.

So in the end, I decided to rely on the simple strategy of disguising myself as quite possibly the most fascinating thing on the planet. But still humble, of course. And creative. And sensitive—but not too much. Fortunately, I wrote terrible poetry and carved my own furniture. And that seemed to work.

The world according to Tom

After the trip, Tom worked hard at being a ski bum for five years, went into a period of which he remembers very little, then in 1977 focused on a career in newspaper photography. He attended San José State University's photojournalism sequence and then moved through a seventeen-year period working for the *Manteca Bulletin, San Francisco Examiner, East Bay Express,* and the *Associated Press,* culminating in five years at the *Oakland Tribune.*

It was while working for the *Oakland Tribune* that he was part of the team that won the 1990 Pulitzer Prize for their coverage of the 1989 Loma Prieta earthquake. During this period, he taught photography and photojournalism at San Francisco State University and later at the Academy of Art in San Francisco. After the *Tribune* folded in 1992, a hobby dealing in vintage photographic equipment became a full-time business. An interest in astronomy prompted him to add telescopes, and he's been at it ever since.

Starting in 1988, he began a career as an amateur driver in West Coast SCCA Formula Ford road racing competition with good success, and is still driving competitively after more than 400 races, 6 regional championships, and a 15% winning average. He recently added the camera and photography book business, CameraBooks.com, to his portfolio. Tom lives with his wife of 34 years, Patty, along with two dogs and three cats in Northern California. He still shoots photographs for himself.

The secret of my success

As a child, I was given a wide variety of great examples. Everyone in our family went to college, even if they didn't all end up with degrees, so I was expected to go as well. Everyone read incessantly. My father owned a local business. My mother was a teacher. My sister became a teacher and then owned several businesses. My brother ran a mental health organization to help people with problems. I was brought up in the family business, and nobody was too hard on me when I made mistakes; they just pointed them out. I was taught that how I did something was at least as important as what I did. I was taught that failure was just one part of getting it right. Expectations and home environment contribute greatly to a person's character, but overcoming failure is what builds it.

The point is, I was given the tools to succeed; I was trained and coached on how to recognize quality, and I was given a moral charter to keep myself on track. So it was up to me, but I didn't "make my own luck." It was provided by my family and my family's work ethic and history, the friends I made early on, and the people I worked with. That kind of privilege perpetuates, generation after generation, just like money does with the wealthy. If you have it and know how to manage it, you don't tend to lose it. And then you pass it forward, one way or another, and it keeps building.

Good old nepotism

Hey, it was a job, and I had to eat; Los Gatos Office Equipment & Supply was just sitting there, and it got my full attention. Plus, there was my family's collective eye-roll to deal with whenever I spoke of anything else. Refusing high school and the draft, along with what Tom and I had gone through, brought just enough confidence to think I might pull it off. I began to sell business machines, file cabinets and chairs, paper clips and desk organizers. I still expected to face prison time if and when the government ever got its act together, and I had no idea how Ray would cope while I was gone, but my anxiety had waned.

When I took my place in the world of business during the early 1970s, I wasn't exactly a blank slate, but there was a lot to learn. Ray was getting tired, and he wanted to stay at home with the books and have me take over the day-to-day operation of his business.

From the age of fourteen, I had done original entry bookkeeping, posted to the general ledger, and closed the books. I hated it, but Ray insisted. I had straightened shelves, handled rubber stamp orders (including metal dies!), sold typewriters and adding machines, furniture, and office supplies, and had even handled purchasing when Nat Muraco, our buyer, went on vacation.

I was near the jumping-off point to managing the business as a whole, but there was still something I felt I needed to learn. I convinced Ray that part of my education should include some time in our Service Department. I argued that it would give me a deeper understanding of the business machines we sold if I knew how to fix them, and it might be helpful to know what it was like to work in the shop. He was dubious, but let me go ahead. So I put on a green apron and asked Dave Dudey, who was our service manager back then, to show me the ropes.

For each of us, the "good old days" has the same meaning, regardless of when we were born. It's that idyllic time in our lives we fondly recall before the weight of adult responsibilities set in. As long as someone else is making the big decisions, hey—we're happy as clams. Take that away, and... *bingo, bango, bongo,* there goes our endless summer.

My own journey into adulthood began early. That's why I was so determined to take that motorcycle trip, despite the risks. I had a pretty clear sense of what awaited me at the Department of Justice, and I craved those last few months of freedom to simply be myself. And it worked. But I knew that when I returned to take over for Ray, everything would change. It would be time for me to grow up, take control, and steer my own course.

The day I stopped working in the shop and sat down at my father's desk was sickening, exhilarating, scary stuff. It made me think about what I was doing and why, especially since I still wanted to be a painter and a writer, find true love, and maybe stand up for truth, justice, and The American Way. But mostly I wanted to avoid bankrupting my parents and looking as inept as I suspected myself to be.

So, there I was, the young hotshot in charge of Los Gatos Office Equipment. My father's company had been chugging along nicely before I came along, so we had a solid foundation and momentum, but I was suddenly in charge of keeping it upright. I was the boss, but I was also the youngest of the bunch. We had six employees, all older than me. I was pretty sure they were shaking their heads in dour bemusement when I took charge of operations. I had to pretend I didn't know about their skepticism, make my voice heard, and not screw up. I had a clear duty to our staff and my parents to see that we remained viable despite my lack of wisdom and experience. Keep calm and carry on indeed.

It was necessary to somehow balance ego and humility. I had to drive the company forward, listen with both ears to my people, keep Ray happy with the bottom line, and keep a watchful eye on the future—particularly with electronics, which were evolving on a monthly basis. I also had to put enough people in charge to help me manage things like inventory, customer relations, maintenance, and staff issues. Fortunately for me, the company had a momentum of its own. I just couldn't let it falter.

I learned how to dance, metaphorically speaking. A critical skill for any business owner. It isn't a waltz either; it's a quickstep. Or perhaps it should be called the "bob and weave." In any case, the ability to make my way through the vagaries of a unique business in a small town was necessary to keep the doors open, and it required something a lot better than two wrong feet in ugly shoes.

But I still had to know more. So, early on, I went down to the library. If there was one thing I knew how to do, it was research a topic, read it to death, and take notes. I checked out books on business management along with a few on the history of typewriters and the companies that made them. I didn't see myself as a businessman, but I didn't want to let anybody down, particularly my parents. I figured if I had enough product knowledge and whatever my father could teach me, plus what I could pick up from my reading, I might fool enough people for long enough to make it work.

For the most part, I got lucky. I never made much money, but I didn't plunge our company into darkness and despair either. And the tightrope I had envisioned between art, writing, and work? That rope broke. Oh, I wrote my monographs and painted, but the quasi-mad creative genius I wanted to grow into became muffled by and sublimated into the constant worry of cash flow management and the responsibility of keeping the company afloat as the world changed.

Passion with boundaries

I didn't wake up to my own inner resolve right away, but my actions rang loudly enough over time. And it was all quite natural. I did not step quietly away from my drive for art and justice, but repurposed that passion to create my own bailiwick out of the town and our family business, making opportunities for women and leveling the commercial playing field where I could.

Our staff grew from six to twenty over the years, and keeping everybody on the same page was sometimes quite a task. Responsibility and creativity cancel each other rather effectively (which took me forever to figure out). I only understood *why* I wasn't able to be artistically creative while running the firm years later, and only after I became conversant with the right-left brain hemisphere dichotomy.

I had to change. I was not unlike that backpacker who fell asleep in a field, only to discover when he woke up that the heat from his body had caused a fast-growing acorn to sprout beneath him, carrying him upward during the night. He found himself lodged in the upper branches of a huge oak the next morning. Not adept at climbing, he braved the situation philosophically. "I cannot," he thought to himself, "adapt circumstances to my will. So, I'll just have to adapt my will to match the circumstances. I choose, forevermore, to live in a tree."

This was a difficult and drawn-out process that drove me nuts with frustration for a number of years, given that I really didn't want my life to be measured out in paperclips. But I eventually changed to fit the situation. Solving other people's problems became my passion, my purpose, my life.

Adding value

Business machines were our big ticket items, but selling one machine at a time to new customers I had to convince over and over again felt like a task for Sisyphus. Businesses bought more than one machine over time, and if I could generate repeat sales that meant better wages all around.

I was also rather tired of being lumped in with all the other firms selling products in the same category (such as department stores that sold typewriters) when I knew we were intrinsically different in attitude, knowledge, and service. We were competing with commodity operations, but we shouldn't be compared to them as equals. I didn't just sell business machines, I sold the best business machines available, including copiers, check protectors, cash registers, and calculators, and backed them with an in-house service department and my own brand of morality. But I wanted to dominate the local market, so I decided to set standards our competition wouldn't try to meet.

I came up with two game-changing ideas. My GUARANTEED TRADE-IN POLICY set future values using a set amortization schedule, and made it an easy decision to come back to our firm when the customer wanted to upgrade or get a newer model. In fact, it made it economically untenable not to. I also came up with the one year RENTAL PURCHASE AGREEMENT, which allowed business clients to equip their office without a long-term financial contract and very little up-front cash — particularly helpful for brand new business owners. And we did it all in-house, which meant almost no paperwork and same-day delivery.

There were a lot of entrepreneurs in Los Gatos. Some grew their companies into solid firms over time, and I was often the first guy they talked to. They usually needed office furniture and a typewriter to start, later on a copier, or a calculator. And I was the friendly guy they already knew who would take anything back if it didn't work out. Other salespeople couldn't follow me down the road I took my clients.

My goal was to make it easier to do business with our firm than with anyone else. All my father had to do was keep up with the cash flow issues I generated.

To make my sales pitch last, I wrote a ten-page brochure highlighting our best-selling machine, our philosophy of business, and how each machine fit the needs of each situation. During our tenure as an Olympia Dealer, we sold more Olympia typewriters than anyone else. We went head-to-head with IBM and won almost every single sale. I changed the playing field by not being a typical salesman.

For one thing, I made a habit of recommending my competition. "Hey, IBM is a great company with a wonderful product! But my company is great too, and our machines are just as good, but in different ways. And our company is scrappy; we'll give you service like you never heard of." (I guaranteed to buy back any machine *with no end date* if the customer wasn't happy.) Nobody was willing to match that kind of service, including IBM. I put our company in a completely different league.

I became a teacher and a knowledgeable partner instead. If someone was unhappy, I made it right, even to giving a full refund on equipment long after the sale. I put the Golden Rule to practical use. Somehow, I knew that making money on every sale was shortsighted, so, like any good gambler, I played the percentages. It was all part of learning how to dance without stepping on anybody's toes. Easy enough to do if you only sell high quality products, want to be well-liked, and think in decades instead of years.

Walking around in downtown Los Gatos, I thought about all the other merchants. Why was I comfortable going into some stores and not others? I realized I had a natural reluctance, a built-in bias against the unknown. To my mind, that meant other people probably had that same irrational reluctance, and overcoming it could be a huge opportunity.

That's what our Copy Center was all about in the beginning: overcoming the initial bias people had of venturing into an unfamiliar place. I let common need and word of mouth do the work for me. Plus some rather cute illustrations I commissioned from Barb Kyger, an artist I knew from the Chamber of Commerce; bunnies and such, plus myself in a magician's outfit. Everybody loves a bit of whimsey.

I created the "copy center as a business" as something completely new to the world of commerce back when the first dry copier was made by the small and obscure Haloid Corporation—before they changed their name to Xerox. The Haloid 914 was bulky, cumbersome, and prone to spontaneous combustion (a fire extinguisher was included, just inside the main cabinet). It weighed 650 pounds and was about the size of two washing machines bolted together.

There were no public copy machines at that time and certainly no copy centers, even in large cities like San Francisco or New York. I could not have been the first kid on the planet to sell copies from a retail outlet, but it sure looked that way. Xerox thought I just wanted to make office copies for my own business. Even they had no idea what I was up to. They sold mostly to lawyers and large corporations.

Every time we made a profit, I either lowered the price per copy or got better machines—usually faster. And as we got more equipment, I kept rearranging the store layout. I soon asked Xerox to qualify me as a technician so I could do my own repairs and get rid of the costly service contracts.

We became a beta site for Xerox when they introduced their new line of *duplicators:* it was just us and Hewlett-Packard. If the technicians weren't at my place, they were over at H-P, drinking coffee and waiting for one of these two machines to break. Our place was *humming,* with customers coming from surrounding cities, and I was buying paper by the pallet.

There was nothing automatic about our success. The cost of the Xerox 9200 was more than a nice house in a big city. I spent uncounted hours, staying up half the night figuring and refiguring the cost-per-impression, service costs, and materials. I used a calculator, pencil, and graph paper to postulate scenario after scenario, projecting volume, income, expense, and potential profit: this went on for years. We could go bankrupt in any rolling six-month period if I didn't get it to work, and there were no guidelines. I was on my own, gambling the family fortune on a calculated hunch.

Decades later, our little company was in the vanguard when the printing and publishing industries adopted digital printing to create the short run | no inventory model for books, fine art, and color printing. What I couldn't do in-house I sent out to other printers—some local, some around the world, depending on turnaround, pricing, and quality.

I drove our firm with single-minded purpose—not to make money particularly (which rarely happened), but to make everything better over time. I promoted capable people and gave them the power to make changes. I was there early enough to push for what I believed in. Nothing grand, but still.

My father was a gambling man, and he passed that skill on to me. As conservative as Ray thought himself to be, he was willing to take on real risk when it came to the company. Ray mortgaged his used car to buy Edith an engagement ring, got a loan on the ring to build our home in Los Gatos, and mortgaged that house and property on at least four occasions to support the business. He bootstrapped his way up the ladder of life and showed me by example how to make it happen.

When I came up with the copy center as a business and our move to a larger location, he was dubious at first, but willing to make the leap. Big gambles for a retail business in a small town. I learned to be pragmatic about change and risk. Standing pat was doomed to failure for anyone but Sees Candy.

Not everything went smoothly; I overstepped, blundered, spent money in the wrong area, and one venture didn't pan out because I didn't know enough. Nobody did; it was a new concept. I had set up a venture to jump-start minority- and women-owned office supply retailers without knowing I'd be competing with my own suppliers at just over cost. I had large firms lined up to buy from us, but the margin of profit was just too slim.

I believe my somewhat comical ability to expound upon almost any subject that interests me dates back to the skills I developed during those years on the sales floor. I knew my products well and honestly believed I was doing everyone a service by providing them to the public. One huge advantage — I was the boss and sold only the finest.

I was preaching the gospel according to me, and I was very focused, usually to the exclusion of everything else. I would interview each client to find out what they were looking for, what their needs were, what their workload was, what their budget was, what problems they might be trying to fix, and then describe one or two business machines that might work well for them — sometimes machines we didn't even carry. After asking more questions and listening further, I would focus on matching a machine to my customer's job, demonstrating the merits of the best machine, showing how the features and benefits would apply to their specific situation.

I listened intently to each of my clients, always looking for clues that would direct me to a solution. I was interviewing my clients to solve problems rather than trying to sell them something to make a profit. Big difference. It transformed a job into a mission.

A few years after Apple invented the personal computer, but before the Macintosh, mouse, and laser printer, I started selling Digital Equipment mini-computers and word processors, alongside our traditional typewriters, calculators, office supplies, file cabinets, and furniture. It became an adventure, because as one of only fifty DEC Dealers in the United States, I had authorized access to some of the world's largest organizations, including federal and state government offices.

My secret weapon

My mother was no longer teaching when we started selling mini-computers; there was just her and my father at home. Ray was involved with the accounting for our firm, and she was helping. She explained it to me one day over lunch; she was bored and housebound — a far cry from all her years as a proactive schoolteacher.

Naturally, I was concerned. So I did the only thing I could do; I hired the woman. I taught her to use a DECmate computer system and put her on the sales floor, tasked with creating sales lists and other files. This worked well for a number of reasons. She was doing something useful, she got to interact with a wide variety of people (both staff and customers), she was learning something quite new, which was exciting and different, and she wasn't stuck in the house all day.

It was all quite novel for her; few people even had access to computers at that time (our systems cost about the same as a new car). Apple had just invented the Apple II, but had yet to release the Macintosh, laser printer, or mouse. Everything was PROMPT>code on a black-and-white screen — sans graphics, photos, email, or internet.

As I watched her chatting with customers one day, I had a sudden moment of clarity. At that time, most people were both curious and afraid of computers. They were considered sophisticated and difficult to learn. Yet here was this nice gray-haired lady, sitting right up front at the keyboard of one of the most complex and expensive business machines available — the type of equipment most people had never seen close up.

People coming into the store felt comfortable talking to her; Edith wasn't a salesperson. She was just this nice lady they could talk to and ask questions of without consequence, partly because they might have thought at first that she was another customer like themselves, and partly because she never tried to sell them anything. She was doing naturally what I had learned long ago — it isn't about sales, it's about helping people.

I never interrupted; I let people talk to her for as long as they liked and just hung about in the background, straightening things, dusting — anything to stay busy while keeping an eye on the situation. And if she started looking around for me, I would walk over (slowly), and keep my mouth shut. Even experienced business people were leary of computers. They were also afraid of salespeople if the product was as expensive as this one looked, so it was critically important to give everyone the space they needed. If they felt any kind of pressure, they would clam up; that's the way it worked. That initial conversation, initiated by Edith, was my introduction.

Many years later, I happened to be at the house when Edith was clearing out some old stuff, and she mentioned she was tossing out all her five-year diaries. I was horrified — this was sixty years of history, not just of her, but of our family, and of me! I came up with a suggestion — that she write the story of her life, using the diaries as source material. I got her a Macintosh and set her up.

Edith attended memoir classes and wrote four books in eight volumes: *Life on a Missouri Farm,* the autobiography of Edith Coffin (her mother); *Meeting Every Challenge,* the life and times of Raymond Robertson (her husband); *Recollections of a Long and Interesting Life,* her own autobiography in five volumes; and *Stopwatch Teacher,* which focused on her twenty-eight years as a grammar school teacher and the unusual techniques she pioneered. I edited and published the first book; Alicia published the rest, just as she has with mine. My aunt LaVerne heard about it and followed suit with another book: *Westward Ho!,* which told the Brookover story and her own life.

I used my new computer skills, along with my knowledge of Digital Equipment systems at NASA and other large organizations to buy and sell terminals, printers, and assorted peripherals. Amazon and eBay wouldn't even be startups for another fifteen years; it was just me, my business license (and history as an ongoing firm, which was critically important), and information technology managers who needed computer systems and peripheral products. At that time, being a "brick and mortar" company with a regular street address was everything.

The 100 foot journey

There were many incidents along the way that tested my fettle as a proper manager and owner. I came to work one rainy day to find everyone gathered outside our front entrance, water flowing out over the sidewalk from under the doorway. (It had been raining all night and an empty soda can was blocking a drainpipe on the roof.) The building was flooded and charged with 200 amps of Pacific Gas & Electric's finest electricity.

Our building at 111 N. Santa Cruz Avenue had been built back in the 1930s. It had a cement floor covered with linoleum, with metal strips of surface wiring—all of which were now submerged beneath an inch or two of water. That wiring carried 110 *and* 220 volts due to our high-speed Xerox equipment. Why the fuses didn't blow, I have no idea.

Somehow, I had to get to the large 200 amp fuse box at the back of the store without electrocuting myself. I had played around with electricity enough to know this wouldn't be like the shocks I'd gotten from house current. There was enough water present to ground me to the center of the Earth.

I climbed over display cases, clung to shelving units, walked on desks, and propelled myself down aisles on chairs with casters. It was like when my brother and I used to circle each new property we moved to without touching the ground, but a bit more risky. I really wondered what the hell I was doing while clambering my way around, balancing on top of machinery, desks, and counters to get to the back of the store. Scary as hell, but somehow part of the geometry of being me.

On another occasion, I got a call at three o'clock in the morning from the Los Gatos Police. When I arrived downtown, the street was dark and quiet except for the police cars blocking the street at crazy angles in front of the store. The police had their rifles trained on the entrance. I got out of my car with my hands up, shouting out, "I'm the merchant!" They even had a police dog inside, checking out the building. An officer on foot had been checking doors, and ours hadn't been locked.

This was the kind of service everyone should get from their police, but I knew that wasn't the case. I'm not disparaging the police for doing their job, but I knew full well that as a business owner in Los Gatos that I enjoyed extraordinary privileges. I left a deposit bag full of money under a table in a restaurant one night. It was brought back to me the next day, still intact.

When our Shop Manager, Maria Harrington, was ready to have her baby, I hadn't been paying attention. Or at least, not to the degree I should have. Lucy Greene (one of the brighter sparks in my life) informed me one night that Maria Harrington had left for the hospital, but I still didn't get it. Then she suggested I might want to show up. Then she said it stronger, that Maria might be having her baby all *alone*. And that's when her voice developed an edge. *Nudge nudge.*

We got to the hospital in time, and Christina was born a few hours later. I happened to met Christina once again, years later and fresh out of college. She was working just a few doors down the street at Sprockets — a soccer equipment store. She introduced herself and referenced that night when she came into the world.

Surviving with grace

For me to thrive in business instead of as an artist, I knew it would be a lot easier if I played out the game with people I liked. A couple of laughs now and again wouldn't hurt either. Since I had control over that, I hired interesting people with intelligence, moxie, and a sense of humor.

A polite description of my managerial style would call me laid back, but honestly? I was lazy. And I hated meetings. So my solution was to hire people who didn't need to be managed. I had a habit of getting very focused on one little area of the business, but still needed all the departments to work.

So I hired people who could figure things out on their own and would only come to me if they had a bright idea that might cost money, or if they needed a bigger hammer. They also took turns warning me when I was about to veer off the map.

Sometimes rules work, and sometimes they don't, but sticking to only one rule book means you only know how to dance in one direction. I didn't know it at the time, but I was creating a new prototype for management—along with a lot of other people around the world. For the most part, it worked. I always felt on the edge of something new, something great. It wasn't writing, it wasn't art, but it was mine.

I really wasn't good at being the ruthless go-getter, so I made sure I worked with people who understood what I was up to and could support me when I needed it. In many cases— such as interviewing someone for a job or negotiating a building lease—I was almost always the youngest and least experienced person in the room. I found that by just stating my goal and shutting my mouth, I could get better results than by trying to fill the silence with conversation (a particular weakness of mine). It was sometimes enough to level the playing field.

Cash flow was an ever-present issue, a clear reminder that I wasn't a public corporation with an endless supply of stock I could issue, like monopoly money. There was no credit line for me to draw down, no credit card I could use to buy now and pay later. If I couldn't pay the bills, it would be the end. I knew business owners who had factored their inventory for operating cash. Huge mistake. It was like getting trapped in some weird game of financial Jenga.

The only flex in my system was based on how I managed my own salary, how long I could ride inventory down, and how quickly I paid vendors. Everyone had to be paid but me, so as the owner, my income was on the line. I went without salary for months at a time—not just once, but many times. Perhaps that's why I have such strong concerns about our national debt; I know where that road goes, and it isn't pretty. It doesn't matter whether you're an individual, a business, or the largest government on the planet; interest payments can eat you alive.

On a more positive note, I was able to lend the weight of our little business to the trajectory of justice as I saw it because I had put in the time and it had become part of my character. If I wasn't to be a writer or an artist, I could at least make a difference in a way that had meaning for me. I learned that when my passion was strong and clearly defined, people either got out the way or teamed up. It made my life far more interesting and meaningful.

Street smarts

My early education provided a foundation for understanding the present, but some things have to be experienced, and there were several specific episodes in business and as a foster parent and guardian that taught me how cultures—both good and bad—can persist over time, and how they can be changed.

- We established a self-perpetuating program for the certification of women as computer trainers within NASA to eliminate waste and allow promotion from within.

  As the primary NASA vendor on business systems for the Moffett Field facility in Sunnyvale, I convinced procurement to have me train and certify their secretarial staff for what I knew they were already doing. Like the Wizard of Oz, I understood how much the world values a scrap of parchment and how difficult it can be to advance without one.

  I held training for a week in one of their conference rooms, and at the end I held a little ceremony, giving all the graduates a signed certificate from a batch Village Printers made for me with gold filigree—just as the Wizard had with the Tin Man. By doing this, we eliminated a ridiculous $500 line item from every system purchased by NASA, but more importantly, did our part to enable and empower underappreciated women. This also educated me as to why our defense spending was so out of whack.

- I worked with a consulting firm charged with helping the United States Forest Service comply with multiple court orders to curtail long-term discrimination against women. I had no idea the forest rangers I had listened to at campfire talks could be so murderous to their own until I saw the documentation.

Apropos to this, an odd turn of events gave me quite a boost. *First Ellipsis...*, the collection of my poetry, prose, and song I had assembled a few years before, found its way into the hands of one of the women working for the U.S. Forest Service. She duplicated the book and audio cassette and they ended up being shared among the women rangers throughout the Forest Service. These people didn't know who I was, but they were listening to my songs and reading my pages. Heady stuff. Suddenly, and without seeking it, I had outside validation. Beauty, thy name is Sequoia sempervirens!

- I helped with a contract to determine why AT&T couldn't manage to promote women and minorities despite long-standing company policy. The study found misogyny and racism throughout middle management, and despite protestations to the contrary, it came from the top echelon.

- I helped start the Coalition of Concerned Parents in 1993, which was a 501c3 nonprofit we formed to address basic problems within the Santa Clara County Department of Family and Children's Services. Our group was perhaps twenty or so parents and grandparents who had been dealing with issues of arbitrary and (we felt) punitive decisions on the part of social workers without reasonable recourse.

This effort was a result of my interaction with social services, first as a foster parent, and later as a legal guardian. I asked for and was trained by Santa Clara County as a mandated reporter, and attended meetings and court cases at the Superior Court for many years, working primarily with Judge Leonard Edwards.

We got the ACLU involved and persuaded the Santa Clara County Board of Supervisors to create an ombudsman position to over-arch systemic bias and intervene. Thirty years later, the program is still in place.

AT&T, the U.S. Forest Service, and Santa Clara County's social services all had stubborn, pernicious issues: systemic racism, misogyny, and an arrogance that came from a lack of credible opposing viewpoints. It made me realize that organizations of any kind can be subject to such issues.

- I promoted a woman to be manager of our service department. I'd hired Maria Harrington to facilitate the flow rate of repair work and to add another pair of skilled hands to a pressured situation, but when customers kept looking past her to get one of our male technicians to answer questions, creating the position of Service Manager and promoting her into that position felt like an appropriately bold move. I had cards printed for her and an engraved name tag. She was the only person who ever got a name tag. I wanted our clients to understand exactly who was in charge.

  It worked a charm, but she got some funny reactions up at the Olympia regional office and training center, near San Francisco. Maria was the first woman to show up there as anything other than a secretary, and the entire building was nothing but men, wall-to-wall. She laughed about it later; "The technicians were nervous as hell adjusting to the new reality." But adjust they did.

- I promoted Andrea Pavellas from the front counter (our entry-level position) directly to Office Manager. We had been growing quickly and I had more staff in the new facility, so I decided to hold a company meeting just to check the temperature. I assembled chairs in a great circle before work one day and I asked everyone to speak their mind, going from person to person.

  There wasn't much said until it was Andrea's turn. She pulled out a little spiral notebook and proceeded to rattle off six to eight issues with precision and detail, consulting her notebook as she went along. She was nervous as hell, but spoke her mind. From staff disputes to delayed orders, she didn't hold back. When she finished, the room fell silent. It was clear that Andrea was a force to be reckoned with. Such wild talent was rare, and I knew it. Like finding diamonds in your backyard.

We'd never had an office manager, but I suddenly realized I needed one. The next day, I put Andrea in charge of correcting all the issues she had in that notebook of hers, plus anything else that caught her eye. She was the perfect fit. Who else to fix such issues than the person who felt so strongly about them?

Business partnerships can be difficult, unwieldy things. I've been in three over the years. They're a democracy of two. Each person gets an equal vote no matter how much it grates, and there's not much you can do about it except quit if it's not working—an existential threat, since the business model can fall apart. It's like divorce in that respect; it can be a clean, amicable break or awkward with emotion.

Ray and I disagreed from time to time, but one dispute was particularly difficult. He wanted to close down our Copy Center. It was taking a lot of my time and not making much money, but I knew it was bringing in new customers. It was a loss leader for a company that normally couldn't afford such luxuries, and sales were going up.

One day, our discussion became unbearable. No matter how I explained it, I just could not get him to see the bigger issue. He was working at his home office with the accounting and wasn't seeing the day-to-day activity first hand, and I knew that was the problem. I strongly felt that a busy store was a happy store, and finally played the only card I had left; I threatened to quit.

Plenty of kids threaten to run away from home or marry their girlfriend anyway. Some refuse to go into the family business. Big whoop. I was telling Ray that he and I were about to walk the plank together and plunge into a briny, shark-infested financial nightmare. Without me, he didn't have a functioning business, and without that business, I didn't have a job. I was desperate.

I knew Ray didn't get it. That if I didn't have something within the company that I had created and could grow, I would be lost. And I simply had to have the creative latitude to run the business. Everything smoothed out in the end, but the power struggle we went through to get there was eye-watering.

People tend to protect themselves. Within organizations and groups they protect their turf. Such thinking often becomes a way of life. The more conservative the ideology, the more each person defends it until the embattled castle walls become so high and mighty that change itself is mistaken for the enemy.

One thing led to another

Everything I did involved some form of communication: office supplies, business machines, word processors and computers, and then typesetting, book editing, printing, large color displays, posters, graphic design, and digital publishing. Los Gatos Sewing Machines was actually my father's business. I started in his fourth venture (which we referred to as LGOE), and ran one company after the other in a natural progression as I tangoed my way between the vagaries of competition and what might be possible. Robertson Publishing is owned and operated by my wife, with over 400 titles as of even date.

> Los Gatos Sewing Machines *begat*
> Los Gatos Office Equipment & Supply (LGOE), *which begat*
> Los Gatos Copy Center, *which begat*
> 1-800 ProColor Print & Design, *along with*
> Ellipsis... (literary magazine), *and then*
> Robertson Publishing

One of these transitions got fairly complex right when retail was going through a major upheaval, and I asked my sister for support. Sheri acted to coordinate the four counter-parties to keep everyone on the same page and negotiated our contracts with the advice of a gifted accountant named Alan Hopkinson while I continued running the store. We sold the building to Ed Stahl, who owned Travel Advisers across the street, then leased it back from him and sublet the rest of the space to Wolf Computer. Ed knew our family and business a lot longer than Wolf, so we ended up being the tail wagging the dog — my little copy center in the back running the whole building.

Sheri and I worked well together; I was just lucky she was available. She ran the Los Gatos Chamber of Commerce out of ProColor for a number of years after that, giving us even more time together. There was a lot going on.

I started by selling sewing machines, hand-crank adding machines, and typewriters; today we publish books. The staff and physical size of the companies would graph as a bell curve, first getting larger, then shrinking as the years wore on. Once we spun off the office supply, the businesses moved progressively down the block and shrank at the same time. In our final move, we transitioned Robertson Publishing and myself, still working for my last and favorite client, Dr. Asher, into our home.

William Faulkner once said that writers have to kill their darlings — meaning that no matter how wonderful your prose, you must delete whatever isn't right for the story. The same can be said in business. If something isn't working, you have to fix it. If you can't fix it, get rid of it. Because if you don't, your business will devolve into mediocre commonality.

This problem plagues large corporations in particular, and issues pile up like driftwood because they are able to ride along on past glory or an established monopoly for a long time. This is exacerbated by the size of their organization (if large) and the automatic buying habits of clients, but sooner or later it catches up with smaller firms also. And it doesn't matter how great you once were, if you can't *stay* relevant you lose.

I went through more than six major changes, not including the initial shift my father made when he moved the business over from Main Street. All over a period of sixty years. Makes me tired just to think about it.

Liz Rogers

Throughout my business career, I was like a forty-niner panning for gold up in the Mother Load, throwing out pebbles and rocks, searching for color in the pan. But I wasn't alone in all this. Somebody jiggled my elbow. Somebody patted me on the back. Somebody else slapped me around a bit and told me to fly straight, damn it. And somebody else said my barnstorming days would never be over and that I needed to keep plugging away until I hit pay dirt. All the glory and wonderfulness of my business success did not happen in isolation. I got help. Sometimes from unexpected sources.

Kinkos moved into Los Gatos right after I'd transitioned the company by splitting off the copy center and selling the rest to McWhorters. It felt like I was staring down the tracks at yet another freight train, like the demise of typewriters and the opening of Office Depot. Kinkos was open 24 hours a day, seven days a week, and I couldn't do that. I didn't want to do that. I had to change, but how?

Liz Rogers was a local designer I'd been working with, and we shared our triumphs and tribulations from time to time. One day, she gave me a brilliant idea. With the purchase of some special software, a server interface, and a few cables, I could plug my Mac into our color copier and go "direct to print" in full color. I would be able to do short-run color printing in-house; exactly what everybody wanted. It was a new technology just breaking through, but a very expensive proposition. Much too risky for most copy centers to gamble on, including Kinkos. But my father had taught me well: "Use your brains, not your heart, and bet the farm when you have to."

So, after seeing the technology in action at a local trade show (with Liz at my side), I took the plunge. But I hedged my bet by asking her to help me transition myself as well, from a copy center owner who did typesetting, into a designer | graphic artist. I offered her free office space and color printing. She became my on-site tutor, guiding and teaching me for several years, and helped transform Los Gatos Copy Center into a full-color design, print, big color, and publishing operation. It was Liz who taught me to design *into* a problem instead of going nuts attempting to fix it. That is: if there is a problem that can't be easily corrected, play it up—make it an intrinsic part of the design. It's like loving someone because of their faults instead of in spite of them. I used her idea from that point on in many areas of my life, and it made a huge difference.

Liz was a creative designer, rather outspoken (as accomplished people often are), and was constantly running afoul of chauvinist attitudes in the marketing departments she needed to work with. In particular, she often couldn't get past the initial presentation, even when she obviously had the best design. She came up with a genius solution. Liz worked with a printer named Scritchfield, who was tall, good-looking, and well-spoken. He presented himself the way the marketing departments expected, even admired.

For the promise of the printing side of whatever jobs she got, Liz got him to go with her on sales calls, acting as point man for their team of two. He would open the conversation and win over the management team, then turn the presentation over to Liz, who would proceed to wow everyone with her brilliance and design expertise. She overcame their resistance by getting in the door with a Trojan horse of her own devising. Brilliant.

1-800 ProColor

Just when I was setting up, AT&T called to ask if I wanted my own 800 number. I said yes — but only if they could come up with a number that spelled out the company name. After several weeks of back-and-forth, we were able to concoct something that worked. The phone number spelling out 1-800 ProColor was available, so I grabbed it, and changed our name to match the number. It gave people the impression I was a much larger company, which didn't hurt. Of course, once clients got inside the door, I had other things to show them, such as all the work I'd done for large corporations and entertainers.

It's interesting that whenever I faced a crisis, somebody helped me over the hump. Sometimes it was a friend, like Tom, or my sister Sheri, or my wife Alicia, but often enough it was someone new in my life, like Liz Rogers, who came along at the right moment to help make things click when I needed to. I was very lucky.

A Chair on My Head?

Dr. James J. Asher showed up at my studio sometime in the 1980s. He was looking for someone to work with him on books that helped students learn a new language. I learned to format for publication and set type in German, Spanish, French, Dutch, and Vietnamese (in addition to English). Jim and I even played around with Yupik at one point, an Inuit language of the arctic.

At first, he just wanted me to update some files so they could be reproduced on our high-speed duplicators, but he kept coming back with larger and more intricate tasks, and I put a second chair next to mine so he could show me exactly what he wanted *while* I worked on his files. We worked side-by-side for about thirty years, often on a daily basis, talking about science, mathematics, history, and social issues in addition to the task at hand. It was a special relationship.

Every labor-intensive business needs a regular income from a reliable source to make it less dependent on attracting new clients. In the office equipment business, I had NASA; in the copy center it was Dr. Asher and Hewlett-Packard; in the design company, it was Dr. Asher and Netflix. Dr. Asher kept me in business when the lights got dim.

Jim had made a simple, yet significant discovery early in his career as a psychologist. It was something any observant parent could have pointed out, but somehow, down through all the ages of man, didn't: Babies don't memorize stuff. They don't even try.

Natural learning comes through emulation and trial and error, and language acquisition erupts naturally by hearing a word while seeing it modeled by the speaker and performing that action. The brain connects the action of our muscles with the word. Jim quantified it, published his findings, and put it to practical use on a large scale. He revolutionized teaching in classrooms around the world.

Asher's method uses right-brain learning (motor activities) to generate long term memory. Students learn through movement instead of memorizing vocabulary lists. While students perform motor activities, the left hemisphere of their brain just observes and learns. Once the right hemisphere has internalized the new information, the student will be able to start producing language. Talking is a left-hemisphere activity, and erupts naturally, just as it does with small children.

Total Physical Response, known worldwide as TPR, was very different from traditional teaching methods since it was based on physical movements. I heard that the classrooms were joyful, even raucous at times, everyone animated with effervescent learning in this ancient way that dated back about fifty-five million years, yet seemed so revolutionary.

Enter Ramiro

I was curious and wanted to understand what I was working on at a deeper level, so I took a private class in Spanish from Ramiro Garcia. He was a retired teacher who had worked with Dr. Asher to develop TPR in the early days, and was the author of several important books on the subject—which I had typeset, designed, and packaged for publication. I'd worked with Ramiro to get the details correct on his books.

I asked Ramiro to come to our house to teach my family Spanish using TPR. After gathering the four of us in the living room and providing an explanation of what was to follow, Ramiro began by saying a word while performing a corresponding action such as *andar* (walk), *parada* (stop), and *de vuelta* (go back), which we imitated *without* speaking. We made use of three props—a plastic cup, a chair, and our own bodies—during the session. After about ten minutes of this, Ramiro sat down and directed us to perform the actions based solely on his spoken instructions.

After forty minutes, Ramiro asked me to leave the house briefly, citing a "trick" he wanted to play on me, and proceeded to inform the family of the plan. Upon my return, I found my family grinning on the couch while I got back to following his instructions—walking, stopping, returning, picking up the cup, sitting on the chair, touching my stomach, touching my head, placing the cup on my head and on the chair—all of which we had practiced earlier. Then Ramiro stopped speaking. I looked at him, waiting for further instructions.

In what I referred to as *Guadalajara Spanish* due to its fast-pace and unintelligible nature to non-native speakers, Ramiro spoke quickly, leaving me bewildered. I had no idea what he'd just said. He then said in a deadpan manner (in English), "Do what your gut tells you to do."

I paused, feeling uncertain. And then, without knowing why and with a peculiar sensation stirring within me, I reached down and grasped the arms of the chair before me. Though I continued to gaze at Ramiro, he remained stoic, but the kids were grinning. With a strange sense of unease churning in my stomach, I lifted the chair higher and higher and finally held it upside down, resting on my head! And there I stood, in the center of my living room, an absurd grin on my face, unsure why I was doing so. Everyone else found this highly amusing.

Suddenly, everyone began speaking at once. Ramiro had apparently forewarned them of what was about to happen, yet they still found it difficult to believe. Nonetheless, we had all witnessed it firsthand. Ramiro proceeded to explain.

Being mute, the *left* hemisphere of our brain has no voice, and thus, we are unable to comprehend its thoughts—at least not consciously. The inner voice we hear originates from the right hemisphere. Physical movement and the flexing of muscles is directly connected to Broca's area in the *left* hemisphere. No wonder I had been so confused; I was unable to hear the conversation taking place in my own mind!

People have a difficult time learning new languages for two reasons. First, they are most often trying to memorize the language, which doesn't work very well. Second, the right side of our brain is telling us that the words we're attempting to learn are gobbledegook because it has no frame of reference for them. But when the left hemisphere anchors the words to muscle movement, it connects the dots just fine.

People learn quickly and easily by *doing stuff*. That was the open secret of Jim's success and something I learned organically that afternoon under Ramiro's tutelage. Learning via our own physical actions truly works, it happens incredibly fast, and it feels like magic. Now I knew why teachers were so enthusiastic about TPR: It transformed their classrooms into incredible learning centers, with joyful, enthusiastic students. To this day, I know what my *cabeza* is, what *la silla* means, and remember vividly how I put one on top of the other to the laughter and excited giggles of my own family.

This also explained why my mother had her fourth graders march around and clap their hands to John Philip Sousa while learning their times tables. Somehow she had figured out that sitting in a chair wasn't the answer for a lot of things; that the chair was, perhaps, the enemy. As she put it to me later, "I know that with young kids, their heinies are connected to their noggins, and when their heinies go dead, so do their brains."

When I told Jim what she'd done with the marching and all, he grinned. "She's a natural," he said. "She was TPRing all her students because she had figured out the same thing I did!" Long-term retention is so high using TPR that the U.S. Navy adopted it for military training, and Japan uses it for all public education.

Jim ended up with a publishing company focused on this method of teaching. Teachers such as Ramiro Garcia and Todd McKay kept inventing new techniques—ideas and methods they'd developed in their own classrooms. Asher published their ideas in addition to his own, plus his books on mathematics, and I was the guy who got to help him do it.

There were always a lot of TPR materials throughout my offices, and occasionally someone new would startle and make a comment. "I taught using TPR in Rumania (or Spain, or the Bronx); what are you doing with it?" Or sometimes, "You actually *know* Dr. Asher?" It was rather wonderful to be part of one great effort to empower teachers throughout the world for some thirty years of my life.

A side lesson I took from my work with Dr. Asher was his insistence on using "native speakers" for translation work. He only used translators who had spoken the language all their life, as opposed to those who had learned it later. He said there were nuances and idiosyncrasies in language that couldn't be taught easily in a classroom setting.

It made perfect sense. How many times had I laughed at something translated into English that may have been correct technically, but was nowhere near how we would say it! That helped when I created brochures in other languages, such as Spanish and Vietnamese. I always explained that issue to my clients, and they appreciated that I was keeping them from looking ridiculous in the eyes of their own customers.

Asher and the Oxford Comma

The only issue that arose between us throughout of all those years was a disagreement over the smallest thing on the page; the second comma in a series of three items. As in apples, pears, and oranges. Commonly known as the Oxford Comma; I was a big fan and Jim was not. He felt it was old-fashioned. I argued for it, feeling that in any series of three, there are instances where the last two items might or might not be viewed as a single compound noun. As in jam, peanut butter and jelly. All items we commonly anoint our bread with. But smooshing the last two into something that sounded very much like a PB&J for the want of a comma just wasn't right. In my humble opinion.

A choice had to be made, but without that differentiating comma, confusion could arise in the mind of the reader, the sea might become boiling hot, and the swallows might never come back to Capistrano. Or maybe it was monarchs to Pacific Grove. Or something, anyway. Bottom line? I knew I was just the navigator, and he owned the pink slip, and if he wanted to drive off a cliff into grammatical ambiguity, I had to just sit there and let it happen. Hey, I warned him.

Several of his books were about mathematical mysteries or the history of science, on which I was conversant. It was a polite tug-of-war between the two of us, brainstorming all those books into proud existence down through the years.

Designer to the stars

I worked with Apple, NASA, San José State University, IBM, the Montalvo Art Center, country singer | songwriter Kenny Butterill, and graphic designers John Danielson (AKA, Johnny Tempo), Gene Faucher, and Rick Tharp. I wholesaled my color work to many other printers and designers in the county, including fine artists such as Amy Konsterlie, Bruni Sablan, and Mark Gray. For a few artists, I was making giclée prints on watercolor paper. Gene Faucher became a close friend, as did Ray

Darrow, who taught me how to create rich black. For many years I worked with a printer named Scritchfield to typeset Hewlett-Packard's Spanish brochures and sell sheets for South America. I made all the full color posters and banners for Netflix.

I produced work for Disney and entertainers such as Cher, Bruce Springsteen, Bon Jovi, Britney Spears, Willie Nelson, Sting, Bette Midler, Janet Jackson, Tina Turner, Ronnie Lot (of the San Francisco 49ers) and the Olympic ice skating champion, Peggy Fleming. Ms. Fleming owned a small winery, and sat next to me while we worked on her advertising and website, just as I did with Dr. Asher. It felt a little surreal at first, sitting next to people I'd seen on television for so many years. If it sounds like I'm name-dropping, I absolutely am. I am proud to have worked for and with such extraordinary talent.

Graphic art for many of these luminaries went through my shop at least in part because I worked with a talent manager named Max Gordon. Max and his wife Joan had managed Tina Turner's bookings, and Tina knew other people, who knew everybody else. And Max lived next door to Steve Wozniak (the co-founder of Apple), up on Cypress Avenue. Word got around.

I worked with Diana Pleasant on the plays at Los Gatos High School, and with Woz while his kids were still in school. I was brainstorming with Diana and Woz one day regarding an effect Diana wanted to create for her next play, *Into The Woods*. I needed a certain kind of software to make it happen, and Woz and I ended up rummaging through the trunk of his car out on High School Court. He had every software title imaginable. (Woz and my wife became Facebook friends because his first wife's name was also Alicia Robertson.)

In many cases, large corporations liked to work with me *because* my shop was small. Small was good because quality control came down to one person—me. Plus, I had quick turn-around times. It also meant they could communicate directly with the person actually doing the work, which meant they could trust us with sensitive documents. I usually mentioned the eight-hundred pound Meilink one-hour fire-resistant cabinet I had to hold their hard drives while they were in my possession, a legacy from earlier years when I used to sell such monsters. Some of the materials I was entrusted with were sensitive, and they appreciated our security.

My initial conversations were often with the Director of Marketing, the lead designer, or the CEO. It felt a little odd getting patched through to someone like Carly Fiorina at Hewlett-Packard. Such conversations were usually short. "Could I do it?" and "Could I do it on time?" about summed it up. They didn't know me, they didn't particularly want to know me, and they had other issues to deal with. Sometimes they asked other questions, mostly about security, or explained a pressing concern, but it was always very much on point.

Small companies and startups kept the doors open: everybody and his brother needed a proper business card, and I could design and print almost anything in one day. But in addition to my design and typesetting work, I also provided a variety of odd job work for all the civic-minded individuals in our very civic-minded little town. If I didn't know how to do something, I either learned quickly or found someone who did. It was Jazz on the Plazz or building the new town library, or the annual Children's Christmas Parade—always something to do.

I did so much work for the Los Gatos Morning Rotary Club they made me an honorary member. And I created brochures for almost every real estate agent in town up until all the real estate firms figured out they could just hire a designer and bring a lot of that work in-house.

Sherlock & Co.

Just as I had done when selling business machines, a great deal of my job involved detective work: figuring out what my client actually needed in order to solve their problem. In some cases they could articulate the inner clockwork in their initial request or they provided examples of previous work, but that wasn't always the case. I often had to interview business owners to get a better sense of their vision, the truth they were trying to convey to their clients. I became a psychoanalyst of sorts, teasing out the fibres of motivation that underlay their goals.

I knew from having watched the process that most designers and ad agencies didn't do anything of the sort. They asked for specifications on a job, got them, and ran with it, eventually coughing up three standard choices: bad | good | indifferent (similar to the *earth* | *god* | *man* methodology for Japanese flower arranging, or *father* | *son* | *holy ghost* triptych used in the Christian religion). Even Liz told me to do it that way.

"It saves time," she said. "You can't make money puzzling out what they *think* they want because they don't really know. Just give them three choices: The bad choice is first, so everything else looks better. Then the one you want them to pick. And finally, one that isn't as good as the second one, which they almost always reject."

But that wasn't always in the client's best interest, and I got new clients time after time who complained about the process. "We didn't get what we wanted," was the most common complaint. Or, "The designer we hired didn't understand. We wasted a ton of money on something we can't use. Someone told us to come to you, that you would help us out."

The competition didn't seem to know how to work collaboratively with their clients. They would just throw three designs at the wall in the hopes that one of them would stick. And I'm not saying they weren't good designers; some of them were very skilled at making unique, eye-catching designs. But they weren't *listening*. I sat with each client until I had a fair idea what they really wanted. I then pitched it back to them until they confirmed that I knew what they were talking about.

I gave my clients any number of iterations—sometimes twenty or thirty—on two or three basic designs, all in a single, page-numbered PDF so they could say, "Well, I like the header font on number three, the color combination on number twelve, and the opening paragraph on number sixteen—but the rest of the text should be more like number eight, with the contact info from number twenty." I charged for my time at about double the going rate, and my clients loved me for it because I was giving them more *choices*.

The main driver of this disconnect with the other designers was a lack of empathy and a superior attitude. Designers seem to self-select with a know-it-all attitude that only a "designer" can know what works, and clients are not that, so we shouldn't listen to them. I don't know if this was instilled during their childhood or if it was some sort of systemic group-think, similar to company cultures that promote false narratives and glass ceilings, but I'd heard it often enough when talking to people in the same line of work. "Clients are idiots. They never know what they want until we tell them." *Completely wrong.*

Thinking inside the box

A lot of my work dealt with typography: the appearance of lettering on a page, poster, or sign. I am very particular about a lot of stuff that may seem esoteric, but actually matters: the space between letter pairs (particularly in headlines or signage), word spacing, and the choice of fonts and font pairing (I detest Times Roman and Helvetica as tired-looking, overused, and indicative of a lazy mind).

It was my facility with language and typography, plus my attention to detail and the passion I brought to each project that allowed me to retain so many clients. It wasn't just typography and tone, but the overall meaning of what each client was trying to convey. This came to a fine point when I became the client.

Very Small Press

When I sold Los Gatos Office Equipment & Supply, I was left with Los Gatos Copy Center and The Service Department (which had been no more than divisions within the parent firm, and fell out of the deal). Almost everyone moved over with the transfer of our company to McWhorter's Stationery. Nobody wants some former boss in a small firm — too many opinions. And Claudia Metivier stayed on. She was our key operator in the copy center, as well as Ki Su Kim — our business machine technician.

At that time I was at a loose end. Claudia was perfectly competent to run the copy center and I had no solid reason to come to work every day. I decided to pursue creative writing.

I set myself up with a word processor, paper, and dictionary in a small shed at the back of my house in Campbell, got a copy of Writer's Digest, and got to work. Writer's Digest said all beginning writers should actually read the publications to which they want to submit, to better understand the type and quality of pieces that would be accepted. So I did.

Some literary magazines are quite famous, including *The Paris Review* and *The New Yorker*, but most are issued by colleges and universities, are published quarterly, and at that time looked like oversized paperbacks. Some are really nothing more than vanity publications to showcase collegiate intellect. And there are many independents as well, run by brave souls on a mission, a number of which go in and out of business on a regular basis. I found a few that looked as if they'd been put together in someone's basement or garage. With the advent of electronic publishing, actual hard copy magazines and books were having a difficult time of it.

As I thought more about it, I began to realize how university publications might be structured. Let's suppose that some university's Board of Regents decides that to help raise money for the university it would be a good idea to publish a literary magazine. Dress the place up a bit. Salt the mine, so to speak. So who do they put in charge of it? The most senior English professor on staff, naturally. And that person is probably a curmudgeonly cliché who believes him- or herself to be *of* the literati, with little reason to try anything new. The mandate from the Regents is probably to *avoid* anything new, because they want their publication to look established, prestigious, and (above all) *intellectual*.

I sent a few of my stories off with a short letter of introduction and the requisite self-addressed, stamped envelope (considered de rigueur by Writer's Digest). And everything came back. Some took their time and came by boat or train, others bounced as fast as bad checks — but like good and faithful chickens, they all came home to roost. There was usually a photocopied rejection slip clipped to the upper left corner, but a few had actual, handwritten notes, most of which said something rather innocuous and vapid, to the effect of, "The story is well-written, but doesn't suit our editorial needs at this time." *Harumph.*

Unwritten but implied was the postscript: You are of course aware, as Imperial Editors to the Nonesuch and Great High Muckamuck, we take a dim view of anyone who does not have a great multitude of publishing credits to their name.

One note I got explained the situation more succinctly and was actually quite helpful:

> "You write funny stuff. We all had a good laugh over your sporadically chaotic and joyful sentence structure (assuming that was intentional), but humor is rarely published on this or any other planet without a successful track record; no puns, no jokes, no coconuts. BTW, you are not alone."

The rejection slips told a tale and I finally understood what Wodehouse had been talking about when he said he'd actually wallpapered his office with rejection slips.

But then it started to niggle at me: How many *other* unpublished writers were there? Probably a lot, and all clamoring for someone, *anyone* to publish their humorous but structurally-challenged short stories that might or might not have correct character development or story arcs with a positive change to the protagonist, or even proper endings — but which, *nevertheless*, were quite wonderful and beautiful and crying out for a voice... This was the stuff that opportunities are made of.

I came to the conclusion that although my writing might not be the radiant beam of enlightened thought I'd striven to create, my efforts might not have been wasted — because my real future would be in *publishing!* I mean, the smart place to be was on the *other* side of the rejection slip, right? It only made sense, and I decided to put myself there as quickly as possible. And I would publish all the great stuff those other magazines were afraid to print and become a powerful voice for reason in a world gone mad!

Publishing

In 1988, Gina Bergamino asked if I could produce a chapbook of her poetry. A chapbook is a booklet, often of poetry, with a dozen or so sheets of quality paper, folded in half, plus a cardstock cover, with two staples "saddle-stitching" the spine. We sat together while I typeset and designed her first publication, just as I was doing with Dr. Asher's books.

I no longer have a copy of *My Name Isn't Richard Brautigan*, but Gina went on to publish many more books of poetry and became well known in the literary world. Her chapbook wasn't difficult to typeset or produce, and it started something.

Jim Dilles was a librarian at the Los Gatos Public Library when he came to me for a short-run publication of his poetry, entitled *To See The World Again As Earth*. That one I have.

I used textured cardstock for the cover, with green endpapers, and premium recycled paper for the inside pages. I set the type using Palatino (also known as Book Antiqua), which is my favorite font for regular text. Mark Grey, a local artist I knew, provided drawings for the cover and inside pages. I used one of my *Ellipsis...* ISBN numbers so it would show up in library computers. I made them in small batches for Jim and also sold them on the front counter in our store.

I produced *Golf 101*, by Mark Rivard. It represented something new. His booklets were small, but they were commercial. Mark was a professional golf instructor. It was a beginning.

The way Gina expressed herself reminded me of some of the Beat poets I'd read years ago. Jim was heartfelt but more traditional in his approach. Mark's book on golf was commercial. Together, these books put me beyond just producing books for Dr. Asher; I had become a bonafide book manufacturer, with the same skill set as much larger firms.

Back to *Ellipsis...*

At this point, I realized that I could produce my own magazine in the form of a slim, but oversized paperback book, just as many other literary magazines did. And I was certain I could make it better than many of the others I'd seen. Well, not *The New Yorker*, perhaps, but I could certainly do a better job than most of the university presses, which had no artwork to speak of, and used text so tight and small that reading was not particularly enjoyable.

At that time *Poets & Writers* magazine allowed any small press publication to run one free ad per year. So I did, and that started an avalanche of submissions. At first just a trickle, but I was soon getting up to twenty enquiries per day. All from that one ad. I soon figured out that my little two-inch ad was being viewed in back issues at the library by thousands of new writers, anxious to get published. And for one reason or another, we clicked.

I wanted to focus on "under-published" authors—writers who had either not been published at all (and we would be their first time in print), or those who had had one or two things out there, but not much more. Along with these authors I hoped to attract more established writers. In addition, I found myself looking for stories that allowed the reader to view the world from a completely different perspective.

One such story was ostensibly written by a severely challenged woman of middle age who didn't understand why she'd lost her job or how she would be able to pay her rent. It put the reader in her shoes for the duration of the story. One poem written by a prison inmate was all about "the seventh wave of the seventh wave," which had scary implications. The introduction letter had been scrawled in red crayon on the cover of an old hardbound book and sent to us along with the poem, also handwritten. I scanned and published it just as it was. I also published drawings. Interesting pieces that would break up the flow a little bit and cause our readership to switch from reading to observing and back again, and in that, rest that part of their brain that dealt with text.

When the mail started pouring in, I had to do something. I had a magazine to publish. Of all the literary magazines I'd purchased when I was sending out my stuff, there was one that stood out in terms of layout and design: *Zyzzyva*. I didn't care about the cover or their editorial style, but I did like how easy it was to *read* and how beautiful each page was to look at. I studied it to find out why I liked it so much.

The pages were clean and it had generous margins, but there was also plenty of white space *between* the lines and words, and I liked their font far better than what everyone else seemed to be using: Times Roman, with its narrow letterforms and tired look. I wanted my publication to look elegant and fresh.

I did the unthinkable. I took a *razor blade* and sliced a page out, right along the gutter. I then set about to reverse-engineer everything on that one page. I had no shame.

I scanned it as an image, but I also used optical character recognition (OCR) software to capture the text from that grayscale scan. I then took that image, cropped it to the edges, and knocked it back to 30% opacity, and placed it in a page layout program (Pagemaker, at that time). I overlayed it with the text I'd captured—letter for letter and word for word—on a page set to the same size and margins. And then I got to work.

First, I had to determine the font, which turned out to be Book Antiqua, also known as Palatino. I then added *leading* to the type (in the old days of cold type, printers used thin sheets of actual lead—the soft gray metal—to add space between the lines). That got the text height to match, line for line. I then calibrated the tracking value—fine incremental spacing between characters and words—until I got a perfect match. I had a page of text, but it was now a perfect overlay to the image underneath. It just looked a little darker and heavier. I wrote down all the values I'd used, and those values became my text formatting style sheet.

I had a style for the inside text, but I still had to create a "look" for the front and back covers, plus editorial guidelines, story headings, and the masthead. Mainly I needed the masthead. I knew it would be the word *"Ellipsis..."* with three dots after it (three dots *are* an ellipsis), but at that time I didn't have the typography skills to manipulate type. I needed help.

Upstairs and right across the street from my business was Patrick Mountain Design, and although I didn't know Patrick that well, I'd seen him on the street enough to wave and say hello. I also knew he had some high-end accounts, like Adobe, Cisco Systems, and Specialized Bicycle. So I took my problem to him and he told me to come back in a couple of days.

He charged me $50 for the masthead and produced it in various sizes in the form of black images on a slick white sheet of photographic paper. Patrick had set the title using the bold version of Book Antiqua, then manipulated it until he had the weight appropriate for a masthead while retaining the elegance of the original font.

This was exactly what I wanted. I scanned them at very high resolution, and that became the masthead and logo font. It was tall, showing our lofty ideals, yet had that lowercase descender on the "**p**", indicating our ability to delve beneath the surface. This was something I would later learn to do for myself as time, software, and my interest in design evolved, but I was very glad to have skilled help create what I needed at the time — and his office was right across the street.

I also had to find a printer who could provide the quality I wanted, in the quantities I needed, at a price I could afford. After getting bids from a number of large printers throughout the United States, I finally settled on a company in Minnesota. I talked to one printer who came highly recommended, asking him why he couldn't produce *Ellipsis...* at a low enough price point; "You don't understand because you've never seen our operation," he said. "It takes fourteen people just to prep and start the main press, which is about half the length of a football field. It would take me the same amount of time to do the setup on your publication as it does for us to prep *Reader's Digest* or *TV Guide*; I can't be competitive with your magazine."

And so I learned about scale in the printing business, which was to serve me well in later years when I started to send out various print jobs. I worked with several local firms, but also sent work to a book printer in Naples, Florida, and quite a bit of work went to a print wholesaler with two facilities — one in Southern California, and another in Gatlinburg, Tennessee.

At that time PDF files didn't exist because Adobe hadn't invented them yet. So I produced my magazine by printing the master for each page as large as I could on legal size paper at 400 DPI on a Postscript laser printer — extremely high resolution at the time. When it was later reduced to the 5x7 text block, the resolution would increase to 640 DPI, which wasn't as good as a Linotype machine at 1200, but it was still quite sharp, and indistinguishable for regular text and line drawings.

I mailed these pages off to Minnesota, where my printer mounted each page with a wax applicator and photographically created a plate, which was then gang-run as a twelve-page signature onto parent-size sheets. The printed sheets were then folded, cut, and bound, the cover applied, then trimmed into finished books, five hundred times. Then shipped to me (the publisher), back in Los Gatos, California.

My friend Tom is a skilled photographer with a discerning eye and a wry sense of humor, and I asked if I could use several of his photos for the new magazine. I share his dry take on the world, and suspected he might have something special I could use for the front cover. We rummaged through his archives and I was right; Tom had a lot of interesting photos squirreled away. I used several of his photographic insights over the next few years. They helped show off the self-deprecating nature of *Ellipsis...*, which is exactly what I wanted.

I typeset a small caption above each photo. *"literature that sticks to the roof of your mouth"* was the first: A fisherman, standing in the open hatchway of his boat, gazing out to sea. Hand to chin, he's wondering where the fish might be, or remembering his wife waving goodbye when he set off that morning. It was all there: the boat, the sea, and the thoughts of a man who had to deal with difficult issues every day. It was wonderful.

The University of Minnesota valued our publication enough to buy several copies of the premier issue for their nitrogen-atmosphere Wangensteen Library for rare books. So Tom is memorialized in there as well, come to think of it.

I was approached individually by Joy Oestreicher and Ruth McCue, two writers who had discovered *Ellipsis...*, and asked if they could help. They wanted to understand how publishing worked by being on the *other* side of the equation. I deputized both as editors, and we worked together for a number of years. We met at each other's homes on weekends to go through the latest batch of submissions, discuss the stories we'd each read since our last meeting, and choose what we wanted for the next publication. I remember using box lids from cartons of paper to carry everything from meeting to meeting.

Most rejections slips are nothing more than a slip of colored paper with a single sentence: *"We are sorry to inform you that we cannot use your material at this time."* Which is horrible. I mean, what good does it do? What does it even mean? Does it mean they'd be happy to publish your story next month? Or was there some other reason, like maybe it just wasn't good enough?

Joy, Ruth, and I all agreed we could come up with something a lot better than that. We sat down to design a *proper* rejection slip. Just a half sheet, but it had a place for at least one line of handwritten explanation and about twenty checkboxes to give some indication of what the author might do to improve their writing and chance of publication. All of which showed the authors that we'd actually read their submissions and we cared enough to acknowledge them in our own handwriting. It was the personal touch, and it worked.

There were some submissions that were very powerful and yet didn't work as written. We wrote letters (not emails), inviting authors to make suggested changes and resubmit. In some cases through several revisions.

The authors flat-out *loved* us. What we were doing was unheard of, especially for writers who were not yet established, and it felt great to be at the other end of such a constructive arrangement.

The last several pages of each issue were devoted to an editorial section, where the three of us wrote our opinions, concerns, and witticisms. It provided a way for our readers to get to know who we were and what we were up to. Since we didn't put any of our own writing in the publication (I did not want *Ellipsis...* to be a vanity press), this helped give the magazine the down-to-earth approach I was striving for, in distinct contrast to the elitist attitude prevailing in many literary magazines at that time.

When I took the first issue out of the box from the printers I felt quite vindicated. My struggles to be a part of a literary world my imagination had so long inhabited had won through. I had seized the rejection slip and turned it around.

After *Ellipsis...*

Mary Foster cut a colorful swath through our little town. She dressed up as Mother Goose for the Los Gatos Children's Parade at Christmas, and she evidently liked poetry. Or thought we should honor poets. Or something. Anyway, she'd heard what I was doing with *Ellipsis...*, and roped me, Sue LaForge, the editor of the *Los Gatos Times Observer* (the "T-O" as we called it), and Leigh Weimers, a columnist for the *San Jose Mercury News*, to name a "Poet Laureate of Los Gatos."

Every year we would go through a stack of poems that had been submitted, pick winners for both Poet Laureate and Poet Laureate Jr. (for our younger poets), and award them in the village square where the railroad used to run.

It was a little tedious because Mary never remembered to get the notices up until about a month before the deadline. But the mayor always read a Town Proclamation at the awards ceremony, and certificates were handed to the two best poets. Leigh Weimers wrote about it in the *Mercury*, the *Times Observer* made mention of it, and then we all waited for next year's scramble to roll around. Small-town living, poets and all.

Staying alive

But life wasn't all beer and skittles. During the middle years of ProColor, I went through a divorce. My finances became rather lean. I lost the house, temporarily became a boomerang boomer to live behind my mother's house, and eventually found lodging through Catholic Charities. Through all of this, the judicial system (in all its vaunted wisdom) decided I had the right sort of skills and attitude, and transitioned me from being a long-term foster parent into the legal guardian of a terribly bright, terribly willful teenage girl who came and went in tune with some undefinable logic. I got her into college at the age of sixteen, but her inner tribulations became too much; she joined the Marines, dropped out, and then left to forge her own life.

In addition to all this, the print engines at my design studio were getting older and breaking down more often. Which meant that I stayed longer to get jobs out, sometimes all night, going home only to shower and change clothes.

And then I met Alicia, who suggested I go into debt one more time to get all new equipment. It worked, and I never looked back. Well, except for now of course.

Meet John Doe

In line with our small-town atmosphere, after Alicia and I had been working together for several years, we came up with something a bit different during a financial downturn. The following article is how our local newspaper reported it:

By **Marianne L. Hamilton**
for **Los Gatos Weekly-Times**
Nov 03, 2008

> Jon and Alicia Robertson frequently tune into Turner Movie Classics. But during a screening of "Meet John Doe" earlier this month, the couple, who own and operate ProColor Printing and Robertson Publishing, had an epiphany. In Frank Capra's Oscar-nominated black and white comedy-drama, the residents of a community, through a series of events, not all of which are legitimate, come together to help each other.
>
> Now, the Robertsons hope to do something similar for the Los Gatos business community. They have pledged to produce a 2-foot by 3-foot full-color poster for each retail merchant in the town, for display in storefront windows—entirely for free.
>
> "A lot of merchants are having trouble in the current economy," Jon Robertson said. "Just as in the movie, we're going to start a 'John Doe Club,' and do something to help local business owners. So many people have helped us over the years, we'd like to return the favor."
>
> Robertson adds that his shop is already equipped to produce the signs, and his paper supplier has agreed to support the program.

"When my vendor heard what we were doing, he offered to sell me the paper at a greatly discounted rate," Robertson said.

Just as in the more modern film, "Pay It Forward," the Robertsons hope their effort will generate a burst of goodwill.

"We're all in this together; we need to help each other. What if every company did something like this? It could be a community challenge," Robertson suggested.

The Robertsons mailed out postcards to local business owners, advising them that the banners will be available through the end of 2008 (one banner per merchant). Though the potential market for the free signs could be as many as 600 businesses, the Robertsons say they are happy to donate as much time, energy and materials to the cause as necessary.

As it turned out, the story was picked up by the *San Jose Mercury News* online edition, and then *Yahoo News* reprinted it as a human interest story. A printer just north of us in Palo Alto called me to ask me how it worked a week or two later. He did the program just as we'd done it and got a similar response. We extended it into 2009, and offered it again a few years later.

Beyond the yellow brick road

Because I worked with language issues, I became interested in the history of English, first via traditional books, then by listening to Kevin Stroud's podcasts as I walked our perpetually cheerful dog, Molly. This was after Alicia joined me with her new firm, Robertson Publishing in 2007. That began the closest collaboration I've had, rivaled only by my long association with Jim Asher.

I had always thought I could create a more interesting life for myself if I tried hard enough for long enough — primarily by riding the coattails of my own curiosity. At some point I would attain all the interesting little nooks and crannies necessary to become utterly fascinating, and intelligent women would be driven by their native curiosity to engage me in meaningful conversation while Patti LaBelle sang in the background. And then, you know, I'd take it from there.

Anyway, everything contributed to the mix, but the motorcycle trip gave me a clear indication that my idea was correct.

Not that I was pursued by hordes of intellectual women attracted en masse to my rough yet sensitive nature, but I was now able to hold my own on a variety of subjects without mumbling or playing with my hair. Which was more than something — it was a quiet breakthrough. Greater than the sum of my parts, I now knew what it was to risk everything in pursuit of a goal. And that I could do it again if I had to. And I was able to leverage *that* self-knowledge into everything else.

Snap out of it!

Alas, I loved not wisely, but too often, soundly rejected by any number of *fascinating* women who were initially mislead by my charismatic personality and rugged good looks, thinking perhaps there was some way I could be fixed. Or at least improved.

In short, I led a somewhat turbulent love life, punctuated at odd intervals by heart-wrenching, soul-searching solitude. But then I met the woman who was to redefine my expectations. She had discerned diamonds wrought by the pressure within, and encouraged me to see the truth of who I was. And that changed everything.

The password was *There will be rain in Salinas tomorrow*. The countersign was *Good for the crops*. And when the time came, we had a Hawai'ian party to a recording of Israel Kamakawiwo'ole (IZ) singing *Over The Rainbow | What A Wonderful World*, and got married on a picking platform in an ancient (and very large) fig tree I once climbed as a child. It was epic. What with one thing and another, years passed, Alicia and I worked side-by-side, she with Robertson Publishing, and I with ProColor.

All of the time I'd spent running businesses instead of writing or painting had put off my inevitable self-confrontation. My literary and artistic aspirations had been both real and not. Alive and dead. As long as I could postpone that part of my life I was able to imagine that the opportunity would always be there, and in that I became the dubious repository of unrealized potential — a sort of Schrödinger's ego of real and unreal talents.

But it was Alicia who germinated the foundation and motivation for *Rebel Without a Clue*. She transcribed the journals that

Tom and I had written during our two months on the road, and presented them to me as a gift. In doing that, she changed the equation. When I sold ProColor and semi-retired from business (I told Dr. Asher I'd keep him as a client for as long as he wanted), I started writing again, beginning with the text of our journals. Her gift became the seed of my resurrection.

Surprise, surprise... the spring steel in my character still held its original form and flex! Suddenly and unexpectedly, I was promethean again, railing at ignorance, irrational fear, and deceit. The coherencies thundered down crashing as I nailed them to the page with everything in me. My voice was back.

These days I write, edit, read, bake, watch movies with Alicia, garden, and play cards with friends. Artwork I've created from wood and canvas are posted on RebelClue.blogspot.com. I have exhibited at the Olive Hyde Art Gallery near Mission San José. I have been reading to others since the 1970s, and continue to do so — everyone from James Barrie and P.G.Wodehouse to Langston Hughes and James Herriot. I currently drive a bright yellow Trihawk: a rather interesting, three-wheeled car.

Despite being lazy from the start, easily bored, and somewhat reserved, I did come out the other side. People say of a young person constantly in trouble, "Well, he fell in with the wrong crowd." That was me, except I somehow managed to engage the reversing engine and fall in with the *right* crowd. I developed friendships, got involved, and became an adult in the process — perhaps even a mensch.

> Most people have an experience at some point in their lives when they go beyond their normal abilities to achieve something improbable. It's interesting what happens next. Do they learn from it, or just think of it as an exciting part of their history?

The Great Teenage Diaspora

When I finally made it home from the motorcycle journey, there were stories to be told and a life to get back to. A life that was about to get a lot more complicated. I finished my Statement of Protest and delivered it to the FBI. Whatever fate awaited me was bound to happen without further intervention until the courts set a date, so to a great extent, I pushed it from my mind.

Tom and I had changed and now we were different. We could taste the color green and smell the darkness of the night. The journey had marked us with our own contemplation, our own measure of life. The belt sander had stopped and our lives continued, but there was a different belt sander now — not of tarmac, but of something less defined. We'd been there, we'd done it. If we didn't understand it completely when we put our left boot down for the last time, it would come to us later.

Zigzagging our way across America had been a journey along the blue-gray ribbons of her existence and conscience. A new dawn was rising like thunder from the Far East, while back home the worry of uncertainty and weight of death hung over kitchen tables where families dealt with their own civil unrest.

Tom and I had met many of these people, shared campfires with them, and eaten together. What did it mean to be American? The old standards were broken and we couldn't live them anymore. Those who tried were stuck in denial. Patriotism didn't include killing people to satisfy a political agenda, and we knew it. America was waking up to its own misbehavior and the possibility that hidden forces might be undermining our destiny.

Into the plains of the Midwest we had ridden, our song of independence disrupted only by the dissonance of a lone hippie in bellbottoms and a fringed vest we'd found in Arco, forlorn and tender, searching for anyone who might care enough to understand. Or the man at the gas station in West Yellowstone who had so much to say about the life he wasn't living that Tom just stood there and listened. The sun beat down on all of us and inked us with the geography of circumstance: the distance between Monterey and Maine, now and the next town, homemade apple pie and a city named Saigon.

The blue-gray ribbons led us to people brave enough to take us in when we were strangers and others who were afraid to speak to us for the same reason.

It wasn't only the Neefe family or the Isralows. We were strangers to everyone we met, yet interesting and somehow worthy of conversation—and we remained that way. We heard it in people's voices and saw it in their faces. What we were doing was tangible, compelling, and full of promise. And we learned something from the other side of human nature as well: *fear*. Fear in the faces at that gas station window. Fear in the restaurant where we never ate, but tasted the peculiar off-balance of being shunned, strangers in our own land.

Tom and I now knew what it felt like to be locked behind bars in a Wisconsin jail. Lucky to be alive after crashing in Chicago, we watched a police cruiser flash its searchlight over us, then glide past as if we were not worth the saving. We knew what a homeless shelter looked like from the inside and what it was to fan out in common cause with other people in search of a lost child. We'd seen the look on a woman's face who didn't know if her husband was coming back alive from the war.

In one small town on the East Coast, we had parked our bikes together at the curb, stopping for an ice cream cone. We were standing there enjoying the sunshine and watching people pass us on the sidewalk, when a guy in his late twenties stopped in front of us, took stock, then introduced himself.

"I'm a reporter for the local paper," he said, "and you guys look interesting. Do you mind if I interview the two of you?"

He handed us a copy of his newspaper, and we looked it over. He glanced curiously at our bikes, then back at the two of us. He seemed genuinely interested in our story and friendly enough, so we told him what we'd been up to with our ride and camping on the road. I told him I had refused to go to war and had been just waiting for the FBI to get its act together. And no, I didn't know what was going to happen next. He jotted in a spiral notebook and took our picture next to the bikes. We clowned for the camera, puffing out our chests, and so on.

"This will run in the next issue," he said. "Human interest."

He asked us to spell our names letter-by-letter while he double-checked his notes, then said goodbye. And then he was off again, down the sidewalk at a brisk clip, looking for something else to write about. While we were looking at America, America had been looking at us. Moments like that filled our days and connected us to everyone else.

Virtual particles pop in and out of existence in matter and anti-matter pairs, entangled with each other, just as Tom and I suddenly appeared on the roadways of America for a brief time, then went back to our regular lives after coming home. In so doing, our lives became entangled with the past, with each other, and with America herself. It may have been only moments out of time, but we packed a hell of a lot into those moments.

The color blue

Tom and I bore witness to an ongoing socio-demographic movement, both during our journey and in its aftermath. The industrial revolution set in motion a remarkable increase in the steady talent drain from rural areas as budding mavericks — anybody with a bit of gumption, actually — bid farewell to the small towns and agrarian communities of their birth, desperate for some other destiny. My parents were perfect examples, moving again and again until they found the right person, the right community, and the right resources to help them grow into who they wanted to be.

The influx of ambitious youth fleeing the Rust and Bible Belts sorted the United States into an uneven patchwork of education, ambition, and ideology. Information management and high technology supplanted assembly-line manufacturing and farming — less obvious changes came later. Values shifted and coalesced. In some cases, they calcified.

When I first took on the job of running Los Gatos Office Equipment, I did what I'd always done: I went to the library over on Main Street and looked up books on business machines. Along with other tidbits, I read some interesting things about IBM, including why they made a habit of transferring people around the country. I had always assumed it was because someone got promoted to a new position and that position was at a different location—but I hadn't been giving them enough credit.

I mean, that happened too, but they also did it as a matter of policy. The idea was that by moving entire families around the country, their people would be exposed to different ways of thinking, and novel ideas could pop out; it was a way for IBM to keep the company fresh, vital, and creative. Other companies may have been doing the same thing, but IBM was rather famous for it; somebody in that company had done their homework.

According to IBM, staying in one place all your life led to complacency, narrow-minded viewpoints, and a deadening of curiosity and creativity. What Tom and I saw at the grassroots level was similar, but without the corporate sponsorship. And the history of it went back a long way, which I discovered during my self-education project on the origins and evolution of the English language, and years later, triggered by *The History of English* podcast by Kevin Stroud.

In the beginning

There were few times and places in history worse to be alive than in Europe during the Middle Ages. War was constant and pointless. The average person lived cradle to grave as an illiterate bumpkin prone to the wildest superstitions. How could they be otherwise? Remember, education and literacy didn't exist outside the clergy and some nobility.

The Catholic Church was still cramming the mediæval mind into a Bible-shaped prison, not that any but a small elite were literate in Latin to read the Good Book. Anyone challenging the status quo was dealt with severely. It was a time of filth and viciousness, a demon-haunted world lit only by sooty candles and torches. Health conditions were atrocious, public sanitation worse, and personal hygiene almost non-existent. People lived and died after short, malodorous lives of profound ignorance. And then life got much worse.

A nasty plague swept through Europe and knocked out half of everybody. This created a big problem — not enough people to do all the work. So the barons and other nobles started paying outside workers just to get their crops in, which was a new concept back then. And it changed history forever.

The Bubonic Plague, known as the Black Death, was the most devastating pandemic in human history, and altered our whole outlook on life. It turned society upside down, leading to the end of feudalism, the creation of the middle class, and a long, slow decline of social conservatism.

People routinely deal with the cycle of life, and a certain degree of attrition is normal. Some die, others live, and the world keeps turning. But there's a line, a breaking point. When death comes too fast, too often, the world falters. Fields go untended and governments stop working. We got near this point when the Covid pandemic was peaking in 185 countries, with people in denial, refrigerator trucks parked ominously next to hospitals, and the use of mass graves to bury the dead.

That kind of disruption in the Middle Ages overwhelmed the people who were in charge, leaving everyone else exposed to chaos. That's when everything really started to break down. However, out of that wreckage something new began — rising from the ruins of what was.

This was the grim reality that unfolded in England and much of Europe in the mid-1300s. The landscape of society was altered irrevocably, with its economy, social structure, and even language reflecting the profound impact of this massive plague. Where and how people lived and worked changed forever, indelibly marked by the memory of devastating loss.

Free enterprise replaced feudalism and workers became more mobile. Hamlets became villages, and villages became towns — and towns are built on trade. In addition to peasants and nobles, we got a merchant middle class. The nobility and church became far less powerful. Education became widespread, secular, and far more varied. People learned to read, and started thinking of themselves as uniquely skilled — and far more capable (hello, Renaissance!). And just like that, hope sprouted up like a happy little flower.

As a result, the best and brightest moved from the farms and small villages where they had been their entire lives, and settled into towns and cities where there was far more economic opportunity and freedom of expression.

This process was still ongoing when Tom and I got our rolling snapshot of America, but the reasons driving it had changed. Farming communities shifted into agribusiness run by conglomerates that marginalized family-run operations. The Rust Belt towns that were once home to factories making everything from refrigerators to televisions lost their economic base as lower cost, better quality products from countries like Japan flooded the market. Then suddenly, almost all the good jobs had vanished. There was a shift in attitude, a bitterness which became incorporated into politics over time.

And the ones who never left the farm? They were the ones who couldn't make it over the speed bump at the edge of town or didn't want to get out in the first place. It was a massive distillation of entrepreneurial moxie from base stock. Which is why frustration and resentment are found in such high concentrations in rural areas — they got left behind.

Economic opportunities are scarce in rural areas, and this disparity affects the entire nation. The divide in economic prospects drives up home prices in thriving regions, deepening the housing crisis and creating a persistent population of people without stable homes. This cycle feeds on itself and isn't just a matter of local politics.

It also drains the country of talented individuals who never get the chance to access a full range of opportunities. The growing concentration of wealth and economic activity in big cities breeds resentment and leaves the nation less equipped to handle economic, political, and social challenges like the ones we face today.

Rural frustrations stem from a deep sense of self-reliance and a belief in solving problems locally, which often clashes with government policies from Washington or even state capitals. On top of that, being told what to do, especially through sweeping changes that disregard local concerns, only fuels the discontent. People know when they're being passed over or boxed into something they didn't ask for, and they don't care for it. Nobody does. Resentment has a ripple effect, and those ripples can become tsunamis—a low swell that looks like nothing until it sweeps everything away.

When water evaporates, the higher energy molecules leave as vapor. The remaining molecules are colder and less energetic. The same thing was happening with people. As the distillation process advanced (with all the high-energy teenagers achieving escape velocity, and no new personalities coming in to replace them), rural communities became more and more socially constrained until the natural parent-to-child-to-parent replacement process concentrated each local community down to whatever was left, like a pot of coffee left unattended.

It was like trying to farm without crop rotation or fertilizer, attempting to refresh their ranks without putting anything back. Such communities were often left with little education or ambition, limited world-view, a narrow range of jobs and income, indifferent health care, and enthusiastically religious—their last and only hope. Rural areas were never fully socialized, nor integrated into American society, which cause feelings of isolation and inferiority to fester.

This resulted in social inbreeding. Similar to the Hapsburg Jaw of Austria, but resulting in a strong distrust and distaste for the outer world. The reverse happened with kids living in cities and suburbs of course; most grew up without knowing the joy and freedom of living in a more natural world with giant trees and open water. The closest they ever got was a couple of precious weeks at summer camp if they were lucky.

Tom and I rode through small towns like these wherever we went, but particularly in the Midwest. There are certainly positive aspects to small-town life, but without local industry, a government facility, or tourist trade, the struggle for survival can degrade whatever character and promise there might have been down to not much more than difficult existence. Walmart, Costco, and the rise of online shopping in recent years has only made things far worse by impoverishing almost all the small family-owned retailers who functioned as the heart and soul of small town life.

Perhaps we just didn't recognize what was going on soon enough. I suspect the assumption that the sheer momentum of capitalism would be great for everyone everywhere all the time played a big part. The sandwich hand didn't know what the milk hand was doing, or even what its motives were. And didn't really care. Then suddenly we had milk all over everything and no easy way to mop it up.

Unintended consequences

One conservative mantra has always been smaller government, including fewer laws controlling commerce. Deregulation in the 1980s, primarily under President Reagan, pounded that catechism home. No longer constrained, bus lines and trains raised their rates or stopped running altogether in less commercial areas. The president of Greyhound bus lines observed that "the rural areas are going to suffer because the bus is a lifeline of many small communities for people just to get to the doctor or to the Social Security office."

Deregulation was a triumph for Wall Street, but a catastrophe for rural America. The data shows that economic opportunities across the heartland plummeted. Entire regions of the country were devastated and left demoralized. It didn't happen overnight, and it didn't happen everywhere, but once the decline began, it was unstoppable.

Commerce increased overall, achieving Reagan's goal, but the sweeping deregulation nearly obliterated rural America. The brightest young minds left, while opioid addiction and "deaths of despair" spiraled out of control. Conservatives got half of what they wanted—less regulation and more wealth at the top—but in their own communities, they were left with very little hope and a hell of a lot more suffering.

At this same time, I began to see how the term *conservative* was being used inappropriately as a catch-all to portray a wide range of ideas and behaviors that didn't match its meaning. Perhaps society had changed faster than our language. I always considered myself a moderately conservative guy. Even my protest against the war was conservative; I was trying to conserve lives, money, and justice. However, it seemed that my views were putting me in the same category as those who ignored people in difficult circumstances or who tried to turn back the natural progression of time and tide.

Nope—not me. Balance the budget, strengthen our social safety net, and save the ocean—all rather conservative ideas—have nothing to do with racism, magical thinking, or angry behavior. Even Reagan recognized our linguistics problem.

> "Preservation of our environment is not a liberal or conservative challenge, it's common sense."   – *Ronald Reagan*
> *State of the Union address, Jan. 25, 1984*

I remembered what I'd read about behavior and cultural anthropology and it made me wonder. It's easy to say that people are one way or another due to this or that issue, but cultural pressures are complex and difficult to nail down. I wondered if personality types might be at work.

Those who had escaped the dust bowl or who had survived a difficult adolescence tended to be both tougher and less empathetic. My mother certainly had no love for chickens, and she thought anyone squeamish enough to concern themselves over livestock was nuts. And that made sense from her perspective. Edith was a farmer's daughter. Killing chickens was a necessary part of life, as far as she was concerned.

But she had worked hard to escape that kind of life, despite the trail of attitudes she carried with her. She was able to look back and understand, but she had no truck with willful ignorance. If she and Ray could do it, anyone could do it. And if they didn't, they were just plain lazy. Or stupid. Or both. She agreed with Cicero: "We reap what we sow."

My mother's family name was Brookover; she was born into a family of seven firm-lipped siblings. Brookies (as we call ourselves) can be an odd bunch, and we come in strong flavors. We are a family of cake bakers, lifelong quilters, entrepreneurs, and dedicated readers. When outraged, willing to stand our ground. I think a lot of who we are stems from the no-nonsense Oklahoma-chicken farmer-hardscrabble-Quaker root stock our parents shared, and how us kids (all the cousins) dealt with it to make our way in the world. I feel that our generation has been a good custodian of our parents' attitudes by keeping the decent parts and channeling a lot of their tough love into productive lives. All rather conservative.

But our values were for the preservation of life, not the ending of it. I have relatives who registered voters in the South and dodged bullets for doing so, helped the mentally ill, stood on street corners with banners and signs that said "Stop the War." Not conservative as most people use the term, but certainly so according to Webster. And Wikipedia, for that matter.

I decided I must have an undiagnosed split personality. I knew our national and state budgets overrode everything, which meant that all our issues had to be framed from a fiscally conservative position. You can't do anything if you can't pay for it. Our main problem seemed uniquely American: we wanted everything, we wanted it all at once, and we didn't want to pay for it. But I also knew that just doesn't work. I also knew that a certain population of wealthy individuals felt incredibly entitled, and really didn't want to participate in the system. But sooner or later the clock runs down, the sand runs out, the well runs dry, and we all run out of metaphors.

Getting the hell out of Arco

This is what Tom and I came home to, became a part of, and observed over the next fifty-odd years as the world changed and reimagined itself. There was a huge contrast between the town we grew up in and most of the small towns we'd passed through; it was a new world. Money, education, and opportunity make a massive difference, not only to the appearance of a town, but the society it fosters. The self-proclaimed "only hippie in the Midwest" had made that contrast even greater in his wistful yearning for a culture beyond the one he was born into, and from which he felt so alienated.

Individualists who left their small towns and family-run businesses to move into the cities and suburbs had three traits that allowed them to make such a drastic change: dissatisfaction with what they had, the ability to think beyond their situation, and most importantly, enough ambition to pull up roots and risk failure in an unforgiving world.

The people left behind didn't have such attributes, or didn't have them in sufficient quantity. By definition, they were the more conservative ones in their community. They were the ones who never rebelled from their parents, or at least not enough to matter. America has been called a melting pot because of our wide variety of cultures and languages, but it also became a threshing mill, separating wheat from chaff.

In addition to all this, there has been a sly selection process at work since the Middle Ages, accelerated by the industrial revolution. In a general way, the young man we met in Arco would prove himself to be one kind of person if he ever left the town where he felt so misunderstood, but another if he stayed. The gas station attendant in Yellowstone talked as if life had passed him by, but there is always opportunity for those willing to reach for it. The fact that he was willing to open up to Tom indicated he was on the cusp. Who knows? Maybe our example provided a catalyst for him, a real indication of what might be possible.

Coming of age in rural America can feel isolating, interminable, and inexorably mired in the past. Everyone knows everything about everyone, or seems to — there's no escaping it. Where you live, who you've been seen with, and the span of your life is forever reflected in the eyes of everyone else.

Girls are little angels or fallen so far they can't get up. You either embrace sin and break your momma's heart or get yourself to church. Alcoholism or abstinence. It's buttoned-up church goers *vs.* good ol' boys, with no room for subtlety, error, or a different point of view. Small towns can be a snakepit of gossip and bullying, like chat sites for teenagers.

Your life echoes all the country songs you've ever heard like a sad cliché that spins out from the far end of Main Street, past the diner, then clear down to the lumberyard—and then doubles back like a bad penny. It was fun when you were little, but you're not little anymore, and your eyes are old enough to see the shadows at the edge of your life.

This is the pressure cooker in which country folk live out their lives, like frogs in one great pot of hot water. If male, too proud to acknowledge that the water is actually boiling. Fully aware if female, but trapped by their sex and almost always powerless to stop it. Except for that singular individual who manages to summon up enough moxie to rise above all of it and slam the screen door on their way out.

It's not known how many millions leave home; the percentage doesn't matter nearly as much as their ability and willingness to find out what really mattered to them in life and work hard to achieve their dream. And the people they leave behind just kept trying harder day by day and year after year to make life work.

I can think of several exceptions of course. Some people may have moved out of sheer desperation, like Black people who fled the South during the Jim Crow era or those who stayed behind to help, such as family doctors and teachers. And there are certainly a few bright ones who stay out of obligation, to work the farm or family business for their parents. So it may not be as simple as it sounds, but the general thesis is right there.

A Chorus Line

When we think of Broadway plays and Hollywood movies, we also imagine a parade of young hoofers and wannabe actors leaving the sticks to make it in the big city. It's the American cliché, dream, and teenage diaspora, all rolled into one. Most come from out-of-the-way places, with Brooklyn accents and River City memories.

The ones who hop on a train or hitch a ride out of nowhere have just enough courage to make that leap of faith. It is not an accident they are some of the more creative and forward-thinking people on the planet. They took themselves out of the doldrums to enter the spotlight, and living one's dream takes a huge effort. Most people can't do it. Whether they survived in their profession or ended up waiting tables forever isn't the issue; they took a risk that others didn't, paving a way for others to follow.

Putting the genie back

The winnowing of rural America stems from systemic social and economic issues. It is a function of our humanity and capitalism itself; larger cities and sprawling suburbs offer more of almost everything, including art, education, and romance. Yes, they are dirty, and in some ways more dangerous. In a few cities, there are homeless encampments because of the huge wealth disparity. But there are far more opportunities, and that tops everything else—including mom's apple pie and the old swimming hole.

Stopping the exodus of ambitious youth from rural regions would take a massive amount of social engineering, and making rural life appealing enough to retain even 25% of the population would require a ton more subsidization—which rural people resent and tend to reject anyway.

Country folk may hate that they haven't been able to find a way to change this long sad story on their own, but it's an impossible task, since conservative attitudes are one of the main drivers. Nobody lives there anymore because nobody wants to. And you can't make people change for no good reason.

Although there's room to support the working class in a general way, it's difficult to revitalize rural communities other than by creating brand new factories ad hoc. Such solutions do not readily exist. As Thomas Wolfe once said, "You can't go home again." People don't return to the Whistle Stop Cafe once they've found their own freedom of expression in Chicago, Los Angeles, or New York. To a great extent, it doesn't exist anymore.

Golden ticket

This isn't far away and long ago stuff. To have watched any of the first audition episodes of *American Idol* is to witness this process in action. It features young vocalists, some no more than fifteen, trying out on a nationwide talent contest, hoping to leverage themselves into a decent life with a guitar and a song. Story after story, each journey of self-discovery unique, yet oddly similar.

It's only during the *audition phase* each year that we can witness this, when it's raw, scary as hell, and untested. For it is in that singular moment when shopgirl and farmboy discover that their dream of a better life in the outer world could actually come true. It is during those first five minutes when we share in the fear, uncertainty, and delight of the new life | old life transition. When they walk into that room and try themselves out in front of three judges and three billion people.

Frightened and brave, they sing their hearts out for a fresh start beyond the confines of county roads or whatever town or suburb they grew up in—music their lingua franca, and that golden ticket, the ultimate passport.

During interviews, contestants tell of their years watching the show, their personal struggle, and how they vowed to get beyond the tangible and emotional limits of their existence. Across more than twenty years, we've witnessed the support of multi-generation families waiting outside the audition doors, or of that one person who stood with them in line—that best friend who understood as completely as they did what it was to be stuck on the wrong side of the mountain.

Given the high percentage of rural contestants, it makes sense that many of these kids show up with a country song for their audition—half about the nobility of being dirt poor yet persevering in the face of it, and the other half about how Jesus saved them. Many dedicate their first song to the momma or a best friend who committed suicide.

America watches from their living rooms, sees these kids fighting irrelevance. Their faces are bright with hope as they reach out during the first and second cut of the auditions. This is their chance. They are the exceptional ones who hammer the odds to show us what it takes to overcome mediocrity's momentum. They are rural America's reflection, singing their own stories right back to where they came from. It's personal. It's important. And they want to be heard.

In many cases, these kids represent generational poverty going back to ancestors who risked everything for an earlier ticket—a ticket that brought them across an ocean and through Ellis Island, scattering to the small towns and inner cities where they existed for generations until one grew up with a cockeyed smile and enough talent, grit, and curiosity to break free.

For all the homilies about country living, family values, and small town life, such paradigms don't always click into place like a Hallmark movie. The whole is sometimes a hell of a lot less than the sum of its parts, and the heartfelt cry, "I'm going to Hollywood!" is now synonymous with the dream of all teenagers in backwaters who want a lot more than the hand they've been dealt. No wonder they light out for parts unknown—their inner life holds an imperative they can no longer ignore.

Be not content

What Tom and I witnessed on our trip wasn't a brain drain; it was an ambition drain, a willingness to take risk drain. The ones left behind had their religion and jobs and status quo and said they were fine with that. But status quo and prayer don't make payments on the harvester when the topsoil blows away. Or when the winter wheat vernalizes too early or gets root rot due to bizarre weather conditions. The flooding, tornadoes, and drops to thirty below combine to make it seem like the rest of the world has passed you by, but idealistic yearning for yesteryear isn't a practical solution.

For those who got out, events and opportunity brought new focus. Part of it was the war. Some escaped to college or into the army. All it took was bus fare and the promise of a job, for the road grants new hope, and dreams of freedom.

> "You can never cross an ocean unless you have the courage to lose sight of the shore."   – *Christopher Columbus*

People sometimes assume that *disruption* refers to a uniquely modern phenomenon involving technology or merchandising that becomes rapidly displaced (like retail stores being overwhelmed by Amazon's long reach and low pricing), but that isn't always the story. Sometimes it happens with belief systems and demographics. Our politics got disrupted because America got disrupted. And now we have to deal with it.

Common Sense

When the Spanish Armada attacked England in 1588, each ship carried a gigantic cross lashed to the masthead. Spain was decidedly religious, and those crosses were symbolic of their anger against the English, with whom they went to war, ostensibly to change their theology and their politics. But that war was also an expression of their long-standing resentment of the English for their unmatched success.

Queen Elizabeth's navy was greatly outnumbered, but her ships were nimble and her guns had more range. Those huge crosses perched at the top made the Spanish ships top-heavy, and their mainmasts acted as giant levers. Any longshoreman could have pointed it out. These mastodons of the ocean wallowed in the heavy seas and foundered easily once their hulls had been breached. England won the battle and the war.

The totalitarian movement in America today is just as top-heavy with religion, and just as dangerous. It is a wayward, reckless thing, and has no actual policies beyond bad-tempered resentment and a list of complaints and grudges against people they suspect have always been looking down on them or living better lives than they are. They are driven without reason like a beast blinded with rage, tearing with its horns. They don't flex their bitterness and anger to any significant purpose, but mostly just because they can and to assuage their frustration.

All of this came from somewhere. Today, we are going through the final throes of a dying ideology that peaked during the Middle Ages. Common parlance calls it conservatism, but that descriptor doesn't fit anymore.

The Civil War put an end to the institution of slavery but it didn't resolve our underlying conflicts. Many of the issues we face as a nation grew out of our history of slavery and racism, reinforced by the dual mythologies of religion and male superiority, which worked together rather neatly. The ancient lessons of fear and male insecurity came down parent to child, parent to child, and now here we are. Hijacked.

We are on the threshold of a uniquely American dystopia, promulgated by the not-so-secret yearnings of wannabe tyrants posing as bread-and-butter politicians and apple-pie leaders who advertise Truth, Justice, and the American Way, yet pull for magical thinking, poverty, and early death without remorse or second thought. They come from the same ideological fever swamp I faced down in 1970.

This vision of America hearkens back to a time before the Civil Rights Act and school integration; before the invention of birth control pills and Roe *vs.* Wade — back before women could get credit cards in their own name. It is driven by people who would just as soon wind the clock back to 1954 and nail it to the side of a barn like a trophy.

This isn't just nostalgia. It is a reactionary backlash driven by what the German psychoanalyst Karen Horney called the "tyranny of the shoulds," caused by the tension between reality and how a person believes things *should* be. To a great extent, that's what religion is based on as well, like one of those colorful Russian dolls that fit inside each other, nesting magical thinking, misplaced patriotism, and existential fear.

When I refused to kowtow to an amoral Uncle Sam in 1970, it wasn't like this. Sure, we were aware of survivalist groups who hid out in the forest and played with guns on the weekend — they were often the ones who joined the Army early, thinking it was going to be "fun." And there have always been people who held religious beliefs over common sense and the well-being of their own families, but it was nothing like we have today, with conspiracy theories galore, and vendetta politics running the country.

Catch me on any number of topics and I'm the guy wearing glasses, but I've avoided conversations dealing with magical thinking, justice, money, and politics most of my life — usually because I didn't know enough or felt it wasn't my place to speak. But it came to me that all of these issues connected like bright dots on a through line that reached back into 1970 and before. In fact, all the way back to the Bubonic Plague, the Crusades, and the invention of stew.

While writing about our motorcycle trip, I came to realize there was a connection between my protest against the war in Vietnam and our nation's current struggles. I also began to see how music, literature, and my own understanding of history combined with what Tom and I experienced to shape my understanding of the social and political issues we are now facing as a nation. My writing shifted as the arc of my life came into context with the history I helped create.

My investigations into the drip-bloop erosion of facts and truth began early in life, when simple curiosity turned into skepticism. It became more pronounced as a result of reading and conversations over the years, which encouraged me to confront various notions I found embedded in our politics and social consciousness. Questions kept popping up for which there didn't seem to be a lot of good answers. At some point I buckled down and began to study the issue. That exploration led me to a new regard for Dr. King's famous arc of history and the nature of its progressively egalitarian curve.

Home truths

I was taught that traditional conservatism was a humane philosophy that *happened* to prefer the familiar to the unknown, fact to mystery, and the actual to the possible. It meant saving for a rainy day and not spending money on frivolous things like exotic vacations if you couldn't afford them. It was all common sense and nothing to get worked up about.

And it's why I've always thought of myself as a conservative. Actually, not *a* conservative. That now carries all kinds of baggage with which I would never identify. Better to say that I always thought of myself *as* conservative, and leave it at that.

To be conservative was to be cautious with resources such as money, clothing, books, housing, water, air, forests, wildlife, and friendships—anything of value. Waste not, want not. Being conservative meant being responsible. You ate your veggies and fruit and avoided junk food most of the time (my father loved Mallomars, pancakes, and raisin snails, but, being a responsible fellow who protected himself to protect his family, only indulged in such things when we went on vacation). You did your best in everything you attempted. Laziness didn't fit in. Being conservative meant not putting up with a bunch of nonsense.

To me, conservatives were somewhat progressive, but with a light hand ready on the brake. It was the pragmatic cooling shed for the more hot-blooded policy ideas that might not work out, particularly if we went too far, too fast. Conservatives were the ones who said, "That's a nice idea, Bob, but did you consider the what-if's?" They were the ones who said, "Your proposed solution has merits, but maybe we should try it as a small test project first, and maybe we should pare that budget down somewhat; it doesn't need to cost *that* much."

For my father, it was numbers, budgets and ethics. To me, conservative means the guy who raps the table and says, "How about we think this through a little more? I have some concerns... Are there other alternatives? Maybe a multi-pronged approach from a couple of other agencies may come up with better results. Has anyone done a cost-benefit analysis?" (To survive in business as long as Ray and I did, such attitudes become automatic because they're necessary to keep expenses within the constraints of cash-flow.)

To me, it also meant everyone had the right to live out their lives in quiet enjoyment without fear, and nobody was put in harm's way unless our lives or liberty were *directly* at stake. It meant we fought together against anything that jeopardized our way of life, such as anarchists, climate change, pandemics, hurricanes, foul water, nut jobs with automatic weapons, or shysters with gold-plated grins selling bogus diplomas. That was my conservatism, and what I fought for by refusing the draft back in 1970.

Mature conservatives accept the rule of law, the norms of democracy, and the legitimacy of opposing voices. They prioritize winning converts over destroying unbelievers. They know full well that governing is impossible without negotiation and compromise. They seek to address the real needs and problems of working-class people while rejecting conspiracy theories, demagoguery, and temptations toward political violence. Basic common sense is their pilot.

Unfortunately, that's no longer our situation. Instead, modern conservatives prefer temper tantrums to governing and fantasies about stolen elections to the hard work of appealing to voters on policy issues. Modern conservatives would rather destroy the federal bureaucracy than use it to implement constructive—even conservative—methodology. Modern conservatives pose a direct threat to our nation's stability.

I'm at the point of saying that these people are not really conservatives, at least not any longer. Maybe they were at one time, but not now. They may still be Republicans out of habit and momentum, I don't know. It seems to me that the Republican Party is now not much more than modern-day fascism with an elephant logo. In any case, there is a massive disconnect between what conservative actually means and how our politics is playing out.

Want Social Security to keep going so grandma can survive her last years in peace? Want her to get medical care when she needs it? How about the Pentagon: want us to continue being the world's peacekeeper to keep Russia, Iran, North Korea, and other meddlers within their own borders? Want higher education and healthcare to be a low-cost option like they are in other countries? *Fine.* Change the tax laws to include the Buffett Rule, take the cap off Social Security contributions, and stop fooling around with wannabe dictators and addlepated nutjobs gumming up the works with their endless prattle and conspiracy theories.

Show me the money

The United States spends more than it takes in. Our national budget has two large areas that consistently run us over budget and increase our national debt: social services and defense.

Over time, the United States and the North Atlantic Treaty Organization became our planet's last good cops, trying to keep

Russia, China, the Middle East, and other aggressive nations from attacking their neighbors. But trying to keep our military as strong as it's been since WWII is creating an economic hole we won't be able to fill unless something changes.

So, do we cut back on Social Security and Medicare and allow 40% of our population to spend their remaining years with less food, housing, and medicine? Do we put a cap on our military with the foreknowledge that at some point we will no longer be able to keep the planet safe? Or do we change our tax structure back to the way it was in 1960?

I was taught that it is important for everyone to be kind, considerate, and helpful, and to deal rationally with all the advances in knowledge and science. When technology got ahead of itself, we restrained it. We needed to have a healthy society, where the strong and corrupt were not allowed to prey upon the weak. We wanted clean water and air, supported by strong laws to protect our health. When there was a medical problem, like the Great Influenza Epidemic of 1918, we dealt with it by wearing masks—no exceptions.

I was also taught we all have a right to keep what we've earned, but as a society we also have a duty to help each other and the less fortunate—and to call this "charity" was sanctimonious; it had to be built into the system or nothing would change. I also learned (in business) that we can't keep piling up debt—the interest becomes unsupportable.

The concept of economic safety nets has been conflated with communism by wealthy conservatives and made into a bogeyman to keep voters in line, but the United States is not a purely capitalistic democracy. It's a mixture of different economic and social philosophies working together for the greater good. Churches, schools, and libraries are not profit centers any more than the police or our military.

When the Coast Guard rescues a sailboat in trouble they don't present the owner with an invoice. Our townships, cities, states, and even the federal government—they all have budgets, but they don't show a profit margin or return on investment. That's because we all support these organizations to support each other. They are all forms of socialistic meritocracies, and they prove how seamlessly socialistic organizations can work within a capitalistic system.

The main issue we have is runaway capitalism without the proper balance of sufficiently robust social services. The entire nation would be happier with a far stronger social safety net as long as we also paid down the national debt. *Guess what?* There is a simple, obvious fix!

Reverse all the tax cuts for the wealthy, enact the Buffett Rule, take the cap off Social Security contributions, and put a serious cap on spending tied to our economic health as a nation.

Capitalism and socialism work together just fine; they are surprisingly synergistic. When people are happy, harmony is possible. Even probable, which improves business. Communism may sound like socialism, but they aren't the same. We don't have a problem with librarians trying to "take over the world" do we? It's conservative propaganda and rank ignorance that conflates them into a political scare tactic.

From the smallest town to the entire nation, good manners and striving for the common welfare are the glue that holds us together. When that fails so does everything else. At some point, compromise is necessary for the common good.

However, that concept of conservatism—of *being* conservative in thought and deed—devolved from the mid-1970s into something quite different today. In my view, there is nothing wrong with being conservative. But being "*a* conservative" is not the same as *being* conservative. Not anymore. It appears to have gone up in smoke. Taking its place is authoritarianism, cleverly disguised as bread and butter conservatism.

Authoritarian anti-social programs would lead to an enormous expansion of the government's role, making it into a quasi-police state. They are starting to dictate which sexual norms to follow, what kind of healthcare should be allowed, and which books students can read. Hate the idea of big government? Our "Land of the Free," will be far more like Russia, Iran, or North Korea. Wealthy conservatives have found a way to tap into a rich vein of American gullibility, and they're mining it with every tool at their disposal.

A pragmatic social contract

There is a fundamental difference in how some people see things like welfare and social programs. Authoritarians tend to think these programs are only for those who benefit directly, and at the expense of those who pay into them. They feel that helping others means hurting themselves. The idea of supporting something financially that has no benefit to them personally seems ludicrous. We see this when conservatives rail against government programs as being socialistic, except, of course, the one or two programs that help them directly, such as Social Security and Medicare. And now healthcare, via the Affordable Care Act, which helps some 40 million Americans, many of whom think of themselves as quite conservative.

And, certainly, the people who directly benefit from social programs are likely to be in favor of them. But there are also a whole lot of people who support the programs for their own sake, even if they'll never personally get a dime out of it.

If you ask them why, you'll usually get answers about empathy and humanity—a basic desire to help others. I agree with that completely, but it always, inevitably, leads to an argument about compulsory charity, and that usually turns into a tug-of-war about libertarian ideals and property rights *vs.* bleeding hearts and bloated government waste.

To make the ideas accessible, I think it's helpful to focus on the more pragmatic idea that social safety nets, if properly implemented, benefit our entire society—not just those on the receiving end.

I remember one of my staff at Los Gatos Office Equipment who wanted to know why he should pay for someone else to receive healthcare. He wasn't argumentative about it; more curious than anything else. He just didn't see the point. I wasn't nearly as succinct then as I am here, but I basically told him that I was happy to pay more taxes to fund such a system, because if I someday lost my job and couldn't afford insurance, and particularly if I had a family, I'd want them to be covered.

I would want to be able to change jobs, or just quit without worrying about whether a lapse in coverage was going bankrupt me or put my life at risk. If I have to go to the emergency room, I don't want it overwhelmed with patients who could have been easily treated if they had been able to go a doctor's office instead of a hospital. And if I get seriously ill, I don't want to have to battle with some insurance company about coverage while I'm just trying to survive.

I focus on this because arguing about empathy and shared social responsibility is largely philosophical. If someone doesn't share my position on it, I'm probably not going to change their mind. But rational self-interest is something everybody understands. And I'm convinced that properly run public programs are in my own self-interest, even if I never personally use them.

Even if I never get my house broken into or my car stolen, I benefit when everyone is protected *carefully*. So I don't mind paying for smarter, well-trained police officers instead of thugs with badges. And even if I never get a deadly disease, I still benefit from science and technology advancing, so I don't mind paying for publicly funded research.

Even if I don't have children, I benefit from living in an educated society, so I don't mind paying for libraries and schools, (including much higher pay for teachers). And I want that education to be universal—not just for the rich kids in "charter" schools, which are siphoning off funds from our public school system. If the poor get a substandard education, we all lose.

More than anything, I want to live in a healthy society of equals, where everyone is treated fairly. But that argument often falls on deaf ears, because some people see "the greater good" as meaning the good for everyone *but* themselves. They really don't see how much they gain by not having people on welfare, especially if getting people off welfare can only be accomplished by providing a range of services.

And without the EPA, FDA, and other federal and state agencies regulating commerce, science, and food (the "administrative state") there would be no check on runaway capitalism. We would be stuck with bad food, bad water, and buildings that wouldn't survive earthquakes. Our lives would be a mess.

The overall cost of these programs and how well they work can be debated, but the basic idea—that helping each other helps everyone—is obvious. We're all in this together, and helping each other out is just the sensible thing to do. It's also the *conservative* thing to do. Which is why I consider myself conservative. In many ways, far more conservative than most modern Republicans.

My understanding of these social and political trends culminated in a collection of monographs called *The Great American Dream Machine*, which is Part II of the book you're reading now. I discuss a triple-whammy of large issues: magical thinking, politics, and the national debt. It contains a fair number of practical suggestions and hope for the future. Considering the two books as one creates a horse of a different color—half paper, half cloud, entangled by intent. Aside from the cost difference, there's another advantage: as a living document, it remains malleable.

My concern is that most people hate the subject matter to begin with. It has all become not much more than *blah, blah,* national debt, bad politicians, complicated charts, *blah, blah, blah,* which doesn't help anybody.

I'll let you in on something. I hate pieces that read well enough, but everything is too rounded or too esoteric. The juice has left the orange, and all I'm left with is the dry husk of an idea (if even that much). No juice running down my chin, no color or flavor, and no seeds. *Blech.*

Excerpts from two of the monographs follow. I included them to give you an idea where I went with this; the rest of my ruminations can be found on the blogsite. I assembled the pieces in a way that describes the puzzle as I see it—juice, rind, seeds, and all. Your mileage may vary.

EXCERPT FROM
The Great American Dream Machine

Thoughts on Thinking

In a philosophy class I took a few months before the trip, the professor asked us to consider a simple idea without judgment. Then he stated it. It was deliberately provocative—an interesting concept I hadn't thought about before. And I liked the idea of what the professor was up to, getting us to consider untried possibilities.

I could see the other students mulling things over, but one kid was in serious trouble. Watching that student's face working with quiet tears was uncomfortable. It was a shock. To realize how hard it might be to reevaluate basic ideas—even to the possibility.

By asking us to consider new information, the class exercise broke that student's confirmation bias—what that student "knew" to be true—at least in part because it had been offered for consideration by a respected source and therefore couldn't be dismissed out of hand. It didn't fit with that person's long-held notions of how the universe worked, and the result was immediate, overwhelming overload.

A lot of the anger some people felt about the social unrest during the 1960s and 70s was triggered that same way. I saw my father get tight-lipped about the race riots in Watts when the city streets of Los Angeles were burning and the police were wielding water cannons like giant insect sprayers against running people—ostensibly to clean humanity off the street like a city worker might clean old chewing gum from sidewalks. Was my father more concerned that his world wasn't perfect or that there were people so miserable they had to take to the streets to be heard? And perhaps he felt a mix of emotions, not the least being America's impotence and loss.

Confirmation bias puts more emphasis on whatever corroborates our existing beliefs while ignoring everything that contradicts them. The illusion of control is the belief that we have more influence over outcomes than we actually do, like believing that if we clutch a Bible verse such as *John 3:16* like a golden ticket, we can somehow cheat death and live forever in some sort of cloud storage arrangement, like photos backed up from our smartphones.

Confirmation bias poses significant challenges to democracy, since it undermines the idea that public agreement can be reached through reason—the give and take of debate and electioneering. People tend to rationalize what they already believe, rather than seeking out the truth. But if our beliefs are false, then failure becomes a self-fulfilling prophecy.

There wasn't any rule about it, but many teachers taught via rote memorization instead of having their students learn logic and abstract thinking. It was easier that way, since it was how they had been taught when young and how they had been trained to teach others. The more students per classroom, the more difficult it is to teach real comprehension.

As an experienced teacher who felt that educating her students was more of a calling than a job, my mother spoke often and long about this issue—that expecting students to learn by rote demeaned them, as if they weren't competent to understand the concepts. To her mind it was an example of lazy teaching, and only mitigated by overcrowding.

If the average person doesn't see a value in education other than as a lever to land a good-paying job, eventually everybody pays a difficult price, as we are right now. Education for education's sake is how we train ourselves to use our brains. If all one learns is how to put *Tab A* into *Slot A*, nothing else can happen. You just become a cog in somebody else's machine.

If I hadn't read myself through a small mountain of books and listened to a tall stack of music, I might never have been *able* to connect the dots. History and civics extend beyond academic subjects like science or math to make our world understandable.

If our kids never learn much more than whatever shows up in front of them by accident, they'll never get the span of human progress or how government actually works. They'll always be frustrated when it doesn't work the way they want it to. They won't understand it, and they won't know how to keep it working. They won't see that autocracy is the *antithesis* of freedom. One of the greatest tragedies of being uneducated is not knowing the difference between opinion and fact.

Thinking is hard, which is why most people don't do it. There are many Hollywood movies featuring workaday people who have wonderful insights and summon up enough gumption to conquer big issues against long odds, but it isn't all that common in the real world.

How many fourth graders have been taught to wonder *why* two plus two equals four, or even why it matters? Students have somehow learned, perhaps from their parents' behavior, that following the ideology of a group (such as church, school, or government) is the same as being able to collaborate and communicate, and that their thoughts hold value even if they're based on nothing more than opinion, something heard on television, or even superstition.

This creates a monstrosity when it comes to human relations: *no one* can negotiate with superstition. It is a self-declarative illogical belief that brooks no common ground, and without common ground there is nothing to negotiate. Relationships (including political ones) simply fall apart.

Think different

I was taught *how* to think rather than *what* to think. It was a chore, but my parents (particularly Edith) believed it was far more important to do everything the correct way than to check things off a list. Issues trip you up with how wet the rain is, or come from an old tree, or taste something like an orange and a woman's laughter in the dark. Nothing fits until it does — or not the way we want, going through all these things twice.

Nevertheless, we all want to know why. It's a function of who we are and how we evolved. Is there something moving in that tall grass over there? Find out or be lunch. People will work hard to explain something they don't understand. From childhood up we focus on cause and effect because without that connection we would never understand how anything works.

The problem is, we attempt to apply that logic to anything and everything, and assign meaning where it doesn't always exist—particularly when we're going through heartache. We got into the habit of reclassifying disturbing issues from bad to good just to make ourselves feel better.

Why did my girlfriend dump me? So I could come alive, smell the roses, and discover you, you lucky thing! Wrong. She dumped me for a good reason, and unless we are living our lives out in a straight-to-internet movie, she wasn't trying to get me together with you. Not only that, there wasn't any great cosmic oversight committee doing that evaluation for the three of us. Life doesn't work that way. None of it does.

We had been told that hell made heaven possible; that some have to die so others can live; the Holocaust was necessary so we could know and recognize evil, and that without such evils good could have no meaning. Lies. All pronounced straight from the pulpit with solemn words and long pauses to let the "truth" of it sink into our tiny little noggins. And then we were told, "Listen to your heart, not your intellect," like that made any sense. It's what you do when you're baking cookies perhaps or skiing down a mountain, but it is not a philosophy of life.

People who "listen to their heart" instead of using their brains end up with abusive partners, buy timeshares they can't afford, embrace superstition and conspiracy theories—the list of stupid decisions based on emotion is endless.

People sometimes say "everything happens for a reason," because that explains away all the hurtful, broken things that happen. Life can be difficult, and it makes sense to create meaning out of pain because it's the perfect hat trick. It makes us feel better; it lessens the pain. But in so doing, we often create a lot more meaning to situations than they merit.

> "People change so that you can learn to let go. Things go wrong so that you appreciate them when they're right. You believe lies so you eventually learn to trust no one but yourself, and sometimes good things fall apart so better things can fall together. Everything happens for a reason."
> *— Attributed to Marilyn Monroe*

Sounds great, doesn't it? Baloney. It's a logical fallacy. An argument that creates conclusions not supported by reality, and a great example of wishful thinking. Sometimes people learn to let go and sometimes they change, and one thing *can* lead to another, but it doesn't happen *for a reason* because activities and things cannot *think* because they don't have *brains* and there is absolutely nothing sitting in loco parentis to make certain that there is meaning in every little thing that happens in our fraught little lives. *Oh, the drama! It must have meaning or I'll die!*

Same for everything else in her little cause-and-effect speech. I always liked Marilyn Monroe; I even painted her portrait once. She was a brilliant woman with incredible talent, but that kind of thinking is just wrong.

Hearts and flowers

The Greeks believed that the heart was the seat of reason. I'm not sure what they thought the brain was for, but that big muscle in the chest was where we figured stuff out. And even today, people refer to the heart as the seat of emotion. It may feel that way sometimes when we say our heart is breaking because it can feel like something in our chest has been torn. It *hurts*. Except the heart isn't the seat of anything but a constant flow of blood, and everybody knows it.

So why do we go on pretending something is true when we know it isn't? Is it an unwillingness to break with the status quo? Peer pressure? Perhaps it's the fear that if we change something we'll end up shattering it beyond all repair. *Pay no attention to that man behind the curtain!*

Just think of it: misinformation passed down person-to-person and generation-to-generation for thousands of years, still capable of tricking us into thinking something that simply isn't true. The Greeks were pretty smart people, but they got that one completely wrong. But it wasn't magical thinking, just a lack of medical knowledge.

Does Valentine's Day hurt anyone? No. But similar beliefs and belief systems passed down through history certainly do. We have killed and maimed millions with the ignorance of the ages, and it's still going on. Witness all that death in the Middle East, including the current genocide in Gaza. All in retribution for pogroms, wars, and family feuds enacted over the past 3,000 years, and started often enough either by dire instructions from someone's sacred cow or in defense of same.

The real problem isn't whether people think a woman in a colorful robe and turban laying out some cards with pictures on them can tell their future or whether pieces of paper with pictures on them in green and gray ink are worth anything to an institution we call a "bank," but the kind and quality of thinking behind such beliefs and whether people start shooting to defend them. Just because a man with gold hair and a grin as big as the Grand Canyon tells us to drink disinfectant and inject horse dewormer to counter a deadly virus doesn't mean we should, and people who do so without at least checking with their doctor are nothing but nickle-plated ninnyhammers.

All of these ideas are based on emotional reasoning. It's something that might sound good if you've been brought up on it your entire life, but it doesn't take more than a second to realize you don't have to have tasted a good apple to know a bad one and there is no sky daddy to make death less inevitable.

People have been taught in Sunday School and church to abandon their own reasoning and live on faith as if we were all breatharians, but all that does is create false ideas in the minds of the indoctrinated. There are no zombies, vampires, or guardian angels, and there are no shape-shifting lizard people running Hollywood or our government. There is no Zeus or Apollo. Getting down on our knees and wishing hard for something (remembering to remain humble) doesn't make it happen. And the fact that people are on television, social media, and on radio championing these beliefs is not proof they are true. It's proof of how far the delusion has spread.

"Almost every disaster movie ever made starts with a politician ignoring a scientist." — *Neil deGrasse Tyson*

I wonder if a lot of it isn't the simple human need for love — unconditional, if we can get it. Dogs provide a sterling example, but so does true love. And religion of course, which purports that some gods love us unconditionally. I notice that there are still strings attached however, such as *John 3:16* – an extremely high bar to jump, since it requires us to drive a metaphorical ice pick through our own intellect and abase ourselves to the unthinking adoration of a mystical being who created us for the sole purpose of worshiping him. The original quid pro quo.

Magical thinking is the belief that a person's own thoughts or wishes can bend reality to their will. It's like wishful thinking on steroids; it attempts to make real what wishful thinking only supposes. Apropos to that, we can sometimes see in others what we cannot see in ourselves.

> "Dear God – Our Jessica keeps talking to her invisible friend, and we're worried. She's almost twelve now, and we're wondering when and if she'll ever start to grow up."

Young children are prone to magical thinking. A four-year-old might believe that wishing for a unicorn will cause one to appear at her birthday party in a cloud of glitter. We excuse it in our children because they don't know any better. They are unschooled in the ways of the universe.

It gets kinda silly however, when grown-ups profess that by folding their hands and wishing fervently, an old guy in a flowing robe, floating high up in the clouds, will miraculously alter the result of a football game, a medical diagnosis, or a legal contract. That's just unicorns and glitter, all the way down.

Continued in The Great American Dream Machine

EXCERPT FROM
The Great American Dream Machine

Rich Man, Poor Man

Sometime in the late 1970s, I noticed a shell game in progress that imposed a false alignment of principles on poor and middle class conservatives. Politicians expounded on the evils of our national debt and the overreach of large government to those who were primarily concerned about race, patriotism, and religion—and tied all these concepts together.

Wealthy conservatives had evidently decided they weren't wealthy enough, so the politicians they had helped elect, led by President Ronald Reagan and the Heritage Foundation, enacted huge tax cuts and got rid of safety regulations on their behalf. To pay for this, they proposed many changes, including big modifications to Social Security (some wanted to get rid of it altogether). Many went through, but Social Security held. The only other variables were the military budget and the national debt. They didn't cut the military.

They manipulated the values and concerns of middle class and poor Americans by telling them over and over that these different concepts—cutting taxes for the wealthy and removing financial and public health safety nets—were part of the same mindset and belonged in the same basket of American ideals. It was like force-feeding ducks to make paté de foie gras.

It wasn't obvious what was going on, but I had my mother's voice in my head telling me to pay attention when things got out of whack. Politicians were using misdirection to conflate three issues into one. This encouraged people who were conservative on social issues and religion to vote for politicians who would enact favorable tax laws for the wealthy, as if voting that way would address all of their deepest fears.

Poor and middle-class conservatives had made a habit of electing politicians who supported tax policies benefitting the rich for no reason that made sense to me—or to them, that I could figure out. However, with my new understanding of that whole legacy of resentment and anger bubbling up out of the South, I realized there might be something deeper, a construct from our own peculiar history, perhaps. Like slavery—and the twisted relationships it created out of whole cloth. And I thought about Harriet Beecher Stowe.

Uncle Tomism, perpetuated down over the years like a bad penny, showed up in this new, parallel universe, with the collective poor and middle-class white folk abasing themselves to the collective rich—just as African-Americans had been forced to do in the step-and-fetch-it universe of the Old South. The model was a match, but with the twist of enthusiastic servitude. And we all went along for the ride as the rich proceeded to suck the nation dry.

This resulted in a transference of attitude and values from the subjugated to the oppressor as they themselves accepted the position of subservience. They were *happy* to pay for little Julia's massive inheritance and Uncle Carl's apartment in Central Park West. Quite the switcheroo, right? To accompany that shift came an embattled attitude of vigorously defending their role in this bizarre new relationship—the enemy of my friend is also my enemy! All very Stockholm-syndromy.

By pumping our hard-earned directly into the pockets of the rich to be perpetuated through dynasty trusts, we were all fighting communism together. It was god-damned patriotic is what it was—and no one was going to shift it with logic or concerns about a growing wealth imbalance.

Politicians went to work with a single-minded ambition: to write laws designed to reduce or eliminate taxes for the wealthy. All this under the guise that monies not paid out by such individuals as taxes would eventually "trickle-down" to everyone else due to the new factories they'd build with all that extra cash. They somehow managed to convince conservative voters that money worked like that. Even though it absolutely doesn't.

President Reagan's economic policies—centered on reducing government intervention, cutting taxes for the wealthy and corporations, and gutting business regulations—were based on a premise that a rising tide lifts all boats. But it wasn't a rising tide; it was a giant lever. And we weren't boats, we were more like kids on a playground when the big kid decides to suddenly jump off the teeter-totter.

As the money started leaving the system, the wealthy continued to thrive. But our economy was on the other side of that fulcrum, and as it declined, the rest of us went down with it. This led to widening inequality, stagnant living standards, and a decline in life expectancy. Conservatives who now applaud Reagan's policies as their historical watershed still don't get it. They still haven't connected the dots between Reagan's huge tax cuts for the wealthy and their own degraded standard of living. Hook, line, *and* sinker.

America experienced a sharp reversal in income distribution, upward mobility, and public health. The ladder of prosperity broke. Today, a child born in almost any other developed nation has a far better chance of surpassing their parents' success than one born in the United States. We are now living in the Reagan Dystopia.

My father was an accountant, not an economist, but he would read *Time Magazine* and *U.S. News and World Report* and *The Kiplinger Letter* in his big chair every evening and just shake his head. He didn't call it a scam because he really liked President Reagan, but he knew what he knew, and he had a pretty good idea it wasn't going to work. He was dubious at best.

For all the ink and pixels championing the idea that conservatives fight for the future well-being of our country through fiscal restraint, the money flow has almost always been the other way. The hypocracy has been blatant, but not that obvious to the general public, in part because it is a complex issue. Several administrations ended up with a smaller deficit as a percentage of GDP (perhaps the best way to measure this metric) than when their second year began, but only two were conservative.

Over the past seventy-odd years, whenever conservatives have had the absolute power to deliver on their promise of reducing the budget (when they held sway over both the Executive and Legislative branches), they've never done it.

Conservatives argue that "tax cuts pay for themselves," but we know that isn't true. Instead of spurring economic growth and creating more revenue, tax cuts for the rich just increase budget deficits and balloon our national debt, making it that much harder to fund social programs to help everyone else. And the economy suffers, which doesn't help anybody, including the rich. President Clinton famously reduced the deficit by lowering spending and partially reversing Reagan's corporate tax cuts, which had juiced the economy in the short run, but were killing us into the future by running up the deficit.

For Reagan's trickle-down theory to function as advertised, they would have had to funnel the money to ambitious people trying to create or expand small- to medium-sized firms (which can change the economy quickly), so they could hire additional staff, advertise, or open a new location. Which is what the Small Business Administration is all about. So pumping up the SBA into something more robust would have been a good place to start. But giving gratuitous tax breaks to a bunch of billionaires? That helps nobody. Major changes require early course corrections. Ask any pilot.

Give an industrialist a million dollars and they put it in their pocket. Well, stocks, municipal bonds, and real estate — same thing. Where it stays. Forever. Maybe they take a vacation with the dividends, but the principle does not create jobs or make new widgets. Not in the real world. Not in any significant way. The truly rich use *other* people's money via the stock market or a lender to start new ventures. If a corporation gets a windfall of cash, they buy back their own stock to increase its value.

It was the "I made it, I get to keep it, it's mine and you can't have it no matter what" theory of money management, as if they'd made all that money in a vacuum. As if every man was an island, beholden to no one. As if the resources and wealth of the nation were there for the taking and didn't belong in some way to its people. That's how unadulterated capitalism and manifest destiny work when normal governors like empathy and common sense aren't sufficient to stop feedback excesses from overtaking the system. (It's also how we get pirates.)

When Adam Smith wrote "The Wealth of Nations" in 1776, he assumed that capitalism would always be self-correcting, but he wasn't able to foresee multinational corporations or how extreme wealth could subvert democracy to destroy the balancing act of normal self-interest.

There is a common ethos of self-sufficiency and a shared distaste for large government and taxes that runs like a thread among all of us, but that doesn't explain the disconnect among middle-class and poor conservatives. I kept wondering why anyone would want to hurt themselves and their children financially *in perpetuity* to help anonymous rich people by voting for politicians who support them? Poor health care, less education, and an early death are not good tradeoffs for gratuitously lowering taxes for someone else's family and friends.

It's as if they all went to one of those weekend seminars where you "fire walk" across a bed of red-hot coals to prove to yourself that mind over matter works and that anyone can conquer their own common sense. Well, it's not a survival trait.

How did wealthy conservatives manage to hoodwink all their poor and middle-class cousins into embracing tax policies so diametrically opposed to their own best interests? This "us *vs.* them" dichotomy grew over time. President Reagan had fed it to the bursting point by misrepresenting the poor as an evil, conniving Black woman out to steal everything she could get her hands on. Reagan always reminded me of William Zantzinger's casual violence when he killed Hattie Carroll for being too slow and too Black. I thought of Reagan's jokes, his big grin, and his casual cruelty, making fun of the countless poor, most of whom were just trying to get by.

Over time, a huge swath of people who were left without any way to improve their lives grew embittered, became angry, or just gave up. And it didn't help that our two-party system had developed a wide gulf, with one side serving the rich while the other side was left to get everything else done that had to be done to keep the wheels of government from locking up. Unfortunately, positive efforts were often reframed as manipulation and nanny-state coddling.

At first I just assumed that when the lights started to dim, they'd wake up and reverse course, realizing that it wouldn't work in the long run. And hey, this is America, everybody gets a say. We try on different things to see how they fit. And if they don't fit all that well, we tailor them or try something else, right? Well, not for this crowd. They wanted it all and to hell with everybody else. Forget history. Pay no attention to the revolutions fomented as a result of isolated and privileged wealth, like what happened over in France and Russia, and what's going on right now in the United States.

Authoritarians tend to exhibit inflexible thinking, a preference for strict rules and authority, and a deep aversion to change and ambiguity. These tendencies line up with their religious beliefs, fostering a strong sense of cohesion and belonging. Their leaders often champion "moral clarity," a catch-all oversimplification that neatly pigeonholes good and evil: This little piggy goes to heaven, that little piggy goes to hell. Which resonates with everything they've been taught as children — accepted as Truth with a capital T, and never questioned. The self-nesting trifecta of religion, patriotism, and existential fear conflated all their issues into a single, cohesive philosophy.

Chaos theory

For many who never left rural America, the federal government came to be seen as a hulking Goliath, and every man with a hunting rifle was David with his slingshot, ready to take the giant down. This evolved into a battle of good *vs.* evil and emotion *vs.* logic. A distrust of education and science was starting to grow as well — the idea that knowledge itself was foreign, and like some intellectual Pied Piper of Hamelin, had mysteriously stolen their children.

And then things got truly bizarre. A large part of conservative America transformed their pent-up anger into a nihilistic desire to see major parts of the government dismantled — with no real plan to put something better in its place. Get rid of the Department of Education; close the Center for Disease Control; make the FBI and the Department of Justice into bully sticks to punish their enemies; defund the IRS; sell all the National Parks to oil companies and shut everything down. (Well, maybe not the police, who will be needed to quell the rioters, right?)

These drama and destruction enthusiasts are not idealists who want to make a better society from the old, like our Founding Fathers. Nope. They share conspiracy theories as a way to unleash chaos and mobilize people against the established order they think has failed to give them the respect they deserve.

Their desire for chaos and destruction is part fantasy, part bluster, and comes out of nihilistic despair that festered in the Old South. It's been on a slow rise since the Civil War, but found its way into high gear ever since one of their own came unexpectedly into power.

Ever wonder about the need throughout the South for genuflection from Black people, women, and children? It's part of the same white male inferiority complex. I believe it's modelled, at least in part, after their deity. They feel they've been mocked and passed over all their lives, they don't know how to change it, and it makes them want to tear everything down. They want to smoke in public, say anything they like to anybody, and flash their guns like tough guys in the movies. And they want that spontaneous subservience back.

The current conservative movement is motivated by political frustration and impotence. They're so fed up with everybody not like them that all they want to do is piss on everybody and tear it all down — even if it kills them. Which they know it will, but they don't care because to hell with the rules and being polite, and to hell with everybody else.

Bait & Switch

> "From the pharaohs of ancient Egypt to the glorified warlords of mediæval Europe, in nearly every society throughout human history, there have been people who have tried to make their society into an aristocracy. These people and their allies are conservatives." — *Philip E. Agre*

From the beginning of time, somebody has always assumed, "I've got more, and that makes me better." Which has always been a fundamental problem for everybody else. The corollary followed immediately thereafter, that if that one person was better, then they should be in charge—they should have authority over everybody else. It was always about more land or more money or whoever could fight better, and that allowed one person (often including their family) to lord it over everyone else. That fundamental logic created the concept of aristocracy and authoritarianism, with kings and queens and dukes and dictators. Genghis Khan, Napoleon, and Elon Musk.

And it makes sense, particularly for a commercial enterprise. Somebody has to be in charge, and it's usually the biggest stakeholder—whoever owns most (or all) of the company assets. It's their equity at risk, right? And it can be an efficient way to get a lot done—there are examples of commercial barons throughout history who changed our lives for the better.

But what if it's something that everybody should have a stake in—something that isn't privately owned, like a country? Until the Greeks came along, communities of people functioned like a family-run business, only bigger. All of life was a social and psychological condition of inequality. The rich over the poor, the powerful over the weak—the entitled over everyone else.

The ones at the apex of that socio-economic pyramid might argue that it's the natural order. But that's just *Might Makes Right* again, as if we were all chimpanzees. And we agreed from the get-go that there are rights which cannot be taken away. *Inalienable*, we called them because we could not be divided from them. And we said that we ourselves were the government. Not the landed gentry, and not whoever had the most money. Certainly not some local (or national) bully. We were all equal in power. So when some of us lose that franchise, when it gets taken from us somehow, we feel disconnected. We feel powerless. We have become alienated, which is dead opposite from what we said we were about.

Conservatives think of governance as a psychological state in which the common people accept the domination of an upper strata of society—*their* strata. If they happen to love it, all the better. This may sound strange to us now, but it is in the writings of historical conservatives like Edmund Burke, for whom freedom was intricately tied to property and social position. Such people believe the aristocracy rightfully dominates society due to its built-in superiority. This perspective puts conservatism not just in contrast to American ideals, but also in opposition to the very principles of democracy. Rich conservatives reap the rewards of this system, while their lesser cousins share the illusion that they've gained something in the bargain.

When we think about it in this light, Reagan's trickle-down economics was really nothing more than the appearance of largess from his fellow aristocrats that cost nothing, like scraps from a factory floor. Charity for the working poor and middle-class, condescension for the hoi palloi. It connects the dots between modern conservative ideology and the economic structures of the Middle Ages: feudalism and manorialism, which functioned in much the same way. Reagan's thimblerig worked perfectly; the rich got fabulously wealthy while the rest of us got stuck with the tab.

The weird symbiosis between wealthy and poor conservatives is like Lucy van Pelt holding the football for Charlie Brown to run and kick it, then pulling it away at the last minute. Again and again. Charlie gets suspicious over the years, but never gives up. And he never blames Lucy for her behavior.

Continued in The Great American Dream Machine

Final Thoughts

One of my favorite films is *Shall We Dance?* rewritten by Audrey Wells from the original film by Masayuki Suo. This is not *Lawrence of Arabia*, but it has its moments. Aside from the two hottest dance numbers ever filmed at any time in the entire history of movies ever made by any studio in this or any other universe bar none, there is a conversation between two of the *secondary* characters that transcends everything, and presents a subject that I've not seen addressed by any other writer.

A question comes up about why people get married. The first answer, *passion*, is dismissed (most people aren't actually that shallow). The next answer surprised me because it went so far beyond my expectations:

> "Because we need a witness to our lives. There's a billion people on the planet. What does any one life really mean? But in a marriage, you're promising to care about everything — the good things, the bad things the terrible things, the mundane things... All of it. All the time, every day. You're saying, 'Your life will not go unnoticed, because I will notice it. Your life will not go unwitnessed, because I will be your witness.'"

When I was a child, and during all my years growing up, I was aware that Edith (my mother) had a five-year diary she wrote in every night. She'd been keeping a diary since before she was a teenager on a chicken ranch. There were a lot of diaries in her bottom drawer. And every time I got deathly ill with something, she would drag out her diaries and go through them until she could point to an entry and say, "Yep. You had chickenpox when you were five — 103° temp." Then she would look at me. "So this must be something else."

The point is, she *knew*. Edith knew who I was from the day I was born because she'd written everything down, and

I was secure in the knowledge that I would be taken care of. I may not have always liked *how* I was being taken care of, what with all the exercises we did and that Tiger's-Carnation-brewer's-yeast milk-water *dreck* I was given to help me chug down all thirteen vitamin tablets and wash away the taste of fried liver every morning, but I had no doubts about who was doing the caring. Edith had an eagle eye on my life as a child. I may have been a science project, but I was *her* science project.

Fast forward umpty-ump years, and I'm married. So now there are *two* witnesses — each of us making sure the other is taken care of. Until one of us stops due to distraction or inattention or confusion about whatever. It happens. Somebody dropped the ball — and it wasn't our ball to drop, was it? We *promised*. But we saw something shiny and looked the other way. Glance aside for a moment, that's okay; you can pick up the slack if it isn't too great. But what if you haul on that rope and there's nothing at the other end of it but a dirty look?

But there are larger implications to this witness idea. That's what hit me when I first heard Susan Sarandon give her speech in that dimly-lit bar.

I am a witness to my wife's life, just as she is a witness to mine. And so are my friends and other relatives — some more, some less, depending on the amount of time we've spent with each other over the years. It's why we celebrate birthdays and remember anniversaries. It's why we attend Little League games. And this book you're reading is a witness to other lives. Mine certainly, but also to Tom's. And a worried mother we met in Yellowstone, a family living in a suburb of Chicago, and two girls from Albuquerque.

We are all on the same planet breathing the same air. We all have to make it work. And because we're all witnesses to each others' lives, lying and cheating doesn't work. Not really. Because if it keeps up, there won't be an answering tug from the other end of that rope I talked about.

We also expect our government to be a good witness. To see all of us for who we are, to understand and respond to our issues. Wealthy people, large corporations, and politicians seem to get almost all the attention, but that isn't right. It's the man on the street who needs to command the ear of government.

We can accomplish that at the local level, but we need it at the national level as well, because that's how wide-sweeping policies that affect everyone are made. We need our government to stop listening to the rich as though they have any more right than everyone else. Because they haven't. They aren't better, they're certainly not more worthy, and to a great extent, most of them do not "earn" their income stream and did not personally "earn" most of their assets.

Bring your own protractor

Tom and I never had to worry about our country before, at least not in terms of her survival. Not really. There had always been major issues, but as far as we were concerned things felt positive in a general way, as though the world was getting better slowly via Dr. King's long arc of history.

Education, new inventions, and life-saving medicine was on the rise. Aside from too many people causing food shortages, the threat of war, and the long-term pressure of climate change, things have been slowly getting better. They have. But the crocodile of time is stalking all of us, and if we don't keep a sharp lookout we could lose more than just a hand. We could lose our humanity. Or our country. Possibly both.

All of human history lives within us and creates harmonics in what we do, what we think, and the path we choose. There are course corrections from time to time, but the psychohistory of mankind spans millennia, and its trajectory is based more on curiosity and exploration than fear. Science and fact rather than magic. To-do lists instead of prayer.

Mankind has been moving towards altruism and logic ever since we invented stew. It's a far better way to live, but we aren't all there yet. Social change, like natural evolution, comes in fits and starts with punctuated equilibrium. Because of our years of slavery, racism, and the entitlement of wealth, it's as if America was born on the side of a hill, but the sooner we stop walking around with one leg shorter than the other, the better.

When my father taught me how to pluck a typebar to make it sing, it came with an important caveat: I shouldn't pull the typebar too far. If I did, the molecules of steel would lose their springy grip on one another and bend—suddenly and catastrophically. The same thing can happen to a society of people. If too many lose their grip on reality, they will deform us permanently, skew the entire group, and nothing will spring back. Community falls apart when the center no longer holds.

My generation posed stark questions to ourselves and the world. Many of us came to the realization that life didn't have to be as it had been—that we could adopt a new philosophy, a new way of being in the world. We understood that life didn't have to be this cruel, and that we could be the ones to change it. Sometimes just by example.

I would like to believe Dr. King was right, and that the trajectory of social issues throughout the world is headed towards a kinder, gentler community of man. But we carry a hell of a lot of baggage, it's a long process, and it's likely to get worse before it gets better.

The promise of America was always for a brighter tomorrow, and most of us haven't given up on that. We still want to know we're pulling in the right direction and that everybody's kid sister will come out okay. But we have to use logic if we're going to get anywhere; emotions are what we need to rise above.

"Great minds discuss ideas; average minds discuss events; small minds discuss people." —Eleanor Roosevelt

Looking back

Tom and I saw America at her best. And at her worst. We grew up and pursued our dreams as best we could. We made friends, ran businesses, got married, and lived our lives. Both of us worked for a living and became business owners. Between the two of us, the number of interesting cars and motorcycles we've owned is staggering, considering that neither of us ever had much money.

Of all our experiences on that trip, our stay with the Neefe family stands out because it affected us the most. To be taken in as strangers with no real connection other than our common humanity spoke volumes, and Mr. Neefe's parting words stayed with us for all the years that followed: "One day—who knows when—you're going to come across someone who needs help. When that day comes is when you thank me."

Tom and I suddenly appeared on the roadways of America for a brief time. We battled wind, rain, and hail to get past, through, or around whatever came up, then vanished just as fast. Suddenly it was over and consigned to memory. Two months out of a lifetime is not long in the conventional sense, but it meant a great deal to us. It was as if we each carried a backpack of shared experience from that moment forward. It may have been brief in the great scheme of things, but we crammed a hell of a lot into those backpacks.

We took a risk that paid off. Tom feels he became more understanding of others, a better listener, and more patient with people who fall over from time to time. I feel that I became more understanding of others, a better listener, and more patient with people with a short fuse.

We endured sunburn, windburn, and rainfall. We looked down on New York City from the Empire State Building, witnessed our first Grand Prix, and saved two squirrels from hypothermia. We spent the night in jail. We slept in a homeless shelter. Tom and I helped move a piano up two flights of stairs and even joined a manhunt for a lost girl. We rode 9,847 miles in about two months on a couple of street bikes and managed to bring each other back alive.

Knowing what it's like when you're cold and out on your own helps connect the dots when it comes to hiring people or surviving as a guardian to a very angry child. Our experience brought texture to the words and lyrics of our younger days and context to many of the political issues we now face as a befuddled and angry nation.

Of all the things we've done, we agree that this was it: our greatest adventure. We've both been on other motorcycle trips, alone, with each other, and with friends, but this is the one we remember; this is the trip that took our measure. We met the belt-sander and made it our own.

We wandered America's blue-gray ribbons for a time and found ourselves. We were just the right age and naïve enough to try. The trip we took is now a memory to be held like a time capsule — a measure of time and wind and sun and rain and growing up. It's the way we were. We're glad we went, and we're glad we went together.

Denouement

After Tom and I got back, and about a year after I met with the FBI, I got a letter from the Selective Service Administration. *Dear Mr. Robertson*, it read... *blah, blah, blah.* But right in the middle of this piece of paper, away from everything else on the piece of paper, I read the following words:

> **1-H: Registrant is not currently subject to processing for induction or alternative service.**

It took a moment to figure it out. And then it hit me — bam! *I'd won.* There was even an official classification card to carry around in my wallet like I was a member of an exclusive club. So I didn't go to court, I didn't go to prison, and I certainly didn't end up picking any beets.

I have no idea what saved me. Was it the eloquence? My cast-iron logic? The cut of my jib?

I rather suspect they were just leery of letting someone like me create havoc among all the new recruits saluting each other back and forth. "USA *vs.* Obnoxious Kid" was over. I fell into swift water when I stood up to that strip of yellow tape, but somehow managed to swim to shore, dry myself off, and get on with life.

Every year when the rains let up and the sun begins to smile again, I roll out the last motorcycle I'll ever own: my yellow Trihawk. With a bit of fiddling, she rumbles into life. Top down, we thunder into glory — downshifting into every corner, clipping the apex, and accelerating into every straight.

And when I am driving like that, right on the edge of wonderful, I'm sometimes reminded of what it was like when Tom and I took on that big encounter with life. I remember what we saw, who we met, and — miracle of miracles — that we made it back alive (without getting lost or crashing into each other). And I am reminded that, in the process of telling that story and parsing it all out, I discovered something rather interesting. Which in turn, makes me think of Bertrand Russell, Dr. Asher, and my brother Glen.

Russell and Asher showed me I could figure stuff out and share what I'd gleaned by paying attention, asking the right questions, and then writing it all down with logic and consideration. But it was my big brother who encouraged me to explore the realm of ideas and follow each lead wherever it might go. Some found their way into this book.

My question of how we got into our uniquely American sociopolitical impasse (and where it will lead us) came out of and was answered by all those history, science, and religious books I read, the music I listened to, and the moral issues I had to face as a young man. It came from the people Tom and I met on our trip, our conversations in the dead of night in that little blue tent, and my sporadic but ever-increasing encounters with high-toned malarkey. Everything mattered, everything contributed.

So now you have the whole enchilada. How a devious kid pitched his tent outside the pale (and survived to tell about it), how the Bubonic Plague broke the feudal system and triggered social progress, and how that subsequently bent the arc of the moral universe toward justice. Plus my somewhat optimistic view of gray and blue highways, lots and lots of rain, and the ubiquitous belt sander of life.

The End

Good night and good luck.

Shameless Request for a Review

I sincerely hope you enjoyed reading this book as much as I enjoyed writing it. If you did, I would greatly appreciate a short review on Amazon or your favorite book website. Reviews are crucial for any author, and even just a line or two can make a huge difference.

Thank you!

www.ingramcontent.com/pod-product-compliance
Lightning Source LLC
Chambersburg PA
CBHW030238170426
43202CB00007B/35